Stockholm Arbitration Yearbook 2024

Stockholm Arbitration Yearbook

VOLUME 6

Editors

Christer Danielsson is an independent arbitrator based in Stockholm. After fifteen years of mainly transactional work with a leading Swedish firm, he has focused on dispute resolution in the last fifteen years as counsel and now as a full-time arbitrator. He is the previous President of the Swedish Bar Association and the Swedish Arbitration Association and is designated to the ICSID Panel of Arbitrators (Sweden).

Patrik Schöldström is a Judge of Appeal of the Svea Court of Appeal. He is also an Associate Professor of the Faculty of Law of Stockholm University. He has a doctorate in arbitration law and is a former member of the Swedish Bar. He regularly writes articles and case notes. He has extensive experience as an arbitrator – chairman, sole arbitrator, co-arbitrator and emergency arbitrator – in international and domestic disputes, ad hoc and institutional.

Introduction

The Yearbook is published under the auspices of the Stockholm Centre for Commercial Law, a part of the Stockholm University Faculty of Law. It is designed to meet the information needs of arbitration practitioners and parties from all over the world. The first volume was published in 2019.

Objective

The Yearbook is designed to meet the information needs of arbitration practitioners and parties from all over the world. It provides authoritative articles, some of them with a Swedish angle, that address current matters of global concern in arbitration. Each volume includes one or more chapters accounting for developments in Swedish case law and legislation since the previous volume.

Frequency

The publication is annual.

The titles published in this series are listed at the end of this volume.

Stockholm Arbitration Yearbook 2024

Edited by

Christer Danielsson
Patrik Schöldström

Assistant Editor

Philip Mellberg

Editorial Committee

James Hope
Kristin Campbell-Wilson
Niklas Berntorp
Eva Storskrubb
Åsa Waller
Bruno Gustafsson

Stockholm Centre for Commercial Law
Faculty of Law

Stockholm University

Wolters Kluwer

Published by:
Kluwer Law International B.V.
PO Box 316
2400 AH Alphen aan den Rijn
The Netherlands
E-mail: lrs-sales@wolterskluwer.com
Website: www.wolterskluwer.com/en/solutions/kluwerlawinternational

Sold and distributed by:
Wolters Kluwer Legal & Regulatory U.S.
920 Links Avenue
Landisville, PA 17538
United States of America
E-mail: customer.service@wolterskluwer.com

ISBN 978-94-035-4428-1

e-Book: ISBN 978-94-035-4438-0
web-PDF: ISBN 978-94-035-4448-9

Editors

Christer Danielsson is an independent arbitrator based in Stockholm. After fifteen years of mainly transactional work with a leading Swedish firm, he has focused on dispute resolution in the last fifteen years as counsel and now as a full-time arbitrator. He is the previous President of the Swedish Bar Association and the Swedish Arbitration Association and is designated to the ICSID Panel of Arbitrators (Sweden).

Patrik Schöldström is a Judge of Appeal of the Svea Court of Appeal and an Associate Professor of the Faculty of Law of Stockholm University. He has a Doctorate in Arbitration Law and is a former member of the Swedish Bar. He regularly writes articles and case notes. He also sits as an arbitrator and has participated in a number of domestic and international arbitrations (ad hoc and institutional) as chair of the arbitral tribunal, sole arbitrator, emergency arbitrator, wing arbitrator, and counsel.

Contributors

David Akrad is an advokat and associate in the dispute resolution group at Mannheimer Swartling, based in Gothenburg.

Anastasiia Dulska is an associate at Bär & Karrer, Switzerland, with more than ten years of experience in international dispute resolution. She specialises in international commercial and investor-State arbitration, cross-border disputes, internal investigations, and public international law. She is particularly focused on representing governments, state-owned entities, financial institutions, and high-net-worth individuals before international tribunals and courts. She holds Master's and Bachelor's degrees in International Law, and an LLM in International Dispute Resolution from the Humboldt University of Berlin. She also completed directed studies at the Hague Academy of International Law and the Paris Arbitration Academy. Anastasiia is recognised by Who's Who Legal as a Future Leader in Arbitration (2024).

Aleksander Godhe is a research associate (Dispute Resolution) at the Centre of Construction Law & Dispute Resolution, the Dickson Poon School of Law, King's College London. He is also a Visiting Fellow at the Stockholm Centre for Commercial Law, Stockholm University.

Søren Henriksen is a partner at Gorrissen Federspiel's dispute resolution practice in Copenhagen. Søren specialises in international arbitration, and his experience ranges across post-M&A and shareholder arbitration over IT separation disputes through international insurance and construction arbitration.

Lord Hope of Craighead KT is a former Deputy President of the UK Supreme Court. He is currently an international arbitrator at Brick Court Chambers, 7-8 Essex Street, London WC2R 3LD.

Alexandra M.O. Junge is a legal consultant at Gorrissen Federspiel's dispute resolution practice in Copenhagen. She holds a Master's in Economic Law from Sciences Po Paris Law School. Alexandra focuses on international commercial-arbitration matters.

Aksel Kolstad is an associate at Wikborg Rein's Oslo office, where he specialises in international arbitration. He has previously held a position as a research assistant at the Institute for Private Law at the University of Oslo, where he has also lectured on contract law.

Mikael Linton-Wahlgren is an advokat and founder of Linton-Wahlgren Law Firm. He is an experienced arbitrator, mediator, and adjudicator in dispute resolution boards. He has more than thirty years of experience working as in-house and external counsel supporting several multinational Swedish and foreign listed companies, including as General Counsel for the Alfa Laval Group and In-house Counsel for Skanska, ABB, Rolls-Royce and NCC. He is also a former Partner of Lindmark Welinder Law Firm. His background and industry expertise include, e.g., the handling of domestic and international disputes and business legal matters in the construction, infrastructure, energy, manufacturing, M&A, Life Science and MedTech industries.

Kristoffer Löf is an advokat and partner in the dispute resolution group at Mannheimer Swartling, based in Stockholm. He is also the former President of the Swedish Arbitration Association.

Haakon Orgland Bingen is a specialist counsel at Wikborg Rein's Oslo office, where he specialises in international arbitration. For over a decade, he has worked almost exclusively with international arbitration, acting as counsel in numerous arbitration proceedings governed by the ICC, SCC and OCC arbitration rules, as well as ad hoc arbitrations. He also regularly sits as an arbitrator.

Paschalis Paschalidis is a counsel in the dispute resolution practice at Arendt & Medernach. He is also an associate professor of Public Law at the University of Lyon 3 'Jean Moulin' and a Member of the Luxembourg Arbitration Association.

Niels Schiersing is an independent international arbitrator and a member of Arbitration Chambers. He is based in London and Dubai. Dr Schiersing is dual-qualified and admitted to practice law in Denmark and England & Wales. As such, he has in-depth knowledge of common law and civil law systems alike. His arbitrator practice focuses on commercial and construction arbitration, and he has acted as arbitrator in more than one hundred arbitrations in various jurisdictions across three continents (Europe, Asia and Africa), including as co-arbitrator, chairperson and emergency arbitrator in a number of SCC arbitrations. Moreover, Dr Schiersing conducts extensive legal research, particularly in the area of comparative contract law and international arbitration law. He holds the highest achievable Doctorate degree. Dr Schiersing only serves as arbitrator and does not act as counsel.

Catherine Schutz is a legal consultant at Gorrissen Federspiel's dispute resolution practice in Copenhagen. Catherine holds a Juris Doctorate (JD) from Georgia State University College of Law and is admitted to the Georgia State Bar (US). She consults on a broad range of matters related to international commercial arbitration and litigation. Prior to joining Gorrissen Federspiel, Catherine's practice focused primarily on large-scale US litigation, including tort, commercial, contract and real estate litigation.

Christopher Stridh is a senior associate at Advokatfirman Delphi. He specialises in Swedish and international commercial arbitration and litigation.

Petri Taivalkoski is an independent arbitrator based in Helsinki. Before launching his practice as a full-time arbitrator in 2020, he practised as a litigator with a leading Nordic law firm for thirty years, including several years as the head of its dispute resolution practice in Finland. Petri has served as an arbitrator under various laws and rules, such as the ICC, the FAI, the SCC, the DIS and the Swiss Rules. He served as a member of the ICC International Court of Arbitration from 2018 to 2024 and as a member of the FAI Board from 2013 to 2018.

Danna Zhang is a dual-qualified disputes lawyer licensed to practice in Denmark and England and Wales. She is an associate in the Disputes and Investigations practice of Slaughter and May in London.

Summary of Contents

Table of Contents

Preface

Welcome to the sixth edition of the Stockholm Arbitration Yearbook!

You will find chapters on arbitration law in general and Swedish arbitration law in particular. Some contributions are by senior and well-known authors, others by more junior ones.

We are happy to receive – at any time of the year – proposals for future contributions in the form of a short abstract.

Christer Danielsson
Patrik Schöldström

CHAPTER 1

Swedish Arbitration-Related Case Law 2023-2024

Christer Danielsson

§1.01 INTRODUCTION

This chapter will account for court cases relevant to arbitration law from the Swedish Supreme Court and Swedish courts of appeal from 1 May 2023 to 30 April 2024. It does not purport to be exhaustive; the aim is to highlight cases that can be assumed of interest to a non-Swedish reader.

§1.02 BACKGROUND

The Swedish Arbitration Act of 1999[1] (the 'Act') applies to all arbitration proceedings seated in Sweden, whether the parties have any connection to Sweden or not.[2] The Act also sets out, incorporating the 1958 New York Convention, the requirements for foreign arbitral awards to be recognized and enforced in Sweden.[3]

Sweden has a three-tier court system: district courts, six regional courts of appeal and the Supreme Court. However, district courts are only rarely involved in arbitration cases since the appellate courts are courts of first instance for invalidity and set-aside cases, as well as for recognition and enforcement cases.

A Swedish arbitral award can be *declared invalid* if it determines an issue which under Swedish law cannot be decided by arbitrators or if the award, or the manner in

1. Lagen (1999:116) om skiljeförfarande, as amended 1 Mar. 2019.
2. The Act, s. 46.
3. The Act, ss 52 et seq.

which it came about, is clearly incompatible with the basic principles of the Swedish legal system, i.e., *ordre public*.[4]

An arbitral award can be *set aside* (wholly or partially) at the request of a party, *inter alia*, when the arbitrators have exceeded their mandate and when, without fault of the party, an irregularity has occurred in the course of the proceedings which probably influenced the outcome of the case.[5]

An action to invalidate or set aside an arbitration award shall be considered by the Court of Appeal within whose district the arbitral proceedings were seated.[6] The Court of Appeal's permission is required in order to appeal its judgment.[7] Such leave to appeal is denied in the large majority of cases. For the case to be tried by the Supreme Court, leave is also required from that Court.[8]

Historically, invalidity and set-aside actions have very rarely been successful. A statistical survey from 1 January 2004 to 31 May 2014 shows that seven arbitral awards were set aside pursuant to section 34 of the Act, while one award was declared invalid pursuant to section 33 of the Act, equal to only 6% of all decided cases.[9]

In the period covered by this chapter, two awards were declared invalid; none was set aside. Both invalidity cases concerned arbitration proceedings based on the dispute resolution clause in section 26 of the Energy Charter Treaty.

§1.03 *KB COMPONENTS PLASTUNION AB V. HUSQVARNA AB*

In NJA 2023 p. 437 ('Husqvarnas skiljeavtal'),[10] the Supreme Court found that an arbitration clause in a frame agreement covered a later call-off agreement under the frame agreement.

In 2007, Husqvarna and KB Components Plastunion AB ('KB Plastunion') entered into a supply agreement regarding future call-offs made by Husqvarna. The terms of the supply agreement applied to purchases of products delivered by KB Plastunion to Husqvarna in accordance with purchase orders submitted by Husqvarna. The supply agreement contained an arbitration clause pursuant to which disputes 'arising out of or in connection with this Agreement or Purchase Order' shall be settled by arbitration.

4. The Act, s. 33. In addition, under this provision, an award is invalid if it does not fulfil the Act's requirements with regard to written form and signature.
5. The Act, s. 34(1), items 3 and 7. Section 34 provides for five other grounds for setting aside an arbitral award, but the two mentioned are those most frequently invoked in set-aside proceedings.
6. The Act, s. 43(1). The large majority of invalidity and set-aside proceedings are brought before the Svea Court of Appeal. The reason for this is that most Swedish arbitrations are seated in Stockholm.
7. The Act, s. 43(2), which provides that leave to appeal shall be granted 'where it is of importance, as a matter of precedent, that the appeal be considered by the Supreme Court'.
8. The Act, s. 43(2). Such requirement was introduced in an amendment to the Act which entered into force on 1 Mar. 2019.
9. Översyn av lagen om skiljeförfarande ('Review of the arbitration act'), SOU 2015:37, p. 79.
10. *KB Components Plastunion AB v. Husqvarna AB*, decision by the Supreme Court on 17 May 2023 in Case No. Ö 4116-22.

KB Plastunion initiated court proceedings against Husqvarna for payment of products delivered in 2020 pursuant to prior purchase orders. Husqvarna objected to the court's jurisdiction, stating that the dispute should be settled by arbitration. Both the District Court and the Court of Appeal found in favour of Husqvarna and dismissed the case.

The Supreme Court came to the same conclusion. It stated, *inter alia*, the following. The description of the legal relationship established by the parties through a frame agreement can be sufficiently precise (Sw. 'tillräckligt konkretiserad') for an arbitration agreement included therein to cover both disputes concerning the frame agreement itself and subsequent call-off agreements and thus satisfying the requirement in section 1 of the Act that an arbitration agreement 'may relate to future disputes pertaining to a legal relationship specified in the agreement'. The Supreme Court added that it does not follow from section 1 of the Act that an arbitration agreement can only apply to agreements already entered into.

'Husqvarnas skiljeavtal' has been the subject of debate in the legal literature, with authors calling into question whether the Supreme Court, by its decision, has changed the position taken in the landmark 2019 *Belgor* case (NJA 2019 p. 171).[11] This has been disputed by former Supreme Court justice Lars Edlund, one of the justices deciding the *Belgor* case.[12]

In my opinion 'Husqvarnas skiljeavtal' does not limit or change in any way the Belgor precedent.

§1.04 *IRENE LARSSON V. NAKED JUICEBAR AB*

The issue before the Supreme Court in the NJA 2023 p. 1067[13] was whether the cost provisions in an arbitral award rendered under the expedited SCC Rules were enforceable. The sole arbitrator had ruled that Irene Larsson, as between the parties, was liable for the fees of the arbitrator and the Stockholm Chamber of Commerce (SCC).

The enforcement authority (Kronofogden) decided to accept the award as the basis for collecting those fees from Irene Larsson. She appealed that decision to the Nacka district Court. The Court found that since the award contained no explicit order for Irene Larsson to pay Naked Juicebar AB, it was not enforceable in that regard. On appeal, the Svea Court of Appeal found to the contrary, as did the Supreme Court. The Supreme Court held that the arbitral award contained a sufficiently clear obligation for Irene Larsson to compensate Naked Juicebar AB for its arbitration costs. Therefore, the cost award could be enforced.

11. Jacob Frank, Svensk Juristtidning 2023 p. 623, '"Husqvarnas skiljeavtal" och tolkningsprinciper för skiljeavtal – har pendeln svängt igen?' and Lars Heuman, Juridisk Tidskrift 2023-2024 p. 463: 'Skiljemäns behörighet att pröva tvister om tilläggsavtal. Relevanta regler och faktorer.'
12. Lars Edlund, Svensk Juristtidning 2024 p. 538: 'En kommentar till "Husqvarnas skiljeavtal" NJA 2023 s. 437. Jacob Frank has replied thereto, Svensk Juristtidning 2024 p. 543: '"Husqvarnas skiljeavtal" – replik till en kommentar.'
13. *Irene Larsson v. Naked Juicebar AB*, decision by the Supreme Court on 27 Dec. 2023 in Case No. Ä 2885-23.

§1.05 *KINGDOM OF SPAIN V. TRIODOS SICAV II*

The Energy Charter Treaty (ECT) is an international agreement that establishes a multilateral framework for cross-border cooperation in the energy industry. It is an investment protection agreement.

Section 26 of the ECT contains a dispute resolution clause which, *inter alia*, refers to arbitration pursuant to the SCC Rules.

TRIODOS SICAV II (Triodos) is a venture capital fund incorporated in Luxemburg. During 2008-2010, Triodos made four investments in the Spanish energy market.

Spain and Luxembourg are parties to the ECT.

In 2017, Triodos requested arbitration against Spain pursuant to the SCC Rules.

In the subsequent arbitral award rendered in 2022, the tribunal found that Spain had breached Article 10.1 of the ECT and Spain was ordered to pay damages.

The same year Spain initiated proceedings before the Svea Court of Appeal, requesting that the award be declared invalid or set aside.[14]

One of Spain's grounds for invalidity was that the award, or the manner in which it came about, was clearly incompatible with the basic principles of the Swedish legal system (public policy, *ordre public*). Spain referred to the judgments by the European Court of Justice (CJEU) in Achmea,[15] Komstroy[16] and PL Holdings.[17]

With reference to such judgments and the Swedish Supreme Court's judgment in PL Holdings,[18] the Svea Court found that the 2022 arbitral award was invalid; to uphold it would be incompatible with basic principles of EU law and, thus, Swedish law.[19] The Court did not grant leave to appeal to the Supreme Court.

§1.06 *FESTORINO INVEST LIMITED ET AL. V. REPUBLIC OF POLAND*

Festorino Invest Limited and four other investors owned all the shares of the Polish company Blue Gas Holding, which conducted business in the Polish energy sector in the 2010s. Four of the investors had their seats in or were citizens of EU Member States. One of the investors was a Swiss citizen residing in Switzerland.

In 2018, the investors initiated arbitration proceedings under the SCC Rules with reference to section 26 of the ECT and claimed that Poland had acted in breach of the ECT.

In the arbitration proceedings, Poland objected to the tribunal's jurisdiction, referring to case law from the CJEU, i.e., Achmea.

14. Svea Court of Appeal Case No. T 15200-22.
15. Judgment by the CJEU on 6 Mar. 2018, *Slovak Republic v. Achmea BV*, Case No. C-284/16.
16. Judgment by the CJEU on 2 Sep. 2021, *Republic of Moldova v. Komstroy LLC*, Case No. C-741/19.
17. Judgment by the CJEU on 26 Oct. 2022, *Republic of Poland v. PL Holdings Sarl*, Case No. C-109/20.
18. Judgment by the Supreme Court on 14 Dec. 2022, NJA 2022 p. 965.
19. Judgment by the Svea Court of Appeal on 27 Mar. 2024 in Case No. T 15200-22.

In a 2021 award, the arbitral tribunal found that it had jurisdiction but found against the investors on substance and ordered the investors to bear the costs of the proceedings.

The same year, the investors initiated proceedings before the Svea Court of Appeal, requesting that the award be declared invalid or set aside.[20]

In the proceedings before the Svea Court, Poland left it to the Court to decide whether the arbitral award was invalid between Poland and the four EU investors but objected to the cost decisions contained therein being declared invalid, as well as to the award being invalidated in relation to the non-EU investor.

With reference to Achmea, Komstroy, PL Holdings and the Swedish Supreme Court's judgment in PL Holdings, the Svea Court found that the 2021 arbitral award was incompatible with basic principles of Swedish law and therefore invalid between Poland and the four EU investors, including in the cost part.[21]

With regard to the non-EU investor, the Svea Court found that an award can be invalid only in part but concluded that this was not the case here due to the reason for the invalidity (procedural public policy, *ordre public*).

Accordingly, the 2021 award was declared invalid in its entirety.

The Court granted the right to appeal to the Supreme Court. At the time of writing, the Supreme Court has not yet decided on whether to take the case.

20. Svea Court of Appeal Case No. T 12646-21.
21. Judgment by the Svea Court of Appeal on 20 Dec. 2023 in Case No. T 12646-21.

CHAPTER 2

'When in Stockholm, ...':[1] Interpretation, Gap-Filling and Modification of Commercial Contracts under Swedish Law – Some Comparative Reflections for Arbitrators and Counsel

Niels Schiersing

§2.01 INTRODUCTION

Occasionally, a dispute referred to arbitration can be resolved without the arbitral tribunal ('tribunal') engaging with the merits of the case, e.g., based on the tribunal's determination that it lacks jurisdiction.

However, in most cases, the tribunal will be tasked with determining issues of substantive law. In commercial arbitrations, this will – invariably – include matters of contract law, including the formation, interpretation, adaption, modification, performance, termination and/or breach of contract and, in the vast majority of disputes, also include dealing with requests for monetary relief relating thereto.

As one of the world's major arbitral institutions, the SCC Arbitration Institute (SCC) administers, *inter alia*, a large number of international commercial arbitrations, many of which are of considerable legal and/or factual complexity and involve substantial amounts in dispute.

1. The famous proverb: 'When in Rome, do as the Romans do', which inspired the title of this article, is traditionally ascribed to St. Ambrose in a letter to St. Augustine from the 4th Century AD discussing fasting habits in Milan and Rome, respectively. The most well-known iteration of the saying is likely the 18th Century AD letter from Pope Clement XIV to Dom Gaillard: 'The *siesto*, or afternoon's nap of Italy, my most dear and reverend Father, would not have alarmed you so much, if you had recollected, that when we are at Rome, we should do as the Romans do.'

In the vast majority of commercial arbitrations proceeding under the SCC Rules,[2] Swedish law is elected as the *lex causae* and, as such, governs the so-called main or matrix contract, i.e., the contract, except for the arbitration clause. The arbitration clause, although included in the matrix contract, is considered a discrete contract between the parties based on the doctrine of severability.[3]

Commercial arbitrations frequently involve fundamental disagreements between the parties on how to construe or interpret the agreement underpinning and governing their contractual relationship as manifested in the (matrix) contract. This can be due to a number of factors that are not limited to poor drafting.[4]

The above considerations entail that arbitrators (and counsel) involved in commercial arbitrations under the SCC rules will often need to deal with and apply the various principles of Swedish law pertaining to contract interpretation, i.e., how to determine what rights and obligations the contract confer on the parties. This can be viewed as a 'meta' issue: only when the meaning of the contract has been established will arbitrators be able to move on to apply the contractual terms, as construed, to the other facts of the case and decide any other issues in contention.

Often, the arbitrators appointed in commercial arbitrations under the SCC Rules are legal professionals (typically lawyers, academics and judges) educated, trained and admitted to practice law in jurisdictions other than Sweden, including practitioners from common law jurisdictions such as England, USA, Canada, Ireland, Singapore, India, New Zealand and Australia.[5] Hence, if the laws of Sweden apply as the relevant *lex causae*, such 'foreign' arbitrators necessarily need to assimilate and comprehend parts of Swedish contract law, including the principles concerning contract interpretation.

Obviously, the parties' counsel will assist the tribunal by making submissions based on the applicable law and/or they may tender expert evidence regarding certain relevant legal principles, but I – emphatically – hold the view that an arbitrator cannot (and should not) rely exclusively on the parties or experts but will need to self-educate and get informed by studying the core principles of the laws on contracts and the relevant part of the law of obligations applicable in the relevant jurisdiction.

It is the principal purpose of this chapter to provide sitting and prospective arbitrators not familiar with Swedish contract law with a brief introduction to a few of

2. The most recent version of the SCC Arbitration Rules (2023) came into force on 1 Jan. 2023.
3. With respect to cases commenced in 2023, Swedish law was elected as *lex causae* in 140 out of a total number of 175 cases. It should be remembered that the SCC administers both domestic and international arbitrations. Among the residual *lex causae*, English law came in second (nine cases).
4. Frequently, the parties did not (and could not reasonably) envisage or foresee such an issue at the time of contracting, or they did indeed foresee the issue but were unable to agree on a way to regulate a certain issue and, therefore, consciously elected to omit a contractual provision. This may be an entirely valid commercial decision taken by savvy and experienced business people based on, e.g., a plausible *ex ante* assessment of the risk that such an event or instance will occur. The fact that *ex post* such an event did transpire does not negate the rationality of the original decision.
5. Obviously, also practitioners from other professions than law are appointed as arbitrators in SCC arbitrations, e.g., CPAs, engineers, architects, quantum surveyors, etc. This chapter should prove helpful to such professionals as well.

the core principles of contract interpretation and modification that such arbitrators will likely encounter when reviewing written submissions or listening to oral arguments in cases seated in Sweden and involving Swedish contract law.[6]

Moreover, in order to better understand certain initial positions potentially taken by arbitrators from, in particular, common law jurisdictions, it is also important for civil law-trained arbitrators to understand some of the core principles of contract interpretation under common law systems. This will facilitate communication and serve to enhance intersubjectivity within the tribunal and, thereby, hopefully, improve the quality of deliberations.[7] To that effect, I have contrasted the principles in Swedish law with some principles found in common law jurisdictions, predominantly England.

Given the constraints in terms of the length of the chapter, I will focus on some of the recurrent contract law issues pertaining to the interpretation and modification of contracts under Swedish law. Also, these constraints entail that I will only refer to case law and (with a few exceptions) not to relevant doctrine.

§2.02 THE SWEDISH CONTRACTS ACT[8]

The main statutory instrument in Sweden regarding contracts is the Contracts Act (Swedish: 'Avtalslagen')[9] (SCA), which came into force back in 1915.[10]

The SCA does not set out a comprehensive or all-encompassing regulation of the legal principles pertaining to contracts under Swedish law but is limited to dealing with some issues of general relevance,[11] such as the rules governing the formation of contracts (Chapter 1, sections 1-9)[12] and invalidity and contract modification (Chapter

6. I am not Swedish, but I have over the past many years been involved as counsel and arbitrator in numerous cases (arbitrations and litigations) under Swedish law, and my comparative legal research often involves analysing Swedish law. Moreover, a close relationship exists between Swedish and Danish (and Norwegian) law within the area of contract law.
7. The practical importance of this fact is amplified by the fact that English law, as mentioned, is the second most agreed *lex causae* in SCC arbitrations (although a very distant second).
8. The analysis in this chapter is to some (limited) extent based on the 'Länderbericht' account on salient features of Swedish and English law (substantive and evidentiary) contained in my book 'Disruption Claims' (2024) and, as regards English law, also on my book 'Earn-Out Disputes' (2020).
9. Law No. SFS 1915:218. The SCA was the result of a joint effort by the Swedish, Danish and Norwegian governments in the late 19th and early 20th century to promote unified codes in Scandinavia across a number of commercially pertinent areas of contract law (law of obligations). The very similar, but not identical, Danish Contracts Act and the Norwegian Contracts Act came into force in 1917 and 1918, respectively.
10. Like a number of similar statutes, e.g., the Japanese Civil Code of 1898 and the Korean Civil Code of 1958, the provisions of the SCA are, to large extent, inspired by the German Civil Code, i.e., the Bürgerliches Gesetzbuch (BGB). The BGB was promulgated in 1896 with effect from 1 Jan. 1900.
11. Some principles contained in other statutes are of importance to contracts in general. As an example, a number of provisions in the Sale of Goods Act are considered to form a part of dispositive law, also outside the ambit of sale of goods.
12. CISG Part II (Arts 14-24) contains provisions on the formation of contract in international sale of goods.

3, sections 28-38).[13] Due not least to the sparsity of actual regulation and the somewhat archaic language employed in the statute, a prominent late Swedish legal scholar once described the SCA as a 'ruin'.

After entering into force, the SCA was left more or less unchanged for sixty years. However, in the mid-1970s, Sweden (and the other Nordic[14] countries) introduced a novel provision promulgated as a rewording of section 36 of the SCA. Since entering into force, section 36 is frequently invoked and relied upon by parties in contract disputes. The same applies to the other Scandinavian countries. I will deal with section 36 when discussing contract modification at §2.04[C] *infra*.

§2.03 CONTRACT INTERPRETATION UNDER SWEDISH LAW

[A] Introductory Remarks

[1] Freedom of Contract, Party Autonomy and 'Pragmatism'

Swedish contract law is fundamentally rooted in the principles of freedom of contract and party autonomy, alongside the complementary principle of enforceability of contractual rights. This framework allows parties engaging in commercial transactions considerable latitude to negotiate and delineate the allocation of risks, rights and liabilities within their agreements, which are then bindingly and enforceably expressed through a written instrument (contract).

In such a legal system, adjudicators (whether courts or arbitral tribunals) should be reluctant to rewrite or substitute the parties' contract with one deemed fairer or more reasonable by the adjudicator(s).[15] This deference persists unless and until a specific threshold or baseline for business ethics is breached or in cases where the contract fails to express or reflect the parties' intended agreement, e.g., due to a mistake or incorrect drafting. Additionally, intervention may be warranted in limited circumstances where an unforeseen and profound imbalance, typically in the value of deliverables exchanged, is evident and not sufficiently offset by other provisions in the contract. The establishment of such a baseline and identification of such imbalances will be further dealt with below. Conversely, I will not engage with questions about mistakes or drafting issues in this chapter.[16]

---

13. For completeness, it should be mentioned that the SCA Chapter 2 (sections 10-27) concerns rules regarding agency/representation and SCA Chapter IV (sections 39-41) sets out a few general provisions.
14. The Nordic area includes the three Scandinavian countries with the addition of Finland and Iceland.
15. As stated by Wallis JA in the South African Supreme Court case, *Natal Joint Municipal Pension Fund v. Endumeni Municipality, 2012 (4) SA 593 (SCA)*: 'Judges must be alert to, and guard against, the temptation to substitute what they regard as reasonable, sensible or business-like for the words actually used. To do so in regard to a statute or statutory instrument is to cross the divide between interpretation and legislation; in a contractual context it is to make a contract for the parties other than the one they in fact made.' South Africa is a hybrid legal system, namely a combination of common law and Roman-Dutch law.
16. Therefore, I will not deal with questions of rectification/reformation of contracts.

However, in Scandinavian and Nordic legal jurisprudence, it is frequently stated that the approach to contract interpretation is 'pragmatic' – it has even spawned the term 'Nordic Legal Pragmatism,' which includes contract interpretation. The proponents of this approach to contract interpretation are often focused not only on normative concepts found in terms like 'fair', 'equitable' and 'reasonable' but less value-laden expressions such as 'common sense' are also suggested to provide adjudicators with a level of flexibility considered relevant and appropriate as opposed to an excessive 'formalism,' i.e., a too slavish adherence to the words employed.

Ultimately, the application of the law serves a practical purpose, namely, to attach legal consequences to human conduct.[17] When viewed through the prism of practical application, it appears quite obvious that vague and ambiguous terms like 'pragmatism' will inherently be fraught with problems. One such problem is that the concept may lack intersubjectivity outside a core sphere of application. Without clarification and clear demarcation lines, applying a concept like 'pragmatism' entails the risk of ending up doing commercial entities engaged in contractual relationships a disservice by introducing (*ex post*) a level of uncertainty and unpredictability as regards the allocation and apportionment of rights and obligations between the parties which they themselves sought to avoid (*ex ante*) by recording the rights and obligations in a written contract.

Contrasting any notions of 'pragmatism' with English law, reference can be made to the statement by Lord Mansfield, dating back approx. 250 years in *Medcalf v. Hall*:[18]

> Nothing is more mischievous than uncertainty in mercantile law.

More recently, Lord Hodge provided the following policy statement in *Wood v. Capita*,[19] echoing Lord Mansfield:

> The recent history of the common law of contractual interpretation is one of continuity rather than change. One of the attractions of English law as a legal system of choice in commercial matters is its stability and continuity, particularly in contractual interpretation.

For completeness, it should be noted that the indicated 'pragmatic' approach to the contract interpretation concept is mostly found in legal doctrine, and it is not readily discernable in Swedish case law beyond the sparingly applied concept of a 'comprehensive reasonableness test' (Swedish: 'övergripande rimlighetsbedömning') and some potential interpretative 'dithering' by its highest court of law. Both of these issues will be discussed below.[20]

17. *See, e.g.*, Burrows: Remedies for Torts, Breach of Contact, and Equitable Wrongs (4th ed., 2019) p. 19: '(L)aw is a practical discipline and, if its theories are set at such a high level that they cannot answer the practical questions addressed by courts, they are of marginal help.' I agree.
18. *Medcalf v. Hall* [1782] 3 Doug 113.
19. *See infra* n. 39.
20. Moreover, the decision mentioned at n. 46 could be seen as expressing such a standard.

[2] Subjective Versus Objective Interpretation

Overall, contract interpretation seeks to determine what the parties have agreed upon, i.e., the joint will of the parties.

It is well-known that a dichotomy between a subjective and an objective approach to contract interpretation has existed for centuries.[21] Very briefly, this distinction can be described as follows.

The 'subjective' approach focuses on discerning the subjective intent or will of the parties involved in forming a contract. As such, it searches for a 'meeting of the minds'.[22] The view from which this interpretative exercise is carried out can be said to be the will of each of the *promisors*.

Conversely, the 'objective' approach will determine the joint will based on the external manifestations or declarations of intent, i.e., the outward expressions of the parties. The view is said to be that of a *reasonable promisee* or a reasonable *third person* with knowledge of the circumstances.[23]

Under Swedish law, neither principle commands the exclusivity of the adjudicator's attention, but a theoretical hierarchy appears to exist, as will be developed below.

[B] General Principles in Swedish Contract Law: Does An Interpretative Hierarchy Exist?

The SCA does not set out the general principles of contract interpretation applicable under Swedish law.[24]

Instead, these have been established in case law by the Swedish Supreme Court (Swedish: 'Högsta Domstolen') (HD).[25]

In a number of decisions from the last decennium, HD has dealt with questions of contract interpretation and helpfully set out and explained the applicable rules.[26]

21. In German jurisprudence, the underlying thinking of these concepts is aptly referred to as the 'Willenstheorie' and the 'Erklärungstheorie', respectively. In English, they are sometimes called the 'will theory' and the 'reliance theory'.
22. In Roman law known as 'aggregatio mentium' or 'consensus ad idem'.
23. *See, e.g.*, the French Civil Code 1188(2), quoted below.
24. Some provisions can be said by implications to include certain principles of interpretation, e.g., section 32 concerning mistake. Regarding international sale of goods, CISG Arts 7-9 contain provisions on contract interpretation.
25. This is also the case in Denmark and Norway.
26. Swedish law does not recognise a formal rule of *stare decisis* but there is no doubt that the more principled and general statements of the law by HD are considered binding directives and applied as such by the lower courts. A list of HD decisions dealing with issues of contract interpretation is provided by C. Ramberg in SvJT 2022 p. 519, footnote 4. The author concludes: 'There is no longer a drought of precedents in the field of contract law.'

In my view, the most comprehensive exposition by HD of these principles is *NJA 2014 s. 960*,[27] which concerned a design-and-build contract (Swedish: 'Totalentrepenad') for the construction of a commercial building.[28] The decision is also remarkable due to the fact that the overall majority was made up of only two justices (Swedish: 'Justitieråd') (JR), whereas three other JR issued individual dissenting opinions concerning different parts of the decision. As regards the principles for contract interpretation, however, all JR agreed on the following paragraphs (referring to HD's previous decisions in *NJA 2012 s. 597* and *NJA 2013 s. 271*):[29]

> 20. As is the case with *contract interpretation in general*, even when a construction project is governed by a standard agreement within the AB[30] family, the guiding principle is what the *parties have mutually agreed upon*. The discussions between the parties at the time of entering into the contract and similar circumstances are indicative of the *common intention* of the parties.
>
> 21. In this case, it has not been asserted that the parties engaged in any discussions regarding the interpretation of the disputed conditions. Furthermore, there is *no discernible shared understanding*. Therefore, there is *no common intention* among the parties. In such a situation, interpretation should be based on *objective grounds*.
>
> Principles for interpreting the relevant provisions
>
> 22. The starting point for an objective interpretation of a standard contractual term is the *wording of the disputed condition*. When the wording allows for different interpretations or provides no clarity at all, guidance should be sought from *the structure and other conditions of the standard agreement*. This is particularly applicable when the provisions of the contract are intended to form a coherent system.
>
> 23. When the structure of the agreement also fails to provide any guidance, the contractual term should be interpreted in light of mandatory law (see NJA 2013 p. 271 para. 7, which concerned the interpretation of terms in AB 92). The impact of mandatory law may need to be limited in certain cases, for example, when, on one side, the contractual context does not offer direct guidance, but on the other side, the relevant mandatory legal rule fits poorly into the contractual system. Thus, ultimately, a more *overarching/comprehensive (Swedish: 'övergripanda') assessment of reasonableness (Swedish: 'rimlighetsbedömning')* should be made, which may occasionally involve *filling a contractual gap* with a rule tailored to the specific agreement (emphasis by me).

27. NJA is an acronym for 'Nytt Juridiskt Arkiv', available online at lagen.nu (in Swedish).
28. *In concreto*, the contract to be interpreted was the Swedish standard terms for construction contracts designed by the contractor, called ABT 94 (now ABT 06). But, as stated by HD, the principles set out apply equally *mutatis mutandis* to other more bespoke or individual contracts.
29. The translations into English of the excerpts from Swedish case law are made by me. I am lawyer by training and not a translator and the translations are unauthorised. I have made initial use of AI when preparing the translations but considered the quality provided by the software and made corrections or amendments where relevant (in my opinion). Neither Swedish nor English is my first language, but I consider myself fluent in both languages. Needless to say, I am happy to receive suggestions for improvements of the translations.
30. AB is an acronym for 'Allmänna Bestämmelser', i.e., standard contracts for construction and engineering contracts in Sweden. The latest editions are AB 04 (build) and ABT 06 (design-and-build).

Interestingly, the first two steps in the approach adopted by HD concerning Swedish contract law correspond, e.g., to the statutory principles for contract interpretation set out in Article 1188 of the French Code Civil (CC), which provides as follows:[31]

1. A contract is to be interpreted according to the common intention of the parties rather than stopping at the literal meaning of its terms.
2. Where this intention cannot be discerned, a contract is to be interpreted in the sense that a reasonable person placed in the same situation would give to it.

Compared with the most relevant soft law instruments, HD's *ratio decidendi* mirrors Article 4.1 of the UNIDROIT Principles,[32] Articles 5:101(1) and (3) of the PECL,[33] as well as Article II 8-101 of the DCFR.[34]

The quoted part of *NJA 2014 s. 960* clearly suggests that the modalities of contract interpretation are prioritised, thereby establishing an authentic hierarchy of interpretation. Consequently, the interpretation process should be conducted sequentially following the structure or decision tree outlined by HD.

Notably, the structured framework for contract interpretation provided by HD in *NJA 2014 s. 960* does not support the notion of a 'pragmatic' approach to contract interpretation,[35] apart from the final statement that considerations of reasonableness should serve as a final check when interpreting a contract. This part of the decision is further developed at §2.03[C] below.

Later, HD provided a slightly different description of the principles in *NJA 2015 s. 741* concerning a dispute between a partner and a partnership of chartered public accountants regarding breach of a restrictive covenant (non-competition). In that case, HD expressed a related but seemingly more flexible (or less schematic) approach to contract interpretation, not least in a multiparty contractual setting:

> 9. One starting point in a dispute over how a contract should be interpreted is to ascertain what the *parties collectively intended* at the time of contracting. However, this is *not always possible*. Furthermore, the contract and the contractual situation may be of such a nature that it is hardly relevant to attempt to establish a common intention of the parties. This can be the case, for example, with contracts involving

31. Article 1188 is a revision of Art. 1156 in the version of the original CC (or Code Napoleon) promulgated under Napoleon Bonaparte in 1804 which only referred to the supremacy of the common intention of the parties, *vide*: 'One must in agreements seek what the *common intention* of the contracting parties was, rather than pay attention to the literal meaning of the terms.' (emphasis by me). France has been called 'the bastion of subjectivism'.
32. UNIDROIT Rules is short for 'UNIDROIT Principles of International Commercial Contracts' (2016) prepared by the International Institute for the Unification of Private Law (UNIDROIT). UNIDROIT is an independent intergovernmental organisation based in Rome, Italy, and established in 1926.
33. PECL is an acronym for 'Principles of European Contract Law' (2003). The PECL were prepared by prepared by the Commission on European Contract Law (the 'Lando Commission', named after the late Danish comparative scholar, Professor Ole Lando).
34. DCFR is an acronym for 'Draft Common Frame of Reference' (2009), prepared by the Study Group on a European Civil Code and the Research Group on EC Private Law (Acquis Group). These groups comprised legal scholars and experts from various European jurisdictions who collaborated on drafting the DCFR. It can be described as an unofficial EU project.
35. This is also the case in Denmark (*see, e.g., UfR 2012.3007H*) and in Norway (*see, e.g., Rt-2010-961* and *Rt-2014-520)*.

> a *large number of parties*. This is often also the case when the relationship between the parties is governed by a *standard contract*, even though the parties' discussions and similar matters prior to the conclusion of the contract may constitute circumstances that express a common intention of the parties that deviates from what would otherwise apply, cf. NJA 2014 p. 960 para. 20.
>
> 10. When individual circumstances cannot be established or provide guidance, the interpretation or specification of contract terms must be based on *objective grounds*. The starting point is then the *wording* of the contract. When the wording allows for different interpretations, as well as when the wording does not provide any guidance at all, guidance must be sought from other factors. Other relevant interpretative data may include the *structure* of the contract and the specific contractual term's *relationship with other terms*, the *background* to the regulation, i.e., the *purpose* of the term, the *nature* of the contract's subject matter, and sometimes the parties' positions (cf. e.g. NJA 2010 p. 559 para. 9). It is generally also natural to assume that a contractual term should serve a *sensible function* and constitute a *reasonable regulation* of the parties' interests ... (emphasis by me).

The decision provided no reason for not just adopting *verbatim* the principles set out in NJA 2014 s. 960.

The importance of NJA 2014 s. 960 as a legal precedent has since been confirmed on various occasions, including in *NJA 2015 s. 862*, which contained the following more condensed summary of the applicable principles:

> 12. In recent years, [HD] has had occasion, in several decisions, to apply the standard agreements pertaining to construction and engineering works and opined on the interpretation of clauses in such agreements. If no common intention among the parties can be considered to exist, and there are no circumstances outside the contractual text that can clarify how the parties perceived a disputed standard clause, the interpretation should focus on the wording of the clause. When assessing the meaning of the clause, guidance can be drawn from the structure and other conditions of the agreement; the provisions are intended to form a coherent system. In interpreting certain clauses, it may be necessary to consider the specific features of the construction contract. When the structure of the agreement also fails to provide any guidance, it is, therefore, natural to interpret the clauses in light of the mandatory law that would otherwise have been applied, some of which is expressed in the Sale of Goods Act. However, it should be noted that construction contracts differ from, for example, sales contracts, as they typically involve extensive, complex, and long-term work with multiple parties involved. Ultimately, a more comprehensive assessment of reasonableness must be made.

Once again, this was a majority decision, and the majority comprised two JR. Three JR expressed various dissenting opinions and views.

Even later, the principles set out in NJA 2014 s. 960 and NJA 2015 s. 862, were confirmed by HD in *NJA 2018 s. 653* concerning the question of defects in a design-and-build contract.[36]

36. In the decision, reference was made to previous HD decisions in NJA 2013 s. 271, NJA 2014 s. 960 and NJA 2015 s. 862.

In *NJA 2021 s. 643* concerning a commercial framework agreement related to the alleged exclusivity regarding the provision of certain services, HD referred to its decision in NJA 2015 s. 741, in particular, with respect to no discernable joint intention in such standard agreements.

However, a broader or more 'holistic' (for lack of a better adjective) approach to contract interpretation appears in *NJA 2018 s. 834* concerning an insurance policy. In that case, a unanimous HD stated as follows:

> 10. When interpreting a standard insurance condition, for example, in a liability insurance policy, several factors must be taken into account. Some of these are typical for insurance contracts. Other factors are those that are generally significant in interpreting standard conditions. The central aspect is often the wording of the disputed condition. When the wording allows for different interpretations, or when the wording does not provide any clear indication, guidance can be sought from the structure and other insurance conditions. Other factors may also be significant, such as the purpose of the condition to the extent it can be discerned and what is objectively a sensible and reasonable regulation.
>
> 11. Therefore, several different factors must be considered when interpreting an insurance condition. Which interpretation factor or factors should be decisive cannot be stated generally but must be determined based on an overall assessment in the individual case (emphasis by me).

This was followed up in *NJA 2023 s. 630* concerning business interruption insurance and the COVID-19 pandemic, in which HD referred to NJA 2018 s. 834 (but not NJA 2014 s. 960 or, for that matter, NJA 2015 s. 741), *vide* the following:

> Interpretation of Insurance Contracts
>
> 9. In the interpretation of a standard-type insurance provision, several factors must be considered. The central focus is often the wording of the disputed provision. When the wording allows for various interpretations, guidance can be sought from the systematics and other insurance provisions. Other factors may also be relevant, such as the purpose of the provision, to the extent that it can be ascertained, and what is objectively a reasonable and sensible regulation. Which interpretation factors are decisive must be determined based on an overall assessment in the individual case. (See ... NJA 2018 p. 834, paragraphs 10 and 11).
>
> 10. The interpretation should be based on the wording of the provision in an objective sense and the text's normal linguistic meaning (see ... NJA 2017 p. 237, paragraph 14).
>
> 11. Only if a result cannot be achieved through evaluation according to the specified criteria is there reason to resort to more general principles of interpretation (see ... NJA 2001 p. 750). For example, there is normally no reason to consider whether the insurance company could have formulated a disputed provision more clearly when sufficient guidance for interpretation can be derived from other factors.

Moreover, reference can be made to *NJA 2023 s. 680.*[37] Even more recently, HD has confirmed a similar approach in its judgment of 25 January 2024 in case *HD T 4849-22.*[38] Both matters concerned insurance contracts.

37. *See* para. 36 of this decision which makes reference to NJA 2018 s. 834.
38. *See* para. 7 of this decision which makes reference to NJA 2023 s. 630.

At first glance, it may seem challenging to reconcile the principled, albeit differently framed, approaches in NJA 2014 s. 960 and NJA 2015 s. 741 (referred to in NJA 2021 s. 643), with the more holistic approach delineated in NJA 2018 s. 834 (referred to in NJA 2023 s. 630, NJA 2023 s. 680 and HD T 4849-22). These decisions appear to reflect distinct approaches to the hierarchical structure of the interpretative process.

However, reconciliation is possible if NJA 2018 s. 834, NJA 2023 s. 630, NJA 2023 s. 680 and HD T 4849-22, as suggested by the wording of the decisions themselves, are considered limited to insurance policies and thus offer a discrete and separate interpretative framework pertaining to such contracts.

Hence, it appears reasonable to maintain that the general exposition in NJA 2014 s. 960 applies as expounding the overall applicable principles to contract interpretation in general commercial contracts albeit, perhaps, in a slightly less rigid or schematic way as suggested by NJA 2015 s. 741.

Before contrasting the above with some decisions under English law, I note that in a number of cases, HD, unsurprisingly, has explained that the interpretation of the words employed in the contract must be based on their natural/ordinary linguistic meaning (Swedish: 'normala språkliga betydelsen'). I refer to the quote from NJA 2023 s. 630, *supra*. Also, reference can be made to *NJA 2007 s. 35* concerning the interpretation of standard terms in a consultancy agreement regarding architect and engineering services, called ABK 96:

> The interpretation must, therefore, be based on the contract's wording in an objective sense, starting from the text's natural linguistic meaning. When interpreting, the contract should be viewed as a cohesive whole, and the specific contractual provision should be read in conjunction with the other provisions in the contract.

Moreover, reference can be made to *NJA 2013 s. 271*.

These cases concerned terms in various standard contracts, but in my view, there is nothing to suggest that a different approach will apply to more bespoke contracts unless specific and singular parts of the factual matrix merit a departure from this commonsensical starting point.

The overall principles governing contract interpretation in Swedish law can be contrasted with the approach adopted in English law,[39] which can be illustrated by the decision of the Supreme Court (SC) in *Arnold v. Britton*[40] concerning service charges pertaining to holiday chalets in Wales. Here, Lord Neuberger[41] provided the following

39. In a number of decisions spanning the past more than fifty years, the Supreme Court (formerly the House of Lords) has had the opportunity to restate the principles of contract interpretation under English law, not least as regards commercial contracts. In this regard, reference can be made to the seminal decisions in Prenn *v.* Simmonds [1971] WLR 1381, *Schuler AG v. Wickman Machine Tool Sales Ltd* [1974] AC 235, *Investors Compensation Scheme v. West Bromwich Building Society [1998] WLR 896, Chartbrook Ltd v. Persimmon Homes Ltd [2009] UKHL 38, Rainy Sky SA v. Kookmin Bank [2011] UKSC 50, Arnold and Ors v. Britton [2015] UKSC 36* and *Wood v. Capita Insurance Services Ltd* [2017] UKSC 24.
40. *See supra* n. 39.
41. David Neuberger was president of the SC between 2012 and 2017.

enumerated restatement of the method applicable to contract interpretation under English law (internal quotations and references omitted):

> 15. When interpreting a written contract, the court is concerned to identify the intention of the parties by reference to what a reasonable person having all the background knowledge which would have been available to the parties would have understood them to be using the language in the contract to mean ... And it does so by focussing on the meaning of the relevant words, ... in their documentary, factual and commercial context. That meaning has to be assessed in the light of (i) the natural and ordinary meaning of the clause, (ii) any other relevant provisions of the lease, (iii) the overall purpose of the clause and the lease, (iv) the facts and circumstances known or assumed by the parties at the time that the document was executed, and (v) commercial common sense, but (vi) disregarding subjective evidence of any party's intentions.

As recently as in February 2024, the Judicial Committee of the Privy Council (JCPC)[42] in *National Commercial Bank Jamaica v. NCB Staff Association*[43] helpfully updated the approach to contract interpretation in a case concerning a profit-sharing scheme ('scheme') for employees of the bank:

> 31. The modern approach of the common law to the interpretation of contracts has been clear at least in its outline since the judgment of Lord Wilberforce in the House of Lords in [Prenn v. Simmond][44] ...
>
> 32. First, the court's task is to ascertain the objective meaning of the language which the parties have chosen to express their agreement, having regard to the contract as a whole. Secondly, in so doing the court has regard to the factual background known to the parties at or before the date of the contract, but excluding evidence of prior negotiations. Thirdly, where there are rival meanings of the relevant contractual provision considered in its context, the court can give weight to the implications of the rival meanings, by considering which construction is more consistent with business common sense. But, fourthly, the court does not depart from an interpretation of the natural language of words just because the contractual arrangement has proven to be a bad bargain for one of the parties. Fifthly, the weight to be attached to the precise words used in the contract will vary depending upon the sophistication of the contractual drafting and whether skilled professionals have been involved in creating the contract. But, sixthly, even where there has been a process of sophisticated professional drafting, the court must be alive to the possibility that the text of a provision, which has been accepted to conclude a contract, is a compromise between parties with conflicting aims or the result of a failure of communication between the parties. Where that is so, the court may give more weight to the factual matrix or the purpose of similar provisions in contracts of the same type. Finally, events and the actions of the parties after the conclusion of the contract are not relevant to its interpretation. The court has regard to the facts and circumstances which existed at the time the contract was made and which were known or reasonably available to both parties.

42. The JCPC is *the court of final appeal for the UK overseas territories and Crown dependencies. The current twelve members of the panel are all justices of the English Supreme Court.*
43. *National Commercial Bank Jamaica Ltd v. NCB Staff Association (Jamaica)* [2024] UKPC 2.
44. *See supra* n. 39.

First, it is evident from the quote that English law applies the objective theory to contract interpretation, i.e., that the perceived joint intention of the parties is derived from and established by the objective meaning of the words, namely what the words would convey to a reasonable third person with all the requisite knowledge of the factual matrix.

However, this apparent distinction between Swedish and English law should not be overstated. First of all, it is rarely the case that a joint intention (other than the one expressed by the wording employed in the contract) is discernable. Second, the applicable principles regarding contract interpretation show considerable similarities, including the emphasis on the actual wording, the linguistic approach to determining the meaning of the words in the contract, the importance and role of the context in which the employed words appear, as well as the purpose of the clause to be interpreted.

However, some notable differences are apparent. First, the Swedish law concept of a 'comprehensive reasonableness test' is not the same as the English law concept of 'business common sense.' Second, the parol evidence rule does not apply in Swedish law. These two issues will be briefly discussed *seriatim*.

[C] 'Comprehensive Reasonableness Test'

A characteristic feature of Swedish law on contract interpretation is the explicit inclusion of an 'overarching' or 'comprehensive' (Swedish: 'övergripande') test for reasonableness as the final element in the intellectual process, *vide* NJA 2014 s. 960 quoted above. As will be seen from the quotation, the principle or its application is not further explained in the decision. I will, inartfully, refer to this as the 'comprehensive reasonableness test' (CRT).

The only instance (that I am currently aware of) in which HD expressly engaged with the CRT is the aforementioned decision in NJA 2015 s. 862.[45]

The case concerned another design-and-build contract, this time regarding the conversion of a part of a building into a hostel. The standard terms of ABT 94[46] were adopted by the parties. The dispute turned on whether the commencement of the prescription period of three months for additional claims by the contractor was predicated on a final inspection (Swedish: 'slutbesiktning') being performed.

45. The Svea Court of Appeal (Swedish: 'Svea Hovrätt') ('SH') considered reasonableness in its decision of 22 Oct. 2020 in T-7981-19 (*Nordic Railway Construction Sverige AB v. Trafikverket*) concerning the question of whether the contractor was entitled to additional payment for geodesic measurement or that deliverable was included in the contract price. SH found in favour of the employer. Towards the end of its decision, SH stated: '(T)he contract interpretation put forward by the [employer] appears as both the most reasonable and the most consistent with the contract's systematics. On the other hand, [the contractor's] strictly semantic interpretation does not appear as reasonable or particularly well-adapted to the factual circumstances.' This could, potentially, be viewed as a singular example of the 'pragmatism' referred to earlier in this chapter.

46. As mentioned, the standard terms in ABT 94 have since been replaced by ABT 06.

In this regard, ABT 94 6§13 included, *inter alia*, the following wording:

> The contractor's claims regarding the works, a prescription period of six months applies, calculated from the approval of the works.

However, in the individual terms and conditions, the parties had, *inter alia*, deviated from ABT 94 6§13 by including the following provision:

> Final Settlement
>
> Amending [ABT94 6§13], the final settlement shall take place no later than 3 months after the approved final inspection (Swedish: 'Slutbesiktning').

After applying the 'decision tree' set out in NJA 2014 s. 960, the majority of the JR[47] noted, *inter alia*, as follows regarding the CRT:

> 18. In the more overarching reasonableness assessment that ultimately must be made, the question arises, among other things, whether the purpose of the relevant rule may lead to it being interpreted in a way that is not supported by its wording. What applies in this regard is related to the type of rule in question. Here, it concerns a prescription rule.

In the decision, HD then made a distinction between long-term and short-term prescriptions and added:

> 20. In this case, it concerns a rule regarding short-term prescription. The purpose can be assumed to be that the parties quickly clarify what applies regarding compensation for changes or additional work. It is an appropriate arrangement. The rule in ABT 94 [6§13] also clearly states that the contractor's claims for compensation for variations or additional work are subject to short-term prescription. Thus, such a prescription scheme should *not come as a surprise to either party*.
>
> 21. The function of the starting point is primarily to provide a clear indication of the endpoint for the short prescription period but also to indicate when it is time for the parties to discuss additional compensation for changes and additional work. This suggests that in a situation like the present one, it is an appropriate arrangement for the prescription period to be linked to the time when the construction works are considered completed. However, the question is whether purposes of that kind carry enough weight to *warrant an interpretative extension* in that direction. This assessment shall be made in light of the specific interpretative principles applicable to prescription provisions.
>
> 22. A prescription rule, due to its *drastic right-depriving effect*, may not be applied analogously and must be *interpreted restrictively*. This applies to both statutory and *contractual provisions*. Restrictiveness applies not only to the provision's scope but also to its application conditions, including the starting point for the prescription period. With respect to a contractual prescription rule, an interpretative extension should only be accepted if there are clear indications for it.
>
> 23. The foregoing has established that if no final inspection has taken place, it is *appropriate* for the prescription period, according to ABT 94 [6§13], to start running when the contractor has *completed their work*. However, there are no clear indications for such an arrangement in the general provisions, and neither does such a time seem to be determinable in an unambiguous manner without closer contractual regulation. In this situation, the conclusion is that the relevant

47. In this case, the majority consisted of three JR, and the minority comprised two JR.

> prescription rule cannot be applied when no final inspection has taken place. (emphasis by me).

When arriving at the opposite conclusion, the minority relied not least on a 'systematic reasoning' regarding, in particular, a coherent and unitary application of the various terms in such standard terms (Swedish: 'avtalssystematiska skäl'). In the case before HD, this approach included a uniform application of the concepts of performance period (Swedish: 'entreprenadtid') and warranty period (Swedish: 'garantitid'). This could be said to correspond to an interpretation based on considerations regarding the '*structure and other conditions of the standard agreement*', *vide* NJA 2014 s. 960.

The somewhat nebulous language employed in the decision makes it difficult to ascertain with certainty exactly what the CRT implied in the case, but it would appear that the strict consequences (loss of a payment claim) made the majority attach additional importance to the term 'final inspection' employed in the individual terms. Put differently, the wording of the *ratio decidendi* suggests that considerations of reasonableness in the view of the majority merited a deviation from otherwise applicable considerations of purpose and contractual coherence in favour of a restrictive interpretation. The minority held the opposite view.[48]

As a general guideline for arbitrators, the decision may serve primarily as an illustration of the mentioned inherent risk associated with a lack of intersubjectivity and linguistic relativism when applying broadly worded normative legal concepts to a factual matrix.

The CRT can be contrasted with the legal concept of 'Business Common Sense' (BCS), which features as an integral part of contract interpretation under English law, *vide* the quote from *Arnold v. Britton*.[49]

In *Rainy Sky v. Kookmin Bank*,[50] which concerned the interpretation of a guarantee, Lord Clarke provided the following guidance regarding contract interpretation:[51]

> 21. The language used by the parties will often have more than one potential meaning. I would accept the submission made on behalf of the appellants that the exercise of construction is essentially one unitary exercise in which the court must consider the language used and ascertain what a reasonable person, that is a person who has all the background knowledge which would reasonably have been

---

48. *See also* Herre & Johansson SvJT 2020.821 et seq., especially pp. 880-881 and 886. They consider that 'reasonable gave way for a restrictive interpretation' of the disputed clause. Based on the wording of the decision, this is, in my opinion, a debatable conclusion. On another view, the majority relied on reasonableness to deviate from the more unitary or systematic arguments emphasised by the minority.
49. *See supra* n. 39.
50. *See supra* n. 39.
51. Earlier, Lord Diplock had stated as follows in *The Antaios Compania Neviera S.A. v. Salen Rederierna A.B. [1985] A.C. 191*: '(I)f detailed semantic and syntactical analysis of words in a commercial contract is going to lead to a conclusion that flouts business commonsense, it must be made to yield to business commonsense.' In my view, this hardly reflects the current state of the law of England and Wales which appears more restrictive in respect of the application of business common sense. However, it may well *pro modo* express the state of Swedish law.

> available to the parties in the situation in which they were at the time of the contract, would have understood the parties to have meant. In doing so, the court must have regard to all the relevant surrounding circumstances. If there are two possible constructions, the court is entitled to prefer the construction which is consistent with business common sense and to reject the other.

In *Wood v. Capita,*[52] Lord Hodge provided further context to the application and place of the principle of BCS when interpreting commercial contracts (internal references omitted):

> 11. ... Interpretation is ... a unitary exercise; where there are rival meanings, the court can give weight to the implications of rival constructions by reaching a view as to which construction is more consistent with business common sense. But, in striking a balance between the indications given by the language and the implications of the competing constructions the court must consider the quality of drafting of the clause ... and it must also be alive to the possibility that one side may have agreed to something which with hindsight did not serve his interest ...Similarly, the court must not lose sight of the possibility that a provision may be a negotiated compromise or that the negotiators were not able to agree more precise terms.

From recent case law, reference can be made to the Court of Appeal decision in *Nord Naphtha v. New Stream*[53] concerning a buyer's claim for repayment of an advance on the purchase price when delivery of the product (diesel) was not made due to force majeure and subsequent termination of the contract. In this case, the Court of Appeal (LJ Whipple) arrived at the following conclusion regarding the claim:

> 57. I conclude that the reasonable person reading clause 14.5, armed with the information available to [the seller] and [the buyer] as they entered the Contract, would have no real doubt that that clause provided Nord Naphtha with a right of repayment of the Advance in the event of non-delivery for force majeure reasons. The right is expressed by that clause, in words which are clear enough when read objectively.
>
> 58. I do not consider the clause is reasonably open to conflicting interpretations. But if I am wrong about that, then I am sure that the construction which is consistent with *common sense and the wider commercial context* is that advanced by [the buyer], and upheld by the Deputy Judge.
>
> 59. I do not in the circumstances need to consider the alternative of an implied term.

In that case, the court found no contractual ambiguity but stated that common sense would have resolved the matter in favour of the buyer if such ambiguity had been afoot. Conversely, it appears safe to assume that, had the wording of the contract been unambiguous in favour of the seller, notions of BCS would not have prevailed. In that event, the court would have had to resort to gap-filling in order to reach the result.[54] Under Swedish law, the CRT would almost certainly have entailed the same result. If

52. *See supra* n. 39.
53. *Nord Naphtha Limited v. New Stream Trading AG* [2021] EWCA Civ 1829.
54. In this regard, it should be noted that both the High Court and the Court of Appeal noted that the contract in question was poorly drafted.

not, the clause would have been exposed to modification under section 36 of the SCA, *vide* below.

Since the case law pertaining to the CRT is so sparse, it is hard to assess its relationship with the BCS principle with any degree of certainty. However, they appear to be similar in underlying thought, although the principle in Swedish law appears to be based on a more normative underpinning than the BCS-test.

It merits mentioning that BCS is explicitly limited to an *ex ante* perspective, as emphasised in *Arnold v. Britton*:

> 19. The third point I should mention is that commercial common sense is not to be invoked retrospectively. The mere fact that a contractual arrangement, if interpreted according to its natural language, has worked out badly, or even disastrously, for one of the parties is not a reason for departing from the natural language.

The same principle, i.e., an *ex ante* view, should, in my view, apply in Swedish law; otherwise, the demarcation lines between contract interpretation and contract modification are completely blurred, not to say compromised.

[D] Parol Evidence Rule

Most common law systems include a legal principle that extrinsic evidence is not admissible if the text of the contract is unambiguous. This is known as the 'parol evidence' rule (PER).[55] The PER is not a term of art, and it is applied differently in various common law jurisdictions.

At its core, however, the PER provides that where a written agreement between the parties exists, and its terms are considered unambiguous, evidence concerning the pre-contractual phase, typically concerning the negotiations between the parties, is inadmissible. The same applies to evidence regarding the subjective belief of a contractual party. The excluded evidence is often termed 'extrinsic evidence'.

It must be emphasised that the PER is considered to be a part of substantive law and is part of the methodology for contractual interpretation, *vide* Lord Neuberger's speech in *Arnold v. Britton*,[56] quoted above. Hence, a tribunal sitting in an SCC arbitration in Stockholm concerning an agreement governed by English law as *lex causae* shall apply the parol evidence rule if and when engaging in contract interpretation.[57]

55. The term has its origin in the peculiar ancient jargon in English law known as 'legal French,' (the word 'parole' means word or speech in French).
56. *See supra* n. 39.
57. A potential clash of principles may be considered to exist if, under Swedish law, contrary to English law, the parol evidence rule is considered a procedural principle. In such circumstances, one can imagine a scenario where a losing party that has had evidence declared inadmissible under the parol evidence rule challenges the final award before the Swedish Courts, arguing that the party was not given a reasonable opportunity to present its case, *vide* section 34(1)(7) of the Swedish Arbitration Act viewed in conjunction with section 24(1) thereof. As far as I am aware, no Swedish court decision has yet grappled with this issue.

In *Nord Naphtha v. New Stream*, the court had to compare two contracts that were not identical. One of the parties argued (unsuccessfully) that considerable interpretative weight should be attached to this difference. LJ Whipple stated as follows:

> As to the second argument, the two contracts are self-evidently different, but why they are different is unknown. There is no evidence to explain the course of negotiations leading up to the Contract or to explain why a counterpart clause (an equivalent to clause 10.18) was not included – leaving aside for the moment the issue of whether such evidence would, in any event, be relevant or admissible to the question of construction. The reasons for the differences are not explained; this is a matter on which the Court cannot sensibly draw inferences, and the Court will not embark on speculation.

In my view, this quote aptly demonstrates the potential weakness of the PER. If you have to consider the evidence before deciding whether it is admissible, the principle is of limited value.[58]

Under Swedish law, a tribunal's ability to consider parol evidence is unfettered without any limitations apart from the requirement of timeliness, and HD, in a number of cases, expressly relied on pre-contractual negotiations when engaging in contract interpretation and also post-contractual conduct to discern the meaning of the contract.[59] Hence, common law-trained arbitrators should forget any notion of limiting the admissibility of parol evidence when deciding a dispute under Swedish law. The probative weight of such evidence is for the tribunal to assess.

[E] Implication of Terms under Swedish Law

To me, it is obvious that interpretation of a contract and implication of terms into a contract (also known as gap-filling) are separate, albeit related, intellectual exercises. Interpretation involves determining the meaning of the words and sentences employed in the contract. If these words and sentences make it possible to arrive at a coherent meaning with respect to the disputed issue, there is no need for any implication of terms. It follows from this observation that considerations of gap-filling are relevant only when it is not possible to derive a meaning without implicating a pertinent additional contractual term.

58. A similar statement by Lord Neuberger can be found in *Arnold v. Britton*, at para. 12.
59. Whether an 'entire agreement clause,' potentially in combination with a 'non-reliance clause' will render extrinsic evidence inadmissible or rather limits the weight (or rather lack thereof) that the adjudicator can place on such evidence is, to my knowledge, not settled in Swedish law. Under Swedish law, the freedom of the courts to assess the evidence is well established. In my view, the principle of freedom of contract and party autonomy should provide the answer to the question; however, given that the point of departure is unlimited admissibility, such a provision must state with clarity and in an unambiguous manner that the parties agree that such evidence is inadmissible, not merely of no (or low) probative value.

A similar view was taken by the *English Supreme Court in Marks & Spencer v. BNP Paribas*.[60] Here, Lord Neuberger explained the difference as follows:

> 27. Of course, it is fair to say that the factors to be taken into account on an issue of construction, namely the words used in the contract, the surrounding circumstances known to both parties at the time of the contract, commercial common sense, and the reasonable reader or reasonable parties, are also taken into account on an issue of implication. However, that does not mean that the exercise of implication should be properly classified as part of the exercise of interpretation, let alone that it should be carried out at the same time as interpretation. When one is implying a term or a phrase, one is not construing words, as the words to be implied are *ex hypothesi* not there to be construed; and to speak of construing the contract as a whole, including the implied terms, is not helpful, not least because it begs the question as to what construction actually means in this context.
>
> 28. In most, possibly all, disputes about whether a term should be implied into a contract, it is only after the process of construing the express words is complete that the issue of an implied term falls to be considered. Until one has decided what the parties have expressly agreed, it is difficult to see how one can set about deciding whether a term should be implied and if so what term. ...

In Swedish law, however, HD has expressed doubts as to the possibility of (always) maintaining a clear and sequential approach to the implication of terms, *vide NJA 2010 s. 416*:

> 5. The question of how an agreement should be interpreted is not uncomplicated, and the boundary between contract interpretation and gap filling is somewhat blurred. ...

In the quoted part of the ratio decidendi from *NJA 2014 s. 960, HD* noted that the 'overarching test for reasonableness' could 'occasionally' merit gap-filling. No further indications were made with respect to the requirements. To me, what is more likely to be 'blurred' is the demarcation lines between questions of gap-filling based on such overarching considerations of reasonableness and a subsequent modification (Swedish: 'jämkning') of the contract based on a test for unreasonableness or unconscionability, *vide* SCA section 36. Although contract interpretation and contract modification are distinct exercises taking place at different stages of the intellectual process, they are ultimately both expressed by the adjudicator in the same decision (unless these issues have been bifurcated, which rarely happens, if ever). I deal with contract modification at §2.04[B] *infra*.

I am aware that some Swedish scholars consider the distinction between interpretation and implication moot and prefer to include both exercises under the umbrella term interpretation and, more importantly, deal with them in a unitary manner. I, with due respect, disagree. To me, it is always possible to operate the distinction between these two parts of the intellectual process, and the distinction should be respected. The reason is straightforward: Interpretation is mandatory on the part of the adjudicator, whereas the implication of a term (gap-filling) is only relevant

60. *Marks and Spencer plc v. BNP Paribas Securities Services Trust Company (Jersey) Limited* [2015] UKSC 72.

and permissible if and when the words found in the contract do not provide an answer to a question of contract interpretation relevant to determining the issue in dispute.

This can be contrasted with the very principled approach to gap-filling adopted and maintained by the English courts.[61]

Reference can be made, in particular, to *Shirlaw v. Southern Foundries*,[62] in which the courts introduced the 'officious bystander' as an intellectual concept. At its core, the concept entails that the implication of a term should only be considered *'if, while the parties were making their bargain, an officious bystander were to suggest some express provision for it in their agreement, they would testily suppress him with a common "Oh, of course!"'*. In a number of subsequent cases, courts have pondered what question the officious bystander would likely have asked the parties and how the parties would have answered that particular question.

The overall substantive test for implication of terms was formulated by *Lord Simon in the JCPC's decision in BP v. Shire of Hastings*:[63]

> For a term to be implied, the following conditions (which may overlap) must be satisfied: (1) it must be reasonable and equitable; (2) it must be necessary to give business efficacy to the contract so that no term will be implied if the contract is effective without it; (3) it must be so obvious that 'it goes without saying'; (4) it must be capable of clear expression; (5) it must not contradict any express term of the contract.

More recently, in *Marks & Spencer v. BNP Paribas*,[64] the SC revisited, maintained and slightly developed the relevant criteria in English law. In that decision, Lord Neuberger added a number of interesting considerations. He stated, inter alia, as follows (internal references and quotations omitted):

> 21. In my judgment, the judicial observations so far considered represent a clear, consistent and principled approach. It could be dangerous to reformulate the principles, but I would add six comments: ... *First*, ... the implication of a term was not critically dependent on proof of an actual intention of the parties when negotiating the contract. If one approaches the question by reference to what the parties would have agreed, one is not strictly concerned with the hypothetical answer of the actual parties, but with that of notional reasonable people in the position of the parties at the time at which they were contracting. *Secondly*, a term should not be implied into a detailed commercial contract merely because it appears fair or merely because one considers that the parties would have agreed it if it had been suggested to them. Those are necessary but not sufficient grounds for including a term. However, and *thirdly*, it is questionable whether Lord Simon's first requirement, reasonableness and equitableness, will usually, if ever, add anything: if a term satisfies the other requirements, it is hard to think that it would not be reasonable and equitable. *Fourthly*, ... although Lord Simon's requirements

61. The origin of the principle in English law is usually considered to be The Moorcock (1884) 14 PD 64.
62. *Shirlaw v. Southern Foundries Ltd* (1926) 1939 2 KB 206.
63. *BP Refinery (Westernport) Pty Ltd v. President, Councillors and Ratepayers of the Shire of Hastings* (1977) 16 A.L.R. 363.
64. *Marks and Spencer plc v. BNP Paribas Securities Services Trust Company (Jersey) Limited and another* [2015] UKSC 72.

> are otherwise cumulative, I would accept that business necessity and obviousness, his second and third requirements, can be alternatives in the sense that only one of them needs to be satisfied, although I suspect that in practice it would be a rare case where only one of those two requirements would be satisfied. *Fifthly*, if one approaches the issue by reference to the officious bystander, it is vital to formulate the question to be posed by [him] with the utmost care, ... *Sixthly*, necessity for business efficacy involves a value judgment. It is rightly common ground on this appeal that the test is not one of absolute necessity, not least because the necessity is judged by reference to business efficacy. It may well be that a more helpful way of putting Lord Simon's second requirement is, as suggested by Lord Sumption in argument, that a term can only be implied if, without the term, the contract would lack commercial or practical coherence.' (emphasis by me)

Unsurprisingly, the more professional the parties and the more complex and comprehensive the contract, the more reluctant English law will be with regard to the implication of further terms in the contract.

As is evident from the quotes above, English law employs a very strict test for gap-filling in commercial contracts that does not allow for the broader normative considerations of 'reasonableness' found in Swedish law.

It follows from the above that arbitrators have considerably more leeway under Swedish law to imply terms into contracts than most common law-trained arbitrators will be familiar with from cases proceeding under English law. Whether arbitrators should do so when dealing with reasonably sophisticated parties in a commercial contract dispute is a different question.

§2.04 CONTRACT MODIFICATION (INCLUDING SETTING ASIDE) UNDER SWEDISH LAW

[A] Introductory Remarks

As mentioned, any notion of contract modification is necessarily predicated on the meaning of the contract being established through interpretation and, if relevant, gap-filling. Put differently, only when a tribunal, through interpretation and – if relevant and pleaded – gap-filling by implication, has assessed the allocation of rights and obligations between the parties will the tribunal proceed to consider whether this contractual regime should be set aside completely or in part, or whether some provisions should be modified. Hence, conflating these processes should be avoided.

Under Swedish law (as well as under Danish and Norwegian law), two different, but in part related, concepts are of particular relevance when considering the issue of contract modification.

[B] Doctrine of Assumptions

The first concept is most often termed the 'Doctrine of Assumptions' (DoA) (Swedish: 'Förutsättningsläran'). This legal construct originated in German doctrine in the mid-19th century[65] but later (towards the end of the 19th century) gained traction in Scandinavia, and it has been a staple of Scandinavian contract law since then. I consider it safe to say that its 'popularity' as a legal argument has diminished while arguments based on section 36 of the SCA have proliferated. I shall, therefore, deal with it briefly.

Overall, an argument based on the DoA will involve ascertainment of whether a promise can be considered invalid or ineffective due to the promise either being made under assumptions that were incorrect at the time of the promise being made or these original assumptions turning out to be incorrect due to later events.

It is imperative to understand that while subsequent developments may be invoked to demonstrate the incorrectness of a specific assumption, the determination of whether the DoA applies is strictly and solely *ex ante*, meaning it is to be conducted at the moment of contracting. In other words, only those assumptions held by a party at that juncture carry legal relevance.

The application of the DoA is predicated upon the fulfilment of three conditions: First, that the incorrect assumption was essential (Swedish: 'väsentlig') to the promisor; second, that it was apparent (Swedish: 'synbar') to the promisee that the promisor held the assumption in question; and third, that the adjudicator deems the assumption 'relevant', which entails that it is appropriate to allocate the risk of the assumption being or turning out to be incorrect to the promisee.

The effect of the application of the DoA is complete/partial invalidity or ineffectiveness. Reference can be made to HD's decision in *NJA 1989 s. 614* regarding the agreement concerning the division of an estate where a requested amendment could not be based on the principles of the DoA:

> The legal consequences that may arise in the application of [the DoA] are total or partial invalidity or ineffectiveness.

The import of this limitation with respect to the available relief is that the DoA cannot be relied on for a more granular modification of the exchange of deliverables (Swedish: 'jämkning'), e.g., by requesting an increased payment.[66]

As an example of HD dealing explicitly with the DoA, reference is made to *NJA 1999 s. 575* regarding a bank seeking to reverse a payment executed by the bank to a payee. It turned out that the payor had insufficient funds to discharge the payment, and the bank unsuccessfully sought a repayment relying on *condictio indebiti*, fraud, *re integra* and the DoA. As regards the DoA, HD noted as follows:

> The bank has finally argued that the payment should be reversed because it is invalid according to the doctrine of assumptions. In this regard, the bank has claimed that it was an essential assumption/precondition for the payment that

65. Normally attributed to the German scholar Bernhard Windscheid: 'Die Lehre des römischen Rechts von der Voraussetzung' (1850).
66. This remains the position under Swedish and Danish law However, under Norwegian law, the DoA has been applied by the Norwegian Supreme Court (Norwegian: 'Høyesterett') as support for a wider or more granular contract modification, i.e., beyond full or partial invalidity/ineffectiveness, *vide*, e.g., Rt-2010-1345 og Rt-2014-866.

> funds were available in [the payor's] account and that this assumption/ precondition has proven to be incorrect.
>
> A party to a contract or a payment transaction must typically bear the risk that their assumptions are flawed. Occasionally, after an objective assessment, it may be considered appropriate and reasonable to shift the risk of an assumption failing onto the counterparty. However, no reasons for this can be considered to exist in the present case, especially since [payee], as previously noted, lacked an overview of the circumstances affecting the payment.

In *NJA 1999 s. 793*, a bank's incorrect assumptions were similarly considered the risk of the bank and, therefore, irrelevant as a matter of law.

[C] SCA Section 36

As previously noted, section 36 of the SCA was promulgated and incorporated into the statute during the mid-1970s. Its first subsection provides as follows:[67]

> A contract term or condition may be modified (Swedish: 'jämkas') or set aside if such term or condition is unconscionable (Swedish: 'oskäligt') having regard to the contents of the agreement, the circumstances prevailing at the time the agreement was entered into, subsequent circumstances, and circumstances in general. Where a term is of such significance for the agreement that it would be unreasonable to demand the continued enforceability of the remainder of the agreement with its terms unchanged, the agreement may be modified in other respects, or may be set aside in its entirety.

It is trite to state that words and their meaning are of obvious importance when applying the law. In the English language, the word 'unconscionable'[68] carries a certain connotation of immorality or unethical behaviour, especially in a legal context, whereas 'unreasonable' is a more general term indicating a lack of rationality or fairness, including a manifest and substantial lack of equivalence between the deliverables to be exchanged.

From English case law, I refer to *Multiservice Bookbinding v. Marden*:[69]

> (I)n order to be freed from the necessity to comply with all the terms of the mortgage, the plaintiffs must show that the bargain, or some of its terms, was unfair and unconscionable: it is not enough to show that, in the eyes of the court, it was unreasonable. In my judgment a bargain cannot be unfair and unconscionable unless one of the parties to it has imposed the objectionable terms in a morally reprehensible manner, that is to say, in a way which affects his conscience.

Since coming into force, section 36 has become a focal point of contention in a large number of contractual disputes across Scandinavia – also between professional

67. This translation is from JUNO, one of the largest legal information service providers in Sweden.
68. I note that in the 'Swedish-English Glossary' published by the Swedish Courts, the term 'oskälig' is translated as 'excessive, unreasonable.' The glossary is available here: svensk-engelsk_ordlista_2019.pdf (domstol.se).
69. *Multiservice Bookbinding Ltd and Ors v. Marden* [1979] Ch 84.

parties. Frequently, an argument based on section 36 serves as a fallback position as an argument for contract modification should the party‘s primary argument of contract interpretation fail to persuade the arbitrators.

Although the original legislative idea behind section 36 was primarily to provide for an equitable revision clause in contractual relationships involving consumers, there is no doubt that it applies in purely commercial relationships. However, the threshold for modification is considerably higher outside the realm of consumer contracts or contracts between parties of (substantially) unequal bargaining power.

From the travaux préparatoires, the following passage shall be quoted:[70]

> (O)bviously, it is out of the question to modify (Swedish: 'jämka') all agreements that cannot be said to entail a fair balance between the parties. This is certainly true in purely business relationships, which often involve a certain degree of conscious risk-taking from one or both parties.

In my view, it is equally 'obvious' that the words 'often' and 'from one or both parties' should be stricken from the quoted sentence to reflect commercial reality. Put differently, risk and risk-taking are inherent features in all business activities.

Moreover, it will most often be necessary to consider the contract as a whole and not merely focus on a discrete provision which may appear unreasonable but is 'offset' by other provisions in the instrument, *vide* the following quote from the travaux préparatoires:[71]

> (T)he assessment of whether a contractual term is considered unreasonable will often depend on how the agreement is otherwise structured. For example, it may happen that a contractual term that clearly disadvantages one party and which would normally be set aside (Swedish: 'underkännas') may be considered fully acceptable in certain instances because the disadvantages that the condition entails for one party are compensated by benefits for that party in other respects.

It follows from the wording of the provision that the assessment can be made *ex ante*, i.e., at the time of contracting, as well as *ex post*, i.e., considering subsequent events of importance for the normative assessment of the potential unconscionability of the agreement. The arbitrators' assessment is fact-sensitive, but it is important to understand that the clause is not meant as an invitation for tribunals to rewrite the commercial bargain struck by the (professional) parties even in circumstances where this bargain turns out to be disadvantageous to one of them.

In a similar vein, HD in *NJA 2022 s. 354* concerning a limitation of liability clause in a contract for tax advice provided by a major CPA firm (PwC) to a real estate company, provided the following more general statement:

> 33. The application of Section 36 of the Contract Act should always be nuanced, based on factual grounds, and exercised with some restraint. In its application, it should be noted that the provision is primarily intended for consumer relationships. In commercial contract law, the principle of freedom of contract should be given particular weight. Against this background, it should generally require

70. Prop.1975/76:81, p. 119.
71. Prop.1975/76:81, p. 118.

> significantly more for a contract term to be considered unreasonable/unconscionable (Swedish: 'oskäligt') in a commercial relationship, especially between parties of equal strength.

The decision involved HD considering, *inter alia*, the following facts and issues:

> 38. At the same time, it should be noted that [the CPA firm] had undertaken a precise advisory assignment in its own specialized area. The core of this assignment was to provide [the client] with sufficient basis for assessing whether the real estate transfer had any negative tax consequences. Furthermore, it was clearly foreseeable for [the CPA firm] what damage inadequate advice in this regard risked causing, namely a specific expense for stamp duty. It is also worth mentioning that [the CPA firm] could reasonably insure itself against the risk that incorrect or incomplete advice would cause harm. Of significance in this context is also that a limitation of liability to ten times the base amount, approximately 450,000 SEK, appears low in relation to the nature and scope of the entire assignment – including the foreseeable economic risk at stake – and the fee that [the CPA firm] charged for the advice, slightly over 100,000 SEK
>
> 39. However, as indicated, the degree of negligence on the part of the tortfeasor is a central aspect in assessing whether a limitation of liability should be adjusted. For example, in advisory services, it is impossible to entirely avoid occasional harm related to one or more oversights or other minor forms of negligence. It is normally reasonable for a contractor to protect themselves against such damages giving rise to extensive liability through limitations of liability.

The loss claimed was calculated at approx. SEK 1.5 m. In the circumstances, the limitation clause was not set aside or modified.[72]

Moreover, it should be noted that HD in *NJA 2009 s. 672* relied on the principles set out in the DCFR regarding a reasonable notice period in an oral distribution agreement that did not contain any such provision.

Due to the constraints regarding the length of this article, I shall not quote further from Swedish case law. Outside the realm of consumer contracts, some classic areas of application of section 36 across the Scandinavian jurisdictions concern, *inter alia*, provisions regarding the size of liquidated damages, limitation of liability clauses, clauses regarding interest rates and indexation of payments, but the application of the statute is not limited thereto.

The application of section 36 does not, as a necessary feature, require any immoral or unethical behaviour on the part of the party to the contract but can rather be viewed as the legal valve for addressing instances of a profound imbalance in the exchange of deliverables, i.e., in some manner akin to the Roman law principle of '*laesio enormis*'. As such, it can be employed as a method of (re)establishing commutative justice when this has been skewed. However, it is not the function of the

72. The decision was by a majority vote (3-2). The minority would set aside in concreto the limitation of liability based on, *inter alia*, the level of culpability (which the minority found was considerable although not rising to the level of gross negligence, the general qualifications and market position of PwC within the area of tax advice (Swedish: 'kvalificerad och stor aktör') and the fact that PwC, but not the customer, could insure the risk, i.e., the unexpected negative tax implications based on the flawed advice provided.

principles of contract law to offer a party that voluntarily enters into a bargain that turns out to be bad protection from the consequences of such a decision.

If, however, immoral or unethical behaviour is demonstrated, the threshold for legal intervention will be lower, and other provisions in the SCA may apply, in particular section 30, section 31 or section 33. However, unethical behaviour should not in and of itself merit a modification if the resulting contract is considered reasonable but may, in certain circumstances, result in the entire contract being set aside.

There is an obvious risk associated with employing a legal standard of such broad and generic description as 'unreasonable' or 'unconscionable', namely that it lends itself to becoming an 'all-purpose' legal argument for seeking to set aside or subsequently amend the allocation of rights and obligations in the contractual instrument which, perhaps over time, may have turned out to be unfavourable to a party. Some legal practitioners will undoubtedly argue that this is already the case.

Contrasting section 36 with common law systems, the doctrine of 'unconscionable bargains' in common law jurisdictions, although not identically applied and understood, has a much narrower application. It is clearly based on a normative assessment of conduct and basically requires that a stronger person in some way or form exploits or takes advantage of another person's weakness to obtain a bargain that is manifestly unfair. Put differently, it is not sufficient that the bargain is 'unfair', 'improvident' or, in other ways, turns out to the considerable disadvantage of one of the parties. It is generally accepted that notions of commutative justice or 'equivalence' regarding deliverables will not assist a party where the contract was entered into by equals.

Regarding English case law on unconscionability, reference can be made to, e.g., *Fry v. Lane*,[73] *Creswell v. Potter*,[74] *Multiservice v. Marden*,[75] *Lobb v. Total*[76] and *PBS v. Dusangh*.[77]

A summary of the conditions for the application of the unconscious bargain doctrine is provided in the JCPC's decision in *Boustany v. Pigott [1995] 69 P. & C.R. 298*,[78] based on submissions made by the ultimately unsuccessful party (internal quotations and references omitted):

> (1) It is not sufficient to attract the jurisdiction of equity to prove that a bargain is hard, unreasonable or foolish; it must be proved to be unconscionable, in the sense that one of the parties to it has imposed the objectionable terms in a morally reprehensible manner, that is to say in a way which affects his conscience ...

73. *Fry v. Lane* (1888) 40 Ch.
74. *Cresswell v. Potter* [1978] 1 W.L.R. 255. The decision of the Chancery division is actually from 1968 but was only reported ten years later.
75. *See supra* n. 39.
76. *Alec Lobb (Garages) Ltd v. Total Oil Great Britain Ltd* [1985] 1 W.L.R. 173.
77. *Portman Building Society v. Dusangh* [2000] 2 All ER (Comm) 221.
78. *Boustany v. Pigott* [1995] 69 P. & C.R 298.

(2) 'Unconscionable' relates not merely to the terms of the bargain but to the behaviour of the stronger party, which must be characterised by some moral culpability or impropriety ...
(3) Unequal bargaining power or objectively unreasonable terms provide no basis for equitable interference in the absence of unconscientious or extortionate abuse of power where exceptionally, and as a matter of common fairness, it was not right that the strong should be allowed to push the weak to the wall ...
(4) A contract cannot be set aside in equity as 'an unconscionable bargain' against a party innocent of actual or constructive fraud. Even if the terms of the contract are 'unfair' in the sense that they are more favourable to one party than the other ('contractual imbalance'), equity will not provide relief unless the beneficiary is guilty of unconscionable conduct...
(5) In situations of this kind it is necessary for the plaintiff who seeks relief to establish unconscionable conduct, namely that unconscientious advantage has been taken of his disabling condition or circumstances ...

A more recent case comprehensively addressing the doctrine of unconscionability (and related topics) is the decision by the Singapore Court of Appeal (SGCA) in *BOK v. BOM*.[79] The case was unusual due to the fact that it involved the SGCA dealing with a number of legal principles leading to potential invalidity of the contract in the common law, namely misrepresentation, mistake, duress and unconscionability. The SGCA articulated, either as part of the *ratio decidendi* or as *obiter dicta*, its views on all these legal concepts, in particular unconscionability, and ultimately, it adopted a 'narrow doctrine of unconscionability'. The SGCA noted that adopting a 'broad doctrine of unconscionability' would look '*very much like a broad discretionary legal device which permits the court to arrive at any decision which it thinks is subjectively fair in the circumstances*'. In the view of the SGCA, this narrow doctrine of unconscionability was (almost) identical to the legal concept of '*Class 1 undue influence*'.[80]

Unconscionability under English and Singaporean law is more akin to SCA section 31, subsection 1, which provides:

> Where a person exploits the distressed circumstances, lack of mental capacity, irresponsibility, or dependence of another, in order to attain for himself or induce benefits which are manifestly disproportionate to the consideration paid or promised, or in respect of which no consideration shall be paid, such legal act shall not be binding on the person exploited.

It should be noted, however, that unconscionability has statutory expression in American law. Reference is made to § 2-302 of the Uniform Commercial Code (UCC). Subsection (1) thereof provides:

> If the court as a matter of law finds the contract or any clause of the contract to have been unconscionable at the time it was made the court may refuse to enforce

79. *BOM v. BOK* [2018] SGCA 18. The SGCA is a part of the Supreme Court of Singapore. Unconscionability is dealt with at paras 114 et seq. of the decision.
80. In short: Class 1 undue influence is also called 'actual undue influence', i.e., situations where undue influence is proven. Class 2 undue influence is 'presumed undue influence' based on a relationship of trust of confidence between the parties. Class 2 undue influence comes in two subheadings.

> the contract, or it may enforce the remainder of the contract without the unconscionable clause, or it may so limit the application of any unconscionable clause as to avoid any unconscionable result.

The UCC has subsequently been adopted by most states in the US. It is among the most debated provisions of the UCC.

In American law, a dichotomy between 'procedural' and 'substantive' unconscionability is recognised but the import of this dichotomy is debated.

As will be seen, the provision expressly limits the determination of unconscionability to an *ex ante* assessment of the bargain. This is contrary to section 36.

Hence, it is beyond contention that SCA section 36 has a much wider ambit than unconscionability under, not least, English common law, and a tribunal deciding a case governed by Swedish law as the *lex causae* will be vested with considerable discretion to set aside or modify contracts also in situations where, e.g., English law would uphold the parties' bargain.

As an illustrative case in point, reference is made to the exceptional factual matrix in *Arnold v. Britton*[81] concerning an indexation clause regarding service charges pertaining to holiday chalets in Wales. The clause provided for a 10% annual increase based on the applicable service charge for the previous year. The original charge was 90 GBP. In the words of Lord Neuberger: 'If one assumes a lease granted in 1980, the service charge would be over £2,500 this year, 2015, and over *£550,000 by 2072*.' A majority of the SC upheld the clause.[82] In my view, there can be no doubt that had a similar case been brought before HD (or the supreme courts of Denmark or Norway), section 36 could have and would have (if relied upon) been applied to modify such a provision.

Finally, as some uncertainty in this regard appears to be afoot, it should be noted that parties cannot contract out of section 36 as such, i.e., the statute will apply regardless of any contractual provision seeking to exclude it from the contractual relationship. However, the parties may well influence the threshold for its application *in concreto* by the language employed in their contract, in combination with the other parts of the factual matrix.[83]

---

81. *See supra* n. 39.
82. The dissenting opinion by Lord Carnwath forms a stark contrast to the speech by Lord Neuberger for the majority.
83. A different position was adopted by the tribunal in an SCC arbitration regarding the sale of natural gas. In its award, the tribunal stated, *inter alia*, as follows: '(460) (Claimant) ... agreed to waive any potential claims regarding the MinAQ Obligation. It also agreed that this provision could not be the object of modification through subsequent arbitration. (*Claimant*) *knew or ought to have known that by waiving any potential claim it was also waiving claims under Section 36 of the Contracts Act – otherwise it should have specified that this was not its intention* (emphasis by me).' This is, with due respect, wrong as a matter of law. Rather, a decision by the tribunal not to modify the contract based on (i) an assessment of the original valid and binding risk allocation agreed to by the parties and noting (ii) that subsequent events did not *in concreto* merit contract modification according to section 36 would have been the correct approach under Swedish (and Norwegian and Danish) law. The quote is from a recent article by B. Flodgren in SvJT 2024.32 et seq. (*see* p. 53). Whereas, the article as such is in Swedish, certain parts of the *ratio decidendi* in two arbitral awards concerning long-term natural gas contracts are quoted in English (the language of these arbitrations).

[D] Comparing the DoA and SCA Section 36

There is no doubt that the principles of the DoA and section 36 have some overlapping spheres of application.

However, as mentioned the DoA as a legal argument has faded into the background over the past approximately fifty years, in particular in Sweden and Denmark, in favour of section 36 of the SCA.[84]

To me, there can be no doubt that this development is due not least to the fact that section 36 offers increased flexibility with respect to the time for assessment of unreasonableness/unconscionability (DoA: *Ex ante* – section 36: *Ex ante* and/or *ex post*) and the limitations of the DoA with respect to legal consequences and the relief available (DoA: Full or partial invalidity or ineffectiveness – section 36: Full or partial invalidity or ineffectiveness or general or specific contract adaption by amendment of the ratio of exchange of deliverables).

Finally, I shall make the following short observation.

This chapter does not cover issues of procedure or evidentiary matters. However, it is worth mentioning that the DoA and section 36 are *not* applied *sua sponte* by courts or arbitral tribunals. Hence, an argument based on, typically, section 36 must be a part of the pleaded case of a party in the arbitration. The fact that the principle of *jura novit curia* is deemed to apply does not change the fact that a party must invoke and rely on section 36 or the constituent parts of the legal rule in order for an arbitral tribunal to be allowed to consider and potentially rely on it in an award. Nor is such a procedural requirement impacted by the fact that the parties cannot contract out of the application of section 36, *vide* above.

§2.05 FINAL REMARKS

Obviously, the above remarks are not in any way meant to be an exhaustive exposition of the many intricacies of the part of Swedish contract law that deals with interpretation (including gap-filling) and modification of commercial contracts.

It is, however, my stated hope and expectation that this article can serve as an introduction for foreign arbitrators (and counsel) to some of the more pervasive and recurring issues that these will likely face when involved in arbitrations governed by Swedish law as *lex causae* and perhaps even serve as inspiration for further (self)studies. Moreover, I hope that Swedish (or other civil law-trained arbitrators) will derive benefit from the contrasting of the Swedish concepts of contract interpretation with those set out and applicable in common law jurisdictions, in particular England.

84. By comparison, the DoA has, as mentioned, retained some of its 'popularity' in Norway, which is likely due to the fact that Norwegian law has allowed the application of the DoA to include contract modification more generally, i.e., a more granular adjustment of the deliverables, *vide supra* n. 65.

CHAPTER 3

The Meaning and Scope of the Commercial Arbitration Exception in *Achmea*

Paschalis Paschalidis

§3.01 INTRODUCTION

Since the delivery of the *Achmea* ruling by the Court of Justice of the European Union (the CJEU) six years ago, a revolution has occurred in the European Union (EU) with respect to international investment law.[1] All intra-EU bilateral investment protection treaties have been terminated because their Investor-State Dispute Settlement (ISDS) clauses were deemed incompatible with EU law.[2] The CJEU extended the *Achmea* ruling to intra-EU investor-State arbitration pursuant to Article 26 ECT.[3] It also found ad hoc arbitration agreements concluded between States and investors in respect of disputes under intra-EU bilateral investment treaties (BITs) to violate EU primary law.[4] At the same time, the CJEU approved investor-State arbitration clauses in extra-EU

1. *See* Case C-284/16, *Achmea*, 6 Mar. 2018, EU:C:2018:158. The CJEU found that EU primary law, and in particular the principles of autonomy, sincere cooperation and mutual trust, preclude Member States from entering into investor-State arbitration clauses in investment protection treaties concluded with each other.
2. *See* Agreement for the Termination of BITs between the Member States of the European Union [2020] OJ L169/1.
3. *See* Case C-741/19, *Republic of Moldova*, 2 Sep. 2021, EU:C:2021:655, paras 40-66. *See also* Alan Dashwood, *Republic of Moldova v. Komstroy LCC: Arbitration under Article 26 ECT Outlawed in Intra-EU Disputes by Obiter Dictum*, 47 Eur. L. Rev. 1 (2022); Mathias Audit, *Arbitrage international – Extension de la solution de l'arrêt Achmea à l'arbitrage d'investissement intra-européen fondé sur la Charte de l'énergie*, Journal du droit international 231 (2022); Paschalis Paschalidis, *Intra-EU Application of the Energy Charter Treaty: A Critical Analysis of the CJEU's Ruling in Republic of Moldova*, 7 Eur. Inv. L. & Arb. Rev. 3-35 (2022) https://doi.org/10.1163/24689017_0701002.
4. *See* Case C-109/20, *PL Holdings*, 26 Oct. 2021, EU:C:2021:875.

investment protection agreements as being compatible with EU primary law but only subject to very stringent conditions.[5]

Despite the upheaval caused by these developments, arbitration practitioners and investors felt reassured by the CJEU's willingness to distinguish commercial arbitration from investment treaty arbitration in *Achmea* by creating the 'commercial arbitration exception' for it.[6] The meaning and scope of the commercial arbitration exception in *Achmea* was also the subject of intense debate before the CJEU in *PL Holdings* but the CJEU did not seize the opportunity presented to it to define the contours of the exception.[7]

A relatively recent decision of the Greek Council of State (the country's supreme administrative court), rendered in *Athens International Airport*, casts doubt as to whether arbitration clauses contained in State contracts fall within the scope of the exception.[8] The Council of State considered the arbitration clause inserted in the contract concluded between the Greek State and a consortium of German companies exploiting the Athens International Airport to be contrary to the CJEU's rulings in *Achmea* and *PL Holdings*, as well as the principle of autonomy of EU law. According to the Council of State, the arbitration clause enabled the arbitral tribunal to rule on a dispute regarding the application of certain VAT conferred by the Greek State to the consortium through the contract, whereas VAT is a harmonised tax subject to EU Directive 2006/112. As a consequence, the administrative courts were not bound by the arbitral tribunal's decision regarding Athens International Airport SA's entitlement to VAT exemptions.

The purpose of the present contribution is to address the meaning and scope of the commercial arbitration exception in *Achmea* and to examine whether EU Member States can enter into arbitration clauses in their contracts with economic operators. To do so, it first presents the two competing interpretations of the commercial arbitration exception (§3.02) and then examines the conditions under which Member States can conclude commercial arbitration agreements (§3.03).

§3.02 COMPETING INTERPRETATIONS OF THE COMMERCIAL ARBITRATION EXCEPTION

It is established case law since 1982 that commercial arbitration tribunals cannot refer questions for a preliminary ruling to the CJEU because they do not constitute courts or

5. *See* Opinion 1/17, *EU-Canada CET Agreement* EU:C:2019:341. *See also* Emmanuel Gaillard, *CJUE. – ass. plén. – 30 avr. 2019. – avis 1/17. – JCP G 2019, 493,* Journal du Droit international 845 (2019); Paschalis Paschalidis, *CETA: une nouvelle ère pour la protection des investissements,* Journal du droit européen 241 (2019).
6. *See* Case C-284/16, *Achmea,* 6 Mar. 2018, EU:C:2018:158, paras 54-55.
7. *See* Opinion of AG Kokott, Case C-109/20, *PL Holdings,* 22 Apr. 2021, EU:C:2021:321, paras 43-65.
8. *See* Greek Council of State, Second Chamber, 9 Feb. 2022, *Independent Authority of Public Revenue v. Athens International Airport S.A.,* Case No. 246/2022. *See also* Polly Eftratiadi & Evanthia Kasiora, *The Achmea Ripple Effect: Greek Conseil d'Etat Finds That a Commercial Arbitral Tribunal Has No Jurisdiction to Deal with Matters of EU Law,* Cahiers de l'Arbitrage 111 (2023).

tribunals of a Member State within the meaning of Article 267 TFEU.[9] Indeed, Article 267 TFEU applies only to 'courts or tribunals of a Member State'. It is also accepted that Member State courts have to uphold EU public policy when trying an action to set aside or recognise and enforce an arbitral award.[10]

In *Achmea*, the CJEU was confronted with arbitration clauses contained in investment protection treaties for the first time. In his Opinion, AG Wathelet put forward a very different vision than the one adopted by the CJEU, arguing in favour of a system in which intra-EU investment tribunals are considered to be part of the EU's judicial architecture, hence enabling or requiring such tribunals to refer questions for a preliminary ruling to the CJEU.[11] However, the CJEU took a very different view. It held that investment treaty arbitration provided for by intra-EU BITs violated the principles of autonomy of EU law, sincere cooperation and mutual trust. According to the CJEU, intra-EU ISDS removed disputes governed by EU law from the courts and entrusted them to arbitral tribunals that cannot refer questions for preliminary ruling to the CJEU.[12] At the same time, the scope of review exercised by the courts in annulment or enforcement proceedings was not broad enough to guarantee the efficient and uniform application of EU law.[13]

These considerations could have also applied to commercial arbitration. However, in paragraphs 54-55 of the *Achmea* ruling, the CJEU distinguished commercial arbitration from investment treaty arbitration in the following terms:

> It is true that, in relation to commercial arbitration, the [CJEU] has held that the requirements of efficient arbitration proceedings justify the review of arbitral awards by the courts of the Member States being limited in scope, provided that the fundamental provisions of EU law can be examined in the course of that review and, if necessary, be the subject of a reference to the Court for a preliminary ruling [...].
>
> However, arbitration proceedings such as those referred to in Article 8 of the [Netherlands-Slovakia] BIT are different from commercial arbitration proceedings. While the latter originate in the freely expressed wishes of the parties, the former derive from a treaty by which Member States agree to remove from the jurisdiction of their own courts, and hence from the system of judicial remedies which the second subparagraph of Article 19(1) TEU requires them to establish in the fields covered by EU law [...], disputes which may concern the application or interpretation of EU law. In those circumstances, the considerations set out in the preceding paragraph relating to commercial arbitration cannot be applied to

9. *See* Case 102/81, *Nordsee*, 23 Mar. 1982, EU:C:1982:107. *See also* Jürgen Basedow, *EU Law in International Arbitration: Referrals to the European Court of Justice*, 32(4) J. Int. Arb. 367 (2015) https://doi.org/10.54648/joia2015017; Paschalis Paschalidis, *Arbitral Tribunals and Preliminary References to the EU Court of Justice*, 33(4) Arb. Int. 663 (2017) https://doi.org/10.1093/arbint/aiw026, Maciej Szpunar, *Referrals of Preliminary Questions by Arbitral Tribunals to the CJEU*, in *The Impact of EU Lax on International Commercial Arbitration* 85 (Federico Ferrari ed., JurisNet 2017).
10. *See* Case C-126/97, *Eco Swiss*, 1 Jun. 1999, EU:C:1999:269; Case C-567/14, *Genentech*, 7 Jul. 2016, EU:C:2016:526.
11. Opinion of AG Wathelet, Case C-284/16, *Achmea*, 19 Sep. 2017, EU:C:2017:699.
12. Case C-284/16, *Achmea*, 6 Mar. 2018, EU:C:2018:158, paras 39-49.
13. *Ibid.*, paras 50-53.

arbitration proceedings such as those referred to in Article 8 of the [Netherlands-Slovakia] BIT.

This statement gave rise to essentially two competing lines of interpretation: a broad one that builds on 'freely expressed wishes' of the parties (§3.02[A]) and a restrictive one that focuses on the commercial nature of the dispute (§3.02[B]).

Before assessing each of these approaches (§3.02[C]), it is worth recalling that the CJEU had not used the term 'commercial arbitration' until its ruling in *Achmea*. Its previous case law referred to 'contractual arbitration' (*arbitrage conventionnel*),[14] i.e., arbitration based on clauses included in contracts.[15] The CJEU meant any arbitration in which the parties 'are under no obligation, in law or in fact, to refer their disputes to arbitration and the public authorities of the Member State concerned are neither involved in the decision to opt for arbitration nor required to intervene of their own accord in the proceedings before the arbitrator'.[16]

However, commercial arbitration may be broader than contractual arbitration, covering matters arising from all relationships of a commercial nature, whether contractual or not.[17] In the absence of a definition of the terms by the CJEU, 'commercial arbitration' for the purposes of this analysis should not automatically be taken to mean the exact same thing as in arbitration practice. Indeed, subject to one's preference for the broad or restrictive interpretation of the terms 'commercial arbitration', these terms may have an autonomous meaning under EU law and exclude certain types of arbitration that may have otherwise been considered 'commercial'.

[A] The Broad Interpretation of the Commercial Arbitration Exception

The broad interpretation of the commercial arbitration exception grapples with the CJEU's reasoning for distinguishing commercial and investment treaty arbitration. According to the CJEU, commercial arbitration would be different to investment treaty arbitration because, unlike the latter, it 'originate[s] in the freely expressed wishes of the parties', whereas investment treaty arbitration originates in a treaty concluded between two States.[18]

One may find this passage of the judgment confusing insofar as it suggests that commercial arbitration would be based on freely expressed consent of the parties to the dispute, whereas investment treaty arbitration would not be based on consent. This is, of course, not the case. Investment treaty arbitration is as much consent-based as commercial arbitration: an arbitration agreement is formed through the investor's

14. *See, e.g.*, Case, 102/81, *Nordsee*, 23 Mar. 1982, EU:C:1982:107, para. 14; Case C-126/97, *Eco Swiss*, 1 Jun. 1999, EU:C:1999:269, paras 32 and 34; Case C-377/13, *Ascendi Beiras Litoral e Alta, Auto Estradas das Beiras Litoral e Alta*, 12 Jun. 2014, EU:C:2014:1754, para. 27.
15. *See, e.g.*, Case C-701/21 P and C-739/21 P, *Mytilinaios v. DEI and Commission*, 22 Feb. 2024, EU:C:2024:146, para. 101.
16. Case C-377/13, *Ascendi Beiras Litoral e Alta, Auto Estradas das Beiras Litoral e Alta*, 12 Jun. 2014, EU:C:2014:1754, para. 27.
17. *See* Julian D.M. Lew & Loukas A. Mistelis et al., *Comparative International Commercial Arbitration*, §§ 4.2-4.26, 50-57 (Kluwer 2003).
18. Case C-284/16, *Achmea*, 6 Mar. 2018, EU:C:2018:158, para. 55.

acceptance of the State's standing offer to arbitrate contained in the investment protection treaty.

Although perhaps not cast in the clearest possible terms, the idea that the CJEU seems to wish to convey is rather different. Commercial arbitration clauses are of two kinds. They are either (more commonly) arbitration agreements (*clauses compromissoires*) concluded before a dispute arises and normally included in a contract or, less commonly, agreements to submit a dispute that has already arisen to arbitration (*compromis*). In either case, commercial arbitration agreements are not a general, binding agreement to opt out of the judicial system but are limited to a specific existing dispute between two or more parties or to future disputes that may arise under a specific contract or other private-law relationship between two or more parties.

Investment treaty arbitration is not of the same kind. An ISDS clause is not an arbitration agreement but rather the State's advance consent to arbitration that any qualified investor can accept, thereby creating an arbitration agreement. Thus, the State's general submission to arbitration contained in an ISDS clause of an investment protection treaty is given in respect of all disputes that might arise in the future with investors of the other State party to the treaty. In this sense, investment treaty arbitration does not originate in the freely expressed wishes of the parties to the dispute. Rather, as noted by the CJEU, it originates in an *ex ante*, binding commitment given by the State to another State to remove all disputes from the jurisdiction of its courts, should the investors so wish.

AG Szpunar lent the support of his authority to this interpretation of the commercial arbitration exception in his Opinion in the *Republic of Moldova*:

> I would point out that there is a fundamental difference between [commercial arbitration and investment treaty arbitration]. Commercial arbitration proceedings presuppose the exercise by each party of its autonomy. They entail the conclusion of an arbitration agreement, either at the same time as the conclusion of the contract in respect of which related disputes will be subject to arbitration or once the dispute has arisen. In other words, the jurisdiction of a court or tribunal, in commercial arbitration, always derives from an arbitration agreement concerning a dispute specifically defined therein. The jurisdiction of such an arbitral tribunal cannot be regarded as falling within the system of jurisdictional protection established by the State. Rather, it derives from the autonomy of each of the parties involved in a commercial activity. Indeed, it is from that autonomy that the possibility arises for the parties to decide to settle disputes by recourse to commercial arbitration.[19]

In his view, investment treaty arbitration is fundamentally different because ISDS clauses 'constitute[] an offer of general and permanent arbitration, which it will be for the other party to accept or reject'.[20] Through this clause, 'the State waives the possibility that a dispute between it and an investor from another Member State falling within the scope of that agreement may be settled by the national courts'.[21] According

19. Opinion of AG Szpunar, Case C-741/19, *Republic of Moldova*, 3 Mar. 2021, EU:C:2021:164, para. 60.
20. *Ibid.*, para. 61.
21. *Ibid.*

to AG Szpunar, the State's waiver is 'systemic in nature, in that it may relate to all disputes falling within the scope of that agreement' and results in the creation of 'a judicial protection mechanism, external to [the State's] judicial system'.[22]

This interpretation finds further basis in the CJEU's reasoning in *Achmea* according to which investment treaty arbitration is a mechanism through which Member States remove disputes (to which EU law may be applicable) from 'the system of judicial remedies which the second subparagraph of Article 19(1) [of the Treaty on European Union ("TEU")] requires them to establish in the fields covered by EU law'[23] and, hence, from the remit of the CJEU.

The CJEU perceived ISDS as a threat to the integrity of the EU legal order insofar as two Member States install, through a binding promise to arbitrate, an indefinite number of investor-State disputes with an indefinite number of investors having the nationality of the other Contracting State. Given that the cross-border investment lies at the very heart of the EU's internal market and integration project initiated by the 1957 Treaty of Rome, intra-EU ISDS was perceived as creating a system of justice regarding disputes that concern the EU's internal market that is parallel and competing to that established by Article 19(1) TEU, according to which the national courts in cooperation with the CJEU ensure the full effectiveness of EU law through the preliminary reference procedure. In other words, ISDS clauses threaten to empty the pool of internal market disputes of its content and deviate it to another system of remedies that operates outside the control of the EU and the CJEU.

Bearing this in mind, there is little surprise that in *PL Holdings*, the CJEU made clear that the breach of EU law is not committed by the investors but by the Member State.[24] The Member States had a duty not to create dispute resolution mechanisms that allow individuals and States to bypass the EU judicial system. In turn, this gives rise to the question of whether the breach of EU law at issue is sufficiently serious, namely whether the Member States manifestly and gravely disregarded the measure of discretion. If that is so, investors whose intra-EU awards were subsequently annulled could claim the costs of the arbitration procedure in damages for breach of EU law against the Member State pursuant to the *Francovich* and *Brasserie du Pêcheur and Factortame* line of case law. Similarly, a court may annul an award even when the Member State prevailed on the merits. It can thus annul the tribunal's award of costs in favour of the State on the basis that the arbitration was unlawful under EU law due to the Member State's decision to conclude the ISDS clause with another Member State.[25]

22. *Ibid.*
23. Case C-284/16, *Achmea*, 6 Mar. 2018, EU:C:2018:158, para. 55.
24. *See* Case C-109/20, *PL Holdings*, 26 Oct. 2021, EU:C:2021:875, para. 50.
25. *See*, to this effect, Svea Court of Appeal, 20 Dec. 2023, *Festorino Invest Limited and others v. Poland*, Case T 12646-21.

[B] The Restrictive Interpretation of the Commercial Arbitration Exception

The broad interpretation of the commercial arbitration exception is contested by the proponents of the restrictive interpretation. In *PL Holdings*, the European Commission, supported by several Member States, including Poland, Italy, Hungary, the Netherlands, and Slovakia, advocated a much narrower interpretation of the commercial arbitration exception.[26] According to this interpretation, it is not sufficient for the arbitration agreement to be based on an arbitration clause that reflects the 'freely expressed wishes' of the parties, even in the sense described above. Additionally, to be compatible with EU law, an arbitration agreement concluded by the State must concern a 'commercial' dispute.

The Commission considers that the term 'commercial arbitration' requires an autonomous interpretation under EU law.[27] Following the distinction drawn in the Brussels I Regulation (recast) between civil and commercial matters that fall within the scope of the Regulation and administrative matters or the liability of the State for acts and omissions in the exercise of State authority (*acta iure imperii*), that fall outside its scope,[28] the Commission advocated the view that 'commercial arbitration' could only refer to disputes between non-State actors or, insofar as the State is involved, to disputes arising out of State conduct that is commercial in nature (*acta jure gestionis*).[29] The Commission thus accepted that, for example, States can lawfully include arbitration agreements in contracts for the purchase of commercial services, such as the installation of a toll system on highways, or in a concession agreement for the installation of a theme park.[30]

By contrast, according to the Commission, disputes calling into question the exercise of the State's prerogatives or sovereign powers (*acta jure imperii*) are not capable of falling within the scope of the commercial arbitration exception.[31] In its view, when a Member State exercises its sovereign powers, 'it is not free and autonomous in its will [but] acts on the basis of public law powers and, where appropriate, adopts acts (particularly of a coercive nature) that are binding on those subject to its jurisdiction'.[32] Similarly, where the Member States exercise their powers of public authority in areas covered by EU law and apply EU law, they are 'not autonomous and free to dispose of the rules of Union law by means of a civil or commercial law agreement, but is bound by those rules and subject to judicial review

26. *See* Opinion of AG Kokott, Case C-109/20, *PL Holdings*, 22 Apr. 2021, EU:C:2021:321, para. 54.
27. *See* European Commission, Written observations in Case C-284/16, *Achmea*, dated 16 Jul. 2020, § 62.
28. *See* Regulation (EU) No. 1215/2012 of the European Parliament and of the Council of 12 Dec. 2012 on jurisdiction and the recognition and enforcement of judgments in civil and commercial matters (recast) OJ L 351/1.
29. *See* European Commission, Written observations in Case C-284/16, *Achmea*, dated 16 Jul. 2020, § 67.
30. *Ibid.*
31. *Ibid.*, § 73.
32. *Ibid.*

under the second subparagraph of Article 19(1) TEU'.[33] The Commission took the view that in such circumstances, the State's counterparty is 'even less free to choose whether or not to submit to [the State's] prerogatives'.[34] It would thus not be possible to speak of a commercial arbitration originating in the freely expressed wishes of the parties.

It follows from the above that, according to the Commission's restrictive interpretation of paragraph 55 of the *Achmea* ruling, matters which are *acta jure imperii* are non-arbitrable by virtue of Article 19(1) TEU because neither the State nor its counterparties have the power to freely dispose of such matters.[35]

[C] Critical Assessment of the Broad and Restrictive Interpretations

Both interpretations of the commercial arbitration exception have been criticised. The proponents of the restrictive interpretation criticise the broad interpretation as being incoherent and leading to discriminatory treatment:

> Why should Member States be allowed to remove EU-law disputes from the EU judicial system in individual cases if they are not allowed to enter into a foreseeable general obligation of this kind? In addition to the risks to the uniform application of EU law, there would also be the risk of unequal treatment of different investors.[36]

The restrictive interpretation is not free of criticism either.

First, it is based on the flawed premise that States cannot enter into arbitration agreements regarding matters which are *acta jure imperii*. This is plainly wrong. There is no such rule in international law. On the contrary, according to the relevant rules of international law, States do not benefit from jurisdictional immunity in commercial matters, and they can even waive their jurisdictional immunity with respect to *acta jure imperii*, provided that the waiver is unequivocal.[37] Nor is there a rule of EU law preventing Member States from entering into arbitration agreements with economic operators in individual cases where such agreement is freely concluded.

Second, the Commission's restrictive interpretation is unworkable in practice for the reason that the compatibility of the arbitration agreement with EU law depends on the nature of the powers exercised by the State giving rise to the dispute.

During the hearing in *PL Holdings*, the Commission's agents gave the following example of the distinction the Commission wished to draw. In the hypothetical example of a concession to construct and operate a highway that would cross a natural

33. *Ibid.*
34. *Ibid.*
35. *Ibid.*, § 74.
36. Opinion of AG Kokott, Case C-109/20, *PL Holdings*, 22 Apr. 2021, EU:C:2021:321, para. 51.
37. *See* European Convention on State Immunity, 16 May 1972, Art. 7(1); United Nations Convention on Jurisdictional Immunities of State and Their Property, 2 Jan. 2004, not yet in force, Art. 10(1); Yas Banifatemi, *Jurisdictional Immunity of States: Commercial Transactions*, in *The Cambridge Handbook of Immunities and International Law*, 125 (Tom Ruys, Nicolas Angelet and Luca Ferro, Cambridge University Press, 2019); Catherina Amifar, Waivers of Jurisdictional Immunity, in *The Cambridge Handbook of Immunities and International Law*, 167 (Tom Ruys, Nicolas Angelet and Luca Ferro, Cambridge University Press, 2019).

reserve area, the Commission argued that an arbitration agreement contained in the concession contract would be compatible with EU law if it concerned disputes regarding losses incurred by the Member State's violation of the concession agreement. However, if the scope of submission to arbitration included claims arising out of the fact that - contrary to its contractual commitments - the environmental impact assessment required the highway to go around the natural reserve area, the Commission considered that such an arbitration agreement would be contrary to EU law because it would (even indirectly) concern the exercise of sovereign powers by a Member State.

This is a highly problematic position because it makes it impossible to assess whether the arbitration agreement is compatible with EU law. Indeed, it is impossible to predict the manner in which a State may breach its contractual commitments. It may do so by acting as a party to the contract, but it may also do so by exercising its powers as a regulator or a sovereign (e.g., by enacting legislation or other measures nationalising the concession granted by contract). The Commission's position also ignored the fact that, very often, State contracts include provisions pursuant to which States commit to exercise or not to exercise their sovereign powers in a certain way (e.g., stabilisation clauses) or by guaranteeing certain treatment with respect to taxes or customs, etc.

Thus far, the CJEU does not appear to have been swayed by the Commission's position in *PL Holdings*. Indeed, despite the fact that its judgment in that case was not favourable to the investor, the CJEU did not endorse the Commission's restrictive interpretation of the commercial arbitration exception. Rather, its judgment focused exclusively on ad hoc arbitration agreements that have the effect of reinstating investor-State arbitrations under intra-EU BITs.[38]

Subsequent CJEU case law appears to be more in line with the broad than the restrictive interpretation of the commercial arbitration exception. Indeed, in *Mytilinaios v. DEI and Commission*, the CJEU did not take any issue with the fact that DEI, the Greek State-owned Public Power Corporation, had entered into an arbitration agreement with Mytilinaios, one of its industrial clients. Provided that the arbitration agreement had been freely entered into by the parties, the arbitral award setting the price of electricity could not qualify as a State aid measure, held the CJEU.[39] The fact that the arbitrators were selected from a list drawn up by the decision of the president of the Greek energy regulator and should demonstrate their independence and impartiality before their appointment did not alter the fact that the arbitration agreement fell within the commercial arbitration exception.[40]

In distinguishing this kind of arbitration from arbitration pursuant to ISDS clauses contained in BITs, the CJEU appears to have endorsed the understanding of *Achmea*

38. *See* Case C-109/20, *PL Holdings*, 26 Oct. 2021, EU:C:2021:875, paras 48-49.
39. Cases C-701/21 P and C-739/21 P, *Mytilinaios v. DEI and Commission*, EU:C:2024:146, para. 106. It could, however, have been otherwise 'if the arbitration procedure in its entirety, from the conclusion of the arbitration agreement until the arbitration award, had been the product of a scheme imposed by the Greek State on the undertakings concerned in order to use that procedure to circumvent the rules in the field of State aid' (*Ibid.*, para. 114).
40. *Ibid.*, para. 103.

according to which ISDS clauses in intra-EU investment protection treaties are unlawful – under EU law – not because they apply to *acta jure imperii* but because they create a parallel and competing system of justice by providing a general, advance consent to arbitration:

> the consent of a Member State to the possibility of litigation being brought against it in the context of the arbitration procedure provided for by a bilateral investment treaty, *unlike that which would have been given in contractual arbitration proceedings*, does not have its origin in a specific agreement reflecting the freely expressed wishes of the parties concerned, but is derived from a treaty concluded between two Member States in which they have, generally and in advance, agreed to exclude from the jurisdiction of their own courts disputes which may concern the interpretation or application of EU law in favour of arbitration proceedings.[41]

Finally, the commercial arbitration exception should not be interpreted with undue formalism. The fact that neither of the parties to an arbitration agreement contained in a contract are State actors does not automatically bring the arbitration agreement within the commercial arbitration exception or immunise it with regard to EU primary law.

In its judgment in *International Skating Union v. Commission*, the CJEU signalled that arbitration agreements concluded between private actors may also be scrutinised under EU primary law in a manner inspired by the *Achmea* ruling.[42] In its decision at issue in *International Skating Union v. Commission*, the Commission had taken the view that the systematic and exclusive references of disputes between the ISU and professional skaters to CAS arbitration in Switzerland did not constitute per se an infringement of EU competition law. However, they reinforced the infringement of Article 101(1) TFEU resulting from the ISU rules governing prior authorisation of competitions and athletes' eligibility to participate in competitions because it systematically precluded athletes from claiming their rights under Article 101(1) TFEU before the courts of the Member States. Indeed, CAS awards would be subject to an action to set aside only before the Swiss Federal Tribunal. The CJEU held that '[i]n the absence of such judicial review [i.e. judicial review by the courts of the Member States], the use of an arbitration mechanism is such as to undermine the protection of rights that subjects of the law derive from the direct effect of EU law and the effective compliance with Articles 101 and 102 TFEU, which must be ensured – and would therefore be ensured in the absence of such a mechanism – by the national rules relating to remedies'.[43]

Although the CJEU did not scrutinise CAS arbitration by reference to *Achmea*, it is clear that it did not consider CAS arbitration to fall within the commercial arbitration exception recognised by *Achmea*, despite the fact that both the ISU and the athletes are private parties.[44] On the contrary, several elements make the analogy between recourse

41. *Ibid.*, para. 109 (emphasis added).
42. C-124/21 P, *International Skating Union v. Commission*, 21 Dec. 2023, EU:C:2023:1012.
43. *Ibid.*, para. 194.
44. *See* Paschalis Paschalidis, *ISU v. Commission: Arbitration as a Reinforcement of Infringements of EU Competition Law*, Kluwer Competition Law Blog, 9 Jan. 2024.

to CAS arbitration in Switzerland and investment treaty arbitration stronger than with commercial arbitration. By virtue of its position as a regulator or quasi-regulator of international skating as an economic activity, the ISU had exorbitant powers in comparison to the athletes. Furthermore, submission to CAS arbitration was not voluntary. Recourse to CAS arbitration was not provided for in a specific agreement concluded with the athletes but was dictated in the ISU Statute, rules, codes, and communications that the athletes had to accept in order to become professional athletes.[45] Submission to CAS arbitration thus governed all possible disputes that might arise between the ISU and the athletes, without exception, including disputes regarding the rights conferred on the athletes by EU law. However, neither the CAS nor the Swiss Federal Tribunal (which would hear actions to set aside CAS awards) are courts or tribunals of a Member State that can refer questions for preliminary rulings to the CJEU pursuant to Article 267 TFEU.[46]

As the CJEU recalled, the requirement of effective judicial review mandates that the court seized of an action to set aside or, otherwise review the award, satisfy 'all the requirements under Article 267 TFEU, so that it is entitled, or, as the case may be, required, to refer a question to the Court of Justice where it considers that a decision of the Court is necessary concerning a matter of EU law raised in a case pending before it'.[47]

The CJEU case law discussed above suggests that the CJEU does not endorse the Commission's broad interpretation of the commercial arbitration exception. In fact, the position defended by the Commission in *Mytilinaios v. DEI and Commission* begs the question of whether the Commission maintains the position it took in *PL Holdings* with respect to the commercial arbitration exception. However, this does not necessarily suggest that economic operators and Member States can enter into any form of commercial arbitration agreement. Indeed, as will be explained below, several reasons may militate in favour of structuring arbitration agreements in State contracts in a manner that does not systematically or automatically foreclose any form of review of EU law matters by the EU courts.

§3.03 CAN MEMBER STATES INCLUDE ARBITRATION CLAUSES IN THEIR CONTRACTS WITH ECONOMIC OPERATORS?

The ability of Member States to enter into arbitration agreements in their contracts with economic operators has been recently called into question by the Greek Council of State's decision in *Athens International Airport*.[48] The Greek State and a consortium of

45. ECHR, *Case of Mutu and Pechstein v. Switzerland*, applications Nos 40575/10 and 67474/10, 2 Oct. 2018, CE:ECHR:2018:1002JUD004057510.
46. *See* Paschalis Paschalidis, *ISU v. Commission: Arbitration as a Reinforcement of Infringements of EU Competition Law*, Kluwer Competition Law Blog, 9 Jan. 2024.
    C-124/21 P, *International Skating Union v. Commission*, 21 Dec. 2023, EU:C:2023:1012, para. 191.
47. *Ibid.*, para. 198.
48. Greek Council of State, Second Chamber, 9 Feb. 2022, *Independent Authority of Public Revenue v. Athens International Airport S.A.*, Case No. 246/2022.

German companies had signed a thirty-year contract for the development and commercial operation of the Athens International Airport. The contract was ratified by an act of the Greek Parliament and provided for the settlement of disputes through LCIA arbitration in London. The contract also conferred certain treatment to the consortium in respect of VAT, which is a harmonised tax governed by the EU VAT Directive.

In an award rendered in 2013, an arbitral tribunal constituted pursuant to the contract ruled that the consortium did not owe the amounts of the imputed VAT and additional charges. The tribunal declared that the relevant act imposing these charges on Athens International Airport had been issued unlawfully, in breach of the contract and Greek law.

In parallel proceedings, Athens International Airport sought to challenge the validity of the decisions taken by the Greek VAT administration. The Greek administrative courts found that the VAT dispute was arbitrable and fell within the jurisdiction of the arbitral tribunal. According to these courts, the fact that the arbitral tribunal lacked the power to annul the administrative acts imposing VAT did not deprive it of the power to assess whether such act was lawful.[49] Thus, the Greek administrative courts were bound by the arbitral tribunal's findings with respect to the VAT exemptions.

The Greek State appealed to the Council of State, which reversed the decision of the lower courts, finding that investment agreements such as the one at issue in the case at hand could not affect the autonomy of EU law.[50] Basing itself on its understanding of the CJEU's rulings in *Achmea* and *PL Holdings*, the Greek Council of State recalled that, pursuant to Article 19 TEU, only the courts and tribunals of Member States and the CJEU are tasked with ensuring the full application of EU law.[51] Thus, disputes between the Greek State and Athens International Airport arising under the contract and concerning the interpretation and/or application of EU VAT law in the field of VAT could not be settled by arbitration before a tribunal that does not meet the requirements of Article 19 TEU and Article 267 TFEU.[52] For these reasons, the Greek Council of State held that the arbitration agreement was contrary to EU primary law and that the 2013 award had been issued in excess of the arbitral tribunal's jurisdiction.[53] It thus concluded that the award was not binding for the Greek administrative courts and remanded the case back to the Administrative Court of Appeal of Athens in order to give judgment on the merits of the VAT dispute.

While this interpretation of *Achmea* and *PL Holdings* is in line with the restrictive interpretation of the commercial arbitration exception advocated by the Commission, it is doubtful that it is in line with the more recent case law of the CJEU, notably *Mytilinaios v. DEI and Commission*. Pursuant to the more recent line of case law,

49. Polly Eftratiadi & Evanthia Kasiora, *The Achmea Ripple Effect: Greek Conseil d'Etat Finds That a Commercial Arbitral Tribunal Has No Jurisdiction to Deal with Matters of EU Law*, Cahiers de l'Arbitrage 111 (2023).
50. Greek Council of State, Second Chamber, 9 Feb. 2022, *Independent Authority of Public Revenue v. Athens International Airport S.A.*, Case No. 246/2022, § 6.
51. *Ibid.*
52. *Ibid.*, § 7.
53. *Ibid.*, § 8.

arbitration agreements fall within the commercial arbitration exception if they are freely entered into by the parties. Indeed, nothing suggests that the Greek State had imposed LCIA arbitration on the German consortium, nor was recourse to arbitration otherwise mandatory under Greek law. In this sense, the case was not analogous to that of ISU, which systematically and exclusively settled disputes with professional skaters through arbitration in non-EU countries.

Even if one were to adopt the Greek Council of State's view, the mere fact that a contract may grant authority to an arbitral tribunal to assess whether an individual administrative act in the field of VAT law is lawful is not *per se* a violation of the EU principle of autonomy.[54] The purpose of such an assessment is not to declare the act valid or invalid – a power which the tribunal lacks – but to decide whether, in adopting that act, the State breached its contractual commitments.

It is noteworthy that in Opinion 1/17, the CJEU took issue only with the ability of CETA tribunals to award damages to investors for measures of general application enacting policy (that are not otherwise arbitrary or discriminatory) but not with the power of such tribunals to award damages in respect of State conduct concerning individual investors.[55]

At the same time, one must not lose sight of the fact that Member States are not in the exact same position vis-à-vis EU law when they enter into commercial arbitration agreements as private parties. Unlike Member States, which are bound by Article 344 TFEU, private parties are not bound by the principle of autonomy and have not undertaken to respect the jurisdiction of the CJEU with respect to matters that concern the interpretation and application of EU law. Provided that private parties do not find themselves in a position of power such as that of the ISU and impose recourse to arbitration in a manner that systematically prevents their counterparts from having access to the EU courts, the action to set aside awards or the powers of review that courts have in recognition and enforcement proceedings are sufficient to guarantee the autonomy of EU law. The CJEU has recognised as much in *Eco Swiss* and *Achmea*.

However, it is not unreasonable to suppose that the principles laid down by the CJEU in *Eco Swiss* and *Achmea* may apply to the Member States when entering into commercial arbitration agreements in a different manner. There may be circumstances where Member States threaten the autonomy of EU law when they resort to arbitration in their contractual relations with economic operators if the arbitration clauses have the following characteristics: (i) they allow arbitral tribunals to rule on the lawfulness of the State's conduct when it implements EU law because it acts in its capacity as an

---

54. Such disputes may, however, be non-arbitrable under the laws of individual Member States. *See*, for example, French Council of State, 17 Oct. 2023, *Ryanair v. Syndicat mixte des aéroports de Charente*, No. 465761, §§ 3, 8-9, in which the French supreme administrative court recalled that, unless otherwise provided by domestic legislation or international treaty, French public bodies cannot opt out from the jurisdiction of the French courts in respect of disputes to which they are parties.
55. *See* Opinion 1/17 *(EU-Canada CET Agreement)*, 30 Apr. 2019, EU:C:2019:341, paras 137-161. Koen Lenaerts, *Le cadre constitutionnel de l'Union et l'autonomie fonctionnelle de son ordre juridique*, in *Évolution des rapports entre les ordres juridiques de l'Union européenne, international et nationaux: Liber amicorum Jiří Malenovský* 285, 298-306 (David Petrlík et al. eds, Bruylant 2020).

administrative authority or a sovereign; and (ii) the arbitration process is arranged in a manner in which the EU courts will not be able to exercise any sort of supervising authority over the arbitral process. The latter is achieved when, as in the case of the ISU, a Member State accepts to place the seat of the arbitration outside the EU.

Indeed, in *International Skating Union v. Commission*, the CJEU underscored the fact that the ISU's recourse to arbitration was systematic and was arranged in a manner in which only the Swiss courts could review the awards rendered in disputes opposing the ISU with professional skaters.[56] However, in the words of the CJEU, 'judicial review [of awards] must, in any event, be able to cover the question whether those awards comply with the fundamental provisions that are a matter of EU public policy'.[57]

Therefore, the fact that the Greek Council of State may have erroneously considered that an arbitration agreement did not benefit from the commercial arbitration exception for the mere fact that it may have covered matters governed by EU law does not mean that the CJEU would have accepted that Member States entrust the power to review the application of the VAT Directive – even with respect to specific taxpayers only – to arbitral tribunals seated outside the EU, and *a fortiori* if such referral to arbitration outside the EU is systematic. This may be the case where Member States systematically resort to, for example, LCIA arbitration in London in their contracts. It is natural for the economic operator to wish the seat to be in a location that is neutral to the dispute. However, there are several arbitration-friendly locations in the EU. There is thus no need to take the risk of placing the seat outside the EU.

§3.04 CONCLUSION

The meaning and scope of the commercial arbitration exception in *Achmea* has not yet been clarified by the CJEU with respect to arbitration clauses included in State contracts. However, subsequent CJEU case law seems to confirm that States can enter into commercial arbitration agreements without breaching EU law, provided that such agreements are freely entered into by the parties and they are not arranged in a manner that systematically rules out the power of the EU courts to uphold norms of EU public policy. This would be, for example, the case if the seat of the arbitration is placed outside the EU. In this sense, it would be wise for Member States and economic operators to avoid placing the seat of their arbitrations in London or Switzerland.

In this context, a recent decision by the Greek Council of State extending the scope of *Achmea* to arbitration agreements contained in contracts concluded by Member States may be going beyond what was imposed by the CJEU's ruling in *Achmea*. However, it cannot be excluded that the CJEU would take an issue with Member States submitting disputes regarding the application of EU law to arbitral tribunals seated outside the EU and thus limiting or excluding any possibility of review by the EU courts. In these circumstances, a more cautious approach may be warranted

56. C-124/21 P, *International Skating Union v. Commission* EU:C:2023:1012, paras 193, 194 and 198.
57. *Ibid.*, para. 193.

when Member States decide, on a specific occasion, to entrust arbitral tribunals with the task of applying EU law even in a commercial relationship. The fact that such caution may not be required in a dispute between two private parties (as was the case in *Eco Swiss*) does not mean that it may not be required of Member States when they act in their commercial capacity. This is due to the fact that, as Member States, they cannot entirely sign out of their obligations under the TFEU.

CHAPTER 4

The Mandate for Arbitrators to Supplement Contracts under Swedish Law: A Brief Study with Particular Focus on Gas Price Review Arbitrations

Kristoffer Löf & David Akrad

§4.01 INTRODUCTION

As a starting point, arbitration is a judicial endeavour. Under Swedish law, this premise is set out in the first paragraph of section 27 a of the Swedish Arbitration Act (the 'Act'), pursuant to which the dispute is to be adjudicated with application of the law or rules agreed by the parties. Under this mandate, the tribunal's primary role is to resolve disputes by adjudicating facts and applying legal principles to them. Essentially, the parties bring a disagreement to the tribunal, which then establishes the disputed facts and interprets them with application of the legal rules to provide a binding resolution. This exercise of an arbitral tribunal to adjudicate a dispute referred to it with application of law may be referred to as *the ordinary judicial mandate* of a tribunal. In the vast majority of arbitrations, this is the mandate under which the tribunal decides the dispute.

However, according to the Act, tribunals can operate under two other kinds of mandate, which are different from the ordinary judicial mandate. When operating under these mandates, a tribunal is not bound strictly to assess the existence of alleged facts and give the facts legal consequences by applying law, as under the ordinary judicial mandate.

The first type of such 'non-legal mandate' is the mandate provided for in the third paragraph of section 27 a of the Act. Pursuant to this paragraph, an arbitral tribunal may base its award on reasonableness and equity (*skälighet och billighet*), but only if the parties have so agreed. In this role, the arbitrators thus act as *amiable compositeurs* or decide *ex aequo et bono* and resolve disputes not strictly by applying legal principles but by determining what is fair and just in the circumstances. In this capacity, the arbitrators may consider the presented facts more freely without strictly giving consequences to the facts that have legal relevance under the applicable rules. This mandate grants the tribunal broader discretion to achieve equitable outcomes based on the tribunal's perception of fairness than would have been possible if applying rigid legal rules.[1] This mandate will not be further discussed here.

Then, there is a third kind of mandate, which will be the focus of this paper, namely the mandate to supplement contracts (*avtalskomplettering*). The fact that this kind of mandate exists and may be given to arbitrators transpires not in section 27 a, which addresses the two other kinds of mandate, but in section 1 of the Act, which sets out what kind of issues are arbitrable and thus may be adjudicated in arbitration.[2] The second paragraph of the statute provides that parties may 'allow arbitrators to supplement contracts beyond what follows from contract interpretation'.[3] As will be discussed in the following sections of this paper, this essentially means that when parties cannot agree on a specific contractual term, they can authorise an arbitrator to decide the content of the contract on their behalf. Thus, this type of mandate allows the tribunal to go beyond mere application of law and contract and actively shape the contractual terms on the parties' behalf.

The leading academic commentators on Swedish arbitration law have addressed this subject and agree that a mandate to supplement the contract gives the tribunal powers that extend beyond an ordinary judicial mandate and, consequently, beyond what an ordinary court could be tasked to do.[4] However, it is still not entirely simple to define the boundaries of such mandate and what has been written on the subject is almost entirely in Swedish. Hence this attempt to approach the issues here. The perspective will be that of practitioners. We will seek to compensate the lesser academic wisdom that we possess compared to previous commentators with practical examples, starting with a number of arbitrations that have come to public knowledge through challenges of the arbitral awards.

---

1. *See*, for example, Stefan Lindskog, *Skiljeförfarande: En kommentar* (*Eng.* Arbitration: A Commentary), commentary to section 27 a of the Act, paras 5.3.1 and 5.3.2 (3rd ed., Juno 2020), for a further discussion.
2. The boundaries of what is arbitrable is defined positively: all matters that the parties themselves may settle. Section 1, first paragraph of the Act thus stipulates: 'Disputes concerning matters in respect of which the parties may reach a settlement may, by agreement, be referred to one or several arbitrators for resolution. Such an agreement may relate to future disputes pertaining to a legal relationship specified in the agreement. The dispute may concern the existence of a particular fact.'
3. Although section 1(2) refers to supplementing contracts, such mandate may also encompass altering or amending contractual provisions. The preparatory works to the Act and the commentary to the Act by former Chief Justice Lindskog explain that such mandate may for example include the power to determine changed prices or other contractual terms in a long-term contract. Stefan Lindskog, *Skiljeförfarande: En kommentar* (*Eng.* Arbitration: A Commentary), commentary to section 1 of the Act, para. 6.2.2 (3rd ed., Juno 2020); Govt. Bill 1998/99:35, pp. 61-63.
4. Stefan Lindskog, *Skiljeförfarande: En kommentar* (*Eng.* Arbitration: A Commentary), commentary to section 1 of the Act, para. 6.2.2, footnote 803 (3rd ed., Juno 2020); Lars Heuman, *Skiljemäns rätt att komplettera avtal* (*Eng.* Arbitrators' power to supplement contracts), in *Festskrift till Ulf K. Nordenson*, pp. 180-181 (Jure 1999).

In recent years, the Svea Court of Appeal has seen a whole host of challenges against awards in gas price review arbitrations.[5] A price review under a long-term supply agreement (whether for natural gas, electricity or 'power', component supply, or other types of products or commodities) is perhaps the typical situation in which an arbitral tribunal is given a mandate by the parties to supplement the contract, by revising the price terms on the parties' behalf.

In a very brief summary, a long-term supply agreement for natural gas contains an undertaking for the buyer to take a minimum volume of gas each year for the duration of the contract. The price payable for that supply is set at the beginning of the contract term and is typically indexed either to the price of other natural gas products or of other energy products. By the indexation, the parties hope that the price will self-adjust to changes in the market. But the parties also know that circumstances will change during the lifetime of the contract, which sometimes exceeds thirty years, in ways that the indexation will not be able to adjust for and that this will necessitate a renegotiation of the contract price.[6]

Such a renegotiation of the contract price is referred to as a 'price review' or a 'price revision'. Typically, a party to the contract has a right to request a price review at three-year intervals.[7] The requesting party must then first show that circumstances have changed in a way which is not reflected in the applicable price formula in accordance with certain specific conditions set out in the contract ('the trigger criteria').[8] Provided that the trigger criteria are met, the parties are then under an obligation to enter into negotiations to agree on a new price. If those negotiations do

5. The gas dispute awards under review by the Svea Court of Appeal in recent years include: *Gazprom v. Naftogaz of Ukraine*, Case No. T 10191-17 (Svea Court of Appeal 27 Nov. 2019); *Gazprom v. PGNiG*, Case No. T 8990-18 (Svea Court of Appeal 23 Dec. 2020); *Akfel Gaz v. Gazprom*, Case No. T 1806-19 (Svea Court of Appeal 8 Jun. 2021); *Enerco Enerji v. Gazprom*, Case No. T 1040-19 (Svea Court of Appeal 6 Oct. 2021); *Kibar Enerji v. Gazprom*, Case No. T 7865-19 (Svea Court of Appeal 1 Dec. 2021); *Botaş v. Depa*, Case No. T 4182-20 (Svea Court of Appeal 24 Feb. 2022); *Gazprom v. PGNiG*, Case No. T 6254-20 (Svea Court of Appeal 9 Mar. 2022).
6. The account of typical features of a gas price review in this Introduction is based on our practical experience of such disputes, having, in the case of the senior author of this contribution, been involved on the side of about ten different buyers of natural gas in more than twenty gas price reviews in the past 15-20 years (primarily working together with fellow Mannheimer Swartling partner Robin Oldenstam). The involvement has ranged from legal and contractual advice in the trigger and/or negotiation phases, counsel assignments (as lead counsel or for matters of Swedish law) in gas price review arbitrations, to a few cases of challenges of arbitral awards before Swedish courts. The typical features of gas price reviews accounted for here have also been described by other practitioners based on their experience; *see*, for example, Marco Lorefice, *Gas Price Review Arbitrations*, in *The Guide to Energy Arbitrations*, p. 1 (5th ed., GAR 2022); and Mark Levy, *Gas Price Review Arbitrations: Certain Distinctive Characteristics*, in *Global Arbitration Review, The Guide to Energy Arbitrations*, p. 185 (2nd ed., GAR 2017).
7. Marco Lorefice, *Gas Price Review Arbitrations*, in *The Guide to Energy Arbitrations*, p. 1 (5th ed., GAR 2022). *See also* Mark Levy, *Drafting an Effective Price Review Clause*, p. 13, para. 3.1 and Marnix Leijten & Martje de Vries Lentsch, *The Trigger Phase*, p. 34, para. 2.1, both in *Gas Price Arbitrations: A Practical Handbook* (1st ed., Globe Law and Business 2014).
8. Mark Levy, *Drafting an Effective Price Review Clause*, p. 13, para. 3.1, and Marnix Leijten & Martje de Vries Lentsch, *The Trigger Phase*, p. 35, para. 2.2 and p. 37, para. 3.1, both in *Gas Price Arbitrations: A Practical Handbook* (1st ed., Globe Law and Business 2014).

not lead to agreement, the contract typically provides that the matter may be referred to arbitration, thus granting the right to determine a new price to an arbitral tribunal.[9]

In most of the challenges heard by the Svea Court of Appeal concerning price review arbitrations, the question of the nature of the tribunal's mandate when determining a new price has not been addressed or has not played a central role in the decision. However, in two cases determined in 2022, the issue of the mandate was discussed. The authors of this article were part of the counsel teams representing the respective buyers (and respondents in the challenges) in both cases, which gave us reason to reflect further on the nature and scope of the mandate to supplement contracts.

The two cases will be briefly summarised below for context. However, the focus of the discussion in this article is not primarily these particular cases as such but what was not discussed in detail in those judgments (because it was not relevant for the court to go further in order to reach its conclusions).

§4.02 THE MANDATE TO SUPPLEMENT CONTRACTS ACCORDING TO THE SVEA COURT OF APPEAL: TWO GAS PRICE REVIEW ARBITRATIONS

[A] *Botaş v. Depa*

On 23 December 2003, Turkey's Botaş and Greece's Depa concluded a contract for pipeline supply of natural gas by Botaş to Depa. Under the contract, the price of the gas would be calculated using a price formula consisting of two factors: Pc + K. The Pc factor was linked to the agreed purchase price from a specific upstream supplier of gas to Botaş, and the K factor was linked to the market price of oil.

Article 9.6 of the contract provided that either party was entitled, under certain conditions, to request a revision of the price formula by submitting a price revision request, opening up a price review negotiation between the parties. If such a review did not result in agreement, the contract entitled either party to refer the matter to arbitration.

The parties have requested several price revisions, but the request of relevance here is one submitted by Botaş in 2011. On 13 June 2017, Depa requested arbitration against Botaş on the basis of this request since the negotiations under it had not resulted in a new price. Depa asked that the tribunal revise the price formula by replacing the aforementioned Pc and K factors with a direct indexation to the average price of imported gas in one of the larger European economies. Botaş objected to this request. The tribunal issued its award on 10 January 2020 and revised the price by replacing the Pc and K factors with a direct indexation to the average price for imported gas in one of the larger European economies.

9. Mark Levy, *Drafting an Effective Price Review Clause*, p. 15, para. 3.1, in *Gas Price Arbitrations: A Practical Handbook* (1st ed., Globe Law and Business 2014).

Botaş lodged a challenge against the award with the Svea Court of Appeal, seeking partial annulment of the award. Depa opposed Botaş's request. Botaş claimed that the arbitral tribunal exceeded its jurisdiction (*behörighetsöverskridande*) or mandate (*uppdragsöverskridande*) when it changed the structure of the price formula by removing the Pc and K factors.

In support of its claim that the tribunal exceeded its jurisdiction, Botaş essentially argued that the content of Article 9.6, which undisputedly gave the tribunal the right to supplement the contract with a new price, affected the tribunal's jurisdiction. Therefore, the tribunal allegedly exceeded its jurisdiction by modifying the structure of the price formula set out in Article 9.6. Botaş argued that the right of the arbitral tribunal to supplement the contract under Article 9.6 stemmed from section 1(2) of the Act and, as such, was a procedural rule and part of the arbitration agreement.

However, as the Court explained, section 1(2) expresses what is arbitrable, which is not the same as regulating the jurisdiction of a tribunal. No power of the tribunal as such is derived from or based on section 1(2), which merely states that if such power is granted to the tribunal (elsewhere, by the parties), that power may be exercised in arbitration. Moreover, the Court found that if the parties had intended Article 9.6 to limit the jurisdiction of the tribunal, they would have done so in the arbitration agreement.

The Court of Appeal then considered whether the arbitral tribunal had exceeded its mandate. In doing so, it made some observations about a tribunal's mandate to supplement a contract, referring to former Justice Stefan Lindskog's writings on the subject:

> In order for a contract to be supplemented, there must be support in the contract or in an instruction submitted jointly by the parties. The contractual support can be found not only in the arbitration agreement but also in the substantive provisions. A special case of exceeding the mandate is when the arbitral tribunal has supplemented the parties' contract without any support in the contract for a mandate to supplement it.[10]

The parties agreed that the contract supported such a mandate. However, they disagreed as to how far that mandate extended, i.e., how Article 9.6 should be interpreted.

In the arbitration, the tribunal itself found that Article 9.6 was a substantive provision and that, by that provision, the parties had given a third party (the tribunal) the right to revise a contractual provision (the price) in the place of the parties could they not agree themselves. Moreover, the tribunal found that Article 9.6 gave it, as well as the parties, the right to revise some or all elements of the price formula.

The question then naturally arose as to how the Court of Appeal should approach the issue in the light of the tribunal's own assessment of the matter. The Court wrote:

---

10. *Botaş v. Depa*, Case No. T 4182-20, p. 25 (our own translation, Svea Court of Appeal 24 Feb. 2022); and Stefan Lindskog, *Skiljeförfarande: En kommentar* (*Eng.* Arbitration: A Commentary), commentary to section 1 of the Act, para. 6.2.3 and commentary to section 34, para. 4.3.6 (3rd. ed., Juno 2020).

> When reviewing a tribunal's assessment of the scope of its mandate, just as in reviewing the issue of jurisdiction, it is reasonable to assume that the tribunal is in the best position to assess the issue and that the tribunal's interpretation and assessment of the evidence is therefore correct as a starting point.
>
> As noted above, a mandate to supplement contracts may follow from a substantive provision of the contract. The arbitral tribunal's assessment that Article 9.6 constitutes a substantive provision to be applied in accordance with Swiss law is supported by the fact that the parties confirmed this during the arbitral proceedings. The Court of Appeal finds no reason to depart from the arbitral tribunal's assessment in this respect.
>
> Accordingly, the substantive provision in Article 9.6 provided the necessary support for the arbitral tribunal to adjust the price. There was therefore no excess of the mandate. Since the Court of Appeal should not review the tribunal's decision in the context of challenge proceedings, the Court of Appeal should not revisit the tribunal's interpretation and application of Article 9.6.[11]

Based on this analysis, the Court concluded that the tribunal had not exceeded its mandate nor its jurisdiction. Thus, the challenge was rejected.

[B] *Gazprom v. PGNiG*

In the other price review discussed here, the dispute arose under a long-term gas supply agreement between Poland's PGNiG, as buyer, and Russia's Gazprom, as seller. The contract provided that the price of gas was to be determined in accordance with a price formula consisting of several different components related to the market price of alternative energy sources. The contract allowed the parties to request a revision of the price formula if certain trigger criteria were met. If the parties could not agree on a new price, the contract allowed either party to refer the matter to arbitration.

Arbitration was requested by the buyer. In a separate award issued on 29 June 2018, the arbitral tribunal concluded that it had a mandate under section 1(2) of the Act to decide on a price revision under the contract and that such revision could be different from the one requested by the buyer. It also concluded that the conditions for a price revision were met in the present case. The seller protested against these findings and also (unsuccessfully) challenged the separate award.[12]

On 30 March 2020, the arbitral tribunal issued a final award setting out a new price formula. Somewhat simplified, the new price formula included components that had been agreed by the parties in the arbitration, albeit the values to be ascribed to those components were debated. The final award provided for values between those requested by the buyer and the seller for each respective component of the formula.

The seller challenged the final award.[13] In the challenge proceedings before the Svea Court of Appeal, the seller argued that the arbitral tribunal had exceeded its mandate, as the parties had not given the arbitral tribunal any joint instructions, either

11. *Botaş v. Depa*, Case No. T 4182-20, pp. 25-26 (our own translation, Svea Court of Appeal 24 Feb. 2022).
12. *Gazprom v. PGNiG*, Case No. T 8990-18 (Svea Court of Appeal 23 Dec. 2020).
13. *Gazprom v. PGNiG*, Case No. T 6254-20 (Svea Court of Appeal 9 Mar. 2022).

in the contract or during the arbitration, that would allow it to supplement the contract. The seller argued that the arbitral tribunal had engaged in contract supplementation by setting a new price formula, thereby exceeding its ordinary judicial mandate. The seller further argued that in order for the arbitral tribunal to have a mandate to supplement the contract, it must have been given complete discretion to decide on the content of the contract, which was not the case here as the contract included a number of guidelines for how a new price should be arrived at, either by the parties themselves or, failing agreement, by a tribunal.

The buyer opposed the challenge. It pointed to the fact that the arbitration agreement empowered the arbitral tribunal to set a new price (including a new price formula) and argued that the arbitral tribunal had thus been given an express mandate to set a new price (including a new price formula). Irrespective of whether this mandate was to be interpreted as an ordinary mandate to interpret the contract or, instead, as a mandate to supplement the contract, the buyer argued that the tribunal had not exceeded any mandate since the decision had not been outside the scope of the facts argued by the parties.

In its judgment, the Svea Court of Appeal first addressed the concept of a mandate to supplement the contract. The Court noted that section 1 of the Act delineates the scope of arbitrability, that is, the issues that may be referred to an arbitral tribunal. It also highlighted that the second paragraph of the same section, which permits parties to grant an arbitral tribunal a mandate to supplement the contract, was included in the Act to define the boundaries of arbitrability. The Court noted that contract supplementation is permissible regardless of whether the agreement in dispute provides precise instructions for the exercise or whether the mandate is more broadly defined. Consequently, the Court concluded that distinguishing between an ordinary judicial mandate, which includes the right to fill gaps through interpretation, and a mandate to supplement the contract is not always practically possible. The judgment provides:

> Section 1 of the Act sets out what is arbitrable, i.e. what matters can be referred to an arbitral tribunal for adjudication (see Govt. Bill 1998/99:35 p. 210). The second paragraph of the section states that the parties may allow the arbitrators to supplement a contract in addition to what follows from the interpretation of contracts. The provision was introduced so that the arbitral tribunals authority to supplement contracts would be clearly stated by law (Govt. Bill p. 61). It thus aims to clarify the limits of what is arbitrable in this respect.
>
> The competence of an arbitral tribunal may thus include a right to supplement contracts in such respects where there is no basis for how the assessment is to be made and this regardless of whether the mandate may be considered as exercise of law (Govt. Bill p. 61). However, such a lack of guidance for the arbitral tribunal's assessments is not, in the opinion of the Court of Appeal, a prerequisite for a right to supplement the contract within the meaning of the law, but constitutes the outer limit for the matters that may be referred to an arbitral tribunal. It follows from this, that it is not meaningful to maintain any sharp distinction between a right to supplement a contract and a right to, for example, gap-filling (cf. Lindskog, Skiljeförfarande, En kommentar (*Eng.* Arbitration: A Commentary), 2020, p. 281 note 1120). Neither the text of the law nor the

preparatory work contains any definition of a right to supplement contracts or even an attempt to define such a right.[14]

The Court further reasoned that determining whether an arbitral tribunal has a mandate from the parties to supplement the contract, and the extent of that mandate, cannot be based on a theoretical legal definition of what such a mandate encompasses. Rather, it must be ascertained from the arbitration agreement and other pertinent documents.

In the present case, the Court noted that the arbitral tribunal had determined that it possessed a mandate to supplement the contract as per section 1(2) of the Act. Additionally, during the arbitration, the parties concurred that the tribunal was empowered to establish a new pricing formula, subject to certain conditions. The contention arose over whether this authority was to be qualified as such a mandate to supplement the contract that, under section 1(2) of the Act, requires the parties' agreement and, if so, how to define that mandate. Again, the Court repeated that such legal qualification of a mandate has no independent meaning. The Court, applying Swedish arbitration law, agreed with the arbitral tribunal's conclusion that the contract authorised it to supplement the contract by adjusting the price formula. The Court found that there were some points of reference for the arbitral tribunal's assessment in the contract, but these were not particularly guiding for the arbitral tribunal. Thus, the Court concluded that the arbitral tribunal had been given wide discretion to revise the price formula. In the end, it held that the arbitral tribunal had not exceeded its mandate when it determined the new price formula.[15]

[C] Further Questions Remaining

In the two cases discussed above, the issue of contract supplementation was raised, but it was not ultimately decisive for the outcome. In *Botaş v. Depa*, there was no dispute that the tribunal had been given a mandate to supplement contracts; the contentious issue was the scope of the tribunal's mandate and whether it was limited to adjusting existing price components or replacing them. This was deemed a substantive issue determined by the interpretation of the contract and, thus, outside of the Court of Appeal's review.[16] In *Gazprom v. PGNiG*, it was in dispute whether the tribunal had been given a mandate to supplement contracts, but the parties agreed in principle that the arbitral tribunal had a right to adjust the price formula, regardless of whether this was characterised as contract supplementation or as an ordinary application of law and

14. *Gazprom v. PGNiG*, Case No. T 6254-20, pp. 12-13 (our own translation, Svea Court of Appeal 9 Mar. 2022).
15. *Gazprom v. PGNiG*, Case No. T 6254-20, pp. 13-18 (Svea Court of Appeal 9 Mar. 2022). The Svea Court of Appeal gave the parties permission to appeal its judgment to the Supreme Court because it considered that the case involved issues where it is important for the guidance of the application of the law that an appeal be heard by the Supreme Court. However, the judgment was not appealed.
16. *Botaş v. Depa*, Case No. T 4182-20, pp. 25-26 (Svea Court of Appeal 24 Feb. 2022).

contract.[17] In both cases, the Court of Appeal found that the parties' contract provided the tribunal with the power to revise the price formula, that the price formula determined by the tribunal fell within its discretion and, importantly, that it did not deviate from how the issues in dispute had been defined by the parties in the arbitrations through their requests for relief and argued facts.[18]

So the question of what happens if it is established that the parties have *not agreed* on giving an arbitral tribunal a mandate to supplement contracts, but the tribunal is said to have done so in any event, was not asked. How does one then determine whether the arbitral tribunal has engaged in its ordinary judicial mandate or in unauthorised contract supplementation? This will be addressed in section §4.03 below.

In section §4.04, we will look at the boundaries of a mandate to supplement the contract once it has been established that the arbitral tribunal has been provided with such powers. As will be explained, the parties' dispositions[19] in the arbitration are critical in shaping the boundaries of the arbitral tribunal's powers.

§4.03 DISTINGUISHING BETWEEN AN ORDINARY JUDICIAL MANDATE AND A MANDATE TO SUPPLEMENT THE CONTRACT

[A] Contract Interpretation under the Ordinary Judicial Mandate (and in the Grey Zone)

As noted above, the parties may 'allow arbitrators to supplement contracts beyond what follows from contract interpretation' (section 1(2) of the Act). The starting point of the analysis of what this means is thus to determine what 'follows from contract interpretation'.

Contract interpretation is, of course, part of a tribunal's ordinary judicial mandate. It requires no specific agreement by the parties. But evidently, according to the provision in section 1(2), a tribunal can go beyond that and beyond what is possible for a court[20] if the parties have allowed the tribunal to do so. Since this kind of operation thus requires the parties' agreement – and consequently is prohibited absent such agreement – it is relevant to consider where to draw the demarcation line between the

17. *Gazprom v. PGNiG*, Case No. T 6254-20, pp. 13-14 (Svea Court of Appeal 9 Mar. 2022). According to Gazprom, the tribunal was empowered to revise the price formula provided that it kept within an ordinary judicial mandate.
18. *Gazprom v. PGNiG*, Case No. T 6254-20, pp. 13-16 (Svea Court of Appeal 9 Mar. 2022); and *Botaş v. Depa*, Case No. T 4182-20, pp. 25-26 (Svea Court of Appeal 24 Feb. 2022).
19. The Swedish law principle of *party disposition* will be developed in this paper and essentially entails that the powers of a court or tribunal is limited by the parties' dispositions (i.e., requests for relief, instructions given, facts invoked, and positions taken) as presented during the course of the proceedings.
20. Stefan Lindskog, *Skiljeförfarande: En kommentar* (*Eng.* Arbitration: A Commentary), commentary to section 1 of the Act, para. 6.2.2, footnote 803 (3rd. ed., Juno 2020); and Lars Heuman, *Skiljemäns rätt att komplettera avtal* (*Eng.* Arbitrators' power to supplement contracts), in *Festskrift till Ulf K. Nordenson*, pp. 180-181 (Jure 1999).

ordinary filling of gaps through contract interpretation and the extraordinary supplementation of contracts.

To draw that demarcation line, we start by looking at the non-controversial filling of gaps through contract interpretation.

Consider a long-term supply agreement between a manufacturer (seller) and a retailer (buyer) for the delivery of goods. The contract specifies the type of goods, the quantity to be delivered, the price per unit, and the total duration of the contract. However, it omits a crucial detail: the specific delivery dates or intervals. To fill this gap, a delivery schedule must be inferred. This inference could be based on the nature of the business, industry standards, and the parties' past dealings, if any. The parties in the arbitration would argue the normative framework to apply and the facts that correspond to it. The tribunal would then base its interpretation on the argued contractual data (any prior agreements, communications, and practices between the parties) and on non-mandatory legal rules (legal principles and industry norms that provide a framework for filling gaps in contracts). That is in itself a judicial endeavour that requires no specific mandate.

Another situation could be that all terms around a purchase have been agreed - quality, number of units per shipment, place of delivery, duration of the contract - but not the unit price. There may then be legal norms to apply in the situation where the price, or the principles for determining the price, are not agreed on, as in Article 55 of the CISG or section 45 of the Swedish Sale of Goods Act. It naturally falls within the ordinary judicial mandate to apply those norms (if they are applicable), whether the issue is faced by an arbitral tribunal or by a court.[21]

What the above-mentioned examples have in common is that the solution is provided for by legal norms. Perhaps, rather than referring to the filling of gaps through contract interpretation, it would have been more to the point if section 1(2) was phrased: 'The parties may allow the arbitrators to supplement a contract beyond what follows from interpretation and application of law.' This wording would be in line with how the permitted and ordinary filling of gaps, under the ordinary judicial mandate, has been defined by former Justice Lindskog in his commentary to section 1 of the Act:

> However, such supplementation [through contract interpretation] must be based on either contractual data or non-mandatory legal rules.
>
> In other words, there must be a legal basis for the interpretative operation by which the contract is filled out so that the operation can be characterised as administration of justice in the true sense of the word. A filling of a gap may thus not be based on mere considerations of what is appropriate under the circumstances.[22]

21. Stefan Lindskog, *Skiljeförfarande: En kommentar* (*Eng.* Arbitration: A Commentary), commentary to section 1 of the Act, paras 6.2.1 and 6.2.2, footnotes 800 and 804 (3rd. ed., Juno 2020); and Lars Heuman, *Skiljemäns rätt att komplettera avtal* (*Eng.* Arbitrators' power to supplement contracts), in *Festskrift till Ulf K. Nordenson*, pp. 187-188 (Jure 1999).
22. Stefan Lindskog, *Skiljeförfarande: En kommentar* (*Eng.* Arbitration: A Commentary), commentary to section 1 of the Act, para. 6.2.1 (our own translation, 3rd. ed., Juno 2020). In the Swedish original (footnotes omitted): 'En sådan utfyllnad måste dock vila på antingen avtalsdata eller dispositiva rättsregler. Det hela kan uttryckas så att det måste finnas ett rättsligt underlag för den

Accordingly, if the gap can be filled by way of ordinary administration of justice in the true sense of the word, the operation requires no special mandate.

Let us now turn to another example (based on a real-life situation). Consider a supply agreement between a manufacturer and a buyer for the delivery of a specific product. The contract includes the following provisions:

> If, during the term of this agreement, circumstances change in a way that significantly affects the availability and market price of the Product, then the parties agree to negotiate in good faith and reach a mutual agreement on an adjusted price for the Product within 30 days of either party providing written notice of such change. If no agreement is reached within this period, the parties shall continue to perform their obligations under the original terms of this agreement unless and until an adjusted price is agreed upon.

The provision is a classical 'agreement to agree'. It evidently provides no remedy (legal consequence) for the situation that no agreement is reached. Would it still be possible for the party seeking renegotiation to initiate arbitration and request the tribunal to determine an adjusted price? To answer that question, one must, of course, read the whole contract, but for this purpose, let us agree that there is no provision in the contract that provides that if the parties cannot come to agreement on a specific point, they may refer their disagreement to arbitration.

In this situation, unlike the example above where there was no price, non-mandatory provisions in CISG or the Swedish Sale of Goods Act cannot be used to determine a price since there *is* a price (what the requesting party wants is a *new* price). This thus seems like a situation that cannot be resolved through contract interpretation.[23] We are thus at the point where an arbitral tribunal's adjustment of the contract to compensate for the parties' failure to agree would go 'beyond what follows from contract interpretation'. That is therefore something that the tribunal ought not do, absent an instruction from the parties allowing it to supplement the contract.

The problem could be more difficult if the renegotiation clause instead had the following wording:

> If, during the term of this agreement, circumstances change in a way that significantly affects the availability and market price of the Product, then the parties agree to enter into negotiation in good faith within 30 days of either party providing written notice of such change and reach a mutual agreement where (a) the possibility for the Buyer to offtake the Product in a certain month should be restricted if availability of the product is 50 per cent or less of current availability

---

tolkningsoperation varigenom avtalet fyllts ut så att operationen kan karaktäriseras som rättsskipning i egentlig mening. En utfyllnad får således inte vila på rena lämplighetsöverväganden.'

23. There may, however, be other ways to argue a case under the applicable legal rules based on the facts resulting in the situation addressed by the provision, such as hardship, impossibility and unconscionability, even if there is no support for that in the contract clause. A case based on such theories could result in termination, avoidance, adjustment and possibly other remedies, but not in contract supplementation or gap-filling per se. Possibly, if one of the parties would have breached the express obligation in the clause to negotiate in good faith, that could also be seen as a breach of contract entitling the other party to damages and possibly other remedies but not in a new agreement.

> in the preceding month and (b), if the market price has changed by more than 20 per cent and has remained so for more than six months, the price for the Product is to be adjusted upwards or downwards, with a percentage corresponding to the change in market price in average seen over the duration of the contract to date.

Again, the contract includes no provision by which the parties agree that a tribunal may amend the agreement on their behalf should they fail to agree on a revision themselves. The clause still says that an adjustment can take place only by the parties' '*mutual agreement*'. But this situation is still more difficult than in the previous example because here, the provision is normative and sets out the parameters necessary to know what the renegotiation should result in. It would thus be possible for an arbitral tribunal to assess evidence relied on by the parties in support of factual allegations and apply principles of burden of proof to determine whether the facts are established. If they are, the legal consequence could be ascertained.

This kind of provision could thus give ground for a cause of action that would allow a tribunal to establish what the revised contract terms should be had the parties complied with their good faith obligation. That could take the form of declaratory relief and also damages, ordered under the tribunal's ordinary judicial mandate. However, it would likely be to stretch the interpretation to say that a tribunal would have the mandate to actually change the contract based on this contract wording since the legal consequence of the requirements being at hand is that the parties are to agree – not that the contract is to be changed. In other words, it would likely be a case of (prohibited) contract supplementation if a tribunal were to declare a revision of the contract based on the clause.[24]

[B] Revision of the Price Based on a Traditional Price Review Clause

Let us now return to the kind of provisions that were the basis for the arbitrations in the two cases outlined above. Here, it is clear that the tribunal may order a new price to apply and thus change the contract. In both contracts, the parties had included price review clauses that are fairly 'typical' for long-term supply of natural gas (even if every clause is unique and includes its own specific requirements).[25] In order for this chapter

---

24. The existence of normative guidance does thus not itself imply that the tribunal may step into the shoes of the parties and reach the agreement that they should have reached themselves. And conversely, when there is guidance sufficient for a finding of the new contract term based on burden of proof, it may still be a question of contract supplementation that requires the parties agreement. Lindskog explains as follows: 'When the parties enter into an arbitration agreement and leave room in it for the arbitral tribunal to supplement the agreement if the need arises, it may often be appropriate to set out certain normative guidelines for how the supplementation is to be carried out. This is, of course, mainly because if the parties agree on the normative guidelines, it increases the chances that they will be able to reach agreement without having to refer the matter to arbitration. And if they do so, the risk of surprises from the arbitral tribunal is reduced.', Stefan Lindskog, *Skiljeförfarande: En kommentar* (*Eng.* Arbitration: A Commentary), commentary to section 1 of the Act, para. 6.2.2 (3rd. ed., Juno 2020).
25. Mark Levy, *Gas Price Review Arbitrations: Certain Distinctive Characteristics*, in *Global Arbitration Review, The Guide to Energy Arbitrations*, pp. 187-188 (2nd ed., GAR 2017).

to be of general interest and not focused on the peculiarities of individual cases, we have asked ChatGPT 4o to provide a typical price review clause for analysis:

Article 10: Price Review

10.1 Trigger Events for Price Review

If during the term of this Agreement, one or more of the following trigger events occur, either party (the 'Requesting Party') shall have the right every three years to initiate a price review:

a. Significant Market Changes: A substantial change in the market conditions affecting the natural gas industry, such as significant fluctuations in the market price of natural gas or alternative energy sources, which makes the price set forth in this Agreement no longer reflective of the current market value.
b. Regulatory Changes: The introduction, modification, or repeal of any laws, regulations, or governmental policies that materially affect the cost or availability of natural gas to either party.
c. Economic Hardship: A substantial change in economic circumstances that significantly impacts the financial viability of the Agreement for either party.

The Requesting Party shall provide written notice to the other party (the 'Responding Party') of its intention to initiate a price review. The notice shall specify the trigger event(s) and provide reasonable evidence supporting the occurrence of such event(s).

10.2 Good Faith Negotiations

Upon receipt of the notice, the parties shall enter into good faith negotiations to agree on a revised price for the natural gas supplied under this Agreement. The negotiations shall aim to establish a price that is fair and equitable, taking into account:

a. The current market conditions and prices for natural gas.
b. The impact of the trigger event(s) on the costs and revenues of both parties.
c. Any other relevant economic or regulatory factors.

10.3 Referral to Arbitration

If the parties are unable to reach an agreement on the revised price within a sixty (60) day negotiation period, either party shall have the right to refer the matter to arbitration in accordance with Article 12 of this Agreement.

10.4 Continuation of Supply

During the period of negotiations and any subsequent arbitration proceedings, the parties shall continue to perform their obligations under this Agreement, including the supply and payment for natural gas, at the price currently in effect, until a new price is agreed upon or determined by the arbitral tribunal which price is to apply retroactively as from the date of the notice.

The above example coincides well with what, in our experience, may be deemed an 'average' price review clause, particularly in 'East-West' gas supply contracts of a somewhat older vintage.[26] As per the above example, the first step in a price revision arbitration is to determine whether the trigger criteria have been met. The trigger criteria usually require that the party requesting price revision can establish certain conditions relating to changed circumstances which are not reflected in the price formula.

When adjudicating the trigger criteria and thus establishing whether there is a right per se to have a new price, the arbitral tribunal clearly engages in an ordinary judicial determination. The trigger criteria constitute legal norms[27] that can be construed through contract interpretation to include precise requirements that, if proven to be fulfilled, provide for a specific legal outcome. In other words, when arguing that there is a right to a price review, the requesting party can present facts corresponding to requirements of the rule. An arbitral tribunal may apply an ordinary operation of burden of proof to ascertain whether the argued facts are supported by the evidence on the record. It follows that an arbitral tribunal tasked with assessing whether the trigger criteria in Clause 10.1 above have been met may assess and interpret the facts and arguments by applying relevant legal rules in order to reach a binding decision. The tribunal does not need any extraordinary power to fulfil this task; an ordinary judicial mandate authorising it to adjudicate the dispute with application of law is sufficient.[28]

Once it has been established that the trigger criteria are met, the next step is to negotiate the revised contract price formula. As in Clause 10.2 in the example above, the price review clause often contains instructions as to how the revision should be carried out, and there are two very common phrases of relevance here:

(a) The revised contract price shall be '*fair and equitable*' (or alterations of this with a similar meaning).

---

26. Many of the Western-European contracts for supply of Russian (and previously Soviet) natural gas have their origin in the 1970s, although most have been amended and sometimes reinstated as new contracts several times since their conclusion. In our experience, the price review clauses of those contracts are often rather concise but with a few clear themes as per the example provided above. More modern contracts for the supply of Liquefied Natural Gas as well as many of the 'North-South contracts', for supply from the North Sea to Continental Europe, are often slightly more technical in how they are drafted albeit with the same or similar main features. For further examples of price review clauses, *see* Mark Levy, *Gas Price Arbitrations: A Practical Handbook*, pp. 173-177 (Globe Business Publishing Ltd 2014), where Mr Levy has included an appendix with a few other sample clauses, some of which include many but not all the elements included in the example provided above.
27. In Swedish procedural law nomenclature, these elements or requirements are referred to as abstract facts (*abstrakta rättsfakta*) or prerequisites (*rekvisit*). In order for the prescribed legal consequence (*rättsföljd*) to materialise, a party must prove that the facts in the case (*konkreta rättsfakta*) match the abstract facts in the relevant rule. This should all be quite obvious for a lawyer irrespective of legal background, even if the Swedish terminology is confusing and unhelpful (even for most Swedish lawyers).
28. Lars Heuman, *Skiljemäns rätt att komplettera avtal* (*Eng.* Arbitrators' power to supplement contracts), in *Festskrift till Ulf K. Nordenson*, p. 190 (Jure 1999). Professor Emeritus Lars Heuman explains that the power to assess the existence of facts includes the power to make legal qualifications, for example, to decide whether certain acts entail force majeure or whether the goods supplied meet the relevant requirements. Similarly, it naturally falls within an ordinary judicial mandate to find that the trigger criteria in a long-term gas supply agreement have been satisfied.

(b) The revision shall '*take into account*' relevant economic data pertaining to the gas market, as further detailed in the price review clause. Although the provision includes some criteria to be followed, this instruction is hardly a rule, nor is it particularly tangible, as it merely sets out certain facts and circumstances to '*take into account*'.

If the parties are unable to reach agreement in accordance with these instructions, the price revision clause sets out the legal consequence: either party has the right to refer the matter to arbitration. The task of the arbitrators is then to step into the shoes of the parties and revise the price, i.e., to finish what the parties themselves have been unable to do.[29]

What the tribunal has to consider and take into account in revising the contract prices are the same substantive provisions that were before the parties. Accordingly, the tribunal shall '*take into account*' relevant market data and ensure that the revised contract price is '*fair and equitable*'.

The requirement that the revision be '*fair and equitable*' encapsulates that the issue submitted to the tribunal is not a matter that could be resolved by exercising an ordinary judicial mandate. In the words of one president of a tribunal considering a gas price review, when the scope of the mandate came under debate at a hearing: 'this is not a burden of proof exercise … we are not applying burden of proof, we are rewriting the contract … and we will do that as professionally we can on the basis of the data we have'. That the revision shall be '*fair and equitable*' is not a concrete requirement possible to apply the burden of proof to; the requirement does not correspond to specific facts that can be proven.

29. Mark Levy, *Gas Price Review Arbitrations: Certain Distinctive Characteristics*, in *Global Arbitration Review, The Guide to Energy Arbitrations*, pp. 185-193 (2nd ed., GAR 2017). As Lindskog points out, the task of the tribunal in these situations is similar to that of an expert in an expert determination procedure (*godmansförfarande*); *see* Stefan Lindskog, *Skiljeförfarande: En kommentar* (*Eng.* Arbitration: A Commentary), at 0 para. 3.2.1. (3rd. ed., Juno 2020). A typical example of a provision subject to expert determination is a purchase price adjustment clause in a sale and purchase agreement for the sale of a company. The parties often agree in the contract that, should they not agree on how to adjust the contract price following receipt of a closing balance sheet, an independent expert (often an auditor) is to complete the task on their behalf with binding effect. Such a decision is binding in the sense that the parties become contractually bound by the decision. Such a procedure is similar but not the same as contract supplementation through arbitration. Lindskog explains as follows (in our translation): 'When attempting to define what constitutes an arbitration, international literature often emphasise that the award is binding and that arbitration has its own procedure. *See* e.g. Fouchard et al. no. 7 et seq. and Lew, Mistelis & Kröll 1-20. But also an expert determination is binding. What distinguishes the two types of decisions is their respective legal quality: an arbitral award is an enforceable judgment, whereas an expert determination has the character of a contract. A contract can (as a general rule) be concluded informally. For expert determinations there may consequently be full party autonomy. An arbitral award has much more far-reaching legal effects than an expert determination. In the interests of due process, therefore, both the procedure and the award must be subject to special scrutiny. In this context, there is also reason to point out that arbitration is an exception to the principle of the inalienable right to a trial that is recognised by the legal system […]. This is not the case with expert determination.' *See* Stefan Lindskog, *Skiljeförfarande: En kommentar* (Eng. Arbitration: A Commentary), footnote 149 at 0 para. 3.2.1. (3rd. ed., Juno 2020).

Put simply, as the provision reads, there is nothing to test evidence against, and a tribunal cannot determine a revised price formula only by applying the law. One could possibly interpret the directions to '*take into account*' certain data as providing concrete requirements that may correspond to facts that may be proven. However, even if that would be the case, the price revision clause does not set out any legal consequence of establishing such facts.

Instead of merely assessing whether the operative facts correspond to the abstract facts, a tribunal with a mandate to supplement the contract arrives at revised contract prices by also taking into account arguments of economic and commercial nature, just as the parties were supposed to do during their negotiations. Under such a mandate, which goes beyond an ordinary judicial mandate, it is not for the arbitral tribunal to simply assess whether a specific price formula has been entirely proven by one party and, if not, dismiss the entire case. Instead, it is for the tribunal to revise the price formula on behalf of the parties and, in doing so, apply its business acumen based on the presented data. But are there no limits to the discretion? We will turn to that now.

§4.04 LIMITS TO THE POWERS OF A TRIBUNAL EXERCISING A MANDATE TO SUPPLEMENT CONTRACTS

[A] The Boundaries of the Tribunal's Powers Are Set by the Contract and the Parties' Dispositions

There are limits to the tribunal's powers, regardless of whether it has been vested with a mandate to supplement contracts or an ordinary judicial mandate. The starting point for identifying these limits is not section 1(2) of the Act, as explained above, but the contract and the parties' dispositions (i.e., requests for relief, instructions given, facts invoked and positions taken) during the course of the arbitration.[30]

It follows that the task of an arbitral tribunal empowered to supplement contracts is to exercise its power in accordance with the principles indicated by the parties. In the absence of any such principles, the arbitral tribunal is allowed to more freely decide the new content of the parties' contract, however, guided by the nature of the contract and the underlying purpose of the supplementation to be made.[31]

30. In the judgment in *Gazprom v. PGNiG*, the Court of Appeal stated: 'Neither the statutory text nor the preparatory work contains any definition of a right to supplement contracts or even an attempt to define such a right. Consequently, whether the arbitral tribunal has a right to supplement the contract, or how far that right extends, cannot be assessed on the basis of an intended definition of what constitutes a mandate to supplement the contract within the meaning of the law. Instead, it is the underlying arbitration agreement and other documents, and what can be read from the provisions therein concerning the limits of the arbitral tribunal's mandate, that may have an impact on the arbitral tribunal's right to supplement the contract. This is also the starting point in the preparatory works (see Govt. Bill. p. 62 and p. 210 *et seq.*). A limit for the arbitral tribunal in this context consists of what is considered as arbitrable, pursuant to section 1(2) of the Act.' *Gazprom v. PGNiG*, Case No. T 6254-20, p. 13 (Svea Court of Appeal 9 Mar. 2022).
31. Stefan Lindskog, *Skiljeförfarande: En kommentar* (*Eng.* Arbitration: A Commentary), commentary to section 1 of the Act, para. 6.2.4 (3rd. ed., Juno 2020).

The scope of an arbitral tribunal's powers emanating from a contract must be interpreted on a case-by-case basis in accordance with general principles of contract interpretation. Under Swedish law, it is the common intention of the parties at the time of entering into the contract that ultimately determines the content of an agreement.

The scope of an arbitral tribunal's powers arising from the dispositions of the parties within the arbitration may be more difficult to determine, as these dispositions are likely to evolve during the course of the proceedings, requiring, to some extent, a dynamic interpretation of the mandate. Critically, when assessing the parties' dispositions, an arbitral tribunal may not go beyond the prayers for relief or consider facts other than those presented by the parties.[32]

The importance of the parties' dispositions, and not least the requests for relief, is an outflow of the *principle of party disposition* (*dispositionsprincipen*), which is at the heart of the Swedish Act and serves to ensure that the parties remain in control of the proceedings, the issues to be adjudicated and thus, the issues to be addressed by the parties. The Svea Court of Appeal has succinctly summarised this principle in *CMP v. Minmetals* as follows:

> The principle implies that the arbitral tribunal may not act in an inquisitorial manner, but that the content and scope of the proceedings are to be determined by the dispositions of the parties. Thus, there is an excess of mandate if the arbitral tribunal unexpectedly adjudicates matters not covered by the parties' dispositions. The two most obvious situations are that the award goes beyond the underlying request for relief or that the award is based on a fact that has not been adduced.[33]

It follows that a tribunal may not award more than what a party has asked for (*ultra petita*) since such award goes beyond the parties' dispositions and, thus, the mandate. Nor may the tribunal award something different (*aliud*) from what the parties have requested. However, the tribunal may award something less (*infra petita*), pursuant to the principle that the greater includes, the lesser (*majus includit minus*).[34]

Lindskog and Heuman seem to agree that a tribunal exercising a mandate to supplement the contract is not limited to the parties' specific requests for relief but that it may also award a compromise between the parties' respective positions. It is not always easy to find a compromise when the differences between the parties' requests for relief are not only quantitative but also qualitative. We will illustrate this through the lens of price review arbitrations in the following section.

---

32. Lars Heuman, *Skiljemannarätt* (*Eng.* Arbitration law), Nordsteds, p. 336 (Jure 1999). One effect of this is that the exact scope of the arbitration will not always be defined from day one but will, to some extent, develop during the course of the proceedings.
33. *Chelyabinsk Metallurgical Plant v. Minmetals*, Case No. T 1356-18, p. 32 (our own translation, Svea Court of Appeal 4 Nov. 2022).
34. Eric Runesson, *Jura Novit Curia and Due Process with Particular Regard to Arbitration in Sweden*, in *Juridisk Tidskrift nr 1 2017/18*, pp. 187-190.

[B] The Arbitral Tribunal's Room for Manoeuvre Between the Parties' Dispositions

In price reviews, the parties sometimes have different views on the components that should be included in the revised price formula. For example, if one party seeks gas market price indexation and the other prefers oil indexation, finding a middle ground may be challenging.

Already, in ordinary arbitrations, the tribunal has a mandate to render the award it deems appropriate.[35] It may do so as long as it does not exceed the parties' dispositions. It follows that an arbitral tribunal may make awards that represent natural compromises between the parties' prayers for relief, even beyond numerical compromises. However, an arbitral tribunal may not make an award which – on an overall assessment – appears to be more burdensome to the respondent than the claimant's requests for relief.

However, a tribunal exercising a mandate to supplement the contract has an even wider mandate to make compromises and to award something different than requested by the parties. By the time a tribunal is given a mandate to supplement the contract, the parties have typically conducted negotiations for some time and to no avail. In such cases, when the tribunal is tasked to step into the shoes of the parties and finish what the parties themselves have been unable to do, the tribunal's mandate can hardly be limited to strictly amend the contract as requested by the parties. In Heuman's words:

> When supplementing contracts, the parties have typically conducted detailed negotiations without succeeding to agree on how to alter or amend the agreement. In these cases, the task of the arbitrators can hardly be limited to amending the agreement solely in the manner requested by one of the parties.[36]

A tribunal that has been given a mandate to supplement the contract is empowered not only to assess the facts and evidence of the parties but also to develop terms and conditions that it considers appropriate. Such terms and conditions may, for example, be construed by the tribunal using a combination of different components of any specific contract amendment argued by the parties. For example, in a price review,

35. Heuman states in his paper on contract supplementation that there are good arguments why determining a 'reasonable price' in fact does not require a mandate to supplement the contract, but only an ordinary judicial mandate. In Heuman's view, deciding what constitutes a reasonable price falls within an ordinary judicial mandate, because a court can decide such price with reference to section of 45 in the Swedish Sale of Goods Act, which only include vague directions as to what constitutes a reasonable price, Lars Heuman, *Skiljemäns rätt att komplettera avtal* (*Eng.* Arbitrators' power to supplement contracts), in *Festskrift till Ulf K. Nordenson*, pp. 187-188 (Jure 1999). Section 45 of the Swedish Sale of Goods Act reads 'If the price does not follow from the contract, the buyer shall pay what is reasonable having regard to the nature and quality of the goods, the market price at the time of purchase and the other circumstances.' As illustrated in section §4.03[A] above, however, there are several conceivable situations in which the provisions of substantive non-mandatory law do not provide tools to a tribunal to supplement or amend a contract.

36. Lars Heuman, *Skiljemäns rätt att komplettera avtal* (*Eng.* Arbitrators' power to supplement contracts), in *Festskrift till Ulf K. Nordenson*, p. 192 (our own translation, Jure 1999).

the tribunal may adopt certain parts or components of a contract price formula proposed by one or both parties.

In departing from the parties' requests for relief, the arbitral tribunal may not award more or something different than what a party has requested, but it may award something less. It is fairly straightforward to ascertain what is more, less or different when there are only monetary reliefs at stake. However, the task becomes more difficult when the reliefs sought are qualitative in nature, e.g., to determine revised prices or other terms of a contract. In such cases, the parties' submissions will be important in further clarifying the boundaries of the parties' requests.

Lindskog submits that when a tribunal considers different compromises between the parties' positions, a general principle should be that the tribunal needs to stay within the positions presented by the parties so that neither party have reason to be surprised by the result. In Lindskog's words, one could speak of a *range of expectations*. An award is not outside the range of expectations only because the parties did not expect all the specifics of the tribunal's determination. However, an award that is significantly outside the range of expectations may constitute an excess of mandate.[37]

Lindskog's view appears to be aligned with the model developed by Professor Emeritus Peter Westberg for determining whether a judgment falls within or outside the parties' requests for relief (i.e., *infra* or *ultra petita*). Under this model, a deviation in the award from the requests for relief is not something different or more, but something less, provided: (i) that the outcome of the award serves the same purpose as the requests for relief, and (ii) that the award is less onerous for the respondent compared to the reliefs sought by the claimant. This approach is particularly applicable when straying from the requests for relief appears to be a straightforward compromise that readily comes across as a clear and understandable reconciliation of opposing requests for relief.[38]

The rationale for this model ought to be uncontroversial: the parties should be in control of the proceedings and have the opportunity to address all issues that may be

37. Stefan Lindskog, *Skiljeförfarande: En kommentar* (*Eng.* Arbitration: A Commentary), commentary to section 1 of the Act, para. 6.2.4 (3rd. ed., Juno 2020). In footnote 812, Lindskog writes: 'Heuman (FS Nordenson, p. 192 *et seq.*) states that the arbitral tribunal should not be bound by the parties' proposals in relation to the content of the contract supplementation, but should be able to determine the content of the contract in a manner representing a compromise. This is certainly correct, and the parties' proposals should then constitute the framework within which the tribunal must operate. But how can a compromise be reached between two proposals that differ not only in term of quantity but also fundamentally in qualitative terms? It appears that a general principle could be that the arbitral tribunal should stay within the parties' positions in such a way that neither party has any reason to be surprised by the content of the contract supplementation (one can speak of a range of expectations). The parties nonetheless need to accept that they may be surprised; only a supplementation of contracts that is significantly outside the range of expectations should constitute a challengeable error (see footnote 3883 below).'

38. Peter Westberg, *Domstols officialprövning* (*Eng.* Court adjudication), p. 487 (Juristförlaget i Lund 1988). Lindskog and Westberg may well have different views on how far the range of expectations can be stretched, as Westberg's perspective is that of the Swedish courts, while Lindskog's is that of the arbitrators. Nevertheless, they seem to be in agreement on a principal level.

relevant to the award in accordance with the principle of party disposition. Accordingly, the award should not come as a surprise to the parties, even if the tribunal departs to some extent from the parties' specific requests for relief.

The views of Lindskog and Westberg are also in line with the case law of the Svea Court of Appeal. An example of this case law is the challenge of a price review arbitration brought by the Turkish gas purchaser Kibar against Gazprom. In the set-aside proceedings, Kibar argued that the tribunal had exceeded its mandate by awarding something different from what Gazprom had requested. According to Kibar, Gazprom had requested a price revision that included two elements: (i) the removal of a discount, and (ii) a revision of the base price (a separate component). According to Kibar, the two elements were inseparable parts of the same request, and the tribunal could not grant one while rejecting the other. Thus, Kibar claimed that the tribunal exceeded its mandate by only removing the discount and not revising the base price as requested by Kibar.[39]

In its judgment of 1 December 2021, the Svea Court of Appeal found that it was within the tribunal's mandate to assess the individual elements of Gazprom's request for relief and award the discount only. The Court of Appeal emphasised that Gazprom's position in the arbitration was that the tribunal could grant individual elements of Gazprom's request for relief and that this had been made clear to Kibar.[40] Although expressed differently than Lindskog and Westberg, it appears that the Court of Appeal based its reasonings on the parties' range of expectations and, in particular, on what Kibar could reasonably have expected in light of Gazprom's position in the arbitration.

It may be difficult for the tribunal to establish an appropriate range of expectations when only one of the parties clearly presents its position, whereas the other party does not. In such situation, the tribunal may consider providing further directions to the parties and seeking to clarify the procedural framework. Should the tribunal's mandate nevertheless remain unclear, it may be put in question whether it is appropriate for the tribunal to seek a compromise by supplementing the contract in ways that have not been briefed and argued in the arbitration by at least one of the parties.

One could derive from the above that it may be challenging for arbitrators and counsel to ascertain the tribunal's room for manoeuvre when the tribunal has been given a mandate to supplement contracts, not least given that it may vary throughout the proceedings. Nonetheless, we would respectfully submit that at least the principles for exercising a mandate to supplement contracts and conquering this room for manoeuvre are straightforward.

Put simply, the arbitral tribunal should carefully balance the parties' positions and expectations, ensuring that any terms or conditions it develops or adopts are within the range of expectations articulated by the parties. The difficult part is that this requires a meticulous assessment of the facts and arguments alongside the evidence on record, together with a creative yet cautious approach to formulating terms that

39. *Kibar Enerji v. Gazprom*, Case No. T 7865-19, p. 4 (Svea Court of Appeal 1 Dec. 2021).
40. *Kibar Enerji v. Gazprom*, Case No. T 7865-19, pp. 10-11 (Svea Court of Appeal 1 Dec. 2021).

reconcile the parties' differing requests in a manner that does not surprise or unduly burden either party. In doing so, the tribunal ought to honour the principle of party disposition while effectively exercising its mandate to supplement the contract, thereby facilitating a resolution of the parties' dispute that reflects a fair and reasonable adjustment of the original contract terms.

CHAPTER 5

Exclusionary Rules of Evidence in International Arbitration

Aleksander Godhe[*]

'The world isn't fair, Calvin.'
'I know Dad, but why isn't it ever unfair in my favour?'[1]

§5.01 INTRODUCTION AND BACKGROUND

The concept of 'exclusionary rules of evidence' originates from common law. It stemmed out of the need to protect the jury from inappropriate evidence, with the courts having a degree of discretion as to what evidence should be included and excluded, albeit this power is rarely exercised in practice today.[2] Although civil law jurisdictions are said not to have an equivalent concept,[3] they do have principles that yield a similar effect in practice. Take, for example, rules on legal privilege. In common law, privilege pertains to the documents themselves.[4] By contrast, in civil law systems, privilege is, first and foremost, a duty of confidentiality imposed on the lawyer not to

* I am grateful to Professor Renato Nazzini, Mel Schwing and other anonymous reviewers for their comments on earlier drafts. Any errors that remain are my own. Email: aleksander.godhe@kcl.ac.uk.

1. Bill Watterson, The Essential Calvin and Hobbes: A Calvin and Hobbes Treasury.
2. Roderick Munday, Cross & Tapper on Evidence, 194-218 (13th edition, OUP 2018).
3. Chester Brown, A Common Law of International Adjudication, 91 (OUP 2007); For example, document proof is preferred over oral witness evidence, *see* John Jolowicz, On Civil Procedure, 214 (CUP 2000).
4. For example, *see* English law in *Three Rivers District Council v. The Governor and Company of the Bank of England*, EWCA Civ 474 (2003) and EWCA Civ 218 (2004); Canadian law: *R. v. McClure*, 1 S.C.R. 445 (2001).

reveal certain evidence.[5] Therefore, although the legal systems approach the issue from different angles, the result is the same: the evidence is either directly excluded from the record or should never be there to begin with.[6]

International arbitration takes a different approach independent of common and civil law traditions.[7] Instead of being subject to strict rules of evidence, it is characterised by tribunals having far-reaching procedural discretion that gives the parties and arbitrators a considerable degree of control over how disputes are resolved. This is perceived as a strength of the system, making it particularly attractive to commercial parties.[8] Nonetheless, this procedural discretion is not endless and is limited and guided by the application of tribunal duties.[9]

The exercise of tribunal discretion and duties can have the effect of excluding evidence. Staying with the example of privileged documents, there is no single rule of law in international arbitration relating to privilege. Instead, such evidence should be excluded by the tribunal as an exercise of their discretion and the need to protect due process.[10] Same logic would apply when tribunals are faced with other types of evidence that should not be included in the record.

Therefore, this paper employs the terminology of 'exclusionary rules of evidence' not to connote that arbitration practice aligns with common law but rather to recognise that, in some circumstances, tribunals should exercise their discretionary powers to exclude evidence. For this reason, arbitration could be argued to have evolved its own endemic *lex evidentiae* independent of legal traditions.[11] That being said, arbitration does not, of course, reside in a vacuum and is influenced by the legal cultures of the

---

5. For example, *see* German law: section 203(1), Criminal Code and sections 383 and 142(2), Civil Procedure Code; Italian law: Arts 200 and 256, Code of Criminal Procedure; French law: Arts 226-313, New Criminal Code; Swedish law: Chapter 36, section 5, Swedish Procedural Code.
6. Jenia Iontcheva Turner & Thomas Weigend, *The Purpose and Functions of Exclusionary Rules: A Comparative Overview*, 255-257 (Sabine Gleiss & Thomas Richter (eds), Springer Open 2019): noting that the scope of exclusionary rules varies greatly between jurisdictions.
7. *See Glamis Gold, Ltd. v. The United States of America*, UNCITRAL, Decision on Parties' Requests for Production of Documents Withheld on Grounds of Privilege, p. 3 (2005): 'The Tribunal observes that the law of the United States, both as to production of documents or to the privilege enjoyed by some set of documents, is not directly applicable to this arbitration. Rather document production in this arbitration is governed by Article 24 of the UNCITRAL Arbitration Rules and guided by the Parties' own agreements to production as evidenced in their February 24, 2005 letters.'
8. Queen Mary University of London and White & Case, *2018 International Arbitration Survey: The Evolution of International Arbitration*, 7, https://arbitration.qmul.ac.uk/media/arbitration/docs/2018-International-Arbitration-Survey---The-Evolution-of-International-Arbitration-(2).PDF (accessed 29 Jan. 2024).
9. Discussed *infra*; *see also* Franco Ferrari, Friedrich Rosenfeld & Dietmar Czernich, *Due Process as a Limit to Discretion in International Commercial Arbitration*, 1-2 (Franco Ferrari, Friedrich Rosenfeld & Dietmar Czernich (eds), Wolters Kluwer 2020).
10. Of course, the circumstances where such steps should be taken are subject to debate: Patricia Shaughnessy, Dealing with Privileges in International Commercial Arbitration, 451, 469 (Scandinavian Studies in Law 2007).
11. Julian Bickman, Fact-Finding in International Arbitration: The Emergence of a Transnational Lex Evidentiae, paras 1.9-1.47 (Wolters Kluwer 2022).

lawyers practising it.[12] For example, common law style document disclosure is widely accepted in arbitration while tribunals nonetheless tend to attribute more weight to documentary evidence over witness testimonies resembling a civilian tradition.[13]

The subject of this chapter, therefore, contributes to a broader debate as to whether international arbitration has any endemic rules of evidence at all and, if it does, what these rules are. The subject is an important one given that, among many other reasons, the majority of international arbitrations anecdotally turn on facts rather than legal issues.[14] This observation is particularly stark in arbitrating disputes in specific sectors such as construction, which tend to concern a considerable volume of evidence.[15]

The purpose of this chapter is to argue that 'exclusionary rules of evidence' must exist in international arbitration as a standalone concept. This is a necessary consequence of the broad discretion of tribunals and the duties that they are subject to, which are discussed in sections §5.02 and §5.03, respectively. Such a conceptual shift would be helpful to both arbitrators who must determine the exclusion of evidence, sometimes even *sua sponte*,[16] and the parties who bear the burden of proof to raise evidentiary objections.[17]

It should also be added that exclusion of evidence in international arbitration does not pertain solely to admissibility of evidence but also to document disclosure and inspections.[18] Indeed, issues that arise at the disclosure and admissibility stage are closely related.[19] In the context of exclusion, the relevant tribunal duties, categorisation of principles, and the applicable test would be similar. The evidentiary objections that the parties would raise would be equally alike, although some differences exist that are

12. Jean-François Poudret & Sébastien Besson, Comparative Law of International Arbitration, 554 (2nd ed., Sweet & Maxwell 2007); Paul Oberhammer, Evidence: Learning from Arbitration, 243 (C. H. van Rhee and Alan Uzelac, Intersentia 2017).
13. Bin Cheng, General Principles of Law as Applies by International Courts and Tribunals, 318-319 (CUP 1953); Durward V Sandifer, Evidence Before International Tribunals, 197 (University Press of Virginia 1975).
14. Constantine Partasides KC & Alan Redfern, Redfern and Hunter on International Arbitration, p. 347 (7th ed., OUP 2023); Jan Paulsson & Georgios Petrochilos, UNCITRAL Arbitration, 236 (Wolters Kluwer 2018).
15. Queen Mary University of London and Pinsent Masons, *International Arbitration Survey – Driving Efficiency in International Construction Disputes*, 25, https://www.pinsentmasons.com/thinking/special-reports/international-arbitration-survey (accessed 5 May 2024); *see also* Renato Nazzini & Aleksander Kalisz, *Construction Law, the Arbitration Act 1996 and Beyond: The Contribution of the Technology and Construction Court to Arbitration*, 197-199 (Peter Coulson & David Sawtell (eds), Hart 2023).
16. IBA Rules on the Taking of Evidence in International Arbitration 2020 (IBA Rules), Art. 9(2) and (3) state that evidence may be excluded at the tribunals' 'own motion'; Rules on the Efficient Conduct of Proceedings in International Arbitration 2018 (Prague Rules), Art. 3.1 and 3.2.
17. Nathan O'Malley, Rules of Evidence in International Arbitration, 336 (2nd ed., Routledge 2019).
18. IBA, p. 28: 'Articles 9.2 and 9.3 provide the limitations on admissible evidence, whether oral or written. These limitations also apply to the production of documents pursuant to Article 3 and inspections pursuant to Article 7.' On the proximity of admissibility and disclosure in international arbitration, *see* IBA Rules, Art. 9(2) on the exclusion of evidence that relates to both; *see also* Roman Khodykin, Carol Mulcahy & Nichols Fletcher, A Guide to the IBA Rules on the Taking of Evidence in International Arbitration, 425 (OUP 2019).
19. Nathan O'Malley, Rules of Evidence in International Arbitration, 280 (2nd ed., Routledge 2019).

acknowledged below, and tribunals are, of course, at liberty to give consideration to the stage at which evidence is introduced or requested.

Further, the chapter argues in section §5.04 that, in the light of tribunal discretion and duties, the appropriate evidentiary test should be a form of a flexible balancing exercise factoring the circumstances of the case. The section also outlines the possible outcomes of such a balancing exercise and presents them as a menu of options available to tribunals. This would not only include exclusion or inclusion of evidence to the record but involve other measures such as cost sanctions, redaction orders or 'attorneys' eyes only' regimes, to name a few.

Finally, in section §5.05, the chapter discusses what are the different types of exclusionary rules of evidence relevant to international arbitration. It argues in favour of a threefold division based on the circumstances that 'taint' the evidence and put into question its inclusion in the record. Therefore, evidence may be excluded on the basis of its substance (Principle 1), on the basis of how it was obtained (Principle 2) and on the basis of non-compliance with procedural directions of the tribunal (Principle 3).

§5.02 ARBITRAL AUTONOMY AND PARTY AUTONOMY

In the context of arbitral procedure and the treatment of evidence in particular, applicable laws and rules set out two key principles. On the one hand, they afford the tribunals with broad and discretionary procedural authority. On the other hand, that discretion tends to be limited by the principle of party autonomy. After all, arbitration is an inherently private dispute resolution process, and the parties should hence have a say in how their disputes are resolved.[20]

Turning to arbitration rules, the ICC Rules offer hardly any specific guidance to tribunals in relation to evidence, let alone its possible exclusion, noting broadly that '[i]n order to ensure effective case management, after consulting the parties, the arbitral tribunal shall adopt such procedural measures as it considers appropriate, provided that they are not contrary to any agreement of the parties.'[21] The VIAC Rules follow a similar approach.[22] Other arbitration rules take a step further and contain some minimal guidance in addition to broad procedural discretion and party autonomy. The SCC Rules state, for example, that '[t]he admissibility, relevance, materiality, and weight of evidence shall be for the Arbitral Tribunal to determine.'[23] Many other leading arbitration rules contain provisions to a similar effect,[24] but none

20. Michael Pryles, *Limits to Party Autonomy in Arbitral Procedure,* 24(3) JIA 327, 327-328 (2007) https://doi.org/10.54648/joia2007023.
21. International Chamber of Commerce Arbitration Rules 2020 (ICC Rules), Art. 22(2).
22. Vienna International Arbitral Centre Rules of Arbitration 2021 (VIAC Rules), Art. 28(1).
23. Stockholm Chamber of Commerce Arbitration Rules 2023 (SCC Rules), Art. 31(1).
24. For example, *see* London Court of International Arbitration Rules 2020 (LCIA Rules), Art. 22.1(vi); Singapore International Arbitration Centre Arbitration Rules 2016 (SIAC Rules), Rule 19.2; Hong Kong International Arbitration Centre Administered Arbitration Rules 2018 (HKIAC Rules), Art. 22.2; Dubai International Arbitration Centre Arbitration Rules 2022 (DIAC Rules), Art. 25.2; American Arbitration Association Commercial Arbitration Rules 2022 (AAA Rules), Rule 35(b).

prescribe a formal procedure or criteria for the inclusion or exclusion of evidence. This makes the conclusions of the International Law Commission accurate:

> The rules of international courts and tribunals and their constitutive instruments do not address evidence in detail. They make only a general reference to evidence in the form of timelines and presentation. They do not contain any reference to the kinds of evidence, presentation, handling, assessment and conclusions to be drawn from the evidence. Judicial practices of different courts and tribunals have developed rules of evidence that go beyond existing rules of international courts and tribunals.[25]

Therefore, arbitration rules leave such specific matters of evidence to the parties and tribunals. Procedural discretion and party autonomy are also enshrined in the various arbitration laws. For example, the English Arbitration Act states that tribunals have procedural and evidentiary discretion that, subject to party agreement to the contrary, expressly encompasses questions of 'the admissibility, relevance or weight of any material'.[26] The Act is also non-exhaustive in listing such procedural and evidentiary issues, and hence, the arbitral discretion extends to other aspects of evidence, such as document disclosure and inspections.[27]

Other arbitration laws give the tribunals similar broad evidentiary powers. To provide a civil law example, the German Code of Civil Procedure states that 'The arbitral tribunal is empowered to determine the admissibility of taking evidence, take evidence and assess freely such evidence.'[28] Belgium and the Netherlands contain equivalent provisions, while the US courts have also consistently upheld the principle.[29] Most other arbitration laws, including those based on the UNCITRAL Model Law on International Commercial Arbitration ('UNCITRAL Model Law'), follow a similar approach, with little divergence between civil and common law jurisdictions.[30]

For the above reasons, tribunals have a general procedural discretion or arbitral autonomy, which also extends to their treatment of evidence but is subject to party autonomy to decide upon a different procedure. Nonetheless, if the parties do exercise their rights to agree upon a procedure, it rarely concerns the admissibility and

---

25. International Law Commission, *Evidence Before International Courts and Tribunals, Report on the work of the sixty-ninth session*, https://www.un-ilibrary.org/content/books/9789213628720s023-c003 (accessed 2 May 2024).
26. English Arbitration Act 1996, section 34(1) and (2)(f).
27. Robert Merkin & Louis Flannery KC, Merkin and Flannery on the Arbitration Act 1996, 378 (6th ed., Routledge 2020).
28. German Code of Civil Procedure (*Zivilprozessordnung*), section 1042.
29. Roman Khodykin, Carol Mulcahy & Nichols Fletcher, A Guide to the IBA Rules on the Taking of Evidence in International Arbitration, 410-411 (OUP 2019).
30. For example, *see* UNCITRAL (United Nations Commission on International Trade Law) Model Law on International Commercial Arbitration 1985 (as amended in 2006) (Model Law), Arts 19(1)-(2) and 34(1); French Code of Civil Procedure, Art. 1467; George M Von Mehren & Claudia Salomon, *Submitting Evidence in an International Arbitration*, 20(3) JIA 285, 285-286 (2003) https://doi.org/10.54648/joia2003023; however, *see* the Swedish Arbitration Act, section 25 that suggests evidence can only be excluded on the grounds of manifest irrelevance to the dispute or the timing at which the evidence is invoked although, of course, parties can incorporate other grounds through, for example, the selected arbitration rules.

disclosure of evidence.[31] This does not, however, mean that tribunal discretion is unrestricted.

§5.03 DUTIES OF THE TRIBUNAL AND EXCLUSION OF EVIDENCE

Arbitral tribunals are subject to different duties, the source of which is party agreement, application of law as well as ethical obligations.[32] Although their application concerns the entire scope of arbitral procedure and even substantive matters, three duties play a particular role in the context of exclusion of evidence. Their purpose is twofold. They (1) set the outer limits of tribunal discretion and (2) guide the exercise of the said discretion. They will be analysed in turn, starting with the most important: due process.

[A] Duty to Afford Due Process and Render an Enforceable Award

One of the key principles that impacts international arbitration is due process, which supersedes tribunal discretion and party autonomy.[33] It hence sets the outer limit to how tribunals can approach evidence. Due process stems from public policy as a safeguard imposed by states to justify arbitration having a derogatory effect on the jurisdiction of national courts.[34] Although public policy or *ordre public* is a far broader concept, encompassing issues that exceed international arbitration,[35] in the specific context of arbitral procedure, both due process and public policy are closely related.[36]

The multiplicity of terminology does not end there. Rather confusingly, from a comparative standpoint, due process bears several different designations across various jurisdictions. Sources refer to natural justice principles,[37] procedural fairness

31. Patricia Shaughnessy, Dealing with Privileges in International Commercial Arbitration, 451, 459 (Scandinavian Studies in Law 2007).
32. Constantine Partasides KC & Alan Redfern, Redfern and Hunter on International Arbitration, pp. 550-552 (7th ed., OUP 2023).
33. Julian Lew, Loukas Mistelis & Stefan Kroll, Comparative International Commercial Arbitration, 95 (Wolters Kluwer 2003): calling due process one of the 'magna carta' principles of international arbitration.
34. Fabricio Fortese & Lotta Hemmi, *Procedural Fairness and Efficiency in International Arbitration*, 3(1) GJIL 110, 112-113 (2015) https://doi.org/10.21827/5a86a89d8e651.
35. Constantine Partasides KC & Alan Redfern, Redfern and Hunter on International Arbitration, pp. 550-552 (7th ed., OUP 2023).
36. Matti Kurkela & Santtu Turunen, Due Process in International Commercial Arbitration, 17-22 (OUP 2010): this overlap stems particularly from the New York Convention and its references to public policy as a ground to refuse recognition and enforcement of an award in Art. V(2)(b). *See also* Audley Sheppard, *Interim ILA Report on Public Policy as a Bar to Enforcement of International Arbitral Awards*, 19(2) AI 217, 239 (2003) https://doi.org/10.1093/arbitration/19.2.217.
37. Frederick F Schauer, *English Natural Justice and American Due Process: An Analytical Comparison*, 18(1) WMLR 47, 47-48 (1976): while 'due process' origins from the fifth and fourteenth amendments to the US Constitution, 'natural justice' is the English law equivalent developed by the courts.

principles[38] or the rules of fair trial[39] when referring to concepts synonymous with due process. Others mention the right to be heard, the so-called *principe de la contradiction* or equal treatment.[40] None of these approaches are incorrect, but they rather reflect the various municipal terminologies. At the heart of the concept is the notion that parties should be treated fairly and equally.[41] This section of the paper discusses how procedural due process interacts with issues of exclusion of evidence. Indeed, both the inclusion and exclusion of evidence can trespass on this cardinal principle in the right circumstances.

Given the divergence in defining due process and its scope, domestic arbitration laws provide a necessary reference point for understanding the limits to tribunal discretion. For example, the UNCITRAL Model Law does not make an express reference to due process, albeit the mandatory Article 18 states that tribunals should treat the parties with equality and afford them the full opportunity to present their case.[42]

Similar due process obligations are found in non-Model Law jurisdictions. For example, the English Arbitration Act sets out general duties of the tribunal in section 33, including the duty to 'act fairly and impartially as between the parties, giving each party a reasonable opportunity of putting his case and dealing with that of his opponent'. The provision also adds that the adopted procedures should be suitable to the circumstances and 'avoid unnecessary delay or expense'.[43] This has been said to represent the English law notion of due process.[44]

The differences between jurisdictions are not insignificant, but, in essence, violation of procedural due process represents a ground on which an award may be set aside, albeit subject to a high threshold.[45] The Model Law, for example, specifies that an award may be set aside if the party making the application furnishes proof that it was unable to present its case, the procedure was not in accordance with party agreement or contrary to a mandatory provision of the *lex arbitri*.[46] Many other

38. Gary Born, International Commercial Arbitration, 42 (Wolters Kluwer 2020) argues in favour of employing the language of 'procedural fairness' in international arbitration since the other concepts have specific connotations in domestic settings. However, this term also has its origin in domestic law, *see* Sophie Boyron & Wendy Lacey, *Procedural Fairness Generally*, 259-261 (Mark Tushnet, Thomas Fleiner & Cheryl Saunders (eds), Routledge 2013); this chapter hence adopts the terminology of 'due process' as it is prevalent in international arbitration literature.
39. Susanne Knickmeier, *Securing a Fair Trial Through Exclusionary Rules: Do Theory and Practice Form a Well-Balanced Whole?*, 329-347 (Sabine Gleiss & Thomas Richter (eds), Springer Open 2019).
40. Gabrielle Kaufmann-Kohler, *Globalization of Arbitral Procedure*, 36(4) VJTL 1313, 1321 (2003).
41. Audley Sheppard, *Interim ILA Report on Public Policy as a Bar to Enforcement of International Arbitral Awards*, 19(2) AI 217, 239 (2003) https://doi.org/10.1093/arbitration/19.2.217.
42. UNCITRAL Model Law, Arts 18 and 34.
43. Arbitration Act 1996, section 33.
44. Robert Merkin & Louis Flannery KC, Merkin and Flannery on the Arbitration Act 1996, 697 (6th ed., Routledge 2020).
45. Constantine Partasides KC & Alan Redfern, Redfern and Hunter on International Arbitration, pp. 541-545 (7th ed., OUP 2023); However, courts are concerned with trespasses on due process and not the correctness of tribunals' decision. For example, *see* English High Court in *Sonatrach v. Statoil Natural Gas*, 2 Lloyd's Rep 252 para. 11 (2014).
46. UNCITRAL Model Law, Arts 34(2)(a)(ii) and (iv).

arbitration laws follow a similar approach to the Model Law. The English Arbitration Act allows an award to be set aside on the grounds of a serious irregularity, which includes violations of the aforementioned section 33.[47] However, unlike the Model Law, the threshold for such a challenge to succeed is higher as the court must consider that the irregularity was 'serious' and affected the tribunal, the proceedings or the award.[48] The Swedish Arbitration Act also allows awards to be challenged on grounds of an irregularity in the course of proceedings if it 'probably influenced the outcome of the case'.[49]

Similarly, principles of due process can be distilled from the New York Convention and the grounds on which courts can refuse to enforce a foreign arbitral award. These grounds include a party not being afforded the right to be heard or being properly put on notice, the arbitral procedure being contrary to party agreement, and the award being contrary to public policy of the state of enforcement.[50]

Although the domestic sources of due process contain key differences regarding the necessary threshold or extent to which due process considerations can lead to the award being set aside, the general principle remains.[51] An award, therefore, may be challenged on the grounds of lack of due process which essentially functions as a limit to the exercise of tribunal discretion and party autonomy in the area of evidence.[52] By extension, tribunals arguably have a duty to render an award that is not subject to being set aside and/or can be enforced abroad, although the precise scope of this duty is disputed since arbitrators, of course, cannot foresee where the parties will enforce the award.[53]

Having established that due process and its various iterations appear in most, if not all, domestic arbitration laws and the New York Convention, it is worth discussing how the inclusion or exclusion of evidence can trespass on this cardinal principle and potentially challenge the award.

The right to be heard is the first and perhaps most significant manifestation of due process from the standpoint of evidence exclusion. It will come into focus, particularly

47. English Arbitration Act 1996, section 68; UK House of Lords in *Lesotho Highlands Development Authority v. Impregilo SpA*, UKHL 43 para. 27 (2005): stated that section 68 reflects 'the internationally accepted view that the Court should be able to correct serious failures to comply with the "due process" of arbitral proceedings: cf art 34 of the Model Law'.
48. *Ibid.*, section 68(3).
49. Swedish Arbitration Act 1999, section 34.
50. Convention on the Recognition and Enforcement of Foreign Arbitral Awards 1958 (New York Convention), Arts V(1)(b), (d) and V(2), respectively.
51. Constantine Partasides KC & Alan Redfern, Redfern and Hunter on International Arbitration, p. 542 (7th ed., OUP 2023).
52. Franco Ferrari, Friedrich Rosenfeld & Dietmar Czernich, *Due Process as a Limit to Discretion in International Commercial Arbitration*, 1-2 (Franco Ferrari, Friedrich Rosenfeld & Dietmar Czernich (eds), Wolters Kluwer 2020); Patricia Shaughnessy, Dealing with Privileges in International Commercial Arbitration, 451, 460 (Scandinavian Studies in Law 2007); L Yves Fortier, *The Minimum Requirements of Due Process in Taking Measures Against Dilatory Tactics: Arbitral Discretion in International Commercial Arbitration – A Few Plain Rules and a Few Strong Instincts*, 399 (Albert van den Berg (ed.), Wolters Kluwer 1999).
53. Gunther Horvath, *The Duty of the Tribunal to Render an Enforceable Award,* 18(2) JIA 135, 135 (2001) https://doi.org/10.54648/317806; Julian Lew, *The Law Applicable to the Form and Substance of the Arbitration Clause,* 114-115 (Albert van den Berg (ed.), Wolters Kluwer 1999).

if the opponent makes objections to the inclusion of evidence. If tribunals do not discuss the objections but admit the said evidence outright, it could be perceived as a failure to afford the party its right to be heard.[54] Conversely, a decision to exclude evidence could amount to denying the party its 'due opportunity to present proofs and argument'.[55] The right to be heard also underpins tribunal control over the procedural timetable. Evidence that is introduced late and subsequently excluded by the tribunals would typically not amount to a breach of due process,[56] nor must the tribunal afford a party indefinite opportunity to respond.[57] Nonetheless, if the evidence was only uncovered after the expiration of the deadline, due process may require the opposite.[58]

Outright rejection of evidence that is relevant and material might also, without a good reason, amount to tribunal's failure to consider party submissions and hence trespass on the right to be heard.[59] Equally, admitting evidence without giving the opponent the opportunity to produce counter-evidence could also fall short of due process.[60] This being said, tribunals retain a considerable degree of discretion. Determinations of what is relevant and material, as well as decisions on admissibility and disclosure, are a prerogative of the tribunal and, without more, such as perhaps

54. For example, *see* Netherlands Supreme Court in *De Jong/Quaude*, HR 08.11.1963, NJ 1964/139 (1964); *Enron Creditors Recovery Corporation (formerly Enron Corporation) and Ponderosa Assets, L.P. v. Argentine*, ICSID Case No. ARB/01/3, Decision on Annulment, para. 192 (2010).
55. United States Court of Appeals in *Tempo Shain Corp. v. Bertek, Inc*, 120 F.3d 16 pp. 17-21 (1997); *see also* investor-State arbitration proceedings in *Fraport AG Frankfurt Airport Services Worldwide v. Republic of the Philippines (I)*, ICSID Case No. ARB/03/25, Decision on the Application for Annulment of Fraport AC Frankfurt Airport Services Worldwide, para. 185 (2010); Tracey Frisch, *Death by Discovery, Delay, and Disempowerment: Legal Authority for Arbitrators to Provide a Cost-Effective and Expeditious Process*, 17 CJCR 155, pp. 162-165 (2015).
56. For example, *see* in relation to late-filed requests to hear new witnesses in a Court of Arbitration for Sport proceedings: *X v. Jamaican Football Federation and FIFA*, 4A_162/2011 (2011).
57. *Pacific China Holdings Ltd (In Liquidation) v. Grand Pacific Holdings Ltd*, 4 HKLRD para. 77 (2012); *Allianz General Insurance Company Malaysia Berhad v. Virginia Surety Company Labuan Branch*, Originating Summons No. WA-24NCC(ARB)-13-03/2018 paras 31-36 (2020): 'A tribunal is not obliged to slavishly adopt the position of parties but instead it is allowed to pick and choose the arguments it deems necessary for its consideration.'
58. For example, *see* Paris Court of Appeal where such allegations was raised albeit they failed in defeating the award: Paris Court of Appeal in *Revue de l'arbitrage*, 1991, p. 345 (1988).
59. BGH, BGHZ 96, p. 40 (1985); United States District Court for the District of Puerto Rico in *Hoteles Condado Beach, La Concha & Convention Center v. Union De Tronquistas Local 901*, 588 F. Supp. 679 (D.P.R. 1984) 686 (1984): 'The exclusion by an arbitrator of evidence central and decisive to a party's position, so affects the fairness of the proceeding as a whole, that such action must be considered arbitrary, unreasonable, incomplete, improper and capricious. Accordingly, we conclude that the conduct described above is so destructive of plaintiff's right to present his case, that it warrants the setting aside of the arbitration award.' Reasoning was upheld on appeal in *Hoteles Condado Beach, La Concha & Convention Center v. Union De Tronquistas Local 901*, 763 F.2d 34 (1985).
60. *Fraport AG Frankfurt Airport Services Worldwide v. Republic of the Philippines (I)*, ICSID Case No. ARB/03/25, Decision on the Application for Annulment of Fraport AG Frankfurt Airport Services Worldwide, para. 200 (2010): 'The right to present one's case, or "*principe de la contradiction*", in arbitral proceedings includes the right of each party to make submissions on evidence presented by its opponent'; Hague Court of Appeal in *Rice Trading (Guyana) Ltd v. Nidera Handelscompagnie BV*, XXIII Ybk Comm Arb, p. 731 (1998).

outright arbitrariness, would not trespass on the right to be heard.[61] It is also arguable that excluding evidence at the document production stage would be far less likely to offend the right to be heard.[62] After all, the tribunal is not yet in possession of the documents and would not be directly denying the party its right to give evidence.

Second, due process encompasses the principle of equality of arms, also called the principle of equal treatment. It is closely linked to the right to be heard but nonetheless distinct. While the right to be heard is concerned with the mere opportunity to make submissions, the principle of equal treatment connotes a certain standard of adequacy of that opportunity.[63] The investor-State tribunal in *Tulip Real Estate v. Turkey*[64] stated that a party must not be under conditions that place it at a substantial disadvantage vis-à-vis the opponent.[65] For example, allowing one party to produce evidence but not the other could trespass on the equality of arms (as well as the right to be heard).[66] It has also been suggested that tribunals should not uncritically accept the evidence of a party in the face of objections as to its credibility,[67] and parties have a duty not to obtain evidence through improper means.[68]

Although due process provides for equal treatment, it does not require that the parties should be treated identically. The circumstances of the parties not being 'comparable' typically suffice to avoid a successful equality of arms challenge.[69]

Third, another corollary of due process, and often alleged in combination with violation of the right to be heard and equality of arms, is impartiality and independence

61. Franco Ferrari, Friedrich Rosenfeld & Dietmar Czernich, *Due Process as a Limit to Discretion in International Commercial Arbitration*, 7 (Franco Ferrari, Friedrich Rosenfeld & Dietmar Czernich (eds.), Wolters Kluwer 2020).
62. Nathan O'Malley, Rules of Evidence in International Arbitration, 58-59 (2nd ed., Routledge 2019).
63. For example, *see* UNCITRAL Model Law, Art. 18: 'The parties shall be treated with equality and each party shall be given a full opportunity of presenting his case' where the right to be heard and equality of arms are mentioned in parallel; *Dudko v. Australia*, Comm. No. 1347/2005 para. 7.4 (2007): 'The right to equality before courts and tribunals also ensures equality of arms. This means that the same procedural rights are to be provided to all the parties unless distinctions are based on law and can be justified on objective and reasonable grounds, not entailing actual disadvantage or other unfairness to the defendant.'
64. *Tulip Real Estate and Development Netherlands B.V. v. Republic of Turkey*, ICSID Case No. ARB/11/28, Decision on Annulment (2015).
65. *Ibid.* [33].
66. *CBS v. CBP*, SGCA 4, Civil Appeal No. 30 of 2020 para. 61 (2021); Swiss Federal Supreme Court, BGE 142 III 360 para. 4.1.1 (2016); *Central European Aluminium Company (CEAC) v. Montenegro*, ICSID Case No. ARB/14/8, Decision on Annulment, para. 110 (2018).
67. *See Ltd v. De La Rue International Ltd*, EWHC 68 (Comm) para. 41 (2014), albeit this allegation did not succeed since the tribunal did engage with the issue.
68. *OOO Manolium-Processing v. Belarus*, Case No. 2018-0, Decision on Claimant's Interim Measures Request, paras 159-160 (2018).
69. Franco Ferrari, Friedrich Rosenfeld & Dietmar Czernich, *Due Process as a Limit to Discretion in International Commercial Arbitration*, 11 (Franco Ferrari, Friedrich Rosenfeld and Dietmar Czernich (eds), Wolters Kluwer 2020); *Ryan v. République de Pologne* Rev. Arb. 304 (2019): 'Equality of arms implies the obligation to provide each party with a reasonable opportunity to present its case – including evidence – in conditions that do not place a party in a substantially disadvantageous position compared to its opponent.'

of arbitrators,[70] although some sources treat it as a standalone concept.[71] Decisions to include or exclude evidence are typically prejudicial to one party. Therefore, it is not uncommon for that party to challenge the award on grounds of actual or apparent bias. In analysing such a challenge, domestic courts would look for the rationale behind the tribunal decision. Following a principled approach to the exclusion of evidence allows us to mitigate the risk of such allegations succeeding.[72] If the tribunal is found to be biased, the sanction is not just the award being unenforceable but also a possible sanction against them personally, such as a reduction in fees or even personal liability.[73] They may also be removed in such circumstances.[74]

The fourth due process principle relevant to the subject is the duty of tribunals to afford the parties sufficient notice.[75] This element is concerned with the parties being kept informed of procedural developments in the arbitration, such as the submission of new documents by their opponent.[76] Albeit it does not clearly relate to exclusion of evidence, it often relates to the surrounding circumstances in which parties introduce the said evidence.

Despite differences in the scope of due process across jurisdictions, there is a significant degree of convergence. It may be possible, therefore, to discern international due process that is accepted across legal systems.[77] Therefore, the exclusion and inclusion of evidence may trespass on the various manifestations of procedural due process, including:

- the right to be heard
- the right to equal treatment/equality of arms
- independence and impartiality
- the obligation to ensure proper notice.

Due to the severe consequences of the lack of due process, it is easy to see why some tribunals might experience 'due process paranoia'. Its consequence is to reduce

70. Matti Kurkela & Santtu Turunen, Due process in International Commercial Arbitration, 111 (OUP 2010); Ronan Feehily, *Neutrality, Independence and Impartiality in International Commercial Arbitration, A Fine Balance in the Quest for Arbitral Justice*, 7(1) PSJLIA 88, pp. 105-106 (2019).
71. For example, *see* Dominique Hascher, *Independence and Impartiality of Arbitrators: 3 Issues*, 27(4) AUILR 789, 789 (2012) noting that independence and impartiality is derived from the arbitrators' 'essential obligations towards the parties'.
72. For example, *see ABB AG v. Hochtief Airport GmbH*, EWHC 388 (Comm) (2006); *Euroflon Tekniska Produkter AB v. Flexiboys I Motala AB*, Case No. Ö 1590-11 (2012).
73. Gary Born, International Commercial Arbitration, para. 13.05 (Wolters Kluwer 2020).
74. For example, *see* section 24(1)(a) of the English Arbitration Act 1996. If the arbitrator's conduct suggest she has 'a mind that is closed to the consideration and weighing of relevant factors', she could be removed: *Jackson v. Thompson*, EWHC 218 para. 15 (2015); *See* most recently the English High Court in *H1 & Anor v. W & Ors*, EWHC 382 (Comm) paras 70-85 (2024).
75. *CDX and another v. CDZ and another*, SGHC 257, para. 34 (2020).
76. *Lenmorniiproekt OAO v. Arne Larsson & Partner Leasing Aktiebolag*, Case No. Ö 13-09 (2010); Case No. 132, Lebanon Court of Cassation, 5th Chamber 29.10.2002 (2002).
77. Charles Kotuby, *General Principles of Law, International Due Process, and the Modern Role of Private International Law*, 23 DJCIL 411, 424-433 (2013).

the exercise of tribunal procedural discretion to a minimum.[78] This, in turn, leaves scope for parties to raise unmeritorious due process objections in an effort to influence the tribunal to their advantage.[79] The problem is aggravated given that oftentimes, the line between complying and falling short of due process is thin.

However, there is a silver lining. The above examples of due process violations suggest that demonstrating an overall absence of arbitrariness could suffice to satisfy due process. Due process appears to be an obligation of conduct and not of result. What domestic courts are typically looking for is the engagement of tribunals with the arguments put to them by the parties.[80] This suggests that if the tribunals show engagement with the evidentiary objections or requests for inclusion of evidence, they will stay well within the boundaries of due process.

Although the fear of due process is very much a storm in a teacup, it is plain to see why many tribunals view admitting virtually all evidence to the record as the less risky approach. However, this is nothing more than an extension of the due process paranoia problem and can cause injustice to parties where exclusion is warranted. Instead, this paper proposes that the due process paranoia can be addressed if tribunals follow a principled approach to the exclusion of evidence by reference to its other duties as well, which are discussed further below.

[B] Duty to Conduct the Procedure Efficiently

Although due process represents a central element of international arbitration and the duties of the tribunals, it is not the only consideration that arises in relation to exclusionary rules of evidence. More evidence inevitably means more work to the tribunal, the parties and the arbitral institutions, who are often committed to strict deadlines and a tight procedural calendar. This translates to increased costs and delays.

Provided that due process requirements are met (this is typically the easy part), the duty that guides tribunals in excluding evidence the most is ensuring procedural efficiency or economy.[81] It consists of two limbs: the avoidance of unnecessary delay and expense.[82] The principle is significant and has been treated by some sources as an

78. Klaus Peter Berger & Ole Jensen, *Due Process Paranoia and the Procedural Judgment Rule: A Safe Harbour for Procedural Management Decisions by International Arbitrators*, 32(3) AI 415, 415-416 (2016) https://doi.org/10.1093/arbint/aiw020.
79. Franco Ferrari, Friedrich Rosenfeld & Dietmar Czernich, *Due Process as a Limit to Discretion in International Commercial Arbitration*, 1-2 (Franco Ferrari, Friedrich Rosenfeld & Dietmar Czernich (eds), Wolters Kluwer 2020); Lucy Reed, *Ab(use) of due process: sword vs shield*, 33(3) AI 361, 364-365 (2017) https://doi.org/10.1093/arbint/aix022.
80. For example, *see Shin-Etsu Chem. v. Xinmao Science*, Min Si Ta Zi No. 18 (2008); *LKSur S.A v. Fichtner GmbH & Co. KG*, Case No. 08/16276 (2009).
81. For example, *see* English Arbitration Act 1996, section 33(1)(b): 'The tribunal shall – ... adopt procedures suitable to the circumstances of the particular case, avoiding unnecessary delay or expense, so as to provide a fair means for the resolution of the matters falling to be determined.'
82. Nadia Darwazeh, *Chapter 7: Is Efficiency an Arbitrator's Duty or Simply a Character Trait?*, 58-60 (Patricia Shaughnessy & Sherlin Tung (eds), Wolters Kluwer 2017).

iteration of due process.[83] After all, a procedure that is grossly inefficient can be viewed as depriving the parties of due process. The overlap between the two principles might, hence, be a question of scope and practical effect. Nonetheless, procedural efficiency certainly affects the exclusion of evidence in its own right. Many arbitration laws attribute special importance to procedural economy. The Swedish Arbitration Act[84] and the English Arbitration Act[85] are possible examples, expressly establishing the connection between procedural economy and the exercise of tribunal discretion. Indeed, without a duty to conduct the procedure efficiently, one of the key advantages of arbitration and dispute resolution would be lost.[86]

However, while a breach of due process may lead to the award being set aside or unenforceable, what are the sanctions to tribunals that prompt them to observe procedural economy? The answer lies in targeting the tribunal personally, subject to the laws on immunity. For instance, a forfeiture of remuneration is one possible avenue permissible under some arbitration rules. The ICC, for example, envisages a forfeiture of arbitrators' fees if the award is rendered after the deadline prescribed by the arbitration rules.[87] Several arbitration laws also envisage the removal of the arbitrator in cases of undue delay.[88] Principles on expediency would be inevitably violated if the tribunal indefinitely allowed parties to introduce new evidence and hence delay the proceedings. After all, most domestic legal systems regulate how evidence is gathered given that 'too zealous pursuit of evidence can easily transform institutions designed to resolve conflict into a rationalization and a setting for possibly even more rancorous conflict'.[89]

In this context, the line between violating the duty to conduct the procedure efficiently and the duty to afford due process is blurred. An arbitrator's pursuit of efficiency can be easily argued by a party to trespass on due process and, in particular, the right to be heard. For instance, that party may seek to introduce last-minute

83. For example, *see* various approaches considered in Gabrielle Kaufmann-Kohler, *Globalization of Arbitral Procedure*, 36(4) VJTL 1313, 1321 (2003).
84. Swedish Arbitration Act 1999, Art. 21: 'The arbitrators shall handle the dispute in an impartial, practical, and speedy manner.'
85. English Arbitration Act 1996, section 1(a): '[T]he object of arbitration is to obtain the fair resolution of disputes by an impartial tribunal without unnecessary delay or expense (...).'
86. Queen Mary University of London and White & Case, *2018 International Arbitration Survey: The Evolution of International Arbitration*, 8, https://arbitration.qmul.ac.uk/media/arbitration/docs/2018-International-Arbitration-Survey---The-Evolution-of-International-Arbitration-(2).PDF (accessed 29 Jan. 2024).
87. Jose Ricardo Feris, *New Policies and Practices at ICC: Towards Greater Efficiency and Transparency in International Arbitration* (Emmanuel Jolivet & Philip Kucharski (eds), ICC 2016).
88. Norwegian Arbitration Act 2004, section 16: 'If an arbitrator becomes de jure or de facto unable to perform his functions or if an arbitrator for other reasons fails to act without undue delay, his mandate shall terminate if he withdraws from his office or if the parties agree on the termination. Otherwise, any party may ask the courts to decide by way of interlocutory order whether the mandate shall terminate for one of the said reasons.' *See also* similar provisions in the Swedish Arbitration Act, section 17; Polish Code of Civil Procedure, Art. 1177(2); German ZPO, section 1038(1); UNCITRAL Model Law, Art. 14(1).
89. W Michael Reisman & Eric E Freedman, *The Plaintiff's Dilemma: Illegally Obtained Evidence and Admissibility in International Adjudication*, 76(4) AJIL 737, 737 (1982) https://doi.org/10.2307/2201551.

evidence. Although the tribunal could, for example, include such evidence and revisit the procedural timetable in an effort to ensure the opponent's opportunity to respond, it is clear that due process does not require the tribunal to afford the parties unrestricted opportunities to respond.[90] The solution must, hence, be a balancing exercise, weighing the circumstances of the case.

The rationale of procedural economy dictates perhaps the most common exclusionary rule of evidence – the evidence having poor relevance to the case or materiality to the outcome. This is perhaps the most common reason for documents to be excluded. It is a general requirement present in the IBA Rules[91] as well as many of the domestic laws and arbitration rules mentioned above.[92]

'Relevance' requires a party seeking to obtain documents to prove to the tribunal that they are likely to be relevant to the case or they have a prima facie relevance in relation to the contention in the case.[93] Put differently, relevance is proven by showing that the evidence may be important for the requesting party to meet its burden of proof.[94] For example, a tribunal may exclude a part of a witness testimony if it is not relevant to the issues raised.[95] In this context, the authenticity and accuracy of evidence play a role, as they impact the extent to which evidence has any value or relevance at all.[96]

'Materiality', on the other hand, requires the evidence to bear upon the final decision in the case.[97] A document could be relevant to the case, meaning that it pertains to one of the key contentions in the dispute, but be non-material since, for example, the tribunal already has dozens of similar documents proving the identical point.

Although determinations of relevance and materiality are firmly within the discretion of the tribunal, persistent refusals by tribunals to order document disclosure or admit documents can lead to perceptions of bias, leading to subsequent challenges to the award on the grounds of due process. Courts, however, will typically be able to

90. *Mme Sergent c/ SCA Coopérative Agricole Agraly*, n° 14/14277, Rev. Arb. (2015) 961 (2015): stating that documents submitted after the deadline under the procedural timetable could be excluded; *BSG Resources Limited v. Vale S.A., Filip De Ly, David A.R. Williams, Michael Hwang*, EWHC 3347 (Comm) paras 12-20 (2019): documents submitted three weeks after the hearing were excluded, which did not amount to a violation of due process under the English Arbitration Act 1996.
91. IBA Rules, Arts 9.1 and 9.2(a).
92. For example, *see* Swedish Arbitration Act 1999, section 25: 'The arbitrators may refuse to admit evidence presented if it is manifestly irrelevant to the dispute ....'
93. Bernard Hanotiau, *Document Production in International Arbitration: A Tentative Definition of 'Best Practices'*, 117 (Bernard Hanotiau (ed.), ICC 2006).
94. Nathan O'Malley, Rules of Evidence in International Arbitration, 62 (2nd ed., Routledge 2019).
95. *Ibid.*, 282-283.
96. For example, *see EDF (Services) Limited v. Romania*, ICSID Case No. ARB/05/13, Award, para. 225 (2009); *ConocoPhillips Petrozuata B.V., ConocoPhillips Hamaca B.V. and ConocoPhillips Gulf of Paria B.V. v Bolivarian Republic of Venezuela*, ICSID Case No. ARB/07/30, Interim Decision, paras 115-120 (2017).
97. Peter Ashford, The IBA Rules on the Taking of Evidence in International Arbitration: A Guide, 71 (CUP 2013).

distinguish between the two.[98] What follows is that evidence which is irrelevant and non-material can be outright excluded. Such measures are well within the boundaries of due process and procedural efficiency.[99]

It is worth noting that, in relation to the disclosure of evidence, another exclusionary principle stemming out of procedural economy is that the search and handover of documents would be unreasonably burdensome.[100] This is essentially a fact-based proportionality analysis linked to the grounds of procedural efficiency.[101]

[C] International Public Policy

Another duty that becomes relevant in the context of exclusion of evidence stems from international public policy. In this area of evidence, the line between substantive and procedural rules becomes blurred. After all, international public policy is typically considered a substantive principle that affects jurisdiction of arbitral tribunals and admissibility of claims. Nonetheless, in the area of exclusion of evidence in particular, it would also apply to procedure.[102]

Much like due process, this duty stems from not only domestic practice but also the need to preserve the integrity of international arbitration and the public function of tribunals.[103] There are various circumstances in which it could be invoked in the context of evidence. For example, evidence could be obtained through corruption in breach of the said international public policy. Investment tribunals have persistently held that corruption is contrary to most if not all, domestic laws as well as international law.[104]

Furthermore, several authorities have emphasised that investment tribunals have the duty to actively combat corruption,[105] and hence, it would be inconceivable to retain evidence obtained by bribery in the record on the grounds of international public policy. The approach towards other evidence obtained in breach of *jus cogens* principles should be similar, torture being another example, as evidence obtained by it

98. For example, *see ABB AG v. Hochtief Airport GmbH*, EWHC 388 (Comm) (2006); *Euroflon Tekniska Produkter AB v. Flexiboys I Motala AB*, Case No. Ö 1590-11 (2012).
99. *Rosenweig v. Morgan Stanley*, 494 F.3d 1328 (2007).
100. IBA Rules, Art. 3(3)(c)(i).
101. Jeffrey Waincymer, Procedure and Evidence in International Arbitration, 866-867 (Wolters Kluwer 2012).
102. *Ibid.*, 749.
103. Walter Mattli, Thomas Dietz & Ralf Michaels, Roles and Role Perceptions of International Arbitrators, 68-72 (OUP 2014).
104. *Mr X, Buenos Aires v. Company A*, YCA 1996, ICC Case No. 1110 (1963); *Himpurna California Energy Ltd. v. PT. (Persero) Perusahaan Listruik Negara*, UNCITRAL, Volume XXV, Yearbook Commercial Arbitration, Volume 25 (1999); *Westacre Investments Inc. v. Jugoimport-SPDR Holding Co. Ltd and Others*, Q.B. 288 p. 315 (2000); *World Duty Free Co Ltd v. Republic of Kenya*, ICSID Case No. ARB/00/7, Award, paras 142-143 and 145 (2006).
105. Bernarde Cremades & David Cairns, *Transnational Public Policy in International Arbitral Decision Making: The Cases of Bribery, Money Laundering and Fraud*, 65 and 79 (Kristine Karsten & Andrew Berkeley (eds), ICC 2006); Michael Hwang & Kevin Lim, *Corruption in Arbitration – Law and Reality*, 8(1) AI 1, 14 (2012) https://doi.org/10.54648/aiaj2012001.

is excluded in most if not all, jurisdictions.[106] As Article 15 of the Convention against Torture provides:

> Each State Party shall ensure that any statement which is established to have been made as a result of torture shall not be invoked as evidence in any proceedings, except against a person accused of torture as evidence that the statement was made.[107]

Therefore, international public policy considerations can give rise to some of the most difficult issues of evidence. An award that is tainted by violations of international public policy would inevitably be challenged in follow-on proceedings.[108]

§5.04 BALANCING EXERCISE FOR DETERMINING EXCLUSION

Against the background of the broad evidentiary discretion and its duties, the tribunal should engage in a balancing exercise weighing the evidence in the light of the circumstances of the case before them. The exclusion of evidence is inherently a case-by-case exercise involving primarily questions of fact. Given the nature of discretion, the types of circumstances that tribunals can find persuasive in the exclusion of evidence are potentially endless.[109] Whatever considerations tribunals deem relevant, however, they must remain within the boundaries of the duties outlined above.

Nonetheless, certain trends and patterns can emerge from international and domestic practice. For instance, tribunals can consider the public availability of documents when considering the exclusion of illegally obtained evidence.[110] Tribunals also appear to fiercely protect privilege and give weight to the scope of privilege that parties and their representatives are subject to under relevant domestic laws.[111] There

---

106. Wojciech Jasiński, *Admissibility of Evidence Obtained by Torture and Inhuman or Degrading Treatment. Does the European Court of Human Rights Offer a Coherent and Convincing Approach?* 29(2) EJCCLCJ 127, 127-152 (2021) https://doi.org/10.1163/15718174-bja10022; Anne Veronique Schlaepfer & Philipe Bartsch, *A Few Reflections on the Assessment of Evidence by International Arbitrators*, 3 IBLJ 211, 214 (2010).
107. Convention against Torture and Other Cruel, Inhuman or Degrading Treatment or Punishment, Art. 15, General Assembly resolution 39/46.
108. For example, *see* most recently the UK Supreme Court setting aside an award on the grounds of fraud and corruption: *The Federal Republic of Nigeria v. Process and Industrial Developments Ltd*, EWHC 2638 (Comm) (2023).
109. Jeffrey Waincymer, Procedure and Evidence in International Arbitration, 411-413 (Wolters Kluwer 2012).
110. For example, *see* Aleksander Kalisz, *Illegal and Inappropriate Evidence in International Investment Law: Balancing Admissibility*, 6(1) CLR 60, 72-76 (2021); Peter Ashford, *The Admissibility of Illegally Obtained Evidence*, 85(4) Arbitration 377, 387 (2019); *R (on the application of Bancoult No 3) v. Secretary of State for Foreign and Commonwealth Affairs*, [2018] UKSC 3 para. 20 (2018): 'First, the document must constitute or remain part of the mission archive, and, second, its contents must not have become so widely disseminated in the public domain as to destroy any confidentiality or inviolability that could sensibly attach to it.'; *Matter of Dampman v. Morgenthau*, 158 Misc. 2d 102 (1993).
111. Klaus Peter Berger, *Evidentiary Privileges: Best Practice Standards Versus/and Arbitral Discretion*, 22(4) AI 501, 506-512 (2006) https://doi.org/10.1093/arbitration/22.4.501.

are many such trends and patterns that can be discerned from available tribunal practice that may point tribunals towards relevant considerations. This being said, proposing an exhaustive evidentiary test is outside the scope of this chapter which focuses on drawing conceptual boundaries of 'exclusionary rules of evidence' as a whole.

Once the tribunal engages in such fact-sensitive balancing exercise, what should it do with the findings? In *Libananco*, the tribunal said that it 'may consider other remedies available apart from the exclusion of improperly obtained evidence or information'.[112] Indeed, empowering tribunals to stay in control of the process by using procedural management tools at their disposal represents an important element in solving the issue of due process paranoia.[113] The various sources hence provide a range of options that are not mutually exclusive:

- include evidence
- exclude evidence
- exclude a part of the evidence[114]
- include evidence but order redactions[115]
- include evidence but lower its probative value[116]
- order a costs sanction on grounds of party bad faith conduct[117]
- order interim measures to preserve evidence[118]
- take adverse inferences[119]

112. *Libananco Holdings Co Limited v. Republic of Turkey*, ICSID Case No. ARB/06/8, Decision on Preliminary Issues, para. 80 (2008).
113. Klaus Peter Berger & Ole Jensen, *Due Process Paranoia and the Procedural Judgment Rule: A Safe Harbour for Procedural Management Decisions by International Arbitrators*, 32(3) AI 415, 431-432 (2016) https://doi.org/10.1093/arbint/aiw020.
114. For example, *see* IBA Rules, Art. 9(2): 'The Arbitral Tribunal shall, at the request of a Party or on its own motion, exclude from evidence or production any Document, statement, oral testimony or inspection, *in whole or in part* (...)' (emphasis added).
115. For example, privileged documents, *see Bank for International Settlements, Reineccius v. BIS*, PCA Case No. 2000-04, Partial Award, p. 11 (2002); *Caratube International Oil Company LLP and Devincci Salah Hourani v. Republic of Kazakhstan (II)*, ICSID Case No. ARB/13/13, Award, paras 166, 171 and 220-230 (2017).
116. For example, *see* in relation to including hearsay evidence *EDF (Services) Limited v. Romania*, ICSID Case No. ARB/05/13, Award, paras 223-237 (2009).
117. IBA Rules, Art. 9(8); *Reliastar Life Ins. Co., N.Y. v. Emc Nat. Life Co*, 564 F.3d 81 (2009); William W Park, *National Law and Commercial Justice: Safeguarding Procedural Integrity in International Arbitration*, 63 TLR 647, 674-679 (1989).
118. Power to order interim measures to preserve evidence is enshrined in many arbitration rules but recognised expressly in the UNCITRAL Arbitration Rules, Art. 26(2)(d); *Churchill Mining and Planet Mining Pty Ltd v. Republic of Indonesia*, ICSID Case No. ARB/12/40 and 12/14, Procedural Order No. 14, para. 72 (2014); *Mr Hassan Awdi, Enterprise Business Consultants, Inc and Alfa El Corporation v. Romania*, ICSID Case No. ARB/10/13, Decision on the Admissibility of the Respondent's Third Objection to Jurisdiction and Admissibility of Claimant's Claims, paras 1-11 (2013).
119. For example, tribunals can draw inferences from the misconduct of parties in adducing evidence: IBA Rules, Art. 9(6); Nathan O'Malley, Rules of Evidence in International Arbitration, 224-225 (2nd ed., Routledge 2019).

- permit the opponent to submit counter-evidence[120]
- adopt an 'attorneys' eyes only' regime[121]
- resignation of the arbitrators.[122]

Tribunals should consider combining several of the above measures in appropriate circumstances. For example, if the balancing exercise strongly suggests that evidence should be included in the record, the party that applied for its inclusion might also be subject to a costs sanction to account for the bad faith conduct in procuring the evidence.[123] Conversely, if the balancing exercise favours exclusion of illegally obtained evidence, the tribunal may consider ordering interim measures to prevent a party from further procurement of similar evidence. Such measures can assist the tribunal in preserving due process, as well as exercising their duties.

§5.05 THREE CATEGORIES OF EXCLUSIONARY RULES OF EVIDENCE

Despite the exclusion of evidence in international arbitration being a case-by-case exercise guided and limited by tribunal duties, it is possible to predict the typical circumstances in which such questions arise. Therefore, the following question is: in what circumstances are such steps warranted? What are the exclusionary rules of evidence?

Perhaps the most widely used set of guidance in this area is the IBA Rules, which can be adopted by the parties or tribunals but which predominantly tend to be treated as non-binding guidance.[124] The IBA Rules can be considered 'soft law' as they are not per se binding and must be adopted by the parties or tribunals. They are, nonetheless, a reflection of an internationally acceptable compromise between various jurisdictions in relation to evidentiary rules in arbitration and are widely used as non-binding but

---

120. For example, *see Fraport AG Frankfurt Airport Services Worldwide v. Republic of the Philippines (I)*, ICSID Case No. ARB/03/25, Decision on the Application for Annulment of Fraport AG Frankfurt Airport Services Worldwide, para. 200 (2010): 'The right to present one's case, or "*principe de la contradiction*", in arbitral proceedings includes the right of each party to make submissions on evidence presented by its opponent.'
121. For example, *see* in relation to commercial arbitration *China Machine New Energy Corp. v. (1) Jaguar Energy Guatemala LLC, (2) AEI Guatemala Jaguar Ltd*, SGCA 12 Civil Appeal No. 94 of 2018 paras 19, 109-115 (2020).
122. Although this is arguable, some authorities state that if the arbitrators cannot uphold the key principles of due process or international public policy, they should be able to resign: Emmanuel Gaillard & John Savage, *Applicable Law Chosen by the Parties*, p. 824 (Emmanuel Gaillard & John Savage Gaillard (eds), Kluwer Law International 1999).
123. Bernard Honatiau, *Complex – Multicontract-Multiparty – Arbitrations*, 14(4) AI 369, 373 (1998) https://doi.org/10.1093/arbitration/14.4.369; Nigel Blackaby KC, Constantine Partasides KC & Alan Redfern, Redfern and Hunter on International Arbitration, p. 311 (7th ed., OUP 2023).
124. The IBA Arbitration Guidelines and Rules Subcommittee, *Report on the reception of the IBA arbitration soft law products*, https://www.ibanet.org/document?id=Subcommittee-on-Arbitration-Guidelines-and-Rules-IBA-soft-law-products-Sept-2016 (accessed 1 May 2024): The IBA Arbitration Guidelines and Rules Subcommittee, pp. 8-9: estimating in the 2016 Report that although the IBA Rules were considered in 48% of arbitrations, in 80% of these cases the IBA Rules were referenced by tribunals as guidance only rather than binding.

authoritative guidance.[125] In fact, they attempt to 'preserve the lines of distinction between the rights of the parties and the authority of the arbitral tribunal'.[126] The IBA Rules hence contain a list of factors that tribunals 'shall' consider in relation to admissibility and disclosure of evidence:

(1) Relevance and materiality
(2) Legal impediment or privilege
(3) Unreasonable burden to produce the evidence
(4) Loss or destruction of the document
(5) Confidentiality
(6) Political or institutional sensitivity
(7) Procedural economy, proportionality, fairness or equality of the parties.[127]

The inclusion of the word 'shall' suggests a mandatory exclusion of evidence, although tribunals nonetheless retain discretion to determine whether one of the above exclusionary rules applies in the circumstances. By contrast, in another provision, the IBA Rules state that tribunals 'may' exclude evidence if it was illegally obtained.[128] Nonetheless, the IBA Rules rather list the circumstances in which exclusion is warranted than set out specific criteria for exclusion and the exercise of tribunal discretion. They are also non-exhaustive.[129]

Many other sources link rules of exclusion to some of the duties of tribunals, mainly stemming out of due process.[130] The difficulty around such division is that the evidence rarely trespasses on a single principle, such as equality between the parties or international public policy. These principles can also often favour both the inclusion and exclusion of evidence depending on the specific circumstances. This chapter, hence, proposes a change in taxonomy to divide exclusionary rules of evidence against the circumstances that 'taint' the evidence and put exclusion into question. In doing so, three principles are proposed:

(1) Exclusion of evidence on the grounds of its substance
(2) Exclusion of evidence on the grounds of how it was obtained

125. Nathan O'Malley, Rules of Evidence in International Arbitration, 8-9 (2nd ed., Routledge 2019).
126. 2020 IBA Rules of Evidence Review Task Force, *Commentary on the revised text of the 2020 IBA Rules on the Taking of Evidence in International Arbitration*, p. 28, https://www.ibanet.org/MediaHandler?id=4F797338-693E-47C7-A92A-1509790ECC9D (accessed 30 Jan. 2024).
127. IBA Rules, Art. 9(2).
128. *Ibid.*, Art. 9(3).
129. The list appears exhaustive although several grounds of exclusion have been omitted: Roman Khodykin, Carol Mulcahy & Nichols Fletcher, A Guide to the IBA Rules on the Taking of Evidence in International Arbitration, 425-426 (OUP 2019).
130. Bruce A McAllister & Amy Bloom, *Evidence in Arbitration*, 34(1) JMLC 35, 35-36 (2003); Jeffrey Waincymer, Procedure and Evidence in International Arbitration, 792-797 (Wolters Kluwer 2012); Frederic G Sourgens, Kabir A N Duggal & Ian A Laird, Evidence in International Investment Arbitration, 237-239 (OUP 2018); *see also* domestic practice in Theodore Perlman, *Due Process and the Admissibility of Evidence*, 64(8) HLR 1304 (1951) https://doi.org/10.2307/1337083.

(3) Exclusion of evidence on the grounds of non-compliance with procedural directions of the tribunal.

The first exclusionary principle concerns the substance of the evidence. In fact, most of the exclusionary grounds listed in the IBA Rules relate to it.[131] As was discussed above, evidence having little relevance to the case or poor materiality to its outcome is a key example.[132] Privileged and confidential documents are also a frequent issue, and there are many cases in which such evidence was excluded.[133]

The second and third principles of exclusion are concerned not with the substance of the evidence but with the procedure. Therefore, second, some evidence is excluded solely on the basis of how it was obtained – for example, through illegality.[134] Such circumstances often involve an analysis of party conduct in question with the analysis of the substantive value of the evidence. The component, hence, fits with Article 9(3) of the IBA Rules that allows tribunals to exclude such evidence. The ground of 'unreasonable burden to produce the requested evidence'[135] would also fall under this category in the context of document disclosure and involve considerations of proportionality of the request.[136]

The third exclusionary principle of evidence concerns non-compliance of the evidence with procedural directions of the tribunal. Tribunals may, for example, set hard deadlines for submitting documents. In *Zeevi Holdings v. Bulgaria*, the claimant attempted to introduce new evidence despite an earlier procedural order stating that no further documents shall be admitted. The tribunal subsequently excluded the said documents.[137] Against this background, procedural economy appears to be the primary

131. IBA Rules, Art. 9(2)(a)-(b) and (e)-(g). Interestingly, the IBA Rules in Art. 9(2)(d) list 'loss or destruction of the Document that has been shown with reasonable likelihood to have occurred'. However, this cannot be an exclusionary rule of evidence as there is nothing to exclude – the evidence does not exist.
132. For example, *see Generica Ltd. v. Pharm. Basics, Inc*, 125 F.3d 1123, p. 1131 (1997); *Economy Forms Corporation v. The Government of the Islamic Republic of Iran; the Ministry of Energy; Dam & Water Works Construction Co. ('Sabir'); Sherkat Sakatemani Mani Sahami Kass ('Mana'); and Bank Mellat (formerly Bank of Tehran)*, IUSCT Case No. 165 (1983).
133. For example, *see* in relation to privilege *Bank for International Settlements, Reineccius v. BIS*, PCA Case No. 2000-04, Partial Award, p. 11 (2002); *Vito G. Gallo v. The Government of Canada*, PCA Case No. 55798, Procedural Order No. 3, para. 49 (2009); *see* in relation to confidentiality *Euroflon Tekniska Produkter AB v. Flexiboys I Motala AB*, Case No. Ö 1590-11 (2012).
134. For example, *see* Aleksander Kalisz, *Illegal and Inappropriate Evidence in International Investment Law: Balancing Admissibility*, 6(1) CLR 60, 61-63 (2021); Peter Ashford, *The Admissibility of Illegally Obtained Evidence*, 85(4) Arbitration 377, 377-378 (2019).
135. IBA Rules, Art. 9(2)(c).
136. Nathan O'Malley, Rules of Evidence in International Arbitration, 47 (2nd ed., Routledge 2019); *INA Corporation v. The Government of the Islamic Republic of Iran*, IUSCT Case No. 161, Award, para. 37 (1985): 'The Respondent's attempt to excuse its non-compliance with the Tribunal's Order [to disclose documents] by merely stating that the documents were "voluminous" is not convincing. The Respondent did not raise this asserted excuse until the hearing, long after the date for submission of these materials had passed; even then, the Respondent gave no indication of the actual amounts of material involved or any description of the alleged problems involved which prevented submission of the materials by the Respondent or their inspection by INA.'
137. *Zeevi Holdings v. The Republic of Bulgaria and the Privatization Agency of Bulgaria*, Case No. UNC 39/DK, Award, para. 61 (2006).

consideration in the area. In fact, in another case before the English courts, the exclusion of a 2,000-page document three months after the hearing did not amount to a violation of due process.[138] The tribunals acting contrary to their own procedural directions in order to include new evidence might, however, trespass on due process. In the *Fraport v. Philippines* investment arbitration, a party applied to introduce new evidence after the close of the hearing, which the tribunal admitted. The Decision on Annulment found that this decision breached due process as it restricted the opponent's right to be heard and respond to the new evidence.[139]

To summarise the point, and in an effort to remedy the lack of systematisation in the area, there is a need to reopen how exclusionary principles are categorised in international arbitration. Having considered practice and doctrinal sources, this paper argues that exclusionary rules of evidence should be divided into three categories depending on the circumstances that taint the evidence:

(1) **Principle 1: The substance of the evidence excludes it from the record**: covering circumstances where nothing was procedurally questionable in relation to the evidence, but rather the evidence itself was privileged, confidential, politically sensitive or otherwise should be excluded due to its substance. Most importantly, this principle addresses evidence that simply does not meet the threshold of relevance and materiality.
(2) **Principle 2: How the evidence was obtained excludes it from the record**: addressing whether the evidence was obtained inappropriately or whether its production was overly burdensome. It stretches from evidence obtained in breach of *ius cogens* principles such as torture, through evidence obtained through corruption, to evidence obtained through domestic civil wrongs.
(3) **Principle 3: The evidence does not comply with a procedural direction of the tribunal**: concerning issues such as the phase in which evidence was introduced, for instance, during the hearing or even moments before the final award. Other considerations include non-compliance with the language requirements, submission of overly voluminous evidence contrary to tribunal directions and other similar factors.

These categories of exclusionary rules are not mutually exclusive and can be argued and analysed in parallel. For instance, in *Rompetrol v. Romania*, the tribunal dealt with evidence procured through wiretapping that was allegedly contrary to confidentiality and national security.[140] The same piece of evidence, therefore, triggered two possible exclusionary rules - one concerning Principle 1, relating to the

138. *BSG Resources Limited v. Vale S.A., Filip De Ly, David A.R. Williams, Michael Hwang*, EWHC 3347 (Comm), paras 12-20 (2019).
139. *Fraport AG Frankfurt Airport Services Worldwide v. Republic of the Philippines (I)*, ICSID Case No. ARB/03/25, Decision on the Application for Annulment of Fraport AG Frankfurt Airport Services Worldwide, paras 218-247 (2010).
140. *The Rompetrol Group N.V. v. Romania*, ICSID Case No. ARB/06/3, Award, paras 255-261 and 270-280 (2013).

substance of the documents (confidentiality and national security) and Principle 2, namely how the evidence was procured (wiretapping).

Moreover, it is conceivable that a single piece of evidence triggers all three principles. Say, for example, that one party employs hackers to break into the investor's servers for the purpose of finding documents it can use in the arbitration (possibly making it inappropriately obtained under Principle 2) and the documents that were subsequently obtained are covered by client-attorney privilege (possibly excluding the evidence in relation to its substance under Principle 1). The party then only attempts to admit the evidence days before the deadline for the final award, restricting the opponent's ability to respond (possibly excluding the evidence on the grounds of failure to comply with tribunal procedural directions under Principle 3). Naturally, the more principles of exclusion are infringed by the introduced evidence, the stronger the argument that it should be excluded, although the test is inevitably a case-by-case one, subject to the relevant burden and standard of proof of the evidentiary objection.

Finally, it is worth emphasising that the three principles mentioned above are also relevant to document disclosure/production, not just admissibility. However, the exclusionary principle relating to non-compliance with the tribunal's procedural direction (Principle 3) would be less relevant to document disclosure since it involves a party applying for tribunal permission to request evidence from the opponent that may be simply refused, although the tribunal can prescribe a specific procedure for requesting documents, such as a Redfern Schedule.[141] Other principles would apply to disclosure unchanged. Indeed, by way of example, parties may and do raise arguments of privilege at the document production stage.[142]

§5.06 CONCLUSIONS AND OUTLOOK

This chapter sets out exclusionary rules of evidence as a standalone concept in the procedural practice of international arbitration which stems out of tribunal discretion and the various duties of the tribunals. Due process serves as the minimum standard that must be observed, but other principles, such as procedural economy and the observance of international public policy, should be factored in by tribunals to guide the exercise of their discretion.

That being said, resolving the issue of exclusion of evidence is an inherently case-by-case exercise. As a consequence of evidentiary discretion tribunals can, subject to their duties, give weight to any considerations they deem relevant in resolving the issue. Once the tribunal reaches a decision through a balancing exercise of these various relevant considerations, it has a range of options available to it apart from the

141. *Dunkeld International Investment Ltd. v. The Government of Belize (Number 1)*, PCA Case No. 2010-13, Procedural Order No. 1, para. 9 (2014): 'Document production requests submitted to the Tribunal for decision *must* be in tabular form pursuant to the model included with this Order as Annexure B. The Parties are encouraged to use the model format throughout their exchange of requests, objections, and responses' (emphasis added).
142. *Apotex Holdings Inc. and Apotex Inc. v. United States of America*, ICSID Case No. ARB(AF)/12/1, Procedural Order on Document Production Regarding the Parties' Respective Claims to Privilege and Privilege Logs (2013).

inclusion or exclusion of evidence such as ordering redactions, imposing a costs sanction on the recalcitrant party or permitting counter-evidence.

Finally, the chapter proposes to divide the exclusionary rules of evidence against the circumstances that 'taint' the evidence in question. Therefore, evidence may be excluded on the basis of its substance (Principle 1), on the basis of how it was obtained (Principle 2) and on the basis of non-compliance with procedural directions of the tribunal (Principle 3). Principle 1 relates to the substance while the other two are concerned with questions of procedure.

CHAPTER 6

Integrating New Technologies in International Arbitration: Thoughts on the Future of Our Profession

Danna Zhang

§6.01 INTRODUCTION

Since the launch of OpenAI's ChatGPT in November 2022, conversations about artificial intelligence (AI) have been everywhere. In just a matter of months, ChatGPT became the fastest-growing consumer app in history,[1] and less than a year from its release, OpenAI CEO Sam Altman announced at the company's first-ever developer conference that the service had garnered approximately 100 million weekly users.[2] Around the same time in November 2023, 'AI' was selected by the Collins dictionary as its word of the year,[3] defined as an 'abbreviation for artificial intelligence: the modelling of human mental functions by computer programs'.[4]

It seems safe to say that the rise of ChatGPT has captured the public imagination and fuelled a surge of interest in the promise and potential of new technologies to transform our lives. The implications are as wide-ranging as the expert predictions for an AI revolution, oscillating from the wildly optimistic to the depressingly dystopian.

1. Krystal Hu, *ChatGPT sets record for fastest-growing user base – analyst note*, Reuters (2 Feb. 2023), https://www.reuters.com/technology/chatgpt-sets-record-fastest-growing-user-base-analyst-note-2023-02-01/.
2. Jon Porter, *ChatGPT continues to be one of the fastest-growing services ever*, The Verge (6 Nov. 2023), https://www.theverge.com/2023/11/6/23948386/chatgpt-active-user-count-openai-developer-conference.
3. *'AI' named most notable word of 2023 by Collins dictionary*, The Guardian (1 Nov. 2023), https://www.theguardian.com/technology/2023/nov/01/ai-named-most-notable-word-of-2023-by-collins-dictionary.
4. Esther Addley, *Definition of 'AI'*, Collins, https://www.collinsdictionary.com/dictionary/english/ai.

When it comes to AI and the future of work, the conversation tends to centre on the threat of automation. To what extent will AI displace workers by replicating tasks previously performed by humans? And how will AI impact highly skilled professions such as the practice of law?

The 2023 edition of the OECD's Employment Outlook report,[5] published in July 2023, provided a bleak outlook for the legal profession. The report observed that 'AI's improving ability to complete [...] non-routine tasks raises new worries of job displacement for occupations previously thought impervious to automation'[6] and proceeded to speculate that '[o]ccupations in finance, medicine and legal activities', could be amongst those which 'may suddenly find themselves at risk of automation from AI'.[7] It is perhaps not so strange, then, that the legal profession remains reluctant to fully embrace the use of AI tools in day-to-day practice.

In November 2023, a survey on the use of AI in international arbitration published by law firm Bryan Cave Leighton Paisner[8] (BCLP) reflected widespread scepticism towards AI within the international arbitration community. The survey was based on a total of 221 respondents (including lawyers in private practice, arbitrators, experts, in-house counsel, academics, staff at arbitral institutions, legal tech providers, and litigation funders)[9] and applied a broad definition of AI which included 'systems using technologies such as text mining, computer vision, speech recognition, natural language generation, machine learning and deep learning to gather and/or use data to predict, recommend or decide, with varying levels of autonomy, the best action to achieve specific goals'.[10]

Overall, the survey found that whilst most members of the international arbitration community acknowledge that AI is useful for performing tasks like document review, translation, and text formatting and editing,[11] the majority are opposed to the use of AI tools to 'formulate or draft adjudicatory elements of an award'[12] or in legal submissions. 86%-88% of the survey respondents expressed concerns about cybersecurity risks, AI hallucinations,[13] the potential for breaches of confidentiality, improper delegation, and the danger of AI tools being misused to falsify or tamper with evidence ('deepfakes').[14] But despite these concerns, 73% of the survey respondents expressed no objection to using AI tools for the generation of factual summaries, whilst 65% indicated that they would deploy AI for document analysis, defined in the survey as 'extracting and organising data from documents'.[15] 62%, however, would *'draw the*

5. OECD (2023), *OECD Employment Outlook 2023: Artificial Intelligence and the Labour Market*, OECD Publishing, Paris, https://doi.org/10.1787/08785bba-en.
6. *Ibid.*, section 3.
7. *Ibid.*
8. BCLP, *Annual Arbitration Survey 2023* (2023), https://www.bclplaw.com/a/web/tUW2SW6fjHrpXVrA7AfWkS/102932-arbitration-survey-2023-report_v10.pdf.
9. *Ibid.*, at p. 7.
10. *Ibid.*, at p. 6.
11. *Ibid.*, at p. 13.
12. *Ibid.*, at p. 23.
13. Defined in the survey as 'risk of the technology conjuring up fictitious information.'
14. BCLP, *supra* n. 8, at p. 15.
15. *Ibid.*, at p. 13.

line' at using AI tools to generate texts for use in arbitral awards, whereas 58% expressed reservations in relation to text for use in expert reports.[16] Survey respondents' confidence in arbitrators' technical capability 'to give directions concerning the use of AI tools in arbitration' was similarly low, with 79% rating it at 5 or below on a scale of 1-10.[17]

It would seem, then, that whilst the COVID-19 pandemic pushed the legal profession to embrace technology for remote work and virtual meetings, many arbitration lawyers remain wary of the integration of AI into their practice. However, whether we like it or not, there is little doubt that technological innovations will radically change how lawyers work in the coming years and that AI will accelerate existing trends in digitalisation and virtual work environments. On that basis, this chapter will seek to offer a perspective on the future of international arbitration and, in doing so, will endeavour to move beyond the dichotomy between 'human intelligence' and 'artificial intelligence' ('AI will/will not replace lawyers') to explore the potential of AI and other innovative technologies to improve international arbitration as a practice and a profession. After all, the most exciting possibilities lie not in replacing lawyers with machines but in deploying new technologies to improve client results and lawyer well-being for a better profession overall.

Considering this, *Part I* of this chapter will address the short-term impact of AI on the practice of international arbitration, including the immediate opportunities and challenges likely to arise. *Part II* will then consider the long-term potential of new technologies to improve the profession of international arbitration.

For the purposes of this chapter, 'AI' is defined as 'an umbrella term for a range of algorithm-based technologies that solve complex tasks by carrying out functions that previously required human thinking'[18] and is generally used without distinction between the different types of AI classification.[19]

§6.02 PART I SHORT-TERM IMPACT: IMMEDIATE OPPORTUNITIES AND CHALLENGES

The existing use cases for AI in arbitration (and in the legal profession at large) already cover a variety of tasks, including document review and e-disclosure, legal research, data analysis, and citations,[20] most of which are performed using machine learning

16. *Ibid.*
17. BCLP, *supra* n. 8, at p. 23.
18. A definition first offered by the UK Information Commissioner's Office in its 2020 publication '*Explaining decisions made with AI*,' co-authored with The Alan Turing Institute, https://ico.org.uk/media/for-organisations/uk-gdpr-guidance-and-resources/artificial-intelligence/explaining-decisions-made-with-artificial-intelligence-1-0.pdf.
19. *See, e.g.*, Naveen Joshi, *7 Types of Artificial Intelligence*, Forbes (19 Jun. 2019), https://www.forbes.com/sites/cognitiveworld/2019/06/19/7-types-of-artificial-intelligence/, for a classification of the types of AI.
20. *See, e.g.*, Nigel Blackaby KC, Constantine Partasides & Alan Redfern, Redfern and Hunter on International Arbitration 6.110 (2022).

algorithms.[21] With the rise of generative AI (genAI), future applications now seem virtually limitless, with many promising tools in the works.

Unlike machine learning algorithms that process and analyse data to make predictions, genAI is a type of AI that can create new and original content by learning patterns from training data.[22] Large language models (LLMs) such as ChatGPT, Falcon, and Google's Gemini rely on this technology to produce original text content that mimics the human voice to such a degree it is sometimes difficult to tell the difference. Meanwhile, image synthesis services like Midjourney, OpenAI's DALL•E 3, and Adobe Firefly are generating artwork and design so impressive that it looks set to change the creative industries, along with video generation technologies able to create deepfakes that blur the line between what is artificial and what is real. These innovations bring with them a host of new opportunities and risks set to challenge the current arbitral framework, a number of which will be considered below.

Section §6.02[A] focuses on the procedural issues likely to arise from the increased use of AI tools by parties and their counsel. *Section* §6.02[B] addresses the use of AI by arbitrators. Finally, *section* §6.02[C] considers the regulatory landscape with regard to the use of AI tools in international arbitration.

[A] AI Use by Parties and Related Procedural Issues

As of September 2024, no major institutional arbitration rules[23] contain any mention of 'artificial intelligence'. This means that it is mostly left to the discretion of the tribunal to tailor an appropriate set of rules or guidelines regarding the use of AI if and when the need arises. However, as the use of AI tools becomes increasingly common, universal procedural issues are likely to emerge that may require broader consideration.

The following pages will consider two key issues of particular relevance to international arbitration: disclosure obligations (section §6.02[A][1]) and concerns regarding data privacy and confidentiality (section §6.02[A][2]).

[1] Disclosure Obligations

The growing use of AI tools amongst parties, counsel, and arbitrators raises the question of whether mandatory disclosure obligations are needed to protect the integrity of arbitration proceedings in the future.

---

21. Defined by IBM as '*a set of rules or processes used by an AI system to conduct tasks – most often to discover new data insights and patterns, or to predict output values from a given set of input variables,' What is a machine learning algorithm?*, IBM, https://www.ibm.com/topics/machine-learning-algorithms#:~:text=A%20machine%20learning%20algorithm%20is,learning%20(ML)%20to%20learn.
22. Margaret Rouse, *Generative AI*, Techopedia (15 Jan. 2024), https://www.techopedia.com/definition/34633/generative-ai.
23. Namely the ICDR Rules 2021, JAMS International Arbitration Rules 2021, LCIA Rules 2020, ICC Rules 2021, SCC Rules 2023, HKIAC Rules 2018, SIAC Rules 2016 (and the Draft 7th Edition of the SIAC Rules shared by the SIAC on 22 Aug. 2023), JCAA Rules 2021, DIAC Rules 2022, and UNCITRAL Rules 2021.

There is certainly no shortage of cautionary tales about the issues that can arise when AI use by non-tech-savvy lawyers goes undisclosed. In May 2023, for example, the legal profession enjoyed a collective chuckle when news emerged of a personal injury lawyer in New York who had relied a little too much on ChatGPT in preparing a brief for submission to Manhattan's federal court.[24] With the aid of the AI chatbot, the lawyer had produced a motion replete with '*bogus*' cases, decisions, and quotes, which was promptly filed to the court upon assurance from ChatGPT that the 'cases I provided are real and can be found in reputable legal databases'.[25] Stories such as this are likely why the November 2023 BCLP survey found widespread concern regarding the potential misuse of AI, with 88% of the respondents expressing worry over AI hallucination and 86% concerned about 'deepfakes'.[26] But just how valid are these fears?

With regard to the risk of hallucination (as in the case of the unfortunate New York lawyer), it is clear that technological advances are no substitute for lawyers' existing obligations to verify the accuracy of their court filings.[27] This is not a new problem, however, and is unlikely to be resolved with AI-specific regulation. Lawyers have been delegating work for as long as the profession has existed, and some have always sought to cut corners wherever possible. Just as they have in the past, law firms should continue to address this issue through internal policies to ensure that work produced by non-lawyers (whether by interns, support staff, or AI assistants) is competently done and subject to review and quality control by a lawyer qualified in the relevant jurisdiction.

The risk of deepfakes may be trickier to tackle.[28] Whilst the prevalence of AI tools has made it easier than ever to fabricate or falsify evidence (as well as to obscure any signs of tampering), it is also easier than ever for parties to level unsubstantiated allegations of forgery against the other side. As with many other issues, this ultimately comes down to trust, but in cases where the trust between the parties has deteriorated to the point that it cannot be restored, a set of robust guidelines for the disclosure of AI use may significantly aid the continued progress of the proceedings.

Mandatory disclosure rules would ensure that parties are given the opportunity to familiarise themselves with the tools used by the other side. Depending on the extent of disclosure required, it may also enable parties to assess the underlying algorithms of such tools and to consider and address the ways in which they may affect the scope and

24. Benjamin Weiser, *Here's What Happens When Your Lawyer Uses ChatGPT*, The New York Times (27 May 2023), https://www.nytimes.com/2023/05/27/nyregion/avianca-airline-lawsuit-chatgpt.html.
25. *Ibid.*
26. BCLP, *supra* n. 8, at p. 15.
27. *See, e.g.*, Art. 48 of the Code of Conduct for the Danish Bar and Law Society (2022), Rule 5.4 of the Code of Professional Conduct for Members of the Swedish Bar Association (2023), Rule 1.4 of the England and Wales Solicitors Regulation Authority's Code of Conduct (2023), and Rules 3.3 and 4.1 of the New York Rules of Professional Conduct (2022).
28. *See* Marie-Helen Maras & Alex Alexandrou, *Determining authenticity of video evidence in the age of artificial intelligence and in the wake of Deepfake videos*, International Journal of Evidence & Proof, 23(3), 255-262 (2019) https://doi.org/10.1177/1365712718807226, on the capabilities of deepfake technology and its impact on the process for authentication of video evidence.

nature of evidence and/or legal submissions in the proceedings. It seems reasonable, however, that proactive disclosure should only be required when mandated by the chosen rules (whether ad hoc or institutional).[29] If the tribunal requires further information (or if no specific rules have been agreed), it should be able to obtain this by requesting the parties to disclose further details.[30]

As AI is adopted more widely in the international arbitration community, arbitral institutions may wish to ease the procedural burden by developing registries of pre-approved AI tools that parties are permitted to use without disclosure (i.e., tools that have been vetted and approved with regard to data privacy and other security and regulatory concerns), as well as written policies for how such tools may be used, including any specific restrictions. In the meantime, the following pages will offer some reflections on the scope of any potential disclosure obligations.

Scope of Disclosure Obligations

The first step in any disclosure framework is to determine the extent of disclosure required and make sure that the scope of any mandatory obligations is clear and workable. In relation to the use of AI and other new technologies, this means disclosure rules should acknowledge that machine learning technology is already embedded into most legal practices through such commonplace tools as grammar and spell checkers, tools that check or generate citations, predictive typing software, translation software, and legal research tools. All these tools tend to incorporate at least some AI features and have been available for years, yet only the most cautious rule-sticklers would have thought before 2023 that the use of such programs would require disclosure.

The need for a pragmatic approach is also reflected in the results of BCLP's November 2023 survey, which found that views on the need for disclosure of AI use depended on the nature of the task. Accordingly, 72% of the survey respondents believed that AI use should be disclosed when applied in the drafting of expert reports, whilst 65% believed that disclosure was necessary for tools that provide assistance with document review and production.[31] Meanwhile, 62% believed that disclosure was needed when AI tools were used to translate documents submitted into the arbitration record, whereas only 40% believed that parties should be required to disclose the use of AI tools for legal research.[32] Despite general calls for transparency,[33]

29. This aligns with Guideline 3 of the Silicon Valley Arbitration & Mediation Center's (SVAMC) *SVAMC Guidelines on the Use of Artificial Intelligence in Arbitration* (2024), according to which '[d]isclosure that AI tools were used in connection with an arbitration is not necessary as a general matter,' whereas proactive disclosure applies under the Dubai International Financial Centre (DIFC) Courts' *Practical Guidance Note Number 2 of 2023 Guidelines on the use of large language models and generative AI in proceedings before the DIFC Courts*, which recommends that parties 'declare at the earliest possible opportunity if they have used or intend to use AI-generated content during any part of proceedings.'
30. This aligns broadly with the general approach to document disclosure in international arbitration where the power to request parties to give disclosure of relevant documents will typically fall within the tribunal's general case management powers (*see, e.g.*, Art. 3(10) of the International Bar Association's (IBA) Rules on the Taking of Evidence in International Arbitration (2020)).
31. BCLP, *supra* n. 8, at p. 19.
32. *Ibid.*

however, only half of the respondents believed that the use of AI tools in arbitration should be openly disclosed to 'all those involved in an arbitration', including the survey respondents' own clients, (other) parties to the arbitration, the tribunal, the administering institution, and potential third-party funders/insurers.[34] These findings suggest that it would be difficult to establish a common ground for the extent of disclosure needed,[35] and compromises will have to be made.

Some courts and judges have already responded to the rise of genAI with rigorous disclosure measures. In June 2023, for example, Judge Michael M. Baylson of the U.S. District Court for the Eastern District of Pennsylvania issued a standing order stating that lawyers 'MUST, in a clear and plain factual statement, disclose that AI has been used in any way in the preparation of' 'any complaint, answer, motion, brief, or other paper, filed with the Court'.[36] From a practical perspective, however, it hardly seems sensible to require mandatory disclosure of AI use that does not alter the substance of the final work product and is indeed so commonplace that it is likely to go unnoticed by most users. At the same time, it is key to ensure that guidelines are as clear and unambiguous as possible to minimise room for creative interpretation by overzealous counsel. A reasonable compromise may be an approach based on the type of AI tool and the intended purpose and nature of its use,[37] with mandatory disclosure required for the use of AI tools relying on generative capabilities or otherwise able to create original content, whereas machine learning tools (e.g., tools capable of making decisions, identifying trends, and other forms of predictive analysis by learning from data, but which do not produce original content) may be used freely. This approach would allow parties to make use of programs that do not influence the legal work product in a substantive way, whereas all AI programs designed to generate original text and image-based content would require disclosure, regardless of whether the AI-generated content is altered or amended before being used in submissions.

For analytics tools capable of generating input or whole documents for submission to the arbitration record, the extent of disclosure required may instead depend on the specific intended use. This category of AI systems includes tools for data summarisation used to generate overviews of factual and/or legal subjects, tools that prepare visual aids for complex advice or video reproductions and the like, as well as accounting and finance tools used for, e.g., loss calculations, valuations, and counterfactual simulation. A party may, for example, deploy AI to identify potentially relevant documents in a data room that it might wish to rely on in the arbitration without

33. The survey found that 60% of respondents agreed or strongly agreed that there is a need for greater transparency over the use of AI tools by parties in arbitration (*see* BCLP, *supra* n. 8, at p. 19).
34. BCLP, *supra* n. 8, at p. 20.
35. *See* the SVAMC's Commentary to Guideline 3, SVAMC Guidelines on the Use of Artificial Intelligence in Arbitration (2024), which states that 'defining a set of generally applicable criteria for disclosure of AI does not seem feasible and could create more controversy than it resolves.'
36. Judge Michael M. Baylson in the United States District Court for the Eastern District of Pennsylvania, Standing Order Re: Artificial Intelligence ('AI') in Cases Assigned to Judge Baylson, 6 Jun. 2023.
37. This aligns with the general approach taken in Guideline 3 of the SVAMC Guidelines on the Use of Artificial Intelligence in Arbitration (2024).

disclosing such use to the other side. If, on the other hand, that party were instead to use the same tool in the context of complying with a document request or an order issued by the arbitral tribunal, disclosure may be required. This ties back to the issue of trust, and parties may well wish to err on the side of caution by agreeing to disclose such tools regardless of actual use.

Overall, a disclosure framework based on these general categories should be fairly easy to manage, in addition to being flexible enough to accommodate new innovations and technological developments. It would also allow parties and their counsel a reasonable degree of freedom with regard to commonly used tools whilst making sure that any AI programs capable of generating new input or output for inclusion in material documents are disclosed and subject to scrutiny by the parties and the tribunal. However, to ensure that the parties can fully assess the potential impact of AI use on the proceedings, disclosure may also be required regarding the extent and nature of specific usage in relation to tools within the general scope. In addition, the parties should be required to disclose in each instance how a specific submission has been altered or otherwise influenced by such tools.

One potential solution is a two-pronged approach requiring:

(1) a general disclosure statement at the beginning of the arbitration, followed by
(2) specific disclosure statements prior to parties' submission of any document intended to be materially relied upon in the proceedings (including pleadings, evidence, and expert reports and submissions) that have been produced with the aid of AI tools.

The initial disclosure should cover (at a minimum):

- the type and nature of the AI tool used and its specific intended use (e.g., document analysis or text generation);[38]
- the identity of the supplier(s) of the AI tool, and
- specific information about the data set on which the tool was trained (e.g., size/volume, sources, and/or selection criteria).

Parties (or arbitrators) may also require disclosure of the prompts provided to the AI system,[39] as well as other technical parameters (e.g., neural network architectures or scripts for training and output generation) to be able to fully assess the workings of the underlying algorithms and evaluate how they might affect the integrity of AI-generated output submitted in the arbitration. This would provide parties with the strongest basis for considering (and substantiating) any objections to the use of specific tools, though it would also require significant resources and technical capabilities.

If the parties are not able to agree on a joint list of approved AI tools after the initial disclosure, the party wishing to use a disputed tool should be able to seek

38. *See* Guideline 3 of the SVAMC Guidelines on the Use of Artificial Intelligence in Arbitration (2024).
39. *Ibid.*

permission from the arbitral tribunal for its intended use.[40] Initial disclosures should therefore be followed by a short deadline for parties to object to the use of any disclosed tools, after which disputes should be settled by the arbitral tribunal.

Subsequent disclosures[41] made during the proceedings should be enclosed with each party submission and should at least contain a general outline of:

- specific use in the relevant submission (e.g., by listing the pages and/or sections of a document that include AI-generated output or by integration of a watermark for AI-generated content),[42] and
- the extent and nature of use (e.g., whether the AI-generated output was altered or otherwise amended before being included in the submission).

For the sake of uniformity, disclosures should be made on forms provided by either the arbitral institution (if any), the tribunal, or – if possible – jointly by the parties. Arbitrators may also require that disclosure statements must be signed by both a party representative and their legal counsel to assuage any lingering concerns of dishonesty.

Of course, this leads to the question of how breaches should be enforced and what sanctions should apply (if any), including whether parties should be liable for breaches by, e.g., experts or even fact witnesses. One possible (and fairly straightforward) approach would be to take inspiration from the existing remedies addressing counsel misconduct in international arbitration,[43] including the ability to draw inferences in assessing the evidence relied upon, or the legal arguments advanced by, the party representative,[44] impact on cost allocation,[45] and even potential liability for damages.

[2] Data Privacy and Confidentiality

It is a common characteristic of AI tools that they require large amounts of data to function (or at least to function well). Indeed, many of the long-term future use cases considered in this chapter require the parties to upload data onto AI-powered

40. Such disagreements should be addressed using the existing mechanisms for resolving disputes under the procedural rules applicable to the arbitration.
41. Given that AI tools covered by subsequent disclosures would already have been approved for use at the initial disclosure stage, there would not seem to be any need for the tribunal to consider objections at this stage except in very special circumstances.
42. This approach is consistent with preamble number 134 of the EU AI Act (*see* section §6.02[C] below), which states that '[f]urther to the technical solutions employed by the providers of the AI system, deployers who use an AI system to generate or manipulate image, audio or video content that appreciably resembles existing persons, objects, places, entities or events and would falsely appear to a person to be authentic or truthful (deep fakes), should also clearly and distinguishably disclose that the content has been artificially created or manipulated by labelling the AI output accordingly and disclosing its artificial origin.'
43. *See, e.g.*, Art. 9(8) of the IBA Rules on Taking of Evidence in International Arbitration (2020) and Guideline 26 of the IBA Guidelines on Party Representation in International Arbitration (2013).
44. Guideline 26, IBA Guidelines on Party Representation in International Arbitration (2013).
45. Article 9(8), IBA Rules on Taking of Evidence in International Arbitration (2020), and Guideline 26, IBA Guidelines on Party Representation in International Arbitration (2013).

arbitration platforms.[46] For many clients and lawyers alike, this will understandably raise alarm bells with regard to data privacy and confidentiality.

Common causes for concern include the lack of transparency about where data will end up, as well as reservations about inputting any kind of proprietary or otherwise sensitive information into AI programs, even if the information is not regulated.[47] As with the whirlwind efforts that followed the introduction of the EU's landmark General Data Protection Regulation (GDPR),[48] attention to confidentiality risks is also likely to be heightened in the coming years as the legal community (and the general public) grows to embrace AI. Overall, however, it seems that confidentiality concerns arising from AI integration will not differ too much in nature from those already raised by parties' reliance on other software programs and tech tools provided by third-party suppliers, including email, data rooms, and document management software. As with any other third-party tech tool – and as already established by the GDPR in relation to personal data[49] – it is key for AI users to assess the nature of the information that will be input into the AI model and closely examine their contracts for how that data will (or can) be used by the supplier, including whether information submitted by users may be reproduced in future responses.[50]

In arbitrations involving EU parties and/or EU individuals or governed by EU institutions, there will be a significant overlap between AI use and the GDPR. Unlike the EU's recently adopted Artificial Intelligence Act,[51] which at its heart is a product safety regulation and does not create any direct enforcement rights for individuals,[52] the GDPR is a rights-based regulation that equips individuals with a wide range of rights with respect to their personal data. However, given that the definition of 'processing' under the GDPR is technology-neutral and includes 'any operation or set of operations which is performed on personal data or on sets of personal data, whether or not by automated means',[53] the GDPR will intersect with the AI Act to 'fill the gap' in regard to individuals' rights whenever AI systems make use of personal data (which, given the broad definition of personal data under the GDPR,[54] will almost invariably be the case). This will address some – if not all – of the immediate data privacy concerns arising from AI integration, and the relationship between AI and the GDPR will likely

46. *See, e.g.*, section §6.03[B] below.
47. Similar considerations are reflected in the SVAMC's Commentary to Guideline 2, SVAMC Guidelines on the Use of Artificial Intelligence in Arbitration (2024).
48. Regulation (EU) 2016/679 of the European Parliament and of the Council of 27 Apr. 2016 on the protection of natural persons with regard to the processing of personal data and on the free movement of such data, and repealing Directive 95/46/EC (General Data Protection Regulation).
49. *See, e.g.*, the ICCA/IBA Joint Task Force's Roadmap on Data Protection in International Arbitration.
50. This is consistent with the recommendation given in the SVAMC's Commentary to Guideline 2, SVAMC Guidelines on the Use of Artificial Intelligence in Arbitration (2024).
51. The latest version of which is the European Parliament's Corrigendum to the EU AI Act of 19 Apr. 2024 passed by the European Parliament on 23 Apr. 2024, which corrected errors in the language and numbering present in previous drafts.
52. *See* section §6.02[C] below.
53. *See* Art. 4(2) GDPR.
54. *See* Art. 4(1) GDPR.

continue to grow and mature as more AI- and data-specific regulations are adopted in Europe and globally.

In addition to potential contractual confidentiality provisions and AI-specific regulations, lawyers who make use of AI tools are also likely to be bound by ethical rules and guidelines, which means they will be required to ensure and certify that the technology maintains the confidentiality of client data. Given that genAI is widely viewed as 'black box' technology due to the lack of transparency over its inputs and operations,[55] law firms may need to recruit and/or train technical coordinators or specialist AI lawyers to ensure a full understanding of the technical specifications, and to be able to advise clients on what actually happens with information put into AI programs deployed by the firm.

[B] AI and Arbitrators: Friends or Foes?

With the rise of generative AI, some countries have already begun to integrate AI-driven technologies into their judiciaries and adjudication processes. Estonia, a global digital leader and a frontrunner in public digital infrastructure, was rumoured in as early as 2019 to be piloting an AI judge for adjudication of small-claims disputes worth less than EUR 7,000, though this has since been debunked by the Estonian Ministry of Justice.[56] In the same year, it was widely reported that China had introduced so-called smart courts employing AI to assist judges with routine tasks such as recording testimony, analysing case materials, and verifying information from databases in real-time.[57] The initiative was so successful that four years later, in 2023, those AI assistants had reportedly been promoted to judges and were settling disputes via digital court hearings without human intervention.[58] Finally, just last year, The Guardian reported that a judge in Colombia had caused a stir when he revealed that he had consulted with ChatGPT in deciding an insurance dispute regarding the costs of medical treatment for an autistic child, in addition to relying on precedent in support of his conclusion.[59]

So far, there do not seem to have been any reports of arbitrations presided over by non-human AI tribunals or of parties selecting AI arbitration in their arbitration clauses, but despite the apparent lack of real-world application, much can be said (and indeed has been already) about the prospect of 'robot arbitrators' – good and bad. For many disputants, the appeal of arbitration comes in part from the ability of parties to appoint their own arbitrators (or, at the very least, influence the appointment process), unlike in civil litigation, where cases are typically assigned to judges at random. It is not

55. *See, e.g.*, the SVAMC's Commentary to Guideline 1, SVAMC Guidelines on the Use of Artificial Intelligence in Arbitration (2024).
56. Maria-Elisa Tuulik, *Estonia does not develop AI Judge*, Estonian Ministry of Justice (16 Feb. 2022), https://www.just.ee/en/news/estonia-does-not-develop-ai-judge.
57. *See, e.g.*, Alena Zhabina, *How China's AI is automating the legal system*, Deutsche Welle (20 Jan. 2023), https://www.dw.com/en/how-chinas-ai-is-automating-the-legal-system/a-64465988.
58. *Ibid.*
59. Luke Taylor, *Colombian judge says he used ChatGPT in ruling*, The Guardian (3 Feb. 2023), https://www.theguardian.com/technology/2023/feb/03/colombia-judge-chatgpt-ruling.

unthinkable, however, that the benefits of party appointment could be transferred to AI judges. It may even be possible in the not-so-distant future for parties to be able to 'design' their own arbitrators by mixing and matching elements from a register of (pre-approved) qualities, competencies, and areas of expertise administered by arbitral institutions or an international organ created on the basis of a multilateral treaty. This would fully resolve the potential problem of partisan arbitrators – and could even result in parties being presented with better-qualified and more ideally suited candidates than would be possible with human arbitrators.

Even if the future of (human) arbitrators is not quite so bleak, there can be no doubt that arbitrators have much to gain from integrating AI into their work. An obvious obstacle, however, is the risk of improper delegation of power, which 81% of respondents in BCLP's November 2023 survey reported being at least somewhat concerned about.[60] Unlike civil judges, arbitrators derive their powers from the parties' agreement to arbitrate rather than by virtue of state powers, and they are appointed by name and chosen because of their unique qualities, experience, and personal characteristics to resolve a dispute on the parties' behalf. An arbitrator's mandate is, therefore, an inherently personal mandate that must be fulfilled by the appointed individual, and delegation of the arbitrator's tasks (whether in full or in part) must be disclosed to the parties. The nature of an arbitrator's mandate also suggests that parties may not be too happy with arbitrators being aided in their decision-making by AI tools like ChatGPT.[61] There is no good reason, however, why parties should object to arbitrators seeking assistance from AI, just as they do not typically object to arbitrators relying on assistance or, indeed, advice from tribunal secretaries and expert witnesses, amongst others.

In the very near future, arbitrators will also likely be able to acquire personal AI secretaries who are fully tailored and trained in accordance with their individual preferences. In the autumn of 2023, for example, Microsoft announced its 'Copilot' for Microsoft 365 (branded 'your everyday AI companion'),[62] which promises to integrate GPT-4-based AI across the full suite of Microsoft 365 products, including Windows, Outlook, Teams, Word, Excel, PowerPoint and more, 'to unleash creativity, unlock

60. BCLP, *supra* n. 8, at p. 15.
61. In addition to the general reflections outlined in section §6.02[A][1] above, arbitrators' use of AI tools will also raise particular issues regarding the need for – and potential extent of – disclosure obligations, which are not further addressed in this chapter. Suffice it to say that whilst a flexible disclosure framework may be warranted for the parties, the nature of an arbitrator's mandate could well merit a stricter approach for arbitrators' use of AI. Parties may find it acceptable for an arbitrator to rely on genAI software in drafting the procedural history of an award but refuse to give consent for use of the same tool to articulate the reasoning behind the arbitrator's decision on the merits of the dispute. Rules regarding arbitrators' duties to disclose the use of AI tools may be best dealt with in institutional rules or by agreement between the parties, with due notice given to the arbitrator at the time of his or her appointment.
62. Yusuf Mehdi, *Announcing Microsoft Copilot, your everyday AI companion*, Microsoft (21 Sep. 2023), https://blogs.microsoft.com/blog/2023/09/21/announcing-microsoft-copilot-your-everyday-ai-companion/.

productivity and uplevel skills'.[63] According to Microsoft, Copilot in Word will 'jump-start the creative process so you never start with a blank slate again', providing 'a first draft to edit and iterate on – saving hours in writing, sourcing, and editing time'. Meanwhile, Copilot in Outlook promises to 'clear your inbox in minutes, not hours' by 'summarizing long email threads' and 'quickly drafting suggested replies'.[64] Many lawyers will recognise these tasks as typical junior-level work: drafting documents or email replies and preparing summaries for seniors to review. And in many cases, this is not too different from the tasks typically performed by tribunal secretaries in international arbitration proceedings. With proper oversight and supervision, there is no reason why an AI secretary should not eventually perform these tasks as well as – if not better than – a human one.[65]

AI assistants will not always be right, of course, and not every draft they produce will be useful, but the same could likely be said of any trainee attorney, junior associate, or young arbitration practitioner, including those trying on the role of tribunal secretary for the very first time. With patience, feedback, and proper training, they are all likely to improve and develop over time into skilful team members. The greatest challenge lies not in the quality of output produced by AI assistants but in making sure that arbitrators develop the technical capabilities and understanding needed to unlock AI's potential and functionality. Indeed, the output produced by AI models is only as accurate and as helpful as the questions asked by their users. Arbitrators – like any other professionals hoping to benefit from AI – will therefore need to learn how to ask the right questions (so-called prompt engineering) to achieve the desired results.

For arbitrators able to master AI, the benefit will be substantial. In addition to considerable time and cost savings,[66] integration of AI into arbitrators' decision-making is also likely to promote consistency and predictability in awards. AI-powered analytics can identify patterns and trends in past orders and awards, helping arbitrators make informed decisions based on the cumulative learnings of every precedent available to the public. In a sense, arbitrators aided by good AI tools will be able to benefit from a form of hybrid intelligence: the arbitrator's personal judgment, skillset, and unique (human) perspective combined with the ability and capacity of AI to consider every source available and find the one 'needle in the haystack' that may be of relevance to the arbitrator's decision. In addition, AI analytics is likely to be helpful

63. Jared Spataro, *Introducing Microsoft 365 Copilot – your copilot for work*, Microsoft (16 Mar. 2023), https://blogs.microsoft.com/blog/2023/03/16/introducing-microsoft-365-copilot-your-copilot-for-work/.
64. *Ibid.*
65. There is still some way to go, though, before AI assistants such as Microsoft's Copilot will be fully and safely integrable into legal practice, particularly when it comes to cybersecurity and data privacy risks. Indeed, the US House of Representatives was reported in March 2024 to have implemented a strict ban on the use of the Microsoft Copilot by congressional staffers over potential security risks identified by the Office of Cybersecurity: Andrew Solender & Ina Fried, *Scoop: Congress Bans Staff Use of Microsoft's AI Copilot*, Axios (29 Mar. 2024), https://www.axios.com/2024/03/29/congress-house-strict-ban-microsoft-copilot-staffers.
66. *See* section §6.03[B] below.

in preventing bias (whether good or bad) and mistakes of fact and/or law that may otherwise be caused by human error.

AI can also assist arbitrators in reviewing party submissions – a very promising use case that is only likely to increase in value as disputes continue to grow in both volume and complexity with legal submissions, exhibits, factual witness statements, and expert reports totalling tens if not hundreds of thousands of pages in many cases. AI models have already demonstrated promising capabilities in summarising content and could potentially assist arbitrators by:

- analysing parties' submissions and providing summaries of key points for each, as well as of each party's overall position and legal arguments;
- assisting arbitrators in researching case histories and identifying relevant evidence for arbitrators to review, and
- accelerating the legal research process by listing out cases and legal authorities cited by the parties (as well as surfacing relevant cases and authorities that the parties may have missed) and analysing trends or tendencies in relevant case law to identify key issues and applicable legal tests.

Of course, any arbitrator worth their salt would ultimately need to review the documents for themselves and conduct their own research, just as they would (or at least should) had they been assisted by a tribunal secretary.[67] But even so, a preliminary AI-generated review and analysis would no doubt be helpful – not only in speeding up the arbitrator's understanding but also by potentially identifying evidence or case law that the arbitrator might otherwise have missed. AI may even be able to add new perspectives to the parties' positions that even their counsel had not thought of.

Sceptics, of course, will claim that AI integration will cause lazy arbitrators to skip any independent review of the record and rely solely on the summaries generated by their AI assistants. As a result, arbitrators would acquire only a superficial understanding of the case rather than the deeper knowledge achievable only by reviewing everything for themselves. Indeed, it goes without saying that arbitrators should retain intellectual ownership of the award and that this requires them not only to review the parties' submissions but also to review, re-review, and re-work any draft awards produced by AI.[68] Just as arbitrators should not confine themselves to considering only what is put forth by counsel in the parties' submissions, they also should not limit themselves to viewing only what was selected by AI for summary. Overall, arbitrators will need to strike a balance between the potential efficiency gains from AI integration and the unique 'human touch' that led them to be appointed in the

67. This is consistent with section 6 of the England and Wales Courts and Tribunals Judiciary's Artificial Intelligence (AI) Guidance for Judicial Office Holders (2023), which states that '[j]udicial office holders are personally responsible for material which is produced in their name' and goes on to note that 'judges are not generally obliged to describe the research or preparatory work which may have been done in order to produce a judgment. Provided these guidelines are appropriately followed, there is no reason why generative AI could not be a potentially useful secondary tool.'

68. *See* section 6 of the England and Wales Courts and Tribunals Judiciary's Artificial Intelligence (AI) Guidance for Judicial Office Holders (2023).

first place. Clear rules and guidelines will also be needed and can likely be modelled on the rules already in place regarding arbitrators' reliance on tribunal secretaries.[69]

If used correctly, AI has the potential to free arbitrators of the busywork currently consuming much of their time and allow them to focus fully on the work that really matters. If anything, that should improve arbitrators' ability to reflect deeply on the legal issues and lead to higher quality awards overall – particularly in complex disputes. And should it so happen that some arbitrators are tempted into overreliance on AI tools, word will no doubt spread quickly throughout the international arbitration community, putting any future appointments in jeopardy.

[C] The Regulatory Landscape

Where technology advances, regulation is sure to follow, and on 13 July 2023, the Cyberspace Administration of China (CAC), along with six other Chinese government agencies, took a swift lead in issuing its Interim Administrative Measures for Generative Artificial Intelligence Services (生成式人工智能服务管理暂行办法).[70] This was followed on 13 March 2024 by the European Parliament's formal adoption of the much-anticipated EU Artificial Intelligence Act.[71] Just two months later, on 17 May 2024, Colorado Governor Jared Polis signed into law Senate Bill 24-205 concerning consumer protections in interactions with AI systems, making Colorado the first U.S. state[72] to adopt broad AI legislation. In addition, legislators in many other jurisdictions are working on similar AI-specific regulations, some of which may altogether prohibit the use of AI in the context of the administration of justice.

The EU AI Act, a landmark piece of legislation for the EU, is the world's first comprehensive regulatory framework on AI and aims to constrain the risks to security and fundamental rights raised by the use of AI systems.[73] In drafting the act, the European Parliament has sought to ensure that all AI systems developed, distributed,

69. In addition to taking inspiration from the England and Wales Courts and Tribunals Judiciary's Artificial Intelligence (AI) Guidance for Judicial Office Holders (2023).
70. 生成式人工智能服务管理暂行办法 (in English: *Interim Administrative Measures for Generative Artificial Intelligence Services*), Cyberspace Administration of China (13 Jul. 2023), https://www.cac.gov.cn/2023-07/13/c_1690898327029107.htm. The Interim Administrative Measures for Generative Artificial Intelligence Services took effect on 15 Aug. 2023.
71. The Act entered into force on 1 Aug. 2024 with a staggered timeline for implementation of its rules and requirements over the course of the next three years.
72. Utah had previously enacted Senate Bill 149 for the Artificial Intelligence Policy Act, which took effect 1 May 2024 and amended the Utah consumer protection and privacy laws to require disclosure of certain uses of AI to consumers, but the Colorado AI Act is the first piece of U.S. legislation to establish broad requirements for developers and deployers of certain AI systems in addition to disclosure requirements for AI systems intended to interact with consumers.
73. Defined in Art. 3(1) of the AI Act as 'a machine-based system that is designed to operate with varying levels of autonomy and that may exhibit adaptiveness after deployment, and that, for explicit or implicit objectives, infers, from the input it receives, how to generate outputs such as predictions, content, recommendations, or decisions that can influence physical or virtual environments.'

and used in the EU are 'safe, transparent, traceable, non-discriminatory, and environmentally friendly'.[74] To this end, the AI Act applies a risk-based approach and defines four levels of risks[75] in AI, which form the basis of its material scope: unacceptable risk,[76] high risk,[77] limited risk,[78] and minimal or no risk.[79]

Territorially, the AI Act applies to providers of AI service systems to EU member states, whether or not the providers are themselves established or located within the EU, as well as to deployers of AI systems established or otherwise located within the EU, importers, distributors, and authorised representatives.[80] In addition, the scope of the Act covers providers and deployers in third countries where the output produced by the AI system is used in the EU.[81]

Of particular interest to the legal profession is the Act's classification of certain AI systems intended to be used in the context of the administration of justice as 'high-risk',[82] which means that providers and deployers of such systems must ensure high levels of transparency and robust governance measures. Though the Act makes no direct mention of arbitration, it does refer to AI systems 'intended to be used by a judicial authority or on its behalf to assist judicial authorities in researching and interpreting facts and the law and in applying the law to a concrete set of facts',[83] further clarifying that 'AI systems intended to be used by alternative dispute resolution bodies for those purposes should also be considered to be high-risk when the outcomes of the alternative dispute resolution proceedings produce legal effects for the parties.'[84] AI tools intended to be used by arbitrators and/or arbitral institutions will almost certainly be captured in this definition of 'high-risk' AI systems and thus be subject to stringent technical and compliance standards such as requirements for detailed record-keeping, 'human oversight', and specific performance metrics.

The requirement for human oversight is particularly onerous and demands that '[h]igh-risk AI systems shall be designed and developed in such a way […] that they can be effectively overseen by natural persons'[85] whilst in use, with oversight measures 'commensurate with the risks, level of autonomy and context of use of the high-risk AI system'[86] either built into the system or 'appropriate to be implemented by

74. *EU AI Act: first regulation on artificial intelligence*, European Parliament (last updated 19 Dec. 2023), https://www.europarl.europa.eu/topics/en/article/20230601STO93804/eu-ai-act-first-regulation-on-artificial-intelligence.
75. Defined in Art. 3(2) of the AI Act as 'the combination of the probability of an occurrence of harm and the severity of that harm.'
76. *See* Art. 5 of the AI Act.
77. *See* Art. 6 of the AI Act.
78. The AI Act offers no clear definition of what constitutes 'limited risk.' However, *see* preamble number 132 and Art. 50 of the AI Act.
79. The AI Act offers no clear definition of what constitutes 'minimal risk' or 'no risk.' However, *see* Art. 2(1) of the AI Act, which excludes 'purely personal non-professional activity' from the material scope of the AI Act.
80. *See* Art. 2 of the AI Act.
81. *Ibid.*
82. *See* preamble number 61 and Annex III, number 8, of the AI Act.
83. *See* preamble number 61.
84. *Ibid.*
85. *See* Art. 14(1) of the AI Act.
86. *See* Art. 14(3) of the AI Act.

the deployer'[87] Amongst other things, such measures must ensure that 'no action or decision is taken by the deployer on the basis of the identification resulting from the system unless that identification has been separately verified and confirmed by at least two natural persons with the necessary competence, training and authority'.[88,89]

Arbitrators and arbitral institutions wishing to make use of AI systems in proceedings within the scope of the AI Act should expect that they will need to observe these requirements. Given the nature of the expert mandate, it seems rather likely that experts appointed to advise the tribunal on matters beyond its expertise will also be captured as deployers in the 'high-risk' classification – particularly where such experts are appointed by the tribunal itself. However, the AI Act provides no guidance as to whether lawyers and law firms acting for clients in arbitration proceedings will be seen to be acting 'on behalf' of tribunals to 'assist' them 'in researching and interpreting facts and the law and in applying the law to a concrete set of facts' when producing legal submissions and/or fact exhibits for submission into the arbitral record. It is not yet known how regulators will approach this issue, but it is worth noting that a broad interpretation may be at risk of clashing with professional regulations and ethical rules, which almost invariably state that lawyers must act 'on behalf of' or as 'representatives of' their clients.[90]

For those covered by the Act's 'high-risk' classification, a potentially helpful mechanism is found in Article 6(3), which sets out exceptions (or 'filters') for AI systems intended to 'perform a narrow procedural task', 'improve the result of a previously completed human activity', 'detect decision-making patterns or deviations from prior decision-making patterns [and] not meant to replace or influence the previously completed human assessment, without proper human review', or 'perform a preparatory task to an assessment relevant for the purposes' of a high-risk activity listed in Annex III of the Act. Whilst the scope of these 'filters' is not yet clear,[91] it is likely that they will include AI models used to structure data, classify documents, review or improve the output of human activity (e.g., by providing stylistic suggestions to a document drafted by a human and/or improving the quality of writing), and review and analyse human decision-making patterns to flag up potential inconsistencies or anomalies (e.g., by identifying logical gaps in an award), as well as tools performing preparatory tasks such as file-handling. This means that the exceptions will likely cover a majority of the use cases considered in this chapter.

87. *Ibid.*
88. *See* Art. 14(5) of the AI Act.
89. Unless 'Union or national law considers the application of this requirement to be disproportionate,' as set out in Art. 14(5) of the AI Act.
90. *See, e.g.*, Art. 3 of the Code of Conduct for the Danish Bar and Law Society (2022), Rule 1 of the Code of Professional Conduct for Members of the Swedish Bar Association (2023), and preamble number 1 of the New York Rules of Professional Conduct (2022), the latter of which suggests in preamble number 3 that 'conflicts [...] among the lawyer's responsibilities to clients [and] to the legal system' must be exercised 'through the exercise of sensitive professional and moral judgment, guided by the basic principles underlying the Rules.'
91. Regulatory guidance will be provided by the European Commission to assist in interpreting the scope of these 'filters.'

It remains to be seen how the EU AI Act will eventually be implemented by the individual Member States and what this will mean in the context of international arbitration. However, as the Act focuses on ensuring the safe technical development and use of AI systems, it will not provide guidance on the specifics around AI use and integration in international arbitration, which is still very much a grey area.

Before the emergence of ChatGPT, the popular opinion in the international arbitration community seems to have been that there was no need for specific regulation on the use of AI. The many new uses now made possible by ChatGPT and other genAI tools have since driven calls for guidelines to address and regulate the use of AI, and this is likely to develop rather rapidly over the coming years. In April 2024, following a lengthy public consultation from August 2023 to February 2024, the Silicon Valley Arbitration & Mediation Center published its SVAMC Guidelines on the Use of Artificial Intelligence in Arbitration,[92] which focuses on: (1) promoting understanding of the uses, limitations, and risks of AI applications; (2) safeguarding confidentiality; (3) disclosure and protection of records; (4) duty of competence or diligence in the use of AI; (5) respect for the integrity of the proceedings and evidence; (6) non-delegation of decision-making responsibilities; and (7) respect for due process. The guidelines offer broad guidance intended to assist participants in arbitrations in navigating the potential risks and uses of AI, though they do not set out detailed standards or requirements for AI applications.

Beyond the SVAMC, there is currently little guidance to be found within the major institutional arbitration rules,[93] none of which address the use of AI or the challenges and procedural issues likely to arise as lawyers begin to incorporate AI tools within their workflows – and it appears that many would prefer to keep it that way. Indeed, BCLP's November 2023 survey found that, whilst 63% of the respondents were generally in favour of regulatory measures on the use of AI in international arbitration, only 26% believed that such regulation should be embedded within institutional arbitration rules.[94] The suggestion seems to be that institutions are not generally viewed as the best choice for dealing with the challenge of regulating AI. But even so, it would likely be useful for future amendments to the major institutional arbitration rules to include at least some general guidelines regarding the use of AI, particularly on issues like data protection, cybersecurity, and ethical concerns, which would benefit from a systemic solution. Other (more specific) AI risks may instead need to be dealt with on an ad hoc basis and are perhaps best left for arbitrators to address through procedural orders.

Overall, it seems likely that regulation of the use of AI in international arbitration will come from many different sources, including national legislation, institutional rules, and tribunal orders, all of which will come together to form a patchwork of rules

92. The guidelines are referenced throughout this chapter, as applicable.
93. That is, the ICDR Rules 2021, JAMS International Arbitration Rules 2021, LCIA Rules 2020, ICC Rules 2021, SCC Rules 2023, HKIAC Rules 2018, SIAC Rules 2016 (and the Draft 7th Edition of the SIAC Rules shared by the SIAC on 22 Aug. 2023), JCAA Rules 2021, DIAC Rules 2022, and UNCITRAL Rules 2021.
94. BCLP, *supra* n. 8, p. 27.

that parties and arbitrators will need to consider to ensure that proceedings are conducted in accordance with the laws of the seat and the place of enforcement and that any final awards are enforceable. Similarly, arbitration practitioners will need to ensure that any use of AI complies with applicable regulations, not only in their home jurisdiction but potentially also at the seat and place of enforcement. As the regulatory landscape evolves, it is also worth noting that differences in regulations across jurisdictions may be grounds for parties to resist enforcement of an award on the grounds of equal treatment and/or equality of arms if AI regulations in their respective home jurisdictions mean that one party had access to AI tools whilst the other did not. Whether or not this is likely to happen (and whether or not such challenges would stand any chance of success) will depend on the legal and regulatory developments in the coming years.

AI use is also likely to give rise to ethical considerations for counsel with regard to their duties towards their clients and the tribunal. Regulators such as bar associations and law societies around the world are already considering the need for specific guidance on AI use. In March 2022, the Council of Bars and Law Societies of Europe issued guidance on the use of AI-based tools by law firms and lawyers in the EU,[95] and in August 2023, the American Bar Association announced the creation of a task force to examine the impact of AI on law practice and the ethical implications for lawyers.[96] As counsel in international arbitration proceedings are typically bound by the ethical rules applicable in their home jurisdictions regardless of the seat of the arbitration or the substantive law of the dispute, they will be required to observe any AI-specific guidance or rules issued by their regulation authority, even if the same rules do not apply to opposing counsel. Such rules may require lawyers to disclose the use of AI to their clients and will almost certainly require them to verify any output produced by AI tools to ensure accountability and compliance with their ethical duties. In some circumstances, the use of AI to perform legal research or answer factual enquiries may not be in line with other duties lawyers have towards their clients, including the duty of confidentiality.

§6.03 PART II LONG-TERM PROSPECTS: THE FUTURE OF ARBITRATION

Once the international arbitration community (and the broader legal profession) begins to truly embrace AI and integrate it into day-to-day practice, the potential impact and possibilities are virtually endless and extremely exciting, to say the least – particularly with the dawn of quantum computing on the horizon, which will significantly reduce the training time required for the development of new AI and thus further accelerate

95. *See* the Council of Bars and Law Societies of Europe and the European Lawyers Foundation's 'Guide on the use of Artificial Intelligence-based tools by lawyers and law firms in the EU' (2022).
96. *ABA forms task force to study impact of artificial intelligence on the legal profession*, American Bar Association (28 Aug. 2023), https://www.americanbar.org/news/abanews/aba-news-archives/2023/08/aba-task-force-impact-of-ai/.

the developments within AI and other new technologies. The following pages will consider three particularly exciting prospects.

Section §6.03[A] addresses the time and cost savings likely to be achieved through AI integration. *Section* §6.03[B] deals with the prospect of so-called blockchain arbitration. Finally, *section* §6.03[C] reflects on the potential for AI to promote the creation of a truly global profession.

[A] Time and Cost Savings: Faster, Better, and Cheaper Arbitration?

Though lauded for its efficiency compared to the traditional litigation system, arbitration is still often a lengthy and expensive process, with parties spending months, if not years, resolving their disputes. However, with AI-driven legal tech tools poised to take over much of the time-consuming work of document review, data analysis, and legal research currently done by (junior) lawyers, it seems clear that AI and other new technologies will soon bring considerable time and cost savings as hours of manpower are replaced by mere minutes or seconds of processing time. The following pages will take a look at some of the greatest prospects for long-term efficiency gains.

Enabling Increased Complexity Without Increasing Costs

GenAI's ability to rapidly analyse and interpret vast volumes of data has the potential to accelerate the expedition of routine tasks at a rate that cannot be achieved by human effort. In particular, automation of tasks like document review and legal research will allow both counsel and arbitrators to take on larger and more complex cases by freeing up human resources for those aspects of the arbitration process that cannot (yet) be undertaken by AI systems, including effective preparation of evidence, advocacy and arbitrators' decision-making. The availability of AI tools may also encourage arbitrators to take on cases requiring greater technical or industry expertise. In particular, AI has the potential to assist arbitrators with objective analysis and assessment of expert reports, which would be particularly helpful in 'battle of the experts' scenarios. Finally, AI is likely to enable an increased level of sophistication and accuracy in complex delay and quantum analyses, including scenarios requiring, e.g., counterfactual simulation or regression analysis.

Facilitating Settlement Negotiations Through Outcome Prediction

Another promising application for genAI's capacity for data analysis is the potential for AI to predict the likely outcome of a current case by analysing historical data – including an estimate of the potential costs. With recent advances in machine learning algorithms and predictive analytics, this is likely to be possible in the very near future. As early as 2016, researchers had developed an AI model capable of predicting the outcome of cases before the European Court of Human Rights with 79% accuracy.[97] And the following year, in 2017, another research team announced that it had

97. *AI predicts outcomes of human rights trials*, University College London (24 Oct. 2016), https://www.ucl.ac.uk/news/2016/oct/ai-predicts-outcomes-human-rights-trials.

developed a program which could predict with 70.2% accuracy whether the US Supreme Court would follow or reverse a judgment.[98] In straightforward commercial disputes, where similar circumstances have been subject to consideration in previous cases, outcome prediction software will likely be helpful in providing parties with an incentive to settle matters at an early stage of the proceedings.

Possible Use During (Physical) Hearings

The potential use cases for AI during hearings are equally intriguing and could significantly reduce the administrative burden for tribunals and institutions. It seems a matter of time before AI-driven transcription systems become universal, leveraging speech recognition algorithms to capture and transcribe hearings in real-time, thereby improving the accuracy and completeness of the record and potentially eliminating (or at least considerably reducing) the need for manual notetaking. For counsel, another interesting prospect is the possibility of deploying AI to review transcripts in real-time and search for legal authorities, arguments, or evidence (whether on the record or in the public domain) to support or challenge statements made by opposing counsel, witnesses, or experts. Of course, lawyers would need to be mindful of any risk of hallucinations so that they do not inadvertently pass on inaccurate AI responses in the heat of the battle – and arbitrators must equally be careful not to miss any potential inaccuracies in AI-generated transcripts, such that witnesses are not mistakenly cited as having answered 'yes' where they, in fact, said 'no'. However, since such errors are also occasionally made by humans, it is very likely that AI court reporters will soon be just as reliable as their human counterparts, if not more.

Virtual Hearings

Much has been written already about the possibility of virtual hearings replacing traditional oral hearings,[99] but so far, this prospect does not (yet) seem to have gained widespread acceptance within the international arbitration community. One significant challenge is the lack of the required technical framework conditions. Whilst law firms and most offices (whether corporate or at home) are likely to be equipped with the hardware needed for virtual hearings, considerable data protection and cybersecurity concerns remain.[100] But even so, there is good reason to view the digitalisation of arbitration proceedings as an opportunity rather than a threat. First, virtual hearings allow for greater flexibility by eliminating the need for travel and are therefore likely to be a very effective tool in preventing lengthy postponement and scheduling processes, especially in urgent proceedings. In addition, the possibility of digital participation would save substantial resources for individuals who only attend the proceedings for a short time, such as witnesses and experts. This aligns well with the general principle

98. Daniel Martin Katz, Michael J. Bommarito & Josh Blackman, *A general approach for predicting the behavior of the Supreme Court of the United States*, PLoS ONE 12(4): e0174698 (2017) https://doi.org/10.1371/journal.pone.0174698.
99. *See, e.g.*, Mo Egan & Hong-Lin Yu, *Intersecting and dissecting confidentiality and data protection in online arbitration*, Journal of Business 2022, 2, 135-163, for a look at the data privacy and cybersecurity issues raised by 'the digitalisation of international arbitration.'
100. *Ibid.*

of speedy justice which is a cornerstone of the arbitral system. In addition, virtual hearings can promote inclusivity and increase access to justice by making it easier for individuals with limited mobility, or who are otherwise unable to travel, to take part in hearings. A clear negative effect, however, is the risk that the oral hearing, which is viewed by many as the centrepiece of any legal action, may be stripped of some of its authority if taking place via video conferencing.

Many lawyers will also argue that body language, such as facial expressions and gestures, is of great importance for their oral advocacy. Similarly, virtual hearings would make it more difficult for both counsel and arbitrators to rely on physical factors in assessing the credibility of a party or witness.[101] This may not be a bad thing, however, and could even increase objectivity in arbitrators' decision-making processes by eliminating physical factors likely to give rise to bias or other preconceived notions. If virtual hearings are ever embraced by the arbitration community, one could imagine that it might even become standard for parties and witnesses to use 'avatars' that obscure their gender and physical appearance to promote objectivity in the proceedings. Whilst this is unlikely to be a viable option for counsel, arbitrators, and experts, who tend to meet occasionally in the wider legal community and may have long-term working relationships, there seems to be no reason why individuals who appear at hearings as party representatives or witnesses should not be able to assume an avatar to protect themselves from bias.

[B] Blockchain Arbitration

In addition to the many potential uses of AI considered above, another breakthrough that promises to revolutionise the practice of international arbitration is blockchain technology. Blockchain technology emerged in 2009 as the public ledger for transactions made with Bitcoin,[102] the world's first cryptocurrency. In 2014, Canadian programmer Vitalik Buterin pioneered the next great innovation in blockchain when he founded Ethereum, now the second-most valuable cryptocurrency by market capitalisation, and introduced the so-called smart contracts.[103]

In short (and very simplified),[104] the blockchain system can be described as a cryptographically secured chain of information (essentially a digital database of sorts) that works by adding 'blocks' of data to the digital ledger in chronological order. Unlike a traditional database, which usually structures data into tables, a blockchain collects

101. Though AI-powered gesture recognition tools may be able to advise counsel and arbitrators to potential false testimony.

102. Bitcoin was invented in 2008 by one or more anonymous coders known by the pseudonym 'Satoshi Nakamoto'.

103. Vitalik Buterin, *Ethereum: A Next Generation Smart Contract & Decentralized Application Platform* (December 2014), https://ethereum.org/content/whitepaper/whitepaper-pdf/Ethereum_Whitepaper_-_Buterin_2014.pdf.

104. *See, e.g.*, Michael Crosby, Nachiappan, Pradhan Pattanayak, Sanjeev Verma & Vignesh Kalyanaraman, *Blockchain Technology: Beyond Bitcoin*, UC Berkeley Sutardja Center for Entrepreneurship & Technology (16 Oct. 2015), for a comprehensive description of blockchain technology.

information into groups (the eponymous blocks), each of which holds a set of information. Once a block is filled to its storage capacity, it is closed and provided with an exact timestamp, after which it is linked to the previous block. Thus, the blocks come together to form a chain, with each block containing the data of the previous block in its hash. The hash algorithm protects the data inside each block from being replicated. This makes the blocks impenetrable such that once added to the chain, they can no longer be altered or deleted unless all users agree to the change. If a change is agreed, this is reflected by the addition of a new block. The original block, however, remains unaltered and so creates a non-corruptible audit trail that protects against tampering. Blockchain therefore comes with built-in data security that eliminates human error - and because blockchain is built on a distributed model, there is no central point of failure, which makes it highly reliable.

In the context of international arbitration, blockchain technology has sparked discussions of 'blockchain arbitration',[105] a futuristic concept that promises a paradigm shift in dispute resolution. Since blockchain technology makes it possible to process transactions quickly and at low cost, blockchain-based platforms could allow parties and arbitrators to collect, store, and process large amounts of data in a more effective and secure manner than is possible today. The parties would be able to submit all notices, legal submissions, and evidence on the platform, providing them and the tribunal with a complete digital record that is easily searchable and fully verified. As users can control who is able to access the blockchain, such platforms would ensure much greater privacy than exchanging documents via email as is common today - though data privacy is, of course, unlikely to ever be fully guaranteed so long as third-party suppliers are involved.

Another key advantage of blockchain technology is the potential for smart contracts to facilitate the enforcement of arbitral awards by automatically executing awards once the proceedings are complete. Smart contracts are, in essence, electronic transaction protocols programmed to self-execute with the fulfilment of certain predetermined conditions. Simply put, this means that smart contracts offer a form of mathematically secured escrow arrangement. Since enforcement is not facilitated by arbitral institutions in traditional arbitration proceedings and can be a very lengthy and expensive process, automatic enforcement is likely to be highly valued by disputants. This would also reduce or even eliminate the need for securities such as bank guarantees and performance bonds, which would lead to a significant reduction in costs for parties and ease the potential financial strain of arbitration. And because neither party can tamper with the data in the blockchain, there is (at least in theory) limited risk of the award being set aside for fraud, material mistakes, or imperfect form.

In fairly straightforward commercial disputes involving one-off transactions, a smart contract is able to cover the entire spectrum of outcome scenarios between no payment on the one end and the release of full payment on the other. A significant challenge, however, is that smart contracts may not adapt easily to more complex,

105. *See, e.g.*, Dirk Wiegandt, *Blockchain and Smart Contracts and the Role of Arbitration*, Journal of International Arbitration, 39(5), 671-690 (2022) https://doi.org/10.54648/joia2022029.

higher-value disputes within, e.g., the construction and energy sectors, which often involve several contracts, parties, claims and counterclaims. Such transactions may not translate well into simple computer languages – at least until quantum computing becomes widely available. Another challenge is that all stakeholders may not be familiar – or indeed comfortable – with using blockchain and smart contracts and so may not be willing to rely on the technology. As blockchain would eliminate the need for oversight at key stages of the administration of the proceedings, the traditional role of arbitration institutions is also likely to be reduced, which may lead to further credibility concerns. In addition, self-executing smart contracts raise the risk of a potential loss of party autonomy as once entered, they do not give parties the freedom to explore other possibilities, including a potential settlement. Parties may also lose the ability to ask courts to refuse enforcement of awards despite having reasonable grounds, e.g., because of due process violations. It will remain to be seen how such issues will be resolved as the potential of blockchain technology continues to unfold in the coming years.

[C] AI as the Driver of a Truly Global Profession

Because AI systems are created and programmed by humans, who are naturally prone to bias, there is a significant risk that AI algorithms may also be inadvertently designed to replicate conscious and unconscious human biases. Indeed, biases and stereotypes are deeply ingrained in the fabric of our societies and in our ways of thinking, affecting how we perceive and interact with the world around us. They are so subtle that they are sometimes hard to detect, and it often takes considerable time and effort to build awareness of one's own biases. But what if human bias is proactively and consciously acknowledged, addressed, and challenged in the development of new AI? Could AI then have the potential to eliminate bias altogether? This is no doubt one of the most exciting prospects of the 'AI revolution', and therefore the final question considered in this chapter.

The first step (and a substantial hurdle) is to make sure that the data used to train the AI algorithm is itself free of bias – or, rather, that the algorithm is programmed to recognise bias in that training data and filter it out of its decision-making process. With the AI models currently available, this de-biasing process would likely require humans to first identify and categorise potentially biased language and then teach the algorithm to flag words, phrases, and expressions that imply bias. As this would require substantial human intervention it is unlikely to scale easily at present, but as more de-biased training data becomes available, that should considerably accelerate the development of bias-free AI.

In the context of international arbitration, which brings together people of many different nationalities, cultures, personal values and beliefs, the impact is likely to be enormous. Indeed, AI could open the door to a truly global, transnational framework for dispute resolution. There is even the possibility that AI could drive the development of a transnational public policy, which would enable the international arbitration community to assist in defining and protecting fundamental public interests and values viewed as essential in a globalised economy, regardless of differences in national laws and regulations. This would allow arbitrators to develop public policy safeguards based on the broad (albeit not entirely unanimous) consensus amongst states to condemn certain practices, at least within international economic transactions and related regulations (including competition laws, securities regulations, and embargos), where the binding power of the arbitral system is already accepted by courts in many jurisdictions.

In addition, AI could be a driver in developing a truly diverse, inclusive, and equitable profession by eliminating bias in the appointment of arbitrators and increasing access to the profession. The process of selecting an arbitrator is currently based on subjective (and thus inherently biased) methods such as reputation, word of mouth, and simple Google or LinkedIn searches. In the not-so-distant future, however, AI-driven platforms will likely enable parties to quickly and efficiently gather information and feedback about arbitrators worldwide. Based on that data, AI tools can then provide recommendations for qualified candidates whilst promoting objectivity and diversity by filtering out irrelevant factors such as gender, ethnicity, personal background, social identity, socio-economic circumstances, and perhaps even nationality. Unlike human lawyers, whose choices are likely to be influenced by (conscious and unconscious) biases, AI tools can guide parties to the choices deemed to be objectively best suited, regardless of what has usually been done in the past.

AI integration is also likely to be key in eliminating existing language and cultural barriers. Like the fictional 'Babel fish' used by intergalactic travellers in Douglas Adams's science fiction classic 'The Hitchhiker's Guide to the Galaxy', AI-powered live translation tools may soon allow parties, counsel, and arbitrators to communicate with ease despite each speaking in a different language. Such tools may even be trained to recognise and accurately translate the intended meaning of any statements made, taking into consideration cultural differences and customs. This would remove barriers to effective communication and understanding, democratising advocacy for counsel of all nationalities and aiding arbitrators' understanding of the facts by allowing parties and witnesses to give testimony in their native languages (and free from the subjectivity of a human interpreter). In time, such tools could be drivers in creating a genuinely international community where arbitration can truly take place anywhere in the world and involve individuals of any and all backgrounds.

CHAPTER 7

From Supreme Court to Arbitrator: A Challenging but Enjoyable Journey

Lord Hope of Craighead KT

§7.01 INTRODUCTION

I spent twenty-four years of my professional life sitting as a judge before my retirement from that role in 2013. I then turned to sitting as an international arbitrator as a means of occupying some of my spare time during my retirement.

It was never my intention to become a full-time arbitrator, even if I could attract enough business to make that a possibility. I had various other interesting things to do for which I wanted to remain available. Arbitration was to be, for me, very much a part-time occupation, and so it has remained. But, I have been fortunate enough to receive several appointments over the years since that retirement. So, I have, at least to some extent, been able to adapt to this new role. I was soon to find that, although these two methods of applying one's mind to resolving disputes may appear to be very similar, there are some significant differences. I found that the path from one role to the other was not quite as easy as it might seem to be.

I should start by saying a bit more about my role as a judge. It was an unusual career, even for someone who has practised law throughout his career in the United Kingdom. I did not seek or apply to be a judge. Until quite recently, the responsibility for making appointments to the senior judiciary was vested in the Prime Minister on the recommendation of the principal government law officers – the Lord Chancellor for England and Wales and the Lord Advocate for Scotland. Applications were not invited or expected. If, like me, you were among those who were qualified for appointment, you just had to wait for this to happen. In my case, when the invitation came, it was wholly unexpected. I was invited by Mrs Thatcher, then the Prime Minister, to accept appointment direct from the Bar in Scotland, where I had been practising as a self-employed advocate for the previous twenty-four years, to be the President of the Court of Session, Scotland's highest court.

I was very fortunate. I do not believe that this promotion would have been extended to me under the current system, by which appointments are made on the recommendation of a judicial appointments committee following a process of application and interviews. It would never have occurred to me, as someone who had never sat as a judge of any kind, to apply to be appointed directly to the position of the Court of Session's President. As it happened in my case, the Lord Advocate provided the Prime Minister with a list of three names, to which he attached his own assessment of each candidate's suitability for the appointment. It was based on that assessment that Mrs Thatcher chose me. It was then up to me to prove that I was capable of performing the duties of that office.

My function as the Court's President was to sit as an appellate judge, sitting with two and sometimes four other colleagues. There were many interesting issues that I had to deal with in that capacity, but they were always issues of law. It was not our function, as appellate judges, to take evidence from witnesses. And I never sat on my own as a trial judge. So I did not have at any time during my judicial career to assess a witness's credibility. But, the judgments which I delivered always had to be based on an assessment and understanding of the facts with which we were presented. I had the advantage of many years of practice as a trial lawyer behind me when I was performing that exercise.

Then, after sitting for seven years as President of that Court in Edinburgh, I moved to London. I was appointed to sit as a Lord of Appeal in the House of Lords at Westminster. One of its functions at that time was to act as the court of final appeal for the whole of the United Kingdom. So here I was, sitting again as an appellate judge, this time as one of a panel of five and sometimes seven members of the House of Lords' Appellate Committee. Then, in 2009, after thirteen years in that role, I moved again when the appellate role of the House of Lords was transferred to a newly created UK Supreme Court. I remained as an appellate judge in London, but I was now sitting as the Deputy President of that court. It was from that position that I retired after a further four years as an appellate judge.

At no time during my twenty-four years as a judge was it open to me to accept an appointment as an arbitrator. The work I was doing was too demanding for that. In any case, I was required by the nature of my employment to devote my full time to the job for which I was being paid. I had done some arbitration work in Scotland before I was appointed to be a judge. But that was a long time ago. In turning to international arbitration after my retirement, I was, in effect, venturing into new and uncertain territory.

§7.02 MY CV

My first move was to apply to join a set of chambers in London as a door tenant. Unlike some of my English judicial colleagues who turned to international arbitration on their retirement and were able to return to the chambers from which they had practised as barristers before becoming a judge, I had to start anew. My place of work before becoming a judge had been in Edinburgh. But there is not yet much of a market for international arbitration in Scotland, so I decided to place myself in London. I was greatly helped by the fact that Brick Court Chambers accepted my application. I did not have much to offer them other than the fact that I had been a judge at the highest level for so many years. I suppose it was my reputation as a judge that persuaded them to accept me. I had no background as an arbitrator to offer them. But they were kind enough to overlook that fact. I was introduced to the clerk who managed their arbitration business. She gave me a warm welcome. The reality of the task that lay before me was made plain, however, when she asked me to prepare a CV for publication on their website.

This was a bit of a challenge. It was never our practice as judges to prepare CVs. We did not need to advertise ourselves. Indeed, during my time as an advocate, before I became a judge, any form of self-advertisement was forbidden by our professional conduct rules. So I was not practised in the art. I was a beginner. Furthermore, I did not have much to say about myself beyond a listing of the various positions I had held as a judge and a brief reference to aspects of my practice before I became a judge. I did not think that it was relevant to attempt to list the various judgments about arbitration in which I had participated, which included the well-known cases of *Fiona Trust* and *Dallah.*[1] What was being looked for was my experience as an arbitrator. It was, of course, not thinkable that I would just invent one or two entries to try to exaggerate what little I had to say about myself. I looked at some of the CVs that were available under the names of other members of my chambers who were in active practice as international arbitrators. That was enough to show that I would be at a serious disadvantage in the open market until I had at least a few appointments to list under my name.

Now, several years later, I have a list which I can publish, thanks to a number of appointments which have come my way as a result of personal contacts. The list is still very short, but at least it is a start. Furthermore, I can now claim to have had enough experience to venture a few observations about how, in practice, sitting and working as an arbitrator differs from sitting and working as a judge.

The lesson I take from this is that one's CV matters in a way that was entirely alien to me and was indeed entirely contrary to my instincts when I was a judge. But it is an essential aspect of life as a professional arbitrator for reasons that I fully understand. It is, after all, up to those who are advising the parties to an agreement to refer their disputes to arbitration to justify their suggestions as to whom they should seek to appoint as their arbitrators by reference to their qualifications and experience. Especially in the international field, this cannot be done by word of mouth alone. It requires a demonstration of what candidates for appointment have to offer by reference to what they have said about themselves in their CVs.

---

1. *Fiona Trust & Holding Corporation v. Privalov and Others* [2007] UKHL 40; *Dallah Estate and Tourism Holding Company v. The Ministry of Religious Affairs, Government of Pakistan* [2010] UKSC 46.

§7.03 THE PANEL

Throughout my time as a judge, I sat with other judges with whom I worked day after day and whose experience and character I knew very well. It was my responsibility to decide who was to sit with me when I was President of the Court of Session in Scotland, and I shared that responsibility with the President of the UK Supreme Court when I was its Deputy President. Almost all the judges with whom I worked in these courts were permanent members of the court in which I was sitting. So, my relationship with them was a continuous one. We met frequently, and there was never any difficulty in maintaining contact with them when this was needed. Moreover, as the numbers at my level in each court were not large, it was a closed community. There were normally only seven other judges at the appellate level with whom I could work in the court in Scotland, and there are only twelve Justices on the UK Supreme Court.

One of the pleasures of moving to the field of international arbitration is the opportunity that it gives to meet and work with a much wider circle of experienced practitioners. This presented me with new challenges. The majority of those with whom I have worked as arbitrators have been English, but I have worked with two from Canada, one from Sudan, one from St Lucia and one from Trinidad and Tobago. In each case, however, it was for one arbitration only. We were starting from scratch in each case, and there was no continuity. Much of our contact before we met to conduct the hearing was by email or, when these systems became readily available, by Teams or Zoom.

Remote working of that kind is easy if the person with whom the contact is made is someone you already know well. One has to be so much more careful when dealing in that way with people whom you do not know. Of course, things improve when you meet and discuss things face to face. But even then, I sometimes found that time pressures left little time to get to know my colleagues well enough to be at ease with them. Such lack of ease affected the quality of our decision-making, which left me with the feeling that I had not given my best to the process.

I was fortunate in the case, which I shared over a prolonged period with colleagues from St Lucia and Trinidad. We decided at an early stage to meet over a period of four days in Port of Spain for a two-day preliminary hearing and a site visit. The site visit took us far from civilisation into what was rightly described to me as 'the jungle'. After a long and rather bumpy drive, we inspected a variety of installations located in a dense forest beneath which was in an extensive oilfield. This was a valuable bonding process.

Shortly afterwards, COVID-19 reduced us, like everyone else, to remote working as we took the parties to the arbitration through the preliminary stages prior to taking evidence. We had then to conduct a fourteen-day hearing by Zoom with counsel working in Trinidad and London and witnesses speaking to us from various places in the UK and North America. I do not think that we would have been as relaxed as we were throughout that process had we not met and got to know each other beforehand. It was not an easy case, but we were able to reach a unanimous decision in a reasonable time without too much difficulty.

The lesson I take from this is that it is worth spending time to get to know one's colleagues and to feel at ease with them, before getting into the hearing and its aftermath. That was new to me, as I never had that problem when I was sitting in my courts as a judge. Much of the preliminary business has to be conducted online. That saves time and costs. But that is no substitute for the benefits that are to be derived from personal contact, especially with people you have never met.

§7.04 THE INSTITUTIONS

Two of my arbitrations, including the first, were what are best described as ad hoc. With the agreement of the parties, we applied the UNCITRAL arbitration rules. But all the other aspects of the procedure were for us to work out among ourselves. We did not see this as a problem, as we had the advantage in each case, as we had all been judges with many years of judicial experience in common law courts behind us. We stuck to what we knew in those cases, and we did not feel that we needed guidance from anyone else. But, I have had to understand and work with institutional rules in each of my other cases. For me, as a former judge, that was a new and not always comfortable experience.

I am not in the least adverse to the need for rules. On the contrary, much of my time on the courts on which I have served was taken up with keeping our rules of court up-to-date. In the case of the UK Supreme Court, I was closely involved in the formulation of its court's rules and practice directions when that new court was being set up before it opened in 2009. I had the same responsibility when I was appointed Chief Justice of the newly created Abu Dhabi Global Market Courts eight years ago. What was new to me was the people to whom these rules were addressed. In my judicial capacity, I was making, revising or creating rules that were to be observed by someone else. These were the litigants and counsel who were appearing before us in our courts. In the case of the institutions, however, the rules were addressed, in part, to me. It was my responsibility as an arbitrator to read, understand and observe what they were telling me to do.

The first institution whose rules I had to work with was the International Court of Arbitration (ICC). For the most part, its Rules caused me no difficulty. They provide a well-designed template of rules, whose object and effect is to set and maintain a sound system of working for all who make use of them. They are particularly helpful for those who need that kind of guidance, and they do not present any obstacles to those whose background is that of litigation in the courts. But I was surprised by the extent to which the proceedings were subject to the supervision of the Court itself. The most surprising was the provision in what is now Article 34 of the Rules that, before signing any award, the arbitrators must submit it in draft form to the Court. The draft is then open to the making by the Court of modifications as to its form and, without affecting the substance of the arbitrators' liberty of decision, to the drawing of attention by it to points of substance too. Then there is the direction that no award shall be rendered by the arbitral tribunal until it has been approved by the Court as to its form.

I have to confess that this provision did not sit easily with my many years of working as a judge in my own courts. It is true that our practice in the UK Supreme Court was to show our judgments in draft to our court reporter before they were made public. But this was so that they could be checked over for any possible misprints, incorrect references or other mistakes of that kind. We did not expect the reporter to raise any points of substance with us. We had already raised them with the other members of the court before finalising our judgment. The provisions in Article 34 took me into new and uncertain territory.

I was also surprised by what happened when we submitted our award in that case to the Court for scrutiny. Perhaps we were unlucky, but the process took a remarkably long time, given the quality of the modifications that came out of it. Almost nothing of any consequence was raised with us by the official who scrutinised our draft award. That this was so was due very largely to the meticulous care that our chairman took when he was preparing the draft. He recorded each stage in the procedure from start to finish in scrupulous detail. It was obvious to me that had he not done this, our draft would have been regarded as defective and open to many more modifications for us to consider than was in fact the case. His careful attention to all those details, as he built up his draft step by step throughout the proceedings, saved us a lot of bother in the end. But this was a very different process from that which I was used to following as a judge. I felt that I was having to devote more attention to the procedure than to the reasoning behind the substance of our decision.

I was to find out later that the ICC's approach to supervision of the award is not universally followed. The rules of the International Centre for Settlement of Investment Disputes (the ICSID), with which I am working at present, do not require the draft award to be submitted to the Centre for scrutiny. Nor do the London Court of International Arbitration Rules (the LCIA). It is no doubt true that scrutiny of the award by the ICC ensures a high standard of the writing of awards. But I wondered whether too much emphasis was demonstrated in my case on a detailed narrative of the procedure, as compared with the attention that seemed to have been paid to the reasoning that led us to our decision.

§7.05 THE PROCEEDINGS

With very rare exceptions, all the proceedings in which I participated as a judge were held in public. Article 6 of the ECHR requires this to be so, but the tradition in the UK of holding our court proceedings in public was established long before it became a party to the European Convention. This applies throughout the proceedings from the earliest stages in the taking of decisions as to points of procedure to the delivery of judgments in open court and their publication. Only in very rare cases, usually for reasons of national security, is it open to the court to go into what are described as closed proceedings. An important aspect of that way of working is that the judge or judges are normally given a position of pre-eminence in the courtroom. And they are usually dressed in some kind of uniform that distinguishes them from those who appear before them to argue the case as advocates on behalf of the litigants.

The fact that the process of arbitration is, from start to finish, confidential is perhaps the feature that distinguishes it most from my previous existence as a judge. As to procedure, in my own case, the contrast with the way we conducted our proceedings in court in the House of Lords and the UK Supreme Court is not that great. In the House of Lords, we, as the Law, Lords sat as members of a committee, its Appellate Committee. We did not wear any uniform. We were dressed in business clothes, just like the members of any other committee of the House. Furthermore, the room in which we sat was not like a courtroom at all. It was a committee room. We sat at a table which was at the same level as the tables occupied by the counsel who were appearing before us. When our appellate jurisdiction was transferred to the newly established Supreme Court, we decided to adopt the same arrangement. The justices in its courtrooms sit at the same level as counsel and they are dressed in business attire, as too are counsel. So, to the casual observer - if one can imagine such a person as being present in an arbitration - there is a very close affinity between what I was used to as a judge and what I now find myself engaged in when sitting as an arbitrator.

There are, however, some very important differences. The first is that we, as arbitrators, do not have the authority of a court behind us. This means that there is an edge, a tension, that is present in all aspects of court proceedings that is missing in an arbitration. Of course, everyone who appears before a court or a panel of arbitrators must be given a fair hearing. But courts exist to serve the public, and they are subject to many demands on their time. Timetables when set must be adhered to. The convenience of the parties must give way to what the court considers to be the best use of its time. The opportunities that exist for challenging an award or refusing its recognition or enforcement under Article V of the New York Convention[2] are different from those in the case of judgments issued by a court. Arbitrators have to be very much more careful as to the way they conduct the proceedings and the way they treat the parties that appear before them than a judge has to be when sitting in his own court.

Then there is the relationship with the advocates and what, as an arbitrator, one expects of them. In the case of a judge, it is very much at arm's length. The judge and the advocate enter and leave by separate doors. There is no opportunity for a casual conversation between them. Indeed, if any of the advocates happen to meet the judge while the hearing is in progress, any contact between them is kept to a minimum. Keeping one's distance is regarded as necessary to preserve the judge's impartiality.

I soon found that a more relaxed approach was possible when sitting as an arbitrator. This is partly because of the physical layout in the hearing room, which tends to bring the arbitrator closer to the parties than is the case in a courtroom. One can have a conversation with them in a way that a judge cannot do. But it is also due to the nature of arbitration itself. An arbitrator has been described in one of the textbooks with which I was familiar when practising in Scotland as 'an equitable judge ... presiding over an amicable tribunal, in the exercise of a private and voluntary jurisdiction'.[3] It seems to me that the word 'amicable', although written well over 150

2. The New York Convention on the Recognition and Enforcement of Foreign Awards, New York, 19 Jun. 1958.
3. JM Bell, *Law of Arbitration in Scotland,* 2nd ed. (1877), p. 15.

years ago, captures the essence of the difference between a judge and an arbitrator. Arbitration is an amicable process of resolving disputes. Court proceedings, on the other hand, are never amicable.

That is not to say that the process is entirely without formality. Of course, formality, to some degree, is a necessary part of preserving a proper balance between the parties in the conduct of the process. Institutional rules have their part in this process. So too are steps that an arbitrator can take to encourage economy on the part of the advocates in their presentation of their arguments, both written and oral. It is normal practice in the UK Supreme Court to set limits on the number of pages and on the time each side has for the presentation of its oral argument. This is done by directions issued by the court, with which the parties must comply.

The taking of such steps in an arbitration cannot be compelled in the same way. They should normally be done with the agreement of the parties. But that should not be too difficult to achieve. The art of advocacy, after all, is adapting one's presentation to what will best appeal to and hold the attention of the audience. Suggestions by the arbitrators as to what would suit them best should be listened to with close attention. Twenty or thirty pages of written argument are more likely to achieve this than sixty or eighty. So too, in the case of the oral presentation, adhering to an agreed allocation of time between the parties will work to the parties' benefit in a way that an uncontrolled and prolonged presentation will never do.

§7.06 THE AWARD

Here too, the difference between the public nature of court proceedings and the confidential nature of arbitration makes itself felt, as does the need to provide details of the proceedings from start to finish within the award itself.

The judgments that are given by a judge in open court are addressed to a wide audience. In addition to the parties themselves, it includes all those who may be interested in reading it for a variety of reasons, such as other judges, academics, law students, the general public and the press. When they are being given at the highest level, which is what I was used to, they have an important function too. Both English and Scots common law derive their strength and their consistency from the operation of the doctrine of precedent. Each judgment takes its place in the hierarchy of courts according to this doctrine. Every judgment is a binding precedent as regards all courts below that from which it emanated. The certainty that the doctrine gives to the system is central to the existence of the rule of law in those jurisdictions, as they are not bound by codes. If this were not so, the law in their case would become unpredictable, changing from court to court and case by case.

This imposes a particular responsibility on the appellate judges sitting, as I was, at the highest level. We were, in each case, in effect, making law. A friend of mine who is a professor at the University of Passau found this hard to accept. 'The duty of a judge is to apply the law, not to make it', she said. That is not, however, the way the common law operates. As a consequence, it is the responsibility of those who are writing judgments that are to be given in the UK Supreme Court to set out the reasons for the decision in considerable detail. The analysis may involve distinguishing the case from any previous case in which a similar issue arose for decision. It will also provide guidance for the judge in the lower courts, for whom it will be a binding precedent.

Freed of that responsibility, the award given by an arbitrator can be much more concise. It is being addressed, after all, to the parties themselves only and to no one else. The factual basis for the decision will need to be set out very clearly, but the law will not normally need to be analysed or explained. Setting out the law that is being applied should not occupy more than a few paragraphs, unlike a Supreme Court judgment where it can run into a hundred paragraphs or more. This lightens considerably the burden that goes into its preparation.

However, the requirement to include details of the proceedings in the award was, for me, an unexpected challenge. As judges, we left this to the clerks of the court, who maintained a detailed record of the whole proceedings from the start to the end without any input from us. That was their job, and we left it to them to carry out according to the well-established practice. I appreciate that arbitrators can employ clerks, but I have not yet had the benefit of that service in the arbitrations in which I have been engaged so far. In any event, I appreciate that good practice requires a narrative of what happened to be set out in the introductory part of the award.

The question which has troubled me is how detailed that narrative has to be? My first encounter with this requirement was not encouraging. It was in the ICC arbitration that I mentioned earlier. Our chairman was very familiar with what the ICC was looking for, so he erred on the side of caution and left nothing out. Some time later I assumed the responsibility of preparing the award in an ad hoc arbitration. I decided to concentrate on the more important stages of the process, avoiding what I regarded as too much detail. I also decided to set out the reasons for the award in an appendix. I felt more comfortable with this approach, as I was able to draft the Appendix in the same way as I used to do when I was preparing my judgments. I avoided what I felt would be the clutter of the procedural narrative. My colleagues accepted my approach. But I am not sure that the ICC would have approved.

§7.07 COSTS

One of the privileges that I enjoyed as a judge was that I never had to deal with the assessment of costs. There was a clear division in the courts on which I sat between the responsibility of the judge, which was to make the order as to costs, and its application to the facts if the parties were unable to agree. It was left to others to make a detailed assessment. Arbitrators do not have that luxury.

Normally, having to resolve disputes about the detailed assessment of costs should not overburden the arbitrator. But that was not so in my most recent case. The procedure, in that case, was very long drawn out, and there were eminently stateable arguments by both sides, who were not on good terms, for arguing that a detailed examination should be undertaken as to where the fault lay for charges that might be regarded as excessive. Many of them had to be examined one by one. Eventually, the parties settled their differences. But that was not until after a lot of work had been done to prepare a solution that could form the basis of an award. I did not enjoy that experience, which, until the case was settled, we could not avoid.

§7.08 SOME FINAL THOUGHTS

In the Scottish textbook to which I referred earlier,[4] mention is made of a celebrated case that belongs, as the writer said, to fabulous antiquity. This was the award that was delivered on the slopes of Mount Ida by the shepherd Paris on the competing claims for the prize of Beauty between the goddesses Juno, Pallas and Venus.[5] All other means of adjudicating their rival claims had failed. The difficulty was overcome by the parties agreeing to a submission to Paris as their sole arbitrator. A dangerous dispute between such powerful rivals was avoided by his final judgment, which they were all bound to accept.

It has not been my fortune to be asked to be an arbitrator in a case of such charm and delicacy. My cases have all been between state-owned entities and commercial organisations that have undertaken to provide them with goods or services. But they have brought with them the pleasure of working in an amicable environment towards the resolution of their disputes. The procedures that we have adopted, some ad hoc and others under institutional rules, have been easy to use and, for the most part, well-adapted to the cases before us.

In most cases, the fact-finding process was not too difficult, the exception being one in which we had to take the evidence by Zoom, which is not best suited to resolving issues of credibility. The issues of law were interesting and well-argued. When it came to drafting the awards in the cases where I was responsible for doing this, I enjoyed being relieved of the need to frame them in the same very detailed way as I would have had to do had I been sitting in the UK Supreme Court.

Above all, it has been a very real privilege for me to meet and work with the very experienced international arbitrators whom I have met on this unusual journey. I am grateful to them all for their guidance and understanding as I have adapted myself to their ways of working. I hope that I have been able to contribute something in return from my unusual background.

4. JB Bell, *The Law of Arbitration in Scotland* (2nd edn, 1877), p. 1.
5. Known to the Greeks as Hera, Athena and Aphrodite.

CHAPTER 8

Legal Privilege Disputes in International Arbitration in Denmark: A Practical Introduction

Søren Henriksen, Catherine Schutz & Alexandra M.O. Junge

§8.01 INTRODUCTION

Few things in life are certain, but those involved in international arbitration can, with virtual certainty, expect that questions surrounding legal privilege, when they arise, will be extremely difficult to answer. The challenges that questions of legal privilege present in international arbitration are so marked that the following maxim has been applied to the issue: 'the only thing that is clear is that nothing is clear in this area'.[1]

The absence of clear answers is, in part, a result of varying interpretations of legal privilege across jurisdictions and legal traditions. In particular, there are considerable differences between how legal privilege is understood in common law, which has recognised and developed the concept of privilege from the seventeenth century onwards, and civil law, which often traditionally does not explicitly recognise the concept of privilege but can provide comparable protections through other legal mechanisms. A marked example of this is Denmark, a civil law jurisdiction, where it is often said that there simply is no general concept of '*legal privilege*' but where protections analogous to legal privilege can be found in certain statutory provisions.

The absence of clear answers also, in the opinion of these authors, stems from the collision of multiple additional reasonable but conflicting factors at play when questions of legal privilege arise in international arbitration. First, there is the fact that questions of legal privilege are often of central importance to an arbitration, so much

1. Klaus Berger, *Evidentiary Privileges: Best Practice Standard Versus/and Arbitral Discretion*, 2 Arb. Int. 501 (2006), at 501 https://doi.org/10.1093/arbitration/22.4.501.

so that the outcome of the arbitration can sometimes hinge on how they are answered. Second, legal privilege sits at the intersection between central arbitral goals such as fairness, efficiency, and a party's right to present its case. Third, there is the (perhaps understandable and reasonable) lack of a uniform approach to answering questions of legal privilege across individual international arbitrations.

The challenges of applying legal privilege in international arbitrations have been written about extensively by arbitral scholars and practitioners[2] but have not been subject to much attention by commentators in Denmark specifically. The authors of this chapter have engaged with the complexities surrounding legal privilege in international arbitrations in Denmark in various contexts over recent years and gleaned insights regarding how the difficulties might be practically approached. In this chapter, the authors seek to add some clarity on this topic by providing a practical introduction to the application of legal privilege in international arbitration disputes from a Danish perspective.

This chapter begins with a short description of the differing interpretations of legal privilege across jurisdictions (§8.02) and continues with a discussion regarding how questions of legal privilege arise in international arbitrations in Denmark in the first place (§8.03) and why questions of legal privilege are important in international arbitration (§8.04). Following which, this chapter will discuss the various methods tribunals can deploy to determine which national law applies to questions of legal privilege in international arbitration (§8.05) and how questions of legal privilege can be interpreted if the choice of law dictates application of Danish law (§8.06).

§8.02 SUMMARY OF THE CONCEPT OF LEGAL PRIVILEGE IN DIFFERING JURISDICTIONS

A good starting point for any discussion on legal privilege in international arbitration is to define what is meant by the concept of privilege.[3] This is an especially difficult task because privilege has no uniform definition applicable across jurisdictions, with common and civil law jurisdictions often having stark differences in how they define and apply privilege. In the following sections, these differences will briefly be examined.

2. *See*, for example, Tatjana Shterjova, *The Challenges of Taking Evidence in International Commercial Arbitration: The Problem of Legal Privileges*, in *Towards a Universal Justice? Putting International Courts and Jurisdictions into Perspective*, Brill (2016), at 432-445; Corina Gugler & Karina Goldberg, *Privilege and Document Production in International Arbitration: How do Arbitrators Deal with Different Legal Systems' Approaches?*, RBA N53, (2017) https://doi.org/10.54648/rba2017004, Dourtrina Internacional; Craig Tevendale & Ula Cartwright-Finch, *Privilege in International Arbitration, Is It Time to Recognize the Consensus?*, Journal of International Arbitration 26(6) (2009) https://doi.org/10.54648/joia2009043.

3. While common law recognises many different types of privileges, this chapter will, by and large, focus on privileges arising from the attorney-client relationship or legal proceedings (so named legal privilege).

[A] Privilege in Common Law Countries as Exemplified by US Law

The concept or principle of privilege originates in UK common law and is today of central importance in common law rules of evidence. While jurisdictional differences between common law countries can be observed, privilege's overarching themes remain similar. How privilege is defined and interpreted under US law will be discussed here.

Under US law, confidentiality and privilege are related but distinct concepts, which are often mixed up even by US legal professionals. Therefore, teasing out their similarities and differences is vital to understanding how common law countries treat these concepts and how confusion regarding these concepts can arise in international arbitration.

Succinctly put, confidentiality is a *duty* that is owed from one person to another. For example, the duty of client-lawyer confidentiality means that the lawyer has a duty to the client to keep information obtained through the legal representation confidential.[4] Generally speaking, in the US, the duty of client-lawyer confidentiality is enshrined in the bar rules for lawyers.[5] Therefore, if lawyers breach confidentiality, they could be sanctioned by their bar, potentially resulting in the highest penalty of disbarment. They could also face civil charges if their conduct rises to legal malpractice but likely would not face criminal charges or fines (assuming their conduct is not otherwise illegal).

Since confidentiality is a duty, it can generally only be expressly waived by informed consent given by the person to whom the duty is owed. Therefore, for the most part, a lawyer is only permitted to share information that is protected by client-lawyer confidentiality if the client expressly provides the lawyer with informed consent to do so.[6] There are circumstances under the bar rules in which a lawyer can break confidentiality without client permission; however, these are, for the most part, limited to situations in which future harm could occur to the lawyer or third parties.[7]

In contrast, privilege is the *right* under law to keep information that is privileged from being disclosed in a court proceeding.[8] Courts in the US have strong powers to compel the disclosure of evidence in court proceedings, including, in extreme cases, the ability to imprison people unwilling to share compelled information for the crime of contempt of court. However, US lawmakers have decided that the ability to compel information should have limits, as some information should be protected from disclosure for the benefit of society as a whole. The mechanism through which this

4. Rule 1.6(a) of American Bar Association (ABA) Model Rules of Professional Conduct.
5. Each individual bar of each individual state will have individual bar rules that the lawyers practising under that bar must followed. However, they are largely similar to each other and to the ABA Model Rules of Professional Conduct, which will be cited in this chapter.
6. Rule 1.6(a) of the ABA Model Rules of Professional Conduct.
7. Rule 1.6(b) of the ABA Model Rules of Professional Conduct.
8. Black's Law Dictionary Eighth Edition defines privilege as 'A special legal right, exemption, or immunity granted to a person or class of persons; an exception to a duty. A privilege grants someone the legal freedom to do or not to do a given act. It immunizes conduct that, under ordinary circumstances, would subject the actor to liability.'

information is protected is a privilege, which is a statutory right created by the state or federal legislature or by court through case law (and occasionally by constitutions).

The attorney-client privilege is the oldest privilege known to common law.[9] In recognising the attorney-client privilege,[10] US lawmakers deemed it more important to society for clients to be able to freely share information with their lawyers without fear that it would later be disclosed in court than for courts to freely use information obtained via the client-lawyer relationship to decide individual cases. This is because 'sound legal advice and advocacy serves public ends'.[11] Further, given the duty of confidentiality owed by lawyers to their clients, without the attorney-client privilege, lawyers could be placed in a rather unfair situation where they must choose between violating confidentiality and facing disbarment or being imprisoned for contempt of court.

Other privileges exist that are potentially applicable to international arbitration, including the work-product privilege, which protects attorney work-product that has been prepared in anticipation of litigation from disclosure;[12] the joint and common interest privilege, which protects information shared between parties that have a joint and common interest;[13] the without prejudice privilege, which protects information shared in the course of settlement negotiations;[14] the mediation privilege, which protects information shared during mediation;[15] the trade secrets privilege, which protects the confidentiality of a trade secret;[16] and the accountant privilege, which protects information shared with an accountant.[17] As the concept and interpretation of privilege are often closely tied with the public policy considerations in the given jurisdiction, not all types of privileges exist or are applied to the same extent in each jurisdiction.[18]

Another feature of privilege under US law is that it can be waived voluntarily and involuntarily. The holder of the privilege (the client) can always waive the privilege voluntarily if, for example, a client wishes to introduce attorney work-product into a court proceeding. However, the privilege can also be waived involuntarily or inadvertently if, for example, the privileged material is shared with an unnecessary third party.[19] Additionally, subject matter waivers dictate that if the holder of a privilege waives certain communication, all communication related to that subject is also

9. *Upjohn Co. v. United States*, 449 U.S. 383 (1981).
10. Black's Law Dictionary Eighth Edition defines attorney-client privilege as 'The client's right to refuse to disclose and to prevent any other person from disclosing confidential communications between the client and the attorney.'
11. *Upjohn Co. v. United States*, 449 U.S. 383 (1981).
12. Nicolas Grégoire, *Evidentiary Privileges in International Arbitration: A Comparative Analysis under English, American, Swiss and French Law*, Collection Genevoise (Schulthess Éditions Romandes/LGDJ 2016), at 69.
13. *Ibid.*, at 73.
14. *Ibid.*, at 77-78.
15. *Ibid.*, at 87-88.
16. *Ibid.*, at 97.
17. *Ibid.*, at 115.
18. *Ibid.*, at 11.
19. *United States v. Evans*, 113 F.3d 1457, 1462 (7th Cir. 1997).

waived, as the holder should not be able to 'selectively invoke the privilege to their own advantage'.[20]

[B] Privilege in Civil Law Countries as Exemplified by Danish Law

Civil law countries have also adopted the concept of legal privilege, albeit often with a narrower scope. Whereas civil law jurisdictions often do not explicitly apply legal privileges, there are several doctrines that serve the same or similar purposes as the legal privileges found in common law.[21] This includes rules pertaining to witnesses being exempt from giving testimony on topics covered by professional secrecy or the right of a party not to produce evidence that may be adverse to its interest.[22]

The narrower interpretation of legal privilege in civil law jurisdictions arguably derives from civil law jurisdictions' more limited approach to disclosure.[23] For example, under Danish law, non-voluntary disclosure is not a given feature of court proceedings, and there is a comparatively restrictive stance on broad disclosure requests. Courts tend to refuse unspecific document requests and seek to limit potential '*fishing expeditions*' unless the documents sought are very likely to be determinative to the outcome of the case. As a natural consequence of this approach, there is a lesser need to protect parties from wide-reaching disclosure requests by employing specific privilege rules.[24]

However, this doesn't mean that the concept of privilege is entirely irrelevant under Danish law. Various statutory rules apply in Danish law that have similar characteristics to legal privilege as understood in common law that can be applied in Danish civil proceedings to prevent evidence from being disclosed. For example, section 170(1) of the Danish Administration of Justice Act (AJA) (in Danish *Retsplejeloven*) permits lawyers to withhold information from court proceedings if that information is protected by the lawyer's duty of confidentiality.

Attorneys in Denmark, as in most jurisdictions, have a duty of confidentiality towards their clients. Chapter 5 of the Code of Conduct of the Danish Bar and Law Society prescribes this broad duty of confidentiality, pursuant to which Danish attorneys must keep all information confidential that the attorney receives as part of his or her duties to the client.[25] This duty of confidentiality is also found in statutory provisions under Danish law. Pursuant to section 129 of the AJA, which refers to section 152 of the Danish Criminal Code, an attorney can face a fine or imprisonment for up to six months for breach of the duty of confidentiality. Confidentiality is an

---

20. Patricia Shaughnessy, *Dealing with Privileges in International Commercial Arbitration*, 51 Sc.St.L (2007) 451, 468.
21. Richard M. Mosk & Tom Ginsburg, *Evidentiary Privileges in International Arbitration*, Int'l & Comp. L.Q. (2001) 345, at 348 https://doi.org/10.1093/iclq/50.2.345.
22. *Ibid.*
23. Grégoire, *supra* n. 12, at 1.
24. *Ibid.*
25. Lars Økjær Jørgensen & Martin Lavesen, *De advokatetiske regler kommenteret*, (3rd ed. 2022), 126; the Code of Conduct of the Danish Bar and Law Society, Applicable from 1 Sep. 2022, Chapter 5, at 4.

absolute right that is owed to the holder of this right, namely the client, and therefore, generally, only the client can waive confidentiality.

Pursuant to section 170(1) of the AJA, an attorney is not required to testify about matters that are covered by his or her duty of confidentiality. The English translation of section 170(1) of the AJA is as follows:

> Where the giving of evidence would be against the wishes of a person having a right to confidentiality, persons bound by professional secrecy, such as ministers of religion of the Danish State Church or other religious communities, medical doctors, defence counsels, court mediators, patent advisers entered on the list referred to in Article 134(1) of the European Patent Convention and lawyers, must not be demanded to give evidence about matters having come to their knowledge in the course of the exercise of their functions.

This protection also applies to documentary evidence under section 298 of the AJA and is also extended to people who are directly connected with the attorney and people who execute functions specifically covered by section 170(4), such as assistants or trainees.[26]

However, the protection against testifying and disclosure provided in section 170(1) is not absolute. Of course, an attorney may give testimony or disclose matters if the client gives the attorney permission to do so.[27] In addition, a court may also order an attorney to provide evidence that is protected by confidentiality if: (1) the evidence is 'essential to the outcome of the case' and (2) the 'merits of the case and its importance to the party concerned or to society are found to justify the giving of such order'.[28] Case law indicates that lawyers can only be compelled to testify if there are strong and specific arguments that they should under the above criteria.[29] Importantly, the test is not whether the production of the document in question is deemed likely to inflict harm to the party in possession, and it would be insufficient to only argue that

26. While there is limited case law determining the extent of this provision, a recent Supreme Court judgment, in case BS-6234/2021, rendered in July 2021 addressed the scope of who is covered by 170(1). If the Supreme Court found that a legal advisor was not covered by section 170(4), even though the legal advisor was a partner and co-owner of a law firm, because she was not admitted to the bar and because she was not nor was she assisted by an attorney from her law firm who could have been covered by section 170(1).
27. Section 170(1) of the AJA.
28. Section 170(2) of AJA; defence counsel in criminal proceedings are not subject to these exceptions per section 170(2) of the AJA.
29. Michael Kistrup & Bernhard Gomard, *Civilprocessen* (8th ed. Karnov Group 2022), at 594. For further examples, *see also* U 2009 2615, an attorney was ordered to give evidence about matters that had come to his knowledge through dealings with client 'K' who died before the related proceedings commenced. The Supreme Court found that a statement from the attorney on certain matters had to be assumed to be of decisive importance to the outcome of the case. The Supreme Court emphasised that it had to be considered highly probable that K would have waived the attorney's confidentiality to give evidence. In contrast, in U.2016.469H where an attorney had prepared a letter regarding inheritance, the Supreme Court found no basis to assume that the deceased client would have waived the right to confidentiality and allowed the attorney to testify. The Supreme Court found that the nature of the case and its importance to the concerned party, or society, did not justify requiring the attorney to give evidence. The Supreme Court attached particular importance to the fact that it was a matter of legal advice in a case of a personal nature.

the document in question is relevant to the requesting party's case. In addition, even if the above two conditions are met, the court cannot order disclosure of confidential information obtained in connection with a *legal proceeding* or *litigation* in connection with which the lawyer's advice has been sought.[30]

Of course, an attorney can always choose not to give evidence that the court has ordered it to provide. As described above, courts in Denmark do not have such wide-ranging powers as courts in common law countries to compel the production of information, even when the court has specifically ordered its production. However, failure to adhere to the court's directive to disclose information may result in the court favouring the opposing party when assessing evidence, potentially prejudicing the non-compliant party's case.[31]

In Danish arbitration practice, the exemption under section 170(1) has been referenced as a narrow exemption. In the context of a privilege dispute in an arbitration, it might be a somewhat difficult task to satisfy such criteria given that disclosure proceedings most often will take place at the outset of the arbitration proceedings, whereas witness evidence in Danish civil proceedings is almost exclusively given orally only and at the main hearing, i.e., at the end of proceedings. Requests for document production in civil proceedings also need not necessarily be done at the outset of court proceedings. Thus, in arbitration, arbitrators might only (be able to) consider the prima facie relevance of the documents sought, and by extension, an analysis of whether the documents sought might be 'essential to the outcome of the case' is inevitably more difficult.

§8.03 HOW QUESTIONS REGARDING LEGAL PRIVILEGE ARISE IN INTERNATIONAL ARBITRATIONS IN DENMARK

Questions of legal privilege arise in international arbitration in connection with the introduction of evidence. It is generally during the document production phase of the arbitration that most privilege disputes will arise; however, questions of legal privilege may, of course, also arise in connection with the cross-examination of witnesses or at other stages of the arbitration that involve the introduction of evidence.

There are several legitimate reasons why a party or attorney would seek to invoke legal privilege in order to be exempt from disclosing certain evidence. For example, the documents in dispute may be attorney work-product generated for the arbitration in question and therefore revealing them could result in unjustified prejudice to the disclosing party. The party may also fear broader consequences from disclosing the document, for example, that sharing it could result in waiving its privilege, which could impact not only the arbitration but also other legal matters the party is involved in.[32]

30. Section 170(2) of AJA.
31. Kistrup & Gomard, *supra* n. 29, at 615: 'A party's failure to comply with the court's discovery order has the same effect as failure to comply with a request from the court to produce documents, cf. Section 339(3) of the AJA [...] The court may, when assessing the evidence, give the failure effect in favor of the opposing party.'
32. Grégoire, *supra* n. 12, at 204.

The attorney may fear reprisal for violating client confidentiality if the ethical rules governing the attorney's conduct are not aligned with the privilege rules deployed by the tribunal.[33]

However, a party cannot invoke legal privilege without reference to rules that mandate tribunal recognition that the legal privilege is applicable in the arbitration in the first place. What is most common for international arbitrations seated in Denmark is the requirement or choice that institutional rules and/or international arbitral standards will apply to the arbitration, both of which may address privilege directly or indirectly. These rules and standards are, therefore, often the starting point for those seeking to invoke the protection of legal privilege in international arbitration.

It is quite common for the International Bar Association's Rules on the Taking of Evidence in International Arbitration (the 'IBA Rules') to apply to international arbitrations in Denmark as guidelines that the tribunal should follow in deciding questions of evidence, although tribunals normally will not be bound by them. The IBA Rules contain two articles that address legal privilege: Article 9.2(b) that requires tribunals to exclude evidence that is protected by privilege; and Article 9.4 that provides further description of how tribunals should determine whether evidence is protected by privilege. Specifically, Article 9.4 provides that tribunals must first apply any 'mandatory legal or ethical rules' to determine questions of privilege, and in the absence of such rules, tribunals may consider other potentially relevant factors, such as the need to protect the confidentiality of the document, either because the document was created to obtain legal advice or because it was created in connection with settlement negotiations; the expectation of the parties and lawyers in regards the privilege of the evidence; any waiver of the privilege; and the need to maintain fairness and equality as between the parties. While Article 9.2(b) uses the seemingly mandatory term of '*shall*', the use of the term '*may*' in Article 9.4 shows that the IBA Rules provide tribunals with discretion on whether to exclude evidence on the grounds of privilege and how to determine whether evidence is or is not privileged.[34]

The institutional rules governing international arbitrations in Denmark can also pave the way for the introduction of questions of legal privilege in arbitration. While not many arbitral institutions will have rules that directly govern questions of privilege, most institutional rules will have provisions that indirectly permit the application of legal privilege.

This is the case under the rules of the Danish Institute of Arbitration (the 'DIA Rules'). Specifically, Article 28(2) of the DIA Rules provides that:

> The conduct of the arbitration shall be governed by the Rules. Where the Rules are silent, the conduct of the arbitration shall be governed by what the parties have

33. Elisabeth Vanas-Metzler, *Chapter II: The Arbitrator and the Arbitration Procedure, the Tension Between Document Disclosure and Legal Privilege in International Commercial Arbitration – An Austrian Perspective*, in Christian Lausegger, Peter Klein, et al. (eds), Austrian Yearbook on International Arbitration 2015 (Manz'sche Verlags- und Universitätsbuchhandlung 2015), at 259.
34. Peter Ashford, *The IBA Rules on the Taking of Evidence in International Arbitration: A Guide*, (1st ed. Cambridge University Press 2013), at 146.

> otherwise agreed or, failing such agreement, by what the Arbitral Tribunal considers appropriate. The Arbitral Tribunal may, for instance, determine the admissibility, relevance, materiality and weight of any evidence.[35]

This gives tribunals acting under the DIA Rules discretion to apply rules that they consider appropriate to answer questions of the admissibility of certain evidence, including questions of privilege, as long as the parties have not themselves agreed on which rules should apply.

Further, Article 33 of the DIA Rules provides that the tribunal may draw an adverse inference if parties fail to produce evidence the tribunal has ordered to be produced. Article 33 is therefore effectively a mechanism for tribunals to ensure that parties comply with orders to produce documents, and, as such, opens the door for questions of privilege to arise in arbitrations at the DIA.

Similarly, while the current version of the Danish Arbitration Association's Rules on the Taking of Evidence in Arbitration (the 'DAA Rules') does not refer to privilege directly, Article 8.6 does provide that objection can be made against the introduction of evidence if 'there are legal impediments or restrictions' connected with that evidence or if 'the evidence is subject to confidentiality that the Arbitral Tribunal considers compelling'.[36] The DAA Rules thereby clearly mirror the IBA Rules' provisions and nod to the applicability of legal privilege in principle. Finally, Article 8.5 of the DAA Rules provides that a party's failure to produce evidence 'without a valid reason' allows the tribunal to 'let this have evidential influence to the advantage of the other party'.

It is important to note that none of these international standards or institutional rules that either explicitly or indirectly permit the application of legal privilege in arbitration are themselves detailed enough to answer the specific questions of legal privilege that arise in arbitration by design; for example, the IBA Rules are as specific as is possible for guidelines whose purpose is to apply to large volumes of international arbitrations across fora and jurisdictions. This also suggests that these rules anticipate that questions of privilege will 'fall within the tribunal's mandate', meaning that tribunals will be given a large amount of discretion in answering questions of privilege even when these rules apply.[37]

Nevertheless, rules such as the IBA Rules, DIA Rules and DAA Rules provide the starting point for counsel to assert legal privilege in international arbitrations in Denmark, should they wish to protect certain evidence from disclosure and consequently provide the foundational mandate for tribunals to engage with these assertions and not dismiss them outright.

35. Article 28(2), DIA Rules 2021.
36. Article 8.6, DAA Rules 2010.
37. Diana Kuitkowski, *The Law Applicable to Privilege Claims in International Arbitration*, Journal of International Arbitration 32(1) (2015), at 80 https://doi.org/10.54648/joia2015003; Craig Tevendale & Ula Cartwright-Finch, *Privilege in International Arbitration, Is It Time to Recognize the Consensus?*, Journal of International Arbitration 26(6) (2009), at 827 https://doi.org/10.54648/joia2009043.

§8.04 THE IMPORTANCE OF QUESTIONS OF LEGAL PRIVILEGE IN INTERNATIONAL ARBITRATION

Questions of legal privilege are often or at least potentially some of the most important evidentiary questions that can arise in an arbitration and are consequently often fiercely argued by counsel and carefully considered by tribunals when they arise.

Fundamentally, questions of privilege are important in international arbitration because how a tribunal rules on questions of privilege and how counsel and parties behave in relation to those rulings can have a significant impact on the outcome of the arbitration. On the one hand, if a tribunal rules that a document or witness testimony is subject to legal privilege, this could result in a party being unable to obtain or introduce evidence crucial for proving its case. On the other hand, if a tribunal rules that the evidence is not subject to legal privilege and must be shared with the opposing party, it may prove decisive to the opposing party's success. The weight attributed to evidence that was subject to an unsuccessful claim for the application of legal privilege ultimately depends on the actual content of the evidence. However, in practice, such evidence will often become a key part of the opposing party's evidentiary strategy, given the alleged perception of importance created by the unrecognised assertion of legal privilege.

How a tribunal rules on questions of privilege can be dependent on which party has the burden of proof to prove or disprove that the privilege applies. International arbitration commentators generally agree that it is usually the party invoking legal privilege that bears the burden of proving it is applicable.[38] This is because '[a]rbitrators … should not allow a party to escape the obligation to disclose important evidence by making a broad and unsubstantiated claim of privilege'.[39] This burden of proof naturally introduces a risk that the party asserting legal privilege would need to produce the requested documents if the privilege is not established or rendered probable.

However, taking into account the policy considerations underpinning legal privilege and the various legitimate reasons why a party or attorney would seek to invoke legal privilege discussed above, arbitral tribunals have been seen to be reluctant to order the production of documents that are *likely* to be covered by a legal privilege under the applicable law. This reluctance could potentially indicate a lower threshold for satisfying the burden of proof.

Questions of privilege can raise particular challenges for counsel and tribunals because it is sometimes necessary to review the contested evidence to determine whether legal privilege applies, but having the tribunal review the evidence would violate the legal privilege if it does apply. To resolve this challenge, parties and tribunals may agree to make use of an independent lawyer or umpire to rule in place of

---

38. *See, e.g.*, Shaughnessy, *supra* n. 20, at 467; and Roman Khodykin, Carol Mulcahy & Nicholas Fletcher, *A Guide to the IBA Rules on the Taking of Evidence in International Arbitration* (© Oxford University Press 2019) pp. 407-510, at 452, para. 12.170. This position also aligns with the IBA Rules.
39. Shaughnessy, *supra* n. 20, at 469.

the tribunal regarding whether privilege applies to the contested document(s) in cases where the specific document for which privilege is asserted needs to be examined. This practice is codified in Article 3(8) of the IBA Rules and Article 2.7 of the DAA Rules. In international arbitration in Denmark, it has been seen that parties agree to appoint a Supreme Court judge as a neutral candidate to act as an umpire.[40]

It has, however, been questioned whether a tribunal has the authority to order the use of such umpire if one or both parties do not consent. The authors are aware of at least one instance where an international tribunal seated in Denmark ruled that it was empowered to refer the determination of whether a document was subject to a legal privilege to an umpire, as this was considered appropriate in the given circumstances. However, while the tribunal did order the parties to engage an umpire, none of the parties did, in fact, object, so the question remains subject to uncertainty.

Even if a tribunal (or an umpire) rules that a privilege does not apply to a particular piece of evidence and orders a party to share it with the opposing party, that party may elect not to share it. Generally speaking, a tribunal seated in Denmark has little power to compel production. However, the tribunal has the power, subject to, for example, Article 33 of the DIA Rules, to adversely infer that a document is harmful to the case of the party that is withholding it.

Usually, the applicable institutional rules only permit a tribunal to draw an adverse inference if there is no valid reason for the party not to comply with the tribunal's order.[41] It would be counterintuitive for a tribunal to reject a claim of legal privilege and order production *and* simultaneously find it reasonable for a party to withhold the evidence on the same rejected grounds of privilege. It therefore seems reasonable to assume that if a party withholds a document on grounds of legal privilege after a tribunal has determined that no such privilege exists, there is a risk that a tribunal may adversely infer that the evidence is harmful to the withholding party. Consequently, parties must carefully weigh decisions not to produce on the grounds of legal privilege when ordered by the tribunal to avoid the risk of this *catch-22* situation. One author notes, however, that drawing an adverse inference regarding documents withheld on privilege grounds that were argued in good faith but ultimately unrecognised may be inappropriate and that therefore tribunals should tread cautiously in this regard.[42]

The importance of such adverse inference is difficult to measure empirically, and most tribunals would likely not enjoy basing their decisions on the merits solely on adverse inferences. Nonetheless, such inferences may become a key part of the opposing party's evidentiary strategy, given the perception of importance created by the assertion of legal privilege and the subsequent withholding of the document(s). To make a credible substitute for the evidence itself, a party's arguments pertaining to adverse inferences should be thoughtfully presented to the tribunal within the context

40. Section 47(a)(3) of the AJA allows requests to the president of a court to appoint a sitting judge as umpire to act in arbitration.
41. *See* Art. 33 of the DIA Rules or IBA Rules Art. 9(6) and 9(7) and para. 8.5 of the DAA Rules.
42. Shaughnessy, *supra* n. 20, at 454 and 469.

of the substantive matters at hand. This may sometimes prove to be an underestimated task, considering that the content of the evidence will remain unknown.

Consequently, reaching a fair and well-supported decision regarding assertions of legal privilege in international arbitration is obviously extremely important, as the ruling can not only impact the outcome of the arbitration but can also be complicated by specific challenges that legal privilege presents, such as nuances with regard to the burden of proof, the potential necessity of involving third parties, and how parties react to the ruling itself.

§8.05 HOW TRIBUNALS CAN DETERMINE THE APPLICABLE LAW TO ANSWER QUESTIONS OF LEGAL PRIVILEGE THAT ARISE IN INTERNATIONAL ARBITRATION IN DENMARK

As noted above, while international standards and institutional rules provide for recognition of confidentiality and/or legal privilege in principle, they are not detailed enough to answer more specific questions on the extent of any invoked legal privilege.[43] This leaves counsel and tribunals grappling with important questions of legal privilege in a peculiar and challenging situation: they *must or can* apply legal privilege per the international standards or tribunal orders but have limited or no international standards guiding *how* to apply legal privilege to any given document or information.

Since privileges are derived from national rather than international law,[44] rules on legal privilege often necessitate the application of national law to be effective. Counsel and tribunals seeking guidance on how to answer specific legal privilege questions that arise in international arbitration therefore inevitably turn to national law to fill the gap left by international standards and institutional rules. However, the natural question then becomes, which national law should apply?

Should parties agree, either before or during arbitration, on the law to apply to questions of legal privilege, then this will naturally be the applicable law. However, it is unlikely that the parties' arbitration agreement would specifically outline what rules or laws to apply to questions of legal privilege,[45] and it is uncommon for the tribunal's procedural orders to do so either. It is equally unlikely that the parties could agree on what rules to apply after issues of legal privilege arise since they would likely wish to invoke the legal privilege rules that best support their position with regard to the disputed evidence.

In the absence of such agreement, tribunals must decide, with input from parties and counsel, on which national law to apply to questions of legal privilege. However, it can be especially complex to even arrive at the applicable law to determine the extent of any asserted privilege, given that there are several choices of law methods that could be employed to determine the applicable law and that there is a lack of guidance within Danish law and commentary as to which method is appropriate. Further, even though

43. Ashford, *supra* n. 34, at 147.
44. Vanas-Metzler, *supra* n. 33), at 261.
45. Berger, *supra* n. 1, at 509; Grégoire, *supra* n. 12, at 128.

the IBA Rules do not dictate any application of a specific choice-of-law method, they do suggest that tribunals consider general concepts of '*fairness*' and '*equality*', which are relevant when determining the appropriate choice of law, which only adds an additional layer of complexity.[46]

In Danish practice, and likely due to this complexity, parties sometimes fail to effectively argue which law should apply or fail to identify the appropriate legal test for arriving at that conclusion. Instead, parties often assume that a particular law must apply and jump straight to arguing why evidence is protected or not under that law or confine arguments to address specific wording included in procedural orders. The lack of guidance on how to arrive at the appropriate law, coupled with tribunal orders that often address applicable law and the application of privilege simultaneously, may also result in arguments being presented under several substantive laws, further muddling the picture.

This chapter does not attempt to identify which method '*should*' be applied in international arbitrations to determine the applicable law, including in Denmark, for two reasons. First, such a discussion would exceed the scope of this chapter. Second, the appropriate method would likely depend on the circumstances present in the specific arbitration, as tribunals should, as a basic proposition, apply a law that aligns as best as possible with parties' legitimate expectations in accordance with Article 9.4(c) of the IBA Rules, and such expectations will naturally vary from case to case.

This section will instead first address the impact of legal characterisation of legal privilege on potentially applicable privilege rules (section §8.05[A]) and subsequently introduce possible choice-of-law methods (and choice-of-law analyses) to determine which law to apply to disputed questions of legal privilege (section §8.05[B]).

[A] The Impact of Legal Characterisation of Legal Privilege on Potentially Applicable Privilege Rules in Arbitration

Before embarking on a discussion of identifying the applicable privileges rules, it is relevant to first examine whether the qualification of legal privilege should be viewed as a substantive matter or as a procedural matter.[47] In short, the question is whether legal privilege is (mainly) a matter of procedure as it concerns the introduction of evidence or whether legal privilege is (mainly) a substantive matter that concerns parties' rights and obligations. This determination is relevant because the qualification might indirectly affect the applicable privilege rules as, absent party agreement, arbitrators would generally enjoy substantial discretion to determine the applicable rules on matters of procedure while recognising privileges as a matter of substantive law would necessitate a choice-of-law analysis.

Procedural matters in arbitration are generally understood to include procedural steps and conduct, evidentiary and pleading rules, disclosure powers of arbitrators,

46. Ashford, *supra* n. 34, at 160 and 162.
47. Grégoire, *supra* n. 12, 120.

and the form, making and publication of the award.[48] Legal privilege could therefore be understood to be a matter of procedural law because privilege concerns the admissibility of evidence, which is 'usually governed by procedural law'.[49]

Section 19(2) of the Danish Arbitration Act provides that failing agreement on procedure, the arbitral tribunal may conduct the arbitration in such manner 'as it considers appropriate', and as mentioned in section 3, Article 28(2) of the DIA Rules contains a similar rule. It is generally accepted that (absent party agreement otherwise) the law of the seat governs the procedural aspects of the arbitration, as it is said to regulate both the '*internal*' procedural conduct of the arbitration and the '*external*' relationship between the arbitration and national courts.[50] Characterising legal privilege as a procedural matter could therefore mean that the privilege rules of the *lex arbitri* should apply.[51]

Legal privilege could also be understood to be a substantive question because 'the underlying purpose of legal privilege' is 'the protection of the confidential communication between the client and his attorney', which creates a substantive right for the privilege holder.[52] Privilege gives the client (in jurisdictions where the client is the privilege holder) a substantive right that can 'affect parties' behaviour outside of any procedural setting'.[53] As such, privilege should not be described as a procedural or solely procedural matter.

Characterising legal privilege as a substantive question would mean that a tribunal would have to apply conflict of law rules in national arbitration laws to determine the law to apply to the legal privilege question at issue.[54] The Danish Arbitration Act provides in section 28(2) that '[f]ailing any designation by the parties, the arbitral tribunal shall apply the law determined by the conflict of laws rules which it considers applicable'. According to the preparatory works, the determination of applicable conflict of laws rules should be made with regard to the domicile or place of business of the parties, the subject matter of the dispute, and the place of arbitration.[55] It has been said in Danish commentary that when applying this rule, generally the jurisdiction to which the dispute is most closely connected should be chosen as the applicable law.[56] Deviating from the Danish Arbitration Act, Article 26(3) of the DIA Rules states that '[f]ailing a designation by the parties of the rules of law applicable to the decision on the merits of the case, the Arbitral Tribunal shall apply the rules which

48. Gary B. Born, *International Commercial Arbitration, Part II: International Arbitration Procedures* (3rd ed. © Kluwer Law International; Kluwer Law International 2021, at 1651.
49. Grégoire, *supra* n. 12, at 121.
50. Born, *supra* n. 48, at 1651.
51. Berger, *supra* n. 1, at 508.
52. Audley W. Sheppard & Fabian G. von Schlabrendorff, *Conflict of Legal Privileges in International Arbitration: An Attempt to Find a Holisitic Solution, Global Reflections on International Law, Commerce and Dispute Resolution: Liber Amicorum in Honor of Robert Briner – 2005*, (ICC 2022), 742-774, at 763.
53. *Ibid.*
54. Berger, *supra* n. 1, 509.
55. Forarbejderne til Voldgiftsloven, LFF 2005-03-16 nr 127, 16 Mar. 2005, section 28, 100.
56. Niels Schiersing, *Voldgiftsloven med kommentarer*, (Jurist- og Økonomforbundets Forlag 2016), 373.

it considers appropriate after consultation of the parties' thus widening the tribunal's discretion.

There is by no means agreement across jurisdictions on whether privilege is a procedural or substantive matter, and most arbitral laws, including the Danish Arbitration Act, are 'silent on the issue of characterization'.[57] There is even disagreement about whether common or civil law jurisdictions generally perceive privilege as procedural or substantive. Some authors say that common law jurisdictions generally perceive privilege as substantive, and civil law jurisdictions generally perceive privilege as procedural,[58] while other authors say the opposite.[59] There is oftentimes not even inter-jurisdictional agreement on the question – in the US, some courts characterise privilege as procedural while others characterise it as substantive or quasi-substantive.[60] Some authors have suggested that questions of legal privilege are both procedural and substantive in nature, which means that 'arbitral tribunals do not have complete discretion in deciding which privileges should apply in any particular case, because they must recognise and give effect to applicable substantive privileges'.[61]

In practice, it is seen that regardless of whether a tribunal characterises privilege as a procedural or substantive matter (which would rarely be set out explicitly by the tribunal), some form of choice-of-law analysis will take place to determine the applicable law. Even in cases where tribunals have been seen to include in procedural orders, for example, that the tribunal 'retains full discretion' to decide any document production-related dispute or positively described certain criteria for exempting documents from production on grounds of legal privilege, a choice of law still seems to be made, either directly because the choice of law was in dispute or indirectly by reference to the applicable law in the tribunal's order on document production. In one case, the tribunal noted that it had not intended to convey by its previous order that any qualification regarding legal privilege should go beyond what is generally accepted in the applicable law.

The distinction between procedural and substantive characterisation and its potential implications will not be discussed from a Danish perspective any further, given the scope of this chapter. Rather, assuming a choice-of-law analysis needs to be done, the following sections will address possible choices and methods for arriving at an applicable law to determine the extent of any legal privilege.

[B] Choice-of-Law Methods

Many different methods for conducting a choice-of-law analysis to determine what law to apply to answer questions of legal privilege in international arbitration have been

57. Grégoire, *supra* n. 12, at 121.
58. *Ibid.*
59. Ted P. Pearce, *How to handle privileged communications in international arbitration*, International Bar Association, https://www.ibanet.org/how-to-handle-privileged-communications-in-international-arbitration (accessed 27 Mar. 2024).
60. *Republic Gear Co. v Borg-Warner Corp.*, 381 F.2d 551, 555 n. 2 (2nd Cir. 1967).
61. Sheppard & Schlabrendorff, *supra* n. 52, at 767.

proposed by various arbitration scholars and practitioners over time.[62] This chapter will not attempt to address all of them, as this task has already been accomplished by other articles that provide a comprehensive overview of the various methods that can be deployed.[63] Instead, this chapter will focus on describing the methods that, in our experience, have been considered in international arbitrations in Denmark, specifically application of the law of the seat (section §8.05[B][1]), application of the law governing the merits of the dispute (section §8.05[B][2]), and the closest connection test (section §8.05[B][3]).

[1] Application of the Law of the Seat

One approach that can be taken is to determine that questions of legal privilege in international arbitration should be decided with reference to the law of the seat of the arbitration because questions of privilege concern matters of procedural law.[64] In a Danish context, since the Danish Arbitration Act does not contain rules on privilege, the relevant question would be whether the protection under Danish law outlined in section §8.02[B] that is equivalent to legal privilege should apply (the procedural *lex fori*).[65]

There are advantages to conceptualising privilege as a matter of procedure and applying the law of the seat. One benefit is that '*a single law could be applied to the issue of evidentiary privileges*' throughout the arbitration, which could avoid unequal treatment of the parties.[66] Application of a single law also has the benefit of making privilege analyses much more efficient in arbitrations where there are voluminous documents potentially subject to privileges and where a choice-of-law analysis might require application of laws from multiple different jurisdictions.

However, there may be fairness considerations when applying the law of the seat of the arbitration to questions of legal privilege. The seat may have been chosen for different reasons, both legal and strategic, and may not have any connection with one or both of the parties. In practice, this is often the case for international arbitrations seated in Denmark. It is consequently not rare for a situation to arise where the jurisdiction of the seat has no immediate connection with the evidence subject to the question of privilege or the legal background of the parties or counsel involved.[67] This may not be in line with the parties' legitimate expectations, particularly in situations where the invoked privilege arises out of a particular relationship (such as attorney-client privilege) or documents and communication completely unconnected with the

62. *See, e.g.*, Berger, *supra* n. 1; Sheppard & Schlabrendorff, *supra* n. 52, at 767; Pearce, *supra* n. 59.
63. Many commentators on international arbitration also frequently discuss the most or least favoured nation approaches. These methods favour equal treatment in the sense that the law providing the greatest and the least level of protection, respectively, is applied. *See, e.g.*, Berger, *supra* n. 1, at 518 or Grégoire, *supra* n. 12, at 150.
64. Grégoire, *supra* n. 12, at 121.
65. *Ibid.*, at 124.
66. *Ibid.*, at 121, citing Berger, *supra* n. 1.
67. Grégoire, *supra* n. 12, at 124; Sheppard & Schlabrendorff, *supra* n. 52, at 768.

particular seat.[68] Applying a choice of law so misaligned with the parties' expectations could also be contrary to the IBA Rules' mandate to consider '*fairness*' and to avoid parties experiencing '*trial by ambush*'.[69]

[2] Application of the Law Governing the Merits of the Dispute

Another approach, assuming that questions of privilege are deemed to be substantive, is that the applicable privileges should be decided in accordance with the parties' choice of the law governing the merits of the dispute.[70] This will most often be the law identified in the choice-of-law provision of the contract underlying the dispute.

There are some advantages to applying the law governing the merits of the dispute to questions of legal privilege. Assuming the law governing the merits of the dispute is the law identified in the choice-of-law provision of the contract, applying this law potentially could reflect the parties' active choice and also '[meet] the need for predictability'.[71] Further, as with applying the law of the seat, using a single law to answer all questions of legal privilege that arise has the benefit of providing uniform and equal treatment of the parties and is also more efficient.[72]

However, while difficult to say in the abstract, some authors doubt that the parties intended, when agreeing to the law governing the contract, for this law to apply to questions of privilege in a potential arbitration emanating from the contract.[73] Legal privileges do not necessarily arise directly out of the contractual relationship, and as such, it might be difficult to align application of the substantive law of the contract with the parties' legitimate expectations in respect of such privileges, in particular, if the parties come from legal traditions that classify privilege as procedural.[74]

[3] Closest Connection Test

Another approach that can be taken to determine which national law to apply is the so-called *closest connection test*, which mandates application of the law to which the evidence in dispute has the closest connection.[75] In other words, the choice-of-law analysis is derived from the document or communication itself rather than the arbitral proceedings or the contract.

The closest connection test has enjoyed wide recognition as an applicable principle for determining the law governing a contract absent an explicit choice-of-law provision. Article 4(1) of the 1980 Rome Convention on the law applicable to

68. Grégoire, *supra* n. 12, 126; Berger, *supra* n. 1, at 509.
69. Preamble 3, Art. 9.4(e) of the IBA Rules; Ashford, *supra* n. 34, 160.
70. Grégoire, *supra* n. 12, at 122.
71. *Ibid.*, at 126.
72. *Ibid.*
73. *Ibid.*, at 769; Sheppard & Schlabrendorff, *supra* n. 52, at 769.
74. Grégoire, *supra* n. 12, at 125-127.
75. Also called 'most significant relationship' or 'centre of gravity' (Grégoire, *supra* n. 12, at 135).

contractual obligations codifies the closest connection test, and the test also 'corresponds to the 'most significant relationship' test favored in the United States'.[76] In contrast to other jurisdictions,[77] the Danish Arbitration Act and the DIA Rules do not explicitly prescribe application of the closest connection test for determining applicable substantive law in the absence of an agreed choice of law for arbitrations seated in Denmark. However, as mentioned in section 5.1, Article 28(2) of the Danish Arbitration Act is said to effectively prescribe a type of '*closest connection*' test.

Under the closest connection test as applied to questions of legal privilege arising in international arbitration, various factors could be considered to determine which jurisdiction has the closest connection to the information in question. Some connecting factors potentially relevant in determination of the law applicable to privileges are:

> (i) the place where the communication was created, (ii) the place where the communication was sent, (iii) the place where the communication was received, (iv) the place where the communication is stored, (v) the place where the party (or witness) claiming the privilege resides, (vi) the place where the lawyer is admitted, (vii) the place where the lawyer has his professional domicile, (viii) the jurisdiction governing the lawyer-client relationship, (ix) the jurisdiction about which the legal advice was sought, and (x) the place where the party requesting disclosure resides.[78]

Arbitrators in Denmark have been seen to consider all possibly relevant connecting factors to determine the strength of the connection between the evidence in question and the choice of law. In one instance, an array of factors pointing to the same choice of law was considered, including the intended use of the document, what jurisdiction the legal advice pertained to, the jurisdiction of the lawyers that made the documents, the domicile of the instructing company, and the location of the project in dispute. These factors were balanced against the fact that the document in question had also been transmitted to another jurisdiction. The arbitrators in this matter also considered the substantive law of the contract as a relevant factor, indicating that the parties' choice of law can be a relevant consideration in the closest connection test, even if it is not determinative in deciding which law to apply to issues of legal privilege. Some have suggested that the same is true for the law of the seat of the arbitration.[79]

The closest connection test has the advantage of providing 'an easily identifiable and predictable solution' to determining the privilege rules applicable to particular evidence.[80] As such, it has been commended by scholars of international arbitration as a flexible and pragmatic approach to answering the question of which law to apply to issues of legal privilege. Several note that it is the preferred method of determining the applicable privilege rules,[81] and some even comment that using the closest connection test to decide the law applicable to privilege has developed into a transnational rule.[82]

76. Sheppard & Schlabrendorff, *supra* n. 52, at 767.
77. Grégoire, *supra* n. 12, at 135.
78. *Ibid.*, at 138.
79. *Ibid.*, at 125.
80. Sheppard & Schlabrendorff, *supra* n. 52, at 768.
81. *See, e.g.*, Berger, *supra* n. 1, at 519; Sheppard & Schlabrendorff, *supra* n. 52, at 767.
82. Grégoire, *supra* n. 12, at 137.

One eminent practitioner and scholar, although not going as far as to recommend the closest connection test outright, concludes that applying some of the factors described above, such as the law of the place where the lawyer is qualified to practice or the client is based, is generally the better choice-of-law solution, as it is more likely to conform to the parties' expectations.[83]

Nonetheless, the closest connection test is not without its caveats. Application of the closest connection test could be cumbersome to parties, counsel and tribunals if there is a substantial volume of documents that each need to be assessed for any applicable privilege in the jurisdiction to which they are most closely connected.[84] This could, in turn, substantially slow down the procedural process, not least because the arbitrators might not be equipped to decide the question of privilege under the applicable national laws, and as such, the closest connection test could potentially tarnish the fair and efficient conduct of proceedings. Application of the closest connection test could also yield seemingly inconsistent outcomes in, for example, an arbitration involving many actors across jurisdictions, where the same information or document could be considered both privileged and not privileged if it had been generated, possessed or shared by people in different jurisdictions.

§8.06 HOW QUESTIONS OF LEGAL PRIVILEGE CAN BE INTERPRETED IN INTERNATIONAL ARBITRATIONS GOVERNED BY DANISH LAW

The above sections describe how a situation can arise in which Danish law must be applied to answer questions of legal privilege in international arbitration. However, this creates an apparent paradox – how should detailed questions of legal privilege be answered under Danish law when Danish law does not traditionally recognise a concept of legal privilege equivalent to the common law concept?

This particular paradox has gained attention in other larger civil law jurisdictions with large volumes of international arbitration proceedings. However, the issue remains associated with legal uncertainty in Denmark, arguably owing to the restrictive Danish legal tradition on disclosure in civil proceedings, and has not gained much scrutiny in Danish scholarly writings.

While it may be correct to say that Danish law does not recognise '*legal privilege*' in the way that it is recognised and codified under common law jurisdictions, this does not mean that Danish law has no individual laws that protect certain confidential information from disclosure, thereby acting as a comparable mechanism to legal privilege. For example, and as described in section §8.02[B], section 170(1) of the AJA provides that lawyers are permitted to withhold evidence that is protected by confidentiality subject to certain important exceptions, which is akin to the fundamental protection provided by attorney-client privilege under common law.

83. Born, *supra* n. 48, at 2384-2385.
84. Craig Tevendale & Ula Cartwright-Finch, *Privilege in International Arbitration: Is It Time to Recognize the Consensus?* Journal of International Arbitration 26(6) (2009), 823-839, at 832 https://doi.org/10.54648/joia2009043.

The challenge is that the laws that provide for protection from disclosure of confidential information under Danish law are not as developed or specific as the laws governing legal privilege in common law jurisdictions. This makes sense considering the different approaches to evidence introduction and privilege that exist between these jurisdictions, as is described in section §8.02. However, it does mean that when questions of legal privilege arise in international arbitration that must be answered with reference to Danish law, there is a need for interpretation and gap-filling.

While many questions will remain open with regard to applying Danish law to questions of privilege in international arbitration, two issues seen to be contentious in practice are addressed in the following sections, namely whether the equivalent of legal privilege under Danish law can be said to have been waived, and whether communications pertaining to in-house counsel are protected by the Danish equivalent of legal privilege.

[A] Waiver of Legal Privilege

As discussed above, waiver of a privilege is an important component of the concept of privilege under common law. As such, an argument could arise in international arbitration that a document must be produced because any legal privilege that once applied was waived by some circumstance. Since Danish law does not operate with the defined legal concept of '*privilege*', it does not explicitly have rules or legal doctrine governing when the equivalent of a legal privilege is waived either. Nonetheless, there are certain rules that speak to circumstances in which a document's confidentiality is maintained or forfeited.

For example, in Danish administrative law, confidentiality of information is generally forfeited when there is no longer a valid reason to keep it from public view.[85] Information loses its confidential status if the client discloses it publicly or if it becomes widely known, such as through media scrutiny. Accordingly, the lapse of confidentiality can occur when the information has been shared with the public.

Further, a question could arise regarding whether the confidential status has been forfeited if it has been shared with an auditor or accountant. Under Danish law, auditors and accountants are subject to professional secrecy[86] since parties frequently need to divulge sensitive information to them during audits. Parties should in principle be able to share this information with auditors without compromising confidentiality to encourage full disclosure in an audit. However, there is no settled law on this topic, and the status of information shared with auditors may depend on the specific circumstances.

It is important to note that client-lawyer confidentiality does not fall away once the issue to which the legal advice pertains is resolved. This is evident from Chapter 5 of the Code of Conduct for the Danish Bar and Law Society, which is based on section 126 of the AJA, pursuant to which 'the duty of confidentiality applies to all information

85. White paper no. 1500 on exchange of information in the public administration (KBET 2008), 25.
86. Revisorloven, LBKG 2022-08-31 nr 1219, Chapter 7, section 30.

that becomes known to him in the course of his professional activity… The obligation of confidentiality is not limited in time, and also applies following termination of the mandate'. As such, any privilege-like protections afforded by client-lawyer confidentiality remain and should be applied in international arbitration, even after the issue has been resolved.

However, many questions on waivers will remain subject to further clarification in practice. For example, as Denmark does not have principles equivalent to the joint and common interest privilege known in common law systems, it remains unclear whether or to what extent sharing information between different parties, such as litigation funders or other interested third parties, could result in a waiver that would otherwise apply under Danish law. One approach is to say that because there are no explicit rules on waiver of legal privilege in Danish law, waiver of legal privilege is an irrelevant argument to make in international arbitrations that apply Danish law. However, it is more likely that in the absence of Danish law, parties and arbitrators will turn to international practice for guidance on whether legal privilege has been waived in the circumstances present if such guidance is deemed appropriate, aligned with the parties' legitimate expectations, and consistent with the fair and equal treatment of the parties.

[B] Legal Privilege for In-House Lawyers

Another question that can regularly arise in international arbitration is whether communication with, documents prepared for purposes of advice from, and the advice itself from in-house lawyers are subject to legal privilege. If they are subject to legal privilege, this could prevent the disclosure of a wide number of documents, either because they were created by in-house lawyers or because they were shared with in-house lawyers for purposes of receiving in-house legal advice. In particular, the latter scenario could potentially result in large volumes of evidence being withheld.

The extent to which legal privilege may be applicable to an in-house attorney's work-product remains subject to some uncertainty in Danish law. Whereas in-house lawyers are considered covered by the duty of confidentiality in the Code of Conduct of the Danish Bar and Law Society,[87] in-house lawyers are not expressly mentioned in the AJA as being exempt from giving witness testimony or providing evidence under section 170 of the AJA.[88] Whether in-house lawyers are covered by the provisions of section 170 has also not been addressed by Danish case law.[89]

One way to potentially determine the extent to which section 170 of the AJA may be applicable to in-house lawyers is to evaluate the similarity of the status of in-house lawyers, taking into consideration their capacity as employees and this relationship's

87. Mads Bryde Andersen & Lars Lindencrone Petersen, *Advokatretten*, (2nd ed. Ex Tuto Publishing 2022), 400; Article 1 of the Code of Conduct of the Danish Bar and Law Society, Applicable as from 1 Sep. 2022; Økjær Jørgensen & Lavesen, *supra* n. 25, 27-28.
88. Trine Bonde Jensen, *Virksomhedsjuristens tavshedspligt samt fritagelse for vidne- og editionspligt*, Erhvervsjuridisk Tidsskrift (75) (Karnov Group 2007).
89. *Ibid.*; Bryde Andersen & Lindencrone Petersen, *supra* n. 87, at 405.

effect on independence, with the status of other positions that are exempt from providing evidence under section 170(1) and section 170(4). For example, Danish legal scholar Mads Bryde Andersen states that, due to the nature of the work undertaken by in-house counsels, including actively engaging in decision-making processes within a given company, the relationship cannot be considered on par with that of the independent legal mandate of an external lawyer.[90] This indicates that an in-house lawyer would likely not or at least not as often be considered covered in the same way as an external attorney would be under section 170 of the AJA.[91]

Continuing this analysis, one approach might be to suggest that if an in-house lawyer carries out duties comparable to those of an external lawyer, communications in such instances could be granted protection equivalent to that of legal privilege.[92] Alternatively, another approach could be to consider the evidence itself and provide greater protection to evidence that concerns subject matters that are more internal.[93] To our knowledge, the Danish courts have not dealt with these issues yet.

In contrast, the European Court of Justice (the 'ECJ') has considered this issue and does not consider the in-house lawyer's evidence as protected by legal privilege due to the lack of independence between the in-house lawyer and its employer. The ruling of the ECJ in C-155/79 – *AM & S v. Commission* highlighted two fundamental conditions for legal privilege to apply universally across member states: first, the correspondence must pertain to the client's defence; and second, it must involve independent legal counsel not in the employment of the client.[94] Subsequent cases, such as the *Akzo Nobel* case, further affirmed the exclusion of in-house attorneys from the scope of legal privilege.[95] In this decision, the ECJ emphasised the importance of the purpose of the evidence, stipulating that for legal privilege to attach the evidence must have been intended to be shared with external legal counsel for the purpose of seeking legal advice. The ECJ's rationale rested on the lack of independence of in-house attorneys, given their employment status within the client company.[96] These ECJ rulings thus affirm that legal privilege extends exclusively to communications with externally appointed attorneys under EU law, thereby excluding internal exchanges emanating from or involving an in-house counsel.

Given the unsettled status of this question under Danish law, it is by no means certain whether tribunals would consider communications by or shared with in-house counsel as protected by legal privilege in international arbitrations subject to Danish law, and it is likely that their rulings would depend upon the circumstances present in the individual cases. In one Danish arbitration, the tribunal decided that legal privilege

90. Bryde Andersen & Lindencrone Petersen, *supra* n. 87, at 384.
91. *Ibid.*, at 401.
92. Jes Anker Mikkelsen, *Denmark: International Association of Defense Counsel*, https://www.iadclaw.org/assets/1/7/17.8_Denmark.pdf (accessed 27 Mar. 2024).
93. Bryde Andersen & Lindencrone Petersen, *supra* n. 87, at 405.
94. Case 155/79, *A. M. & S. Europe Ltd. v. Commission of the European Communities*, Q.B. 878, 1611 (1983).
95. Case C-550/07 P, *Akzo Nobel Chemicals Ltd and Akcros Chemicals Ltd v. European Commission*, I-08301, 8380-8383 (2010).
96. *Ibid.*

did not apply to documents forwarded for purposes of receiving legal advice from in-house counsel, despite arguments being presented that the in-house legal department, in all material respects, operated as an independent entity from the remaining parts of the company. It was held that the right of audience of in-house lawyers did not suffice to apply legal privilege and that any limitation restrictions applied to the in-house legal department would not render such documents subject to legal privilege either.

§8.07 CONCLUSION

At the beginning of this chapter, we noted that the maxim '*the only thing that is clear is that nothing is clear*' has been used when discussing the issue of legal privilege in international arbitration.[97] While seeking perfect clarity with regard to the application of legal privilege in international arbitration might prove a fool's errand, some lucidity can be gained, particularly by exploring the issue at the level of one individual jurisdiction.

Building on extensive practical experience in recent years, we have sought to examine legal privilege in international arbitration in Denmark from a practitioner's perspective. This chapter has shown how questions of legal privilege can arise in international arbitrations in Denmark through the application of international standards and institutional rules and how to engage in appropriate analysis despite the concept of legal privilege not traditionally being recognised under Danish law. It has shown that when these questions do arise, they can be significant for the arbitration. It has shown that while international standards and institutional rules allow for the introduction of questions of legal privilege, national laws are required to fully implement them. Therefore, this chapter has examined some of the most common methods for deciding which national law to apply in such a scenario. Finally, it has also examined how certain Danish laws may be used to provide useful input on the topic in cases where reference to Danish law is necessary.

Questions of legal privilege in international arbitration, important as they are, will always be subject to some uncertainty due in no small part to the transnational nature of international arbitration and the national nature of legal privilege. This is perhaps especially true in jurisdictions where non-voluntary disclosure is not the main rule, and issues of legal privilege might seem a rare visitor. This does not mean that obtaining answers to these questions will be entirely arbitrary or unpredictable. Instead, to glean answers and prepare a proper strategy, practitioners should consider such issues early on and assess applicable international standards, institutional rules, and national law within the context of fundamental principles of international arbitration. As such, this chapter may serve as a starting point for the exploration of the characteristics of legal privilege disputes in international arbitrations in Denmark and perhaps also more generally in the Nordics.

97. Berger, *supra* n. 1.

CHAPTER 9

Speeding up the Arbitration Process: Dos and Don'ts

Petri Taivalkoski

The criticism against international arbitration that one repeatedly hears relates to time and costs. These two are interlinked in that the longer the proceedings take, the higher is usually the cost. All major arbitration institutes have sought to address these concerns by putting in place mechanisms for the purposes of ensuring efficient conduct of the proceedings and by offering new, speedier alternatives.

Seeking a speedy resolution of a conflict must always be balanced against other considerations. There are conflicts with regard to which the stakes involved and/or the complexity of the issues are such that a very speedy resolution simply is not an option. Due process, the right to be heard, and sufficient opportunity for the arbitral tribunal to consider the merits of the case cannot be sacrificed just to achieve a swift resolution of the dispute.

However, I believe that most readers of this review are familiar with cases that could have been dealt with much faster than they were but were not because the parties and the arbitral tribunal opted for a procedure applied in most other cases without critical consideration of expediency and efficiency of the proceedings. I had the privilege of serving as the presiding arbitrator in proceedings that took more than two years to complete and thereafter as a sole arbitrator in another case of comparable scope and complexity, in which the Final Award had to be—and was—rendered within three months of my appointment because of a fixed time limit set forth in the arbitration clause. This experience gave me some food for thought as to the ways in which the proceedings could—in appropriate circumstances—be expedited.

The topic of this chapter is to examine what could work to speed up the process when all parties to the arbitration are sufficiently willing to commit to contributing to a swift process and which features and techniques perhaps should be avoided. In the following, I will discuss first questions relating to the composition of the arbitral tribunal (1), second the early stages of the proceedings (2), third the features of the arbitration proceedings that are conducive to a swift process (3) and fourth the drafting process of the arbitral award (4). In the last section, I will describe the timeline applied in the arbitration with the fixed three-month time limit mentioned above and discuss the prerequisites that made rendering the final award within the three-month time limit possible for me as the arbitrator (5).

§9.01 COMPOSITION OF THE ARBITRAL TRIBUNAL

[A] On the Benefits of Appointing Jointly a Sole Arbitrator

Without an agreement with the adverse party, the possibility of appointing one of the arbitrators is the only way of making sure that there is at least one person in the arbitral tribunal whose integrity and judgment have the full confidence of the nominating party. Furthermore, the risk of an error of law or fact by a three-member tribunal is likely to be generally lower than it is with a sole arbitrator.[1] Discussion and deliberation between arbitrators, especially when they are from different legal and cultural backgrounds, enriches the reflection on the issues at stake in the matter. However, having a three-member instead of a sole arbitrator tribunal inevitably prolongs the arbitration process. This is due, *inter alia*, to the following factors.

The mechanics of the appointment process. Appointing first one arbitrator for each party, followed by the steps needed to have a suitable presiding arbitrator in place, takes time and could add several months to the formation of the arbitral tribunal. The difference between the parties agreeing directly on a mutually acceptable sole arbitrator and completing the appointment process of a three-member tribunal could, in the case of procedural complications, such as a challenge of a member of the arbitral tribunal, be four to five months or even longer.

Scheduling. It is sometimes challenging to find hearing dates that suit all three members of an arbitral tribunal, as well as all counsel and other necessary participants in the hearing. This is especially true in cases where the hearing requires a week or more and the arbitrators reside in different jurisdictions. Any need to reschedule the hearing at a late stage may seriously exacerbate the problem. In my abovementioned arbitration that took more than two years to complete, a significant part of the delay was caused by scheduling difficulties in a situation where the hearing first had to be changed from the originally decided virtual hearing to an in-person hearing due to an agreement to this effect between the parties, and later had to be postponed one more time. All in all, the oral hearing ended up being postponed by more than ten months from the dates reserved for the hearing in the original procedural timetable, much because of the difficulties in finding dates that suited all arbitrators and counsel located in different jurisdictions.

1. *See, e.g.*, Nigel Blackaby KC, Constantine Partasides KC, and Alan Redfern, *Redfern and Hunter on International Arbitration*, Seventh Edition, 4.23.

The dynamics of decision-making. A three-member tribunal obviously needs to deliberate not only on the outcome of the case but also on various procedural decisions, and sometimes, this takes time simply because of lack of simultaneous availability of the members. The more decisions are to be made, the longer usually the additional time needed, as compared to a sole arbitrator. It is essential to ensure that all members of the arbitral tribunal have a meaningful opportunity to contribute to deliberations and give input on the contents of the decisions taken by the arbitral tribunal. For this to be possible, the time needed for three arbitrators to complete the final award could be significantly longer than for a sole arbitrator. Sometimes, difficulties in reaching a consensus on key issues or dissenting opinions may cause additional delay in the deliberations.

To conclude, a three-member tribunal has obvious advantages but brings with it inherent delay that can, at times, be significant compared to a one-member tribunal. The optimal solution, when expediency is a key factor, is to agree on a sole arbitrator who has the trust of both parties. Where this is not possible, the choice of the sole arbitrator can be entrusted to an arbitral institution with specific knowledge of suitable arbitrators in relevant jurisdictions, possibly with mutually agreed guidance on the qualifications of the sole arbitrator to be nominated.

The general default position under national laws on arbitration is that the number of arbitrators shall be three, as reflected in Article 10(2) of the UNCITRAL Model Law. Given the cost-efficiency benefits of having a one-member arbitral tribunal, the default position in some institutional arbitration rules today is that where the parties have not agreed on the number of arbitrators, the institute will nominate a sole arbitrator. This is the case, e.g., of the International Court of Arbitration (ICC) and the Finland Arbitration Institute (FAI).[2] In ICC Arbitration, where the parties have not agreed on the number of arbitrators, the International Court of Arbitration will normally appoint a sole arbitrator where the amount in dispute is less than USD 10 million and a three-member tribunal where the amount in dispute exceeds USD 30 million.[3]

In ICC arbitration, the time and cost benefits of a sole arbitrator have been considered to be so important that where the monetary interest at stake is relatively low, the ICC Rules on Arbitration provide for the possibility to nominate a sole arbitrator despite the parties' agreement on three arbitrators. Under Article 30 of the ICC Rules, the Expedited Procedure Provisions (EPP) apply in cases where the amount in dispute does not exceed USD 3 million, and the parties have not opted out of the EPP.[4] As to the constitution of the arbitral tribunal, under the EPP, the ICC Court of

2. Pursuant to Art. 12(2) of the ICC Rules, "Where the parties have not agreed upon the number of arbitrators, the Court shall appoint a sole arbitrator, save where it appears to the Court that the dispute is such as to warrant the appointment of three arbitrators." A similar provision is included in Art. 17 of the FAI Rules. According to the FAI Statistics for 2023, 85.9% of the cases were referred to a sole arbitrator in 2023 (*see* the FAI February 2024 Newsletter, available at www.arbitration.fi).
3. *See* the Note to the Parties and Arbitral Tribunals on the Conduct of the Arbitration under the ICC Rules of Arbitration Jan. 1, 2021 # 40, available at www.iccwbo.org.
4. The EPP is regulated by the Expedited Procedure Rules set forth in Appendix VI to the ICC Rules. The USD 3 million threshold applies to arbitration agreements concluded on or after Jan. 1, 2021. The previous threshold of USD 2 million applies to arbitration agreements concluded from Mar.

Arbitration may appoint a sole arbitrator notwithstanding any contrary provision in the arbitration agreement. A vast majority of the EPP proceedings are conducted by a Sole Arbitrator.[5]

Due to the factors discussed above, it is unsurprising that a standard feature in any institutional expedited rules is the nomination of a sole arbitrator, as reflected, e.g., in Article 17 of the SCC Expedited Arbitration Rules.[6]

[B] Finding an Arbitrator with Availability

Many years ago, I acted as lead counsel for a respondent in an arbitration in which claimants were represented by an experienced and knowledgeable opposing counsel from Southern Europe. After lengthy but constructive discussions between counsel, we had managed to agree on a suitable presiding arbitrator, whom I was tasked to give a call on behalf of all parties to inquire about his availability, which I promptly did. In our call, the prospective presiding arbitrator said that he would be delighted to take on the task but asked us to consider that his calendar was quite full: in more concrete terms, the first possible window for a one-week oral hearing would be in approximately two years from our telephone conversation. In that matter, getting the desired arbitral tribunal was such an important consideration that the prospective presiding arbitrator was selected despite his extremely limited availability.

The reality is that many renowned arbitration practitioners have very full calendars. As opposed to cases taken on as counsel, the possibilities of delegating the work involved in an arbitrator assignment are very limited because of the personal nature of the assignment.[7] Nominating arbitrators who do not have the necessary availability may have a significant delaying impact.

For the arbitration procedure to move swiftly, the arbitral tribunal needs to be in a position to acquaint itself with the case and put the procedural parameters in place without delay. The tribunal also needs to have sufficient availability to be on top of the case all the way and to be able to address any procedural and practical issues as needed if and when they arise. How can the parties ensure that this will be the case?

There is nothing wrong in asking the prospective arbitrator about his or her availability when discussing his or her possible appointment as arbitrator. Many

---

1, 2017 to Dec. 31, 2020. EPP provides for a simplified arbitration procedure in that no Terms of Reference are required, the case may be decided on the basis of documents only and the arbitral tribunal may limit the number, length and scope of written submissions and written witness evidence. The time limit for rendering the Final Award is six months of the Case Management Conference, to be held within fifteen days of the transfer of the file to the arbitral tribunal.

5. According to ICC statistics for 2017 to 2023, there have been altogether 713 EPP cases since the introduction of the EPP in March 2017. A three-member tribunal was nominated in only 22 cases.
6. Article 17 of the SCC Expedited Arbitration Rules: "The Arbitration shall be decided by a sole Arbitrator."
7. The arbitral tribunal may engage a secretary to assist in organizational, administrative or preparative tasks. For a comprehensive overview of the role and best practises of the use of tribunal secretaries, *see* Hans-Patrick Schroeder and Wolfgang Junge, *Tribunal secretaries re-examined—comparative legal framework, best practices and terms of appointment*, Arbitration International, 2022, 38, pp. 21-41 https://doi.org/10.1093/arbint/aiac004.

arbitration institutes nowadays require arbitrators to disclose information on their other pending commitments and sometimes also information on reserved calendar dates in the next few years. In a similar manner, if information on the prospective arbitrator's availability is important for the purposes of arbitrator selection, it is entirely appropriate for counsel to inquire about these issues when communicating with the prospective arbitrator.[8] For such a discussion to be as useful as possible, it would be important for counsel to be able to communicate to the prospective arbitrator at least a rough idea of the desired timeline.

§9.02 EARLY STAGES OF THE PROCEEDINGS

A key feature of national laws on arbitration and institutional arbitration rules that are consistent with international practises is that they do not contain detailed provisions on the arbitration procedure. This is the basis for party autonomy and the flexibility of arbitration: as opposed to proceedings in state courts, the parties to arbitration proceedings have the freedom to tailor the proceedings to meet the specific needs of the case in question. In a similar manner, to the extent that the parties have not agreed on the procedure, the arbitral tribunal is at liberty to tailor the procedural features and the timetable.

The early stages of the proceedings are therefore crucial in laying the foundation for the entire arbitration all the way until the final award. As the arbitrator, in deciding how to proceed, I have found it useful to envision where I would like to be once the closing submissions (written or oral, as the case may be) have been delivered by counsel. In an optimal situation, looking back at the completed procedural steps at that stage:

- the parties will have articulated early on the relief sought in a precise and comprehensive manner and responded to the relief sought by the other party;
- the respective positions as to relevant facts will have been clearly set out;
- the parties will have submitted apposite but not excessive evidence in support of their allegations;
- the legal aspects of the case will have been fully pleaded, and there is sufficient evidence on the record on the contents of the applicable substantive law or laws;
- time will not have been wasted on procedural battles of little additional value; and
- the parties' closing arguments provide the arbitral tribunal with a useful roadmap to the factual and legal exhibits on the record.

At times, real life turns out not to be in all respects optimal. When starting to deliberate, the arbitral tribunal may come to realize that the relief sought by a party,

8. *See, e.g.*, the IBA Guidelines on Party Representation in International Arbitration Art. 8(a) and (c) on the permitted ex parte communications with the prospective party-appointed arbitrator and the prospective presiding arbitrator.

despite having evolved several times in the course of the arbitration, is still in some regards unfit for determination. A surprisingly often arising issue is shortcomings in interest claims: the legal basis and the interest claim may be lacking altogether, and/or a party has not explained the legal basis for post-award interest where this is not evident under the applicable law.[9] The adverse party may have omitted to provide any response or comment on the interest claim. A party may have conducted the arbitration with a heavy emphasis on facts and evidence and omitted to furnish evidence on the contents of the applicable law, putting the arbitral tribunal in a rather delicate position in determining the contents of the applicable law to the extent required. The parties may prove to have very different expectations on the rules of the game or even the role of the arbitral tribunal, leading to time-consuming procedural battles and numerous procedural decisions. The early stages of the proceedings are an opportunity for the arbitral tribunal to reduce the possibility of unpleasant surprises by making sure that the parties understand the rules of the game in the same manner and commit to playing by them. The difficulty of this task may vary considerably, depending on the expectations of the parties based on their own legal cultures and the familiarity of counsel on both sides of international arbitration practises, as well as procedural strategies and tactics of the parties.

The first task of the arbitral tribunal after receipt of the case file is usually to organize the case management conference (CMC) for the purposes of determining the parameters of the procedure and the procedural timetable. Where expediency is primary, rather than basing the discussions on Procedural Order No. 1 (PO 1) templates from other cases, it may be more efficient to have a discussion with counsel on what features of the procedure are truly necessary and how each participant can best contribute to a swift process. This may require going a bit deeper into each of the typical topics on the CMC agenda. To give a concrete example, instead of just agreeing that written witness statements will be required for all fact witnesses, it may be useful to have a discussion on the drafting process and the contents of the witness statements. As regards document production, instead of just recording that the arbitral tribunal may use the IBA Rules on the Taking of Evidence in International Arbitration (the "IBA Rules") as guidance when ruling on the requests, it could be useful to have a discussion on what in concrete terms is to be understood by "a narrow and specific requested category of documents" referred to in Article 3.3(a)(ii) of the IBA Rules and what is required for a party to show relevance and materiality of the requested documents.

One of the difficulties for the arbitral tribunal in the early phases is that the request for arbitration and the answer usually contain very little information on the matter at hand and only some key documents. An effective way for the parties to assist the arbitral tribunal and to make the early phase of the arbitration more efficient is to expand on the request for arbitration and the answer by including a more comprehensive account of the factual background, the key legal issues and evidence to be presented in support of the case. The more information the arbitral tribunal has early

9. For a comprehensive analysis of problems with interest claims, *see* Mika Savola, *Awarding Interest in International Arbitration*, Jubilee Publication for Professor Seppo Villa, Alma Talent Oy, 2021, pp. 493-515.

on in the case, the better the tribunal will be able to assist the parties in tailoring the proceedings to meet the needs of the case in question.

As to the CMC and the documentation resulting from it, i.e., usually the PO 1 setting forth the procedural parameters and the Procedural Timetable (PTT), much will depend on the parties and their counsel. Where the counsel know one another and their expectations on the procedure are similar, a lighter documentation may be sufficient. Where this is not the case, it may be prudent to opt for a rather detailed PO1 to minimize the possibility of disagreement on procedural issues later on.[10] However, since it would be an impossible exercise to anticipate in the documentation all issues that may arise, the parties' understanding of and commitment to the rules of the game may be more important than striving at an exhaustive PO 1.

§9.03 FEATURES OF A SWIFT PROCEDURE

In the following, I will discuss in more detail the procedural features that may be helpful in order to streamline and speed up the process and how these can be addressed in concrete terms in the CMC.

Reducing the number of submissions. The default position in most CMCs is to have two rounds of submissions. Unless the respondent presents a counterclaim, this is by no means indispensable. Having only one round of submissions requires a willingness by both parties to commit to a genuinely front-loaded procedure, in which the claimant submits a comprehensive statement of claim with all relevant facts, legal arguments and evidence, and the respondent submits a comprehensive statement of defense meeting the same requirements. When implemented in good faith by both parties, this will lead to significant savings of time. The agreed procedure should entail that further submissions will only be allowed at the request or permission of the arbitral tribunal on specific topics. To the extent that there may be a need to submit new claims, arguments or evidence after the first and only round of submissions, this would be possible on the agreed first cut-off date and, respectively, on the second cut-off date as a response to the submission of new claims, arguments or evidence on the first cut-off date.

Articulating with precision the requests for relief early on. The arbitral tribunal has preliminary information on the relief sought by the parties on the basis of the request for arbitration and the answer. When there is only one round of actual submissions, unclear or inapt requests for relief may prove problematic when the arbitral tribunal starts its deliberations. Different types of requests for declaratory relief that appear to have become more and more common in recent years may pose specific problems.[11] The arbitral tribunal is generally not in a position to reformulate the relief

10. *See* Mika Savola, *Procedural Order No. 1—Trends and Practices*, ASA Bulletin 4/2023 (December) pp. 783-804 https://doi.org/10.54648/asab2023055 making a compelling case in favour of a detailed PO 1 in cases where counsel come from different legal cultures.
11. Generally on non-monetary relief in international arbitration *see* Michael Schneider, *Non-monetary Relief in International Arbitration: Principles and Arbitration Practice*, ASA Performance as a Remedy, JurisNet, LLC 2011, available at www.lalive.law.

requested, at least not without soliciting the views of the parties. One way to anticipate this issue is to have an open discussion on it in the CMC and get commitment from the parties to give the matter special attention and to endeavor to formulate their requests for relief in such a way that they can be included directly in the dispositive section of the award.

Reducing the scope and extent of document production. It appears that the use of very extensive document production requests, still quite unusual in the early 2000s, is spreading to the Nordic Countries not only in arbitration but also in court proceedings. An extreme example is a recent Norwegian case where the order to produce documents issued by a Norwegian Court of Appeal would have led to the production of a data volume of 500 GB, some 2.5 million documents and requiring a workload of some 10 man years from the requested party.[12] While the order was ultimately annulled by the Supreme Court of Norway, the case may be seen as an indication of a radically more permissive approach to requests for document discovery in the Nordic Countries.[13]

In international arbitration, extensive and often excessive document requests have already, for some time, been a significant contributor to delay and costs and a standard topic of discussion in international arbitration seminars and conferences.

In the CMC, the arbitral tribunal has the possibility to encourage the parties to consider critically whether there is a need for a procedure for document discovery in the first place. It is not entirely uncommon that an extensive document production phase requiring several months to complete ends up bringing quite little added value to the proceedings compared to the time and costs needed. Where there is a need for document production, the arbitral tribunal may consider mechanisms to reduce its scope and extent. Such mechanisms may include, e.g., limiting the number of requests, ordering that the arbitral tribunal may only accept or deny a request (i.e., not "correct" it by accepting it partly in a redacted form) and ordering that as a rule, requests for documents on issues where the requested party bears the burden of proof are not permitted. Overly broad requests for documents can also be discouraged by imposing a requirement that the requesting party specify the factual allegations with regard to which the requested documents are suggested to have relevance as evidence.[14]

Efficient use of documentary evidence. Far too often, one as an arbitrator comes to realize that a considerable part of the documentary evidence submitted by the parties does not serve any purpose with regard to the central issues in dispute. It is understandable that counsel may wish to err on the side of caution when deciding whether or not to submit evidence so as not to find themselves barred from doing so

---

12. Presentation of Fredrik Lilleaas Ellingsen at the Norwegian Arbitration Day on Feb. 8, 2024 in Oslo.
13. Supreme Court order 27 May 2019, HR-2019-997-A (case no. 18-186326SIV-HRET). The trend towards more extensive obligation to produce documents is reflected also in a recent decision by the Finnish Supreme Court KKO 2019:7, in which the required evidentiary value of the requested documents was set at a rather low level.
14. In court proceedings in Finland and Sweden, the parties are required to specify an evidentiary topic (in Swedish *bevistema*, "theme of evidence") for each piece of documentary evidence. The requirement of such topic could be a useful tool in international arbitration proceedings as well.

after the cut-off dates. However, when expediency of the proceedings is important and the parties are willing to commit to a swift and front-loaded process, this may also be helpful for the purposes of focusing on the essential and practicing restraint when it comes to the temptation to submit large numbers of documents just in case. In the CMC, the arbitral tribunal may encourage the parties to specify for each piece of documentary evidence the factual allegations that they relate to and to identify clearly the specific parts invoked in support of the allegations in the documents. New kinds of documentary evidence, such as printouts from WhatsApp or chat log exchanges, may require special attention to ensure user-friendliness and verifiability.

Guidance on the contents of witness statements. Virtually all international arbitrations use witness statements, and they may be indispensable for the expediency and efficiency of the proceedings, especially in cases with many witnesses of fact. In any large and complex case, it is hardly conceivable to address witness testimony only orally in the same way as in court proceedings in some jurisdictions.[15] Being informed early on of the contents of the fact witnesses' testimony invoked by the adverse party also reduces the possibility of surprises or "trial by ambush" that may lead to procedural complications or due process concerns. The requirement that written witness statements be submitted for all witnesses is therefore an important feature of a swift process.

In practise, there is quite a lot of variation in the preparation and contents of witness statements. For the witness evidence to serve the efficiency of the proceedings as much as possible, it may be useful to take the issue up for discussion. In a recent publication, it was suggested that the following principles should guide the preparation of witness statements:[16]

(i) subject to providing background context, the witness statement must only contain matters relevant to the issues in dispute of which the witness has personal knowledge;
(ii) the witness statement must not contain any supposition, speculation, conjecture, or commentary on another person's knowledge;
(iii) the witness statement must not contain any argument;
(iv) there should not be any recitation of the documentary record or quotations from contemporaneous documents;
(v) witnesses should only refer to documents which they had received or were aware of before the dispute arose, and only if it is necessary to refer to the document; and
(vi) the witness should identify where documents have been used to refresh the witness's memory (whether or not those documents have been referred to or not in the witness statement).

15. E.g., in Finland and Sweden witness statements are as a general rule not allowed for fact witnesses and the hearing takes place orally also for direct testimony.
16. Doug Jones and Robert Turnbull, *Witness statements and memorials, Reforms to serve parties, arbitrators and arbitrations*, ICC Publication Rethinking the Paradigms of International Arbitration, International Chamber of Commerce 2023, p. 136.

The parties' commitment to observe guidance along the principles outlined above could significantly improve the quality of the witness statements, assist in focusing on the case of each party at an early stage and be conducive to a swift and efficient process.

Submitting appropriate evidence on the contents of the applicable law. Counsel whose practise focuses on proceedings in State courts may not always pay sufficient attention to the need to submit evidence on the contents of the applicable substantive law in international arbitration proceedings. As opposed to state courts in civil jurisdictions that have the power to apply the law ex officio by the application of the *jura novit curia* principle, arbitral tribunals need to be cautious in developing legal arguments not invoked by the parties so as not to risk validity and enforceability of the award because of violation of the right to be heard.[17] It may also be risky for the Arbitral Tribunal to base its decision on a legal source, not on the record, if such a legal source comes as a surprise to the parties.[18] To avoid any surprises in this regard, the issue may benefit from discussion at the CMC, getting commitment from the parties to submit evidence on the contents of the applicable substantive law in a front-loaded manner comprehensively early on as legal exhibits, with translations into the language of the arbitration to the extent needed.

Efficient use of oral hearing. Even in the rare case that no cross-examination will be needed for any of the facts or expert witnesses, an oral hearing serves an important function for the arbitral tribunal to communicate directly with counsel and clarify any unclear issues. This is all the more the case in proceedings with only one round of submissions. A bare minimum oral hearing may consist of brief opening arguments by the parties and questions by the arbitral tribunal, followed by oral closing submissions, which was the case in a recent Expedited Arbitration under the FAI Expedited Arbitration Rules in which I served as the sole arbitrator. However, in the more usual scenario, time will need to be allotted to fact or expert witness testimony. Opting for a fully digital hearing may be the speedy and cost-efficient choice in certain cases.[19] In cases where an in-person hearing is the better option, for the purposes of avoiding delays in the event of surprises, it is prudent to agree on the possibility to allow for the possibility of hearing witnesses remotely or even organize the hearing entirely or partially as a remote hearing, if a compelling need arises.

Opting for oral closing submissions instead of post-hearing briefs. Oral closing submissions are very efficient from the arbitrator's perspective in that they are delivered at the end of the oral hearing when the whole hearing is in the arbitrator's

---

17. For an excellent overview of the topic, *see* Affef Ben Mansour, et al., *Does Jura Novit Curia Apply in Arbitration? ICC Bulletin* 2023 issue 3, pp. 53-61.
18. In ICC Court scrutiny, an often recurring comment to the arbitral tribunal relates to legal sources referred to in the draft arbitral award with regard to which it is unclear whether they are on the record, *see Ten Tips on How to Make an Arbitration Award Work: Lessons from the ICC Scrutiny Process*, ICC Dispute Resolution Bulletin 2022, Issue 2, p. 59.
19. For useful tips in this regard, *see, e.g.*, Niels Schiersing & Tim Robbins, *Digital Hearings, the Arbitrator's Perspective* and Johan Sidklev, *Best practices in conducting a digital arbitral proceeding, in Digital Hearings*. Civil Procedure and Arbitration, ed. Mika Savola, Ylli Dautaj, Bruno Gustafsson & Rolf Åbjörnsson, Norsteds Juridik 2022.

fresh memory, and the arbitral tribunal may start its deliberations right away using the closing submissions as useful guidance. Post-hearing briefs will always cause some delay because of the time needed for their preparation and the arbitral tribunals' review of their contents. Post-hearing briefs may also entail a bigger temptation for the party to come up with new allegations, arguments or evidence that may lead to procedural disputes and further delay. Post-hearing briefs may be necessary from the parties' perspective and valuable also from the arbitral tribunals' perspective in many large and complex cases. Where expediency is key, the parties and counsel should seriously consider opting for oral closing arguments.

§9.04 DRAFTING PROCESS OF THE FINAL AWARD

Once the closing arguments have been delivered and proceedings have been declared as closed, the duration of the arbitration up until the issuance of the final award is in the hands of the arbitral tribunal. The key to a speedy last part of the arbitration is front-loaded work and preparation by the arbitral tribunal. When acting as the sole arbitrator, I have found it useful to start early on preparing a document that will serve as an outline for the final award with all necessary information on the procedure, the relief requested and sometimes also summaries of the parties' positions. In a similar manner, preparing concise summaries of the parties' submissions at the receipt of each submission has been helpful both for the purposes of staying on top of things and preparing for the oral hearing.

The most critical and time-consuming part of the work of an arbitral tribunal is the actual decision-making and drafting of the reasoning explaining why the case has been decided in the manner that it was. The parties to an arbitration may sometimes take the view that in order to have the decision available as quickly as possible after the hearing, the final award should be rendered without reason. Whether the arbitral tribunal can, at the request of the parties, do so or not depends on the applicable arbitration law. Nowadays, under most arbitration laws and rules, the parties may validly agree that the arbitral tribunal shall decide the matter without giving reasons upon which the award is based (§9.04[A]). However, the parties should carefully consider whether sacrificing the reasons of the award for increased expediency is genuinely in their best interest (§9.04[B]).

[A] Most Arbitration Laws Permit Agreeing on the Award Being Issued Without Reasons

Article 31(2) of the UNCITRAL Model Law provides as follows:

> The award shall state the reasons upon which it is based, unless the parties have agreed that no reasons are to be given or the award is an award on agreed terms under article 30.

In the drafting process of the 1985 UNCITRAL Model Law, the reasons for and against requiring awards to state the reasons upon which they are based were considered. In favor of the requirement, it was noted that many national laws required reasons, and this was thought to improve the quality of the award. Against the requirement it was suggested that awards that did not state reasons could be issued more speedily and were less subject to challenge and that issuing awards without reasons was usual in certain kinds of arbitration.[20] The end result was a provision requiring reasons but permitting the parties to agree that no reasons are to be given.

National laws still differ on the requirement of reasons. One example of a law that sets a mandatory requirement of reasons is the Belgian Law on Arbitration of 2013, set out in Book VI of the Belgian Judicial Code (the "BJC"). Article 1713 § 4 of the BJC provides that the award shall state the reasons upon which it is based.[21] Pursuant to Article 1717 § 3 a) iv) of the BJC, absence of reasons constitutes a cause for setting aside an arbitral award. The Belgian legislator of the 2013 reform decided to deviate on this point from the UNCITRAL Model Law, considering that Belgian public policy requires that all judgments and awards be reasoned because of the jurisdictional nature of arbitration.[22]

It should nevertheless be noted that under Belgian law, the requirement for reasons is a formal one. It is satisfied as soon as the arbitrators have stated the reasons for their decision and responded to the means and pleas developed by the parties. The court seized with setting aside of the arbitral award may neither control the application of the law by the arbitral tribunal nor examine the opportunity or appropriateness of the decision of the arbitral tribunal[23] nor is a contradiction in the reasons a cause for annulment of an arbitral award under Belgian law.[24] The requirement to provide reasons has not been considered part of the international public policy in Belgium either, and consequently, absence of reasons should not constitute grounds for refusing recognition and enforcement of a foreign arbitral award in Belgium.[25]

The Netherlands Arbitration Act of 2015 similarly requires awards to be reasoned—save for arbitrations pertaining to the quality or condition of goods—but allows the parties to agree in writing that no reasons shall be given once the arbitration is pending.[26] Examples of provisions in national arbitration laws that are in substance similar to the UNCITRAL Model Law are, for instance, Article 52(4) of the 1996 English Arbitration Act[27] and Article 189(2) of the 1987 Swiss Private International Law Act.[28]

20. Holzmann H.M., Neuhaus J.E., *A Guide to the UNCITRAL Model Law on International Commercial Arbitration: Legislative History and Commentary*, Kluwer 1989, pp. 837-838.
21. "*La sentence arbitrale est motivée.*"
22. Niuscha Bassiri & Maarten Draye (eds.), *Arbitration in Belgium. A Practitioner's Guide*, Wolters Kluwer 2016, p. 473.
23. *Ibid.*
24. *Ibid.*, p. 474.
25. *Ibid.*, p. 523.
26. Albert Marsman, *International Arbitration in the Netherlands: With a Commentary on the NAI and PCA Arbitration Rules*, Wolters Kluwer 2021 at 14-050.
27. England, like many other common law countries, has a long tradition of unreasoned awards. The practise started to change with the passing of the 1979 English Arbitration Act and was completed in the 1996 English Arbitration Act. For more information on the historical background, *see* Noam Zamir and Neil Kaplan, *To reason or not to reason: arbitral awards—the conflict between conciseness and the duty to provide reasons under national laws and international rules*, Arbitration International, 2024, XX, pp. 2-4.

As to the Nordic countries, Norway and Denmark, as UNCITRAL Model Law countries, have adopted the solution set forth in the Model Law.[29] Conversely, the Finnish and Swedish Arbitration Acts do not contain specific provisions on reasons. The reasoning of the Finnish and the Swedish legislators is similar to the points made against the requirement of reasons in the drafting process of the UNCITRAL Model Law referred to above. As to Finnish *travaux préparatoires*, the rationale for not including such provision in the 1992 Arbitration Act was not to encourage post-arbitration disputes on the adequacy of reasons in the award.[30] As to Swedish law, according to the *travaux préparatoires*, the rationale for not requiring reasons is, on the one hand, cost-efficiency and, on the other hand, keeping down the number of challenges to the arbitral tribunal's reasons. However, even without an explicit requirement for reasons, it is hardly conceivable that an arbitral award would be rendered in Finland or Sweden without reasons unless the parties have explicitly agreed so. Both the SCC Arbitration Rules and the FAI Arbitration Rules contain an explicit requirement that the award be reasoned, and proper reasoning is, without any doubt, the expectation of the parties in ad hoc arbitration in Finland and Sweden as well.[31]

Parties may agree that the award is rendered without reasons by agreeing on arbitration under certain rules on expedited arbitration. As to the Nordic countries, the SCC Expedited Arbitration Rules permit the award to be rendered without reasons unless a party requests a reasoned award no later than at the closing statement. Under Article 41.1 of the Finland Arbitration Institute (FAI) Rules for Expedited Arbitration, rendering the award without reasons is the default position unless a party has requested reasons to be given:

> An award shall be made in writing. It shall not contain reasons, unless a party has requested a reasoned award within the time limit set by the sole arbitrator.

According to information received from the FAI, there have been only a handful of cases in recent years where the award has been given without reasons.[32] The situation is very similar in arbitrations conducted under the SCC Expedited Arbitration Rules in recent years.[33]

The validity of an agreement under Finnish law to the effect that the arbitral award shall not contain reasons was recently tested in the District Court of Helsinki. In the matter in question, the parties to the arbitration had, in the course of the arbitration, agreed to apply the FAI Rules for Expedited Arbitration. At the first Case

---

28. Daniel Gisrberger and Nathalie Voser, *International Arbitration, Comparative and Swiss Perspectives*, Fourth Extended Edition 7/1520 and 1507.
29. Article 31(2) of the Danish Arbitration Act of 2005 is identical to the corresponding provision in the UNCITRAL Model Law. As to the Norwegian Arbitration Act of 2004, Art. 36(2) sets a requirement that the award be reasoned, but Art. 36(6) provides that the parties may contract out of such requirement.
30. Government Bill HE 202/1991 vp., p. 8.
31. For Swedish law, *see International Arbitration in Sweden, A Practitioner's Guide*, second edition, eds. Annette Magnusson, Jakob Ragnwald and Martin Wallin, Wolters Kluwer 2021, p. 311 #358. For Finnish law, *see* Mika Hemmo, *Välimiesmenettely*, Alma Talent 2022, p. 944.
32. Telephone conversation with Sanna Kaistinen, General Secretary of the FAI on Mar. 7, 2024.
33. Information received from Evelina T. Wahlström, Head of Quality at the SCC on Mar. 8, 2024.

Management Conference, the parties had specifically agreed that there is no need to give reasons in the arbitral award. After the sole arbitrator had found for the claimant, the respondent initiated setting aside proceedings claiming, *inter alia*, that the arbitral award violated the public policy of Finland and the European Convention of Human Rights because no reasons for the award had been provided. In its judgment rendered on January 5, 2024,[34] the District Court of Helsinki correctly held that neither Finnish public policy nor the European Convention of Human Rights prevents a party from waiving its right to a reasoned award, rejecting the action for setting aside.

To conclude, there appears to be a wide consensus in national laws and rules that the parties can validly agree on an award without reasons. However, a totally different question is whether agreeing so is in the parties' best interest.

[B] Agreeing on an Award Without Reasons Is Rarely in the Interest of the Parties

An award without reasons may be in the interest of the parties in case they are in agreement that there is only a need for a swift resolution of the dispute and that reasons for the decision will not serve any purpose. This could be the situation in relatively straightforward matters, e.g., where the dispute turns on a single issue of fact, such as the quality or condition of commodities delivered.

However, in more complex cases, the situation is quite different. As in the Finnish court case referred to above, the losing party may come to regret its decision to agree that the award shall be given without reasons. Without reasons, the losing party may only make assumptions as to why the case has been decided as it was. It may nevertheless also be important for the winning party for future purposes to understand why some arguments or evidence have not convinced the arbitral tribunal. All this benefit for present and future purposes is lost with an award without reasons.

Also, from the arbitrator's perspective, agreeing to render the award without reasons is far from optimal. As an arbitrator, one has a strong desire to explain the findings and decisions and demonstrate that the evidence presented in the matter has been given appropriate consideration and the legal arguments have been adequately assessed. Writing is an important part of making sure that the logic of the decision holds water and that all relevant aspects have been taken into consideration. In the words of an eminent practitioner:

> We all know what the reasons for providing reasons for arbitral awards are. Probably the most important one is to oblige the arbitrators to think carefully of every aspect of the dispute and to allow them to come to a decision that is fully thought through and respectful of the rules by which they have to abide in

34. L 706/2023/344, decision number 1014 6972. The respondent appealed the decision to the Court of Appeal of Helsinki, which rejected the appeal by its decision rendered on May 8, 2024 (decision number 705, matter number S 24/203) and upheld the decision of the District Court of Helsinki.

> reaching their decision, and that has the cogency, intellectual rigour and persuasiveness that only writing can provide.[35]

To conclude, agreeing that the award shall be rendered without reasons is rarely in the interest of the parties or the arbitral tribunal. Such option may be appropriate for very straightforward disputes such as quality arbitrations. For disputes of any degree of factual, technical or legal complexity—and it is submitted that this applies to most international arbitrations—it is hard to see how the gain in time could outweigh the downside of the parties not being provided with an explanation as to why the case has been decided as it has.

A middle ground between fully reasoned awards and awards without reasons is provided, e.g., in Article 42(2)(f) of the Swiss Rules of International Arbitration. Under the said provision, where the Expedited Provisions apply, the arbitral tribunal may state the reasons for the award in a summary form. Summary reasons are certainly better than no reasons at all. However, explaining in a summary manner may not be a satisfactory solution in that summary reasons may fall short of convincing the reader. Stating the reasons in a summary form may be a workable solution in straightforward disputes or, e.g., in decisions on disclosure of documents rendered in a Redfern-schedule format. To the extent it is possible to dispense the arbitral tribunal with giving reasons for its final award, the same applies *a fortiori* to procedural decisions.

§9.05 APPLICATION IN PRACTISE OF A THREE-MONTH TIMELINE

Below, I have set out as a listing the timeline applied in the three-month arbitration referred to in the introduction as a list of the essential procedural steps from the nomination of me as the sole arbitrator on day 1 until the rendering of the Final Award on day 85:

Day 1 Appointment of the Sole Arbitrator (SA)
Day 1 SA's proposal of times for the CMC and for the agenda
Day 3 CMC (Teams)
Day 3 SA provides draft minutes of the CMC and the PTT to the Parties
Day 7 Parties' comments to draft CMC minutes and the PTT
Day 8 SA provides signed CMC minutes and the PTT to the Parties
Day 23 Statement of Claim, Documentary Evidence and Witness Statements
Day 42 Statement of Defense, Documentary Evidence and Witness Statements
Day 49 First Cut-off date submissions
Day 56 Second Cut-off date submissions
Day 56 Claimant's request to submit additional evidence
Day 57 Respondent's response and request to submit additional evidence
Day 57 SA's decision on additional evidence

35. Luca G. Radicati di Brozolo, *Reasons in International Commercial and Investment Arbitration Awards—How Much and How?* in Explaining Why You Lost—Reasoning in Arbitration—Institute Dossier XVIII—2020, published by the International Chamber of Commerce (ICC).

Day 67 Oral Hearing
Day 71 Cost Submissions
Day 73 Reply Cost Submissions
Day 73 Closing of the Proceedings with regard to the matters to be decided in the Final Award
Day 85 Final Award

Put briefly, the factors and features of the procedure that made the exceptionally compact procedure possible can be summarized as follows:

(i) The professional and constructive attitude of counsel on both sides.
(ii) Quick kick-off of the proceedings after receipt of the case file, CMC on day 3 and putting together the minutes (replacing the usual PO 1) and the PTT without delay thereafter.
(iii) Agreeing on only one round of submissions.
(iv) The parties agreeing on and committing to a genuinely front-loaded procedure in which the Statement of Claim and the Statement of Defense provided a comprehensive account of the facts and legal argumentation of the respective party, accompanied with all documentary evidence, all witness statements, expert evidence and legal exhibits of that party.
(v) Concise Oral Closing Arguments that provided me with a useful roadmap to the evidence and legal argumentation of each party and permitted immediate start of decision-making after the closing of the oral hearing.
(vi) Arbitrator availability throughout the procedure and in particular at critical points.

It is unlikely that we would have agreed on such a speedy process without the necessity to do so because of the fixed three-month time limit in the arbitration clause. I would nevertheless strongly advise against agreeing to the arbitration clause on a time limit without the possibility of extending the time limit. It is very risky and may, in the worst case, lead to the arbitration clause being in practise inoperative. A better option would be to refer to expedited clauses providing for a possibility to transfer to a full-fledged process if the situation so requires, empowering the arbitral tribunal or the arbitration institute to grant extensions if there is a compelling need.

CHAPTER 10
Document Production in Scandinavia

Haakon Orgland Bingen[*] *& Aksel Kolstad*

§10.01 INTRODUCTION

Documents are the most important source of evidence the parties to an arbitration may have available to them.[1] However, it is not always the case that the parties to an arbitration have all the documents required to plead the case as they would like. For this reason, a party may have to request the production of documents from the opposing party or parties[2] in order to illuminate its case.[3]

A proper document production phase may substantively affect the outcome of the dispute.[4] However, document production procedures may also be abused, e.g., as a procedural tactic to impose costs, delay, and undue burdens or in an attempt to substantiate a case which, from the outset, was not supported by documentary

* Thank you to Marcus Johansson for his invaluable input to the Swedish law aspects, and Karsten Kristoffersen, Lasse Mikkelsen and Jakob Bue Sørensen for their helpful comments on Danish law.

1. Nigel Blackaby, Constantine Partasides & Alan Redfern, *Redfern and Hunter on International Arbitration*, N 6.88 (7th ed. Oxford University Press 2022); Gary Born, *International Commercial Arbitration*, p. 2421 (3rd ed. Kluwer International, 2021); Jean-Francois Poudret & Sébastien Besson. *Comparative Law of International Arbitration*, p. 554 (Sweet and Maxwell 2006).
2. This chapter only deals with requests from parties to the Tribunal, not requests directed towards third parties or the tribunal's competence to request the parties to produce evidence.
3. In the *2012 International Arbitration Survey: Current and Preferred Practices in the Arbitral Process*, by the Queen Mary University of London https://arbitration.qmul.ac.uk/media/arbitration/docs/2012_International_Arbitration_Survey.pdf (accessed 3 Mar. 2024), 62% of the respondents said that more than half of their arbitrations involved requests for document disclosure, while only 22% said that less than one-quarter of their arbitrations involved such requests (p. 24).
4. In the *2012 International Arbitration Survey*, 59% stated that documents obtained through document production materially affected the outcome of at least one-quarter of their arbitrations (p. 24), while 29% believe this happened in at least half of their arbitrations (p. 27).

evidence available to the requesting party. A common understanding of the correct application of the document production rules is, therefore, important.

We observe an increased focus on document production in arbitral proceedings seated in Scandinavia. This development may in particular be attributed to digitalisation and the availability of an ever-increasing amount of exchanged e-mail correspondence and compilation of data. The availability of, and relatively easy access to, extensive documentation may also lead to requests being formulated too broadly and/or concerning issues of little or no relevance.

This chapter explores the features of document production commonly found in Scandinavian arbitral proceedings and whether there may be differences between 'national' and 'international' arbitrations seated in Scandinavia.

We focus in particular on the respective countries' arbitration acts[5] and principles from domestic civil procedure established in jurisprudence and legal works and compare the result of our analyses of national principles with the IBA Rules on the Taking of Evidence (the 'IBA Rules'), as an expression of best practice in international arbitration.

In the next sections, we first perform a comparative study of the regulation of document production in arbitral proceedings in the three Scandinavian countries.[6] We then proceed with a presentation of how three main principles of particular practical significance, namely *specificity, relevance* and *proportionality,* are understood in the respective Scandinavian jurisdictions while also comparing them to the requirements in the IBA Rules.[7] Finally, we set out our conclusions.[8]

§10.02 GENERALLY ON DOCUMENT PRODUCTION IN ARBITRATIONS IN SCANDINAVIA

[A] Introduction and Some Starting Points

The relevant starting point under the Norwegian Arbitration Act of 2004 (NAA), the Danish Arbitration Act of 2005 (DAA), and the Swedish Arbitration Act of 1999 (SAA) is that it is for the parties to submit the evidence on which they intend to rely.[9] The parties are otherwise free to agree on the procedure, including for document production.[10] Notably, neither the NAA, the DAA, nor the SAA regulate the procedure of

5. The Norwegian Arbitration Act of 2004 (N. '*Lov om Voldgift*') (the 'NAA'), The Swedish Arbitration Act of 1999 (SW. *Lag (1999:116) om skiljeförfarande*) (the 'SAA'), and the Danish Arbitration Act of 2005 (D. Voldgiftsloven: Lov nr. 553 af 24. juni 2005) (the 'DAA').
6. *See* §10.02 below.
7. *See* §10.03 below.
8. *See* §10.04 below.
9. SAA § 25; NAA § 28. Jakob Juul & Peter Fauerholdt Thommesen, *Voldgiftsret* (3rd ed. Karnov, 2017), p. 237.
10. NAA §§ 43(1) litra e and 46(1) litra e, stating that an award may be set aside or refused recognition and enforcement if the procedure is contrary to the parties' agreement. *See* similarly, DAA § 37(2) no. 1, litra d, and § 39(1), no. 1, litra d, and SAA §§ 34(1)(3) and 54(4).

document production in the arbitration.[11] Rather, all three acts only regulate the situation in which the tribunal, or a party with the consent of the tribunal, requests the regular courts to assist in document production.[12] In this latter context, it has been established in Swedish jurisprudence that the regular courts shall rely on the tribunal's assessment of whether the request for the production of documents should be granted.[13]

In addition, the arbitration rules of both the Danish Institute for Arbitration (the 'DIA Rules') and the SCC Arbitration Institute (the 'SCC Rules') entitle the tribunal to order document production in the arbitral proceedings.[14]

As regards the relevance of national civil procedure acts, we recall that an agreement to arbitrate is an agreement to divert the dispute away from the regular courts and their procedural rules. Thus, unless specifically agreed between the parties, the national civil procedural act is not applicable to the arbitration procedure. This overall principle applies in all three Scandinavian countries.[15] However, to the extent that the arbitration act of the respective jurisdiction and the institutional rules, insofar as these are applicable, do not regulate the matter, we often see that principles of civil procedure are used as guidance.[16]

In §10.02[B] below, we first establish the tribunal's mandate to govern the document production procedure in the arbitral proceedings. In §10.02[C] we establish the principles commonly applicable in arbitral proceedings seated in Scandinavia.

[B] The Tribunal's Mandate to Govern the Document Production Procedure

Where the parties have not agreed on the procedure, and within the framework of the arbitral acts, the tribunal is entitled to conduct the arbitration 'in such manner as it considers appropriate'.[17] This follows from the NAA § 21 first sentence and the DAA § 19(1) and (2) first sentence. The provisions are equivalent to Article 19(2) first sentence of the UNCITRAL Model Law. Although not as clearly expressed, the same applies in Sweden, where § 21 of the SAA requires and empowers the tribunal to conduct the procedure in an appropriate manner.[18]

The DAA and the Model Law go a step further than the NAA and SAA by also stating that 'the power conferred upon the arbitral tribunal includes the power to

11. NAA § 28 contains a distinctive provision on evidence, but is not meant to encompass requests for document production although it may be analogously applicable in certain cases.
12. NAA § 30, SAA § 26, DAA § 27.
13. NJA 2012 p. 289.
14. *See* Art. 33 of the DIA Rules and Art. 31(3) of the SCC Rules.
15. Denmark: Bernhard Gomard & Michael Kistrup, *Civilprocessen* (8th ed. Karnov, 2020), p. 880.
16. Generally in Luca Radicati di Brozolo, 'International arbitration and domestic law' in Giuditta Cordero-Moss, *International commercial arbitration* (2013, Cambridge).
17. '*På den måte den finner hensiktsmessig*' in Norwegian, *see* § 21 of the NAA and DAA § 19(2).
18. Sw.: Ändemålsenligt, *see* generally Stefan Lindskog, *Skiljeförfarande – En kommentar* (3rd ed. Norstedts Juridik, 2020), 636 et seq. *See also* the SCC Rules, Art. 23(1).

determine admissibility, relevance, materiality and weight of any evidence'.[19] This is also the position under Norwegian law despite it not being expressly set out.

Thus, the starting point under all three arbitration acts is that the tribunal is provided with a mandate to govern the document production procedure in the arbitral proceedings and apply the principles it sees fit. In practice, a tribunal seated in Scandinavia will regularly apply the principles established in the respective countries, and international principles like the IBA Rules. There are also instances where the parties agree that document production shall be regulated by the *lex arbitri*. Finally, there are instances where the tribunal or a party, with the consent of the tribunal, will request assistance with document production from the regular courts. In all three instances, national principles will be relevant.

[C] The National Principles That May Be Applied in Considering a Request for Document Production

It has been argued that the tribunal's assessment, *in lieu* of guidance in the applicable procedural law, the parties' agreements or institutional rules, may be made pursuant to the same principles as applied in the courts under both Norwegian[20] and Danish[21] civil procedural law, at least in '*national*' arbitral proceedings. Under Norwegian law, it is held that the tribunal should be guided by general principles of dispute resolution.[22]

In Sweden, the Supreme Court has concluded that pursuant to § 26 of the SAA, the arbitrators shall perform the same overall legal review of a request as is done by the Swedish courts pursuant to the Swedish Procedural Code before granting an appeal to seek assistance from the courts.[23]

Thus, in respect of which rules the arbitral procedure may be guided by, the commonly held view seems to be that, particularly in 'national' arbitration matters, also the respective principles of the civil procedure act provide guidance with respect to requirements for document production.[24]

However, foreign parties choosing to arbitrate in a Scandinavian country may not have considered whether the domestic civil procedure and its peculiarities may have a bearing on the procedure as such. This could give a locally domiciled party an unfair advantage which the foreign party was not aware of. In respect of document production, it is therefore reasonable that the guidance provided by principles from domestic civil procedural law are restrictively applied. In these cases, it may be more appropriate to make a broader consideration of the parties' reasonable expectations and that the

19. Cf. § 19(2) second sentence of the DAA and the Art. 19(2) second sentence of the Model Law.
20. Per Magne Ristvedt & Sven Eriksrud, *Bevistilgang i voldgift*, Vol. 4. TfF, pp. 275 et seq. (2015).
21. Steffen Pihlblad & Julie Arnth Jørgensen *Bevisoptagelse i voldgiftssager* (ET.2013.177).
22. NOU 2001:33, p. 57.
23. NJA 2012 p. 289; Kaj Hobér, *International Commercial Arbitration in Sweden* (2nd. ed., Oxford University Press, 2021), p. 210; Finn Madsen, *Commercial Arbitration in Sweden* (5th ed., Jure Förlag, 2020), pp. 298-296, fn. 917.
24. Denmark: Pihlblad & Jørgensen, *supra* n. 21, p. 2; Sweden: NJA 2012 p. 289, Norway: Ristvedt & Eriksrud, *supra* n. 20, pp. 285-290.

tribunal seeks guidance from international best practice instruments, such as the IBA Rules, rather than from national law.[25]

In respect of Norway and Denmark, a more international approach would be supported by the preparatory works of the Model Law. The preparatory works first establish that the tribunal's competence to determine evidentiary rules is encompassed by the tribunal's competence to conduct the arbitration as it considers appropriate.[26] As established, the discretionary powers of the tribunal are considerable in evidentiary matters, as the Model Law provides a liberal framework.[27] The preparatory works indicate that the tribunal, where the parties are from similar legal systems, may adopt features similar to the parties.[28] Where the parties are from *different* legal systems, the preparatory works of the Model Law advocate that the tribunal may adopt '*suitable features from different legal systems and relying on techniques proven in international practice*'.[29]

The Norwegian Supreme Court applied a similar reasoning in its judgment HR-2017-1932-A, albeit in another context. In assessing the question of whether an arbitration agreement may be binding on others than the parties, the Supreme Court held that where there is no fixed position under Norwegian law and where Norwegian rules are largely adjusted to international rules, foreign sources of law may be relevant by virtue of their argumentative value.[30] The Norwegian Supreme Court stated that this:

> seems to be in line with an international arbitration trend that these issues are resolved based on what one may refer to as a 'denationalised approach' and more liberal deliberations regarding the parties' common qualifications and fair expectations.

Thus, the Norwegian Supreme Court appears to confirm that where there are international best practices applicable to a legal issue, and Norwegian law does not provide a fixed solution, the courts (and tribunals) may be guided by such international practice. However, as stated by the Supreme Court, '*Norwegian judges' view on which conclusions can be drawn from such a "denationalised approach", will to some extent be coloured by the habitual Norwegian legal approach*'.[31] This approach seems to be

25. *See, e.g.*, Robin Oldenstam & Kristofer Löf, 'Best Practices in International Arbitration' in Borgar Høgetveit Berg & Ola Ø. Nisja, *Avtalt Prosess* (Universitetsforlaget, 2015), pp. 295-297; Amund B. Tørum, 'Best Practice i Norsk og Nordisk Voldgift og NOMAs Guidelines', in Torsten Iversen et al. (eds) *Festskrift til Mads Bryde Andersen* (DJØF Forlag, 2018) expressing some of the same considerations.
26. UNCITRAL, *Report of the Secretary-General on the Analytical Commentary on Draft Text of A model Law on International Commercial Arbitration*, A/CN.9/264, pp. 44-46. On the relationship between the Model Law, its *travaux préparatoires* and the NAA, *see* Borgar Høgetveit Berg (red.)., *Voldgiftsloven: Med Kommentarer* (Gyldendal Akademisk, 2006), pp. 34-36.
27. A/CN.9/264, p. 45.
28. A/CN.9/264, p. 45. The principle is also referred to in the preparatory works to the DAA (LFF 2005-03-16, nr. 127).
29. A/CN.9/264, p. 46.
30. HR-2017-1932-A § 113 (quote from the formal English translation made by the Supreme Court).
31. HR-2017-1932-A § 114 (quote from the formal English translation made by the Supreme Court).

consistent with the position adopted in the preparatory works of the Model Law described above.

When the requesting party in an international arbitration in Sweden does not seek a court-ordered document production pursuant to §26 of the SAA but rather a non-enforceable order by the tribunal, the tribunal has considerable freedom to apply rules and principles for document production that it finds appropriate unless otherwise agreed by the parties. In that context, guidance is regularly found in Article 3 of the IBA Rules.[32] The Swedish Supreme Court's reference to the IBA Rules in the context of §25 SAA[33] and in domestic court proceedings regarding the possession criterion[34] seems to confirm, *a fortiori*, that tribunals seated in Sweden may also look to the IBA Rules when assessing requests for document production orders by the tribunal itself.

More broadly, it seems that also under Swedish law, it is accepted that tribunals may look to international best practice instruments in arbitration in the absence of an agreement to the contrary between the parties. This seems particularly true with regard to international matters and document production.[35]

An analysis of the principles of document production in all three countries reveals that in order for a request for document production to be successful, the request should typically meet the following criteria:

(1) the party who submits a request must state the facts that are intended to be proven by the documents;[36]
(2) the request must concern a physical or electronic *document* that exists (including that it can be printed or easily compiled from a computerised system);[37]
(3) the requested documents must be *properly identified* (the identification requirement; Sw. *identifikationskravet*);[38]

32. Fredrik Andersson et al., *Arbitration in Sweden* (Jure Förlag, 2011), pp. 124-126.
33. NJA 2012 p. 289.
34. NJA 2022 p. 249.
35. *See* Lindskog, *supra* n. 18, p. 270, fn. 2818, with further references to Claes Zettermarck & Rikard Wikström, 'The Impact of Document Production on the Efficiency of Arbitration' in Kaj Hobér, A. Magnusson & Marie Öhrström (eds) *Between East and West: Essays in Hobour of Ulf Francke* (Juris, 2010) pp. 590 et seq. and Lars Perhard, *Något om elektronisk edition i tvistemål och skiljefåorfarande*, in JT 2007/08 p. 395, on p. 410.
36. Sweden: Per Olof Ekelöf, Henrik Edelstam & Lars Heuman, *Rättegång. Fjärde häftet* (JUNO Version 7, 2016), p. 264 Denmark: Erik Werlauff i U 2016 B 205 208 f; U 1968 608 H. Norway: Maria Astrup Hjort, *Tilgang til bevis i sivile saker* (Universitetsforlaget, 2016), pp. 265-271; Jens Edvin Skoghøy, *Tvisteløsning* (4th ed., Universitetsforlaget 2022), p. 337.
37. According to Swedish case law, a document is considered to be any document that can be printed, even though it is not saved anywhere in that particular form. E.g., NJA 2020 p. 664, NJA 2020 p. 373 and NJA 2022 p. 249. Denmark: U.2020.3872 H; Sø- og Handelsrettens dom af 3. Nov. 2023, p. 21; U.2024.1618. Norway: Tvisteloven §§ 26–5 and 26–6, HR-2019-997-A § 28.
38. Sweden: Lars Heuman, *Skiljemannarätt* (1999, Norstedts Juridik), p. 462; Lars Heuman, 'Editionsförlägganden i civilprocesser och skiljetvister. Del II', in *Juridisk Tidsskrift* (1989-1990), pp. 241 et seq.; Madsen, *supra* n. 23, pp. 286-287; Lindskog, *supra* n. 18, p. 719; Hobér, *supra* n. 23, pp. 210-211; Zettermarck & Wikström, *supra* n. 35, p. 594; Ekelöf, Edelstam & Heuman, *supra* n. 36, p. 264; P. Fitger et al. *Rättegangsbalken* (Juno Version 95, 2023), 38:2.
Norway: G. Woxholth, *Voldgift* (Gyldendal, 2013), pp. 639-640 and 669-670; Hjort, *supra* n. 36, pp. 335-337; Jens Edvin Skoghøy, *Tvisteløsning* (4th ed., Universitetsforlaget 2022), pp.

(4) each requested document or most documents in the eligible category must be *assumed to be relevant* to a *specified, invoked* and *disputed factual circumstance*, and the requested document must be *material to the outcome of the case* (the evidentiary requirement; Sw. *bevisrelevanskravet*).[39] It is not possible to request documents for the purpose of seeking to understand the facts better, for the purpose of analysing whether additional arguments can be made or new facts can be invoked, or to prove facts that are not relevant to the outcome of the case;

(5) the requested documents must not be possible for the requesting party to obtain elsewhere, e.g., if they are already in the requesting party's direct or indirect possession or in the public domain;[40]

(6) the party or person who is requested to produce a document must be *in possession of the document* (the possession requirement; Sw. *innehavskravet*);[41]

(7) the document production must be *proportional*, i.e., it shall not be more intrusive and burdensome than is justified by the importance of the evidence (the proportionality requirement; (Sw. *proportionalitetskravet*);[42] and

---

265-271; Amund Bjøranger Tørum & Per Magne Ristvedt, *Provokasjoner, begjæringer om bevistilgang og edisjonsplikt; tvistelovens modifiserte 'discovery'*, Vol. 2 TfF, pp. 103 et seq. (2015) at, pp. 138-149.

Denmark: Steffen Pihlblad et al. *Praktisk Voldgift* (Jurist- og Økonomforbundets Forlag, 2011), p. 147; Pihlblad & Jørgensen, *supra* n. 21; Gomard & Kistrup, *supra* n. 15, p. 611; Lars Lindencrone Petersen & Erik Werlauff *Dansk retspleje* (8th ed., Karnov, 2020), pp. 308-309; Werlauff, *supra* n. 36; J. Møller et al. (eds) *Kommenteret Retsplejelov* (Jurist- og Økonomforbundets Forlag, 2018), pp. 790-792.

Internationally: IBA Rules Art. 3(3)(a)(i) and Born, *supra* n. 1, pp. 2535-2537; Virginia Hamilton, *Document Production in ICC Arbitration*, in ICC Publication Document Production in International Arbitration, 2006 Special Supplement to ICC International Court of Arbitration Bulletin, (ICC, 2006), pp. 71-72; Tobias Zuberbühler et al. *IBA Rules of Evidence. Commentary on the IBA Rules on the Taking of Evidence in International Arbitration* (2nd ed., Schulthess, 2022) p. 66; Hilmar Raeschke-Kessler, 'The Production of Documents in International Arbitration – A Commentary on Article 3 of the New IBA Rules of Evidence', in *Arbitration International* Vol. 18, no. 4 (2002), p. 419; Roman Khodykin, Carol Mulchay & Nicholas Fletcher, *A Guide to the IBA Rules on the Taking of Evidence in International Arbitration* (2019), p. 136; Commentary on the IBA Rules 2020, p. 11.

39. Sweden: Lindskog, *supra* n. 18, p. 697, Fitger et al., *supra* n. 38, 38:6-7. Denmark: Retsplejeloven § 341; Retsplejeloven § 300(1)Sø- og Handelsrettens dom af 3. november 2023, p. 21; Østre Landsrets kendelse av 23. november 2022, p. 266; U 2021.1273 V: Højesterets kendelse af 24. november 2020. Norway: Tvisteloven § 21–7, HR-2019-997-A and Rt. 2013 p. 817.

40. Sweden: NJA 2012 p. 289, Denmark: Retsplejeloven § 341; Sø- og Handelsrettens dom af 3. november 2023, p. 21; Østre Landsrets kendelse av 23. november 2022, p. 258; Petersen & Werlauff, *supra* n. 38, p. 311, U 2021.1273 V. Norway: [XX].

41. Sweden: Heuman (1989/90), *supra* n. 38, pp. 22 et seq. and pp. 247 et seq. *See also* NJA 2020 p. 664 in which the fact that the use of the documents had been restricted by agreement with a third party did not prevent production of the documents and NJA 2022 p. 249, in which '*possession*' was considered intact also when the documents were in another country, Denmark, since the documents could be accessed electronically. Denmark: Sø- og Handelsrettens dom af 3. november 2023, p. 21; U.2020.3872. Norway: Tvisteloven §26–5; HR-2019-997-A.

42. Sweden: NJA 1998 p. 829. Denmark: Retsplejeloven § 298; U.2023.268 V; Petersen & Werlauff, *supra* n. 38, p. 311; Gomard & Kistrup, *supra* n. 15. Norway: HR-2019-997-A paras 79 et seq.; Hjort, *supra* n. 36, pp. 166 et seq.

(8) the documents must not be subject to a legal impediment, e.g., privileges or other confidentiality restrictions.[43] However, in Denmark, internal or confidential documents may only be ordered and produced under exceptional circumstances.[44] In Sweden, memorial notes are not available for document production and business secrets are available only exceptionally.[45]

Of these common requirements, items 3, 4 and 7 are the ones which in our practice are most disputed and which will be further discussed in §10.03 below.

Finally, a decision ordering a party to produce documents takes the form of an '*order*'. In neither of the three jurisdictions is the tribunal mandated to render decisions enforceable by the enforcement agencies.[46] However, the parties' refusal to adhere to the tribunal's order to produce certain documents may have an evidentiary value in and of itself, and the tribunal should, in such circumstances, be permitted to draw adverse inferences as part of its assessment of the evidence.[47] As explained, the alternative in all three jurisdictions would be for the tribunal, or a party with the approval of the tribunal, to request the regular courts to assist in ordering the procurement of the documents that the tribunal has ordered to be produced.[48]

§10.03 KEY PRINCIPLES OF DOCUMENT PRODUCTION

[A] Introduction

The common principles for a request for document production to be successful were set out in §10.02[C] above. Here, we discuss the criteria which, in our experience in practice, give rise to most discussions: that the request should be sufficiently specific,[49] that the requested documents must be relevant to the case,[50] and that the request must be proportional.[51] From a macro-perspective, the principles in the Scandinavian countries broadly set out the same requirements for requesting documents from the opposing party. In the following, we have therefore chosen to focus on the similarities, highlighting where the legal systems deviate from each other and comparing the national principles with international best practices represented by the IBA Rules.

43. Sweden: Chapter 38 § 2 of the Code of Judicial Procedure. Denmark: Retsplejelovens § 298, Gomard & Kistrup, *supra* n. 15, p. 614. Norway: Hjort, *supra* n. 36, pp. 175 et seq.
44. Sø- og Handelsrettens dom af 3. november 2023, p. 21; Østre Landsrets kendelse av 23. november 2022, pp. 257 and 260; U 2023.268 V; Højesterets kendelse af 24. november 2020; U.2002.1734H; U.2010.2808H,.
45. NJA 2012 p. 289 point 11.
46. Sweden: Lindskog, *supra* n. 18, p. 720. Norway: Woxholth, *supra* n. 38, p. 669, Denmark: Niels Schiersing, *Voldgiftsloven med kommentarer* (Jurist- og Økonomforbundets Forlag, 2016), p. 358.
47. Hobér, *supra* n. 23, p. 210, Woxholth, *supra* n. 38, p. 669.
48. *See* § 30 of NAA, § 27 DAA, and § 26 SAA.
49. *See* §10.02[C] above.
50. *See* §10.02[C] above.
51. *See* §10.02[C] above.

We recall that both in the Scandinavian countries and under the IBA Rules, document production is based on the following main principles. First, it is commonly accepted that a far-reaching 'discovery' system is undesirable.[52] Second, while the parties are free to submit requests for production, it is for the tribunal to decide whether the requested party should be ordered to produce such documents.[53] Thirdly, the scope of any possible production must be limited by specific conditions and a possibility for the party against whom the request is made to object to production in certain cases. Finally, it is broadly accepted that arbitral proceedings shall be efficient, economic and fair, considerations which are also applicable to issues of document production.

Beneath these principles lie two conflicting interests that must be balanced against each other: on the one hand, the parties must have full and equal opportunity to present their case. On the other hand, the parties do not have the right to do so at any cost, as this imposes burdens on the opposing party. For reasons of procedural economy, the right to request that documents be produced must therefore be limited.

[B] The Specification Requirement

[1] Introduction

The requesting party does not generally know whether the requested party indeed has relevant documents under its control. Nevertheless, it seems commonly accepted across the Scandinavian countries that a request for document production must be sufficiently specific.[54]

The specification requirement is, alongside requirements of relevance and materiality, a key restriction on the scope of document production in arbitration. The purpose of the specification requirement is to give the requested party the opportunity to locate the relevant document(s)[55] and assist the tribunal in deciding whether to order the production of the requested document(s),[56] making the requirement also practically significant. The requested documents or category of documents have to be

52. Sweden: NJA 1959 p. 230; *see also* dissenting opinion in NJA 2019 p. 289. Denmark: UfR 2015.339 and UfR 2011.413 H. Norway: HR-2019-997-A, paras 30-32, Internationally: Zuberbühler et al., *supra* n. 38, p. 41.
53. *See* §10.02[B] above.
54. Sweden: NJA 1998 p. 590 I and II; Heuman (1999), *supra* n. 38, p. 461; Heuman (1989-1990), *supra* n. 38, pp. 238 et seq.; Madsen, *supra* n. 23, pp. 287-288; Brozolo, *supra* n. 16, p. 23; Lindskog, *supra* n. 18, pp. 719-720; Hobér, *supra* n. 23, pp. 210-211; Zettermarck & Wikström, *supra* n. 35, p. 594; Ekelöf, Edelstam & Heuman, *supra* n. 36, p. 263-264; Fitger et al., *supra* n. 38 p. 38:2.
Norway: Woxholth, *supra* n. 38, pp. 669-670; Hjort, *supra* n. 36, pp. 335-337; Skoghøy, *supra* n. 38, pp. 265-271; Tørum & Ristvedt, *supra* n. 38, pp. 138-149.
Denmark: Pihlblad et al., *supra* n. 38, p. 147; Pihlblad & Jørgensen, *supra* n. 21, pp. 1-3. Gomard & Kistrup, *supra* n. 15, p. 611; Petersen & Werlauff, *supra* n. 38, pp. 307-313; Werlauff, *supra* n. 36; U 1968 608 H.
Internationally: IBA Rules Art. 3(3)(a)(i) and Born, *supra* n. 1, pp. 2535-2537; Hamilton, *supra* n. 38, pp. 71-72.
55. *See, e.g.*, Ekelöf, Edelstam & Heuman, *supra* n. 36, p. 264.
56. Madsen, *supra* n. 23, p. 287.

identified to such an extent that it is possible for public authorities to enforce an order to produce the documents,[57] should the tribunal, or a party with the tribunal's consent, seek assistance from the regular courts.[58]

By providing that a request must be specific, the requirement also limits the opportunity to request excessive amounts of documents, and correspondingly that the requested party produces a disproportionately large volume of documents.[59] As will be set out below, allowing requests for production also of categories of documents may be abused, as one party may make requests that are excessively broad and vague.[60] The specification requirement should therefore be viewed in connection with the requirements for relevance and materiality as a way to prevent '*fishing expeditions*'.[61]

Key issues following this is how specification should be understood. When is a request sufficiently specific? And how specific should a request for categories of documents be, also compared to the 'narrow and specific' test under the IBA Rules?

[2] When Is a Request Sufficiently Specific?

In a Scandinavian context, an *individual* document may be specified by the following information: (i) the author or recipient of the document; (ii) the date or period when the document was prepared, sent, and/or received; and (iii) the presumed subject matter or contents of the document.[62] The same applies under the IBA Rules.[63] The list is not exhaustive; for example, the document's numbering or title may also identify the

57. (SW. *verkställighetsprecision)*.
58. *See* §10.02 above.
59. Madsen, *supra* n. 23, p. 288; Daria Kozlowska-Rautiainen, *Obtaining Documents from the Opponent in International Commercial Arbitration* (2016), pp. 84-85; Bernard Hanotiau, 'Document Production in International Arbitration: A Tentative Definition of 'Best Practices' in *ICC Publication Document Production in International Arbitration, 2006 Special Supplement to ICC International Court of Arbitration Bulletin*, (ICC, 2006), p. 117; Commentary on the IBA Rules 2020, p. 10.
60. *See* §10.03[C][1] et seq.
61. Sweden: NJA 1959, p. 230, *see also* the dissenting opinion in NJA 2012 p. 289; Ekelöf, Edelstam & Heuman, *supra* n. 36, pp. 264 et seq.; Lars Heuman, 'Editionsförlägganden i civilprocesser och skiljetvister. Del I', in *Juridisk Tidsskrift* (1989-1990), pp. 25 et seq. and Peter Westberg, *Anskaffning av bevis i tvistemål* (Norstedts Juridik, 2010), pp. 488 et seq.
   Norway: HR-2019-997-A paras 30-32.
   Denmark: U.2011.431 H; U.2015.3319 H; Gomard & Kistrup, *supra* n. 15, pp. 611-612; Petersen & Werlauff, *supra* n. 38, pp. 308 and 312.
   Internationally, *see, e.g.*, Hanotiau, *supra* n. 59, p. 117.
62. Some of the same elements are considered in, e.g., NJA 1998 p. 510, I and II, as well as in HR-2019-977-A.
63. Gabrielle Kaufmann-Kohler & Philippe Bärtsch, 'Discovery in international arbitration: How much is too much?' Zeitschrift für Schiedsverfahren (2004), p. 18; Raeschke-Kessler, 'The Production of Documents in International Arbitration – A Commentary on Article 3 of the New IBA Rules of Evidence', in *Arbitration International* Vol. 18, no. 4 (2002), p. 418; Zuberbühler et al., *supra* n. 38, p. 60.
   In a Scandinavian context, *see also* HR-2019-997-A para. 69, mentioning the same considerations; & Heuman (1989-1990), *supra* n. 38, p. 240, mentioning, *inter alia*, author.

document.[64] Not all conceivable information needs to be specified for a document to be located, and a document may even then not be adequately identifiable. This depends on a closer assessment of the request and the documents seemingly covered by this.[65]

When assessing what a sufficiently specific request for a *category* of documents looks like, the same elements as described directly above may be of use. A '*category of documents*' is typically understood as several documents which share common features.[66] These are documents that may be difficult to identify individually but that have a natural internal coherence which may make the category itself sufficiently specific, e.g., minutes of meetings, memoranda or reports within a specific period of time. Such documents are often internal by nature, and the requesting party may not be certain that they exist, but it can often be assumed.[67]

All Scandinavian supreme courts have rendered a number of decisions concerning the specification requirement as interpreted in national law, which may provide some guidance in the tribunal's assessment. The following selected cases are illustrative of the specification requirement in a Scandinavian context:

(i) As set out in NJA 1998 section 590(I), it is sufficient for the requesting party to state that the application for an order for production relates to all documents relevant to a carefully described *evidentiary theme* or a certain category of documents, here the credit file held by the bank concerning a specific loan. Crucially, the Swedish Supreme Court held that it would not be difficult to determine which documents were in the requested file and thus covered by the request. In NJA 1998 p. 590 (II), the request concerned all written documentation relating to certain loans relevant to the case. The Swedish Supreme Court found that the documents referred to in the application for a production order were neither sufficiently specified nor sufficiently identified by evidentiary themes.[68]

(ii) In HR-2019-997-A, the Norwegian Supreme Court considered access to evidence pursuant to §§ 26-5 and 26-6 of the Civil Procedure Act, including the requirements of specification, relevance,[69] and proportionality.[70] In respect of the specification requirement pursuant to § 26-6(1) of the Civil Procedure Act, the Supreme Court recalled the strict starting point under the provision that each document has to be individualised, albeit having

64. Reto Marghitola, *Document Production in International Arbitration* (Kluwer Law International, 2015), pp. 37-38.
65. Kozlowska-Rautiainen, *supra* n. 59, pp. 86-87.
66. The IBA Rules Art. 3(3)(ii) lists several in the context of electronic documents.
67. At this point Danish law seemingly departs from Norwegian and Swedish law, and the IBA Rules. Under Danish law, internal documents are as a starting point exempted from production, *see, e.g.*, U.2002.1734 U; Petersen & Werlauff, *supra* n. 38, p. 309; and Peter Bang *Partsedition* in UfR 1997 B pp. 268 et seq.

    In contrast, the IBA Rules additionally require that it is reasonable to assume that the documents exist, as parties cannot request production of documents they merely hope exists.
68. *See also* NJA 1998 590.
69. *See* §10.03[C][1] below.
70. *See* §10.03[D] below.

due regard to the somewhat softer approach in recent case law.[71] With reference to previous case law, the Supreme Court proceeded to highlight that the requirement could not be understood so narrowly as to prevent production of documents which may affect the case. The Supreme Court recalled that requests specifying the sender, recipient, topic and time period have previously been considered to satisfy the specification requirement,[72] that the purpose of the specification requirement is, first and foremost, that the opposing party should know which documents are requested, and that it should be possible for the court (or tribunal) to assess the relevance of the requested documents. Sweeping requests bearing similarities to disclosure would have to be rejected. The Supreme Court also emphasised the opportunity in the specific case to significantly restrict the document requests by focusing on specific persons in the organisation and specific hard drives.

(iii) In U.2015.3319 H, the Danish Supreme Court assessed the specification requirement. The request related to virtually all of the requested party's working material concerning the audit of Roskilde Bank for the financial years 2006 and 2007, including all working papers, draft audit protocols as well as reports received and other documentation. The Supreme Court noted that the request did not specify which facts were to be proven by production of the documents, and the Supreme Court found no basis for ordering the requested party to hand over the documents for the purpose of an investigative review. While we otherwise would consider this as a matter of 'relevance',[73] the Danish Supreme Court considered this as a matter of 'specificity'. This may have been based on a reasoning along the same lines as in HR 2019-997 A, i.e., that the documents must be sufficiently specified to enable the court (or tribunal) to assess the relevance of the requested documents.

In conclusion, requesting production of documents, even if the parties are not able to identify individual documents, is accepted in all three Scandinavian countries. However, the threshold is fairly high, in particular in Sweden, and such requests have to be carefully tailored, focusing on relevant and material documents.[74]

The IBA Rules explicitly require that a request for a category of documents is both sufficiently '*narrow and specific*'. It has been held that this formulation is a key consideration in arbitration which distinguishes international arbitration from the

71. *See* NOU 2001:32B p. 980.
72. Rt-2007-920.
73. *See* §10.03[C][2] below.
74. Sweden: NJA 1998 p. 590 I and II; Heuman (1989-1990), *supra* n. 38, p. 241; Madsen, *supra* n. 23, p. 287; Ekelöf, Edelstam & Heuman, *supra* n. 36, p. 264.
Norway: Tørum & Ristvedt, *supra* n. 38, pp. 138-149.
Denmark: Pihlblad & Jørgensen, *supra* n. 21, section 3.3; U.2022.1661V.

'common law' system and 'discovery'.[75] The commentary on the IBA Rules does not distinguish between the two adjectives.[76] It should be noted that the 'narrow' requirement is not explicitly referred to as a separate principle in Scandinavian practice. However, our impression is that it often is part of the consideration of specificity.[77]

Also, under the IBA Rules, there does not seem to be a clear distinction between the two concepts, and the exact meaning is a matter of interpretation. A possible interpretation of '*specific*' is that it denotes how the category is described as set out above,[78] while '*narrow*' may require the category to be 'reasonably limited in time and subject matter in view of the nature of the claims and defences advanced in the case'.[79] This would presumably also mean that the request should be limited in other senses, e.g., by not having too many authors or consisting of too many different types of documents.

Whether a category is sufficiently narrow does not necessarily say anything about the amount of documents that may be produced. This is particularly true in cases where one request, in reality, is a request for several categories of documents.[80] It is challenging for the party to know the volume of documents within a category, and the tribunal will not be able to determine this either when the request is made. A narrow request can result in the production of large volumes of documents, while expansive requests can result in few documents.[81]

In the context of the IBA Rules, it has been widely discussed what characterises a sufficiently narrow and specific request.[82] The discussion has concerned three main themes. First is the subject matter of the documents.[83] Second is that the request should be narrowly tailored, reasonably limited in time and subject, in light of the claims each party has made in the case.[84] Third is that the request should seek to obtain documents related to a specific requirement or a specific claim in the case and not be loosely connected to a requirement or general point of disagreement.[85] For example, a reference to longer time periods and/or documents 'related to' a broadly described

75. Peter Ashford, *IBA Rules on the Taking of Evidence in International Arbitration* (Cambridge University Press, 2013), p. 70; O'Malley, Nathan D. *Rules of Evidence in International Arbitration: An Annotated Guide* (2nd ed. Routledge, 2021), p. 187; Zuberbühler et al., *supra* n. 38, p. 62.
76. Commentary on the IBA Rules 2020, p. 10.
77. Indications of this may be found in HR-2019-997-A para. 75 in which the Norwegian Supreme Court relies on the opportunity to narrow the scope of the request to certain persons and hard drives, as well as in NJA 1998 p. 590 in which the Swedish Supreme Court did not say that it *suffices* to state a category of documents. It said that it '*may*' suffice. That leaves open the question of how the category needs to be defined.
78. *See* §10.03[B][2].
79. O'Malley, *supra* n. 75, p. 187.
80. Reto Marghitola, *supra* n. 64, p. 41.
81. Kozlowska-Rautiainen, *supra* n. 59, pp. 88-89.
82. Commentary on the IBA Rules 2020, p. 10; Raeschke-Kessler, *supra* n. 38, p. 418; Ashford, *supra* n. 75, p. 69; Zuberbühler et al., *supra* n. 38, p. 61; Kozlowska-Rautiainen, *supra* n. 59, pp. 84-97; Khodykin, Mulkin & Fletcher., *supra* n. 38, N. 6.57; Born, *supra* n. 1, pp. 2535-2536.
83. HR-2019-997-A paras 71-73; *See also* IBA Rules Art. 3(3)(a)(ii).
84. O'Malley, *supra* n. 75, p. 187. *See* to this effect also; Ekelöf, Edelstam & Heuman, *supra* n. 36, p. 264.
85. O'Malley, *supra* n. 75, p. 187; Ashford, *supra* n. 75, p. 70.

subject or point of disagreement will likely be deemed insufficiently narrow and specific.[86]

In principle, it is probably true that most things can be searched only if a search is lengthy enough. However, as previously emphasised, a 'discovery'-like process is not desired, and accepting arrangements that strongly resemble 'discovery' is difficult. This starting point should also apply in complex cases with a significant amount in dispute.

The question is then what a sufficiently narrow and specific request looks like. As pointed out by Ashford, '[t]here is a fine but important distinction between an incoherent and non-specific categorization and a detailed narrow and specific description'.[87] For example, a formulation such as 'all documents being, evidencing, relating to, touching upon or concerning an issue' will likely not be evaluated to meet the criteria of specificity and scope. Meanwhile, a request for 'all emails and letters between A (acting by its employees C, D or E) to B (acting by its employees F, G or H) in the period from J to K relating to L together with any documents attached or enclosed, located in the paper files in the offices at M or on the computer servers at M and containing one or more of the following words N, P or Q', will likely meet the requirements.

[C] Relevance

[1] The Content of the Relevance Requirement, Including Materiality

For the tribunal to order the production of documents, it needs to find that the requested documents are relevant to the dispute.[88] Together with the requirement of specification, this is the most significant restriction on the extent of document production.[89]

The relevance requirement is inseparably linked to the principle that the requested evidence should be able to inform the case, i.e., support the requesting party's claims or

86. HR-2019-997-A para. 71. *See also* Heuman (1989-1990), *supra* n. 38, p. 247, in this regard. As a digression, the Swiss Supreme Court judgment DFT 4A_438/2020 of 15 Mar. 2021, cons 4.2, is also interesting in this regard.
87. Ashford, *supra* n. 75, p. 68.
88. Sweden: Heuman (1999), *supra* n. 38, p. 462; Heuman (1989-1990), *supra* n. 38, pp. 241 et seq.; Madsen, *supra* n. 23, pp. 286-287; Lindskog, *supra* n. 18, p. 719; Hobér, *supra* n. 23, pp. 210-211; Zettermarck & Wikström, *supra* n. 35, p. 594; Ekelöf, Edelstam & Heuman, *supra* n. 36, p. 264; Fitger et al., *supra* n. 38, p. 38:2.
    Norway: Woxholth, *supra* n. 38, pp. 639-640 and 669-670; Hjort, *supra* n. 36, pp. 161 et seq.; Skoghøy, *supra* n. 38, pp. 265-271; Tørum & Ristvedt, *supra* n. 38, pp. 138-149.
    Denmark: Pihlblad et al., *supra* n. 38, p. 147; Pihlblad & Jørgensen, *supra* n. 21; Gomard & Kistrup, *supra* n. 15, p. 611; Petersen & Werlauff, *supra* n. 38, pp. 308-309; Werlauff, *supra* n. 36; Møller et al., *supra* n. 38, pp. 790-792.
    Internationally: IBA Rules Art. 3(3)(a)(i) and Born, *supra* n. 1, pp. 2535-2537; Hamilton, *supra* n. 38, pp. 71-72; Zuberbühler et al., *supra* n. 38, p. 66; Raeschke-Kessler, *supra* n. 38, p. 419; Khodykin, Mulkin & Fletcher., *supra* n. 38, p. 136; Commentary on the IBA Rules 2020, p. 11.
89. Blackaby et al, *supra* n. 1, N 6.95; Born, *supra* n. 1, pp. 2537-2538.

dispute the requested party's claims. In a Scandinavian context, a document is relevant to the dispute when it may substantiate an invoked fact. Typically, a relevant document can illuminate the factual circumstances related to a claim or objection in the case, either by proving facts invoked by the party itself or disproving facts invoked by the opponent. The relevance requirement is interpreted strictly. The parties must be able to justify why they are requesting the particular document. To do this, parties should explain the relationship between the document and the disputed invoked fact.[90]

In Denmark, the requirement that the evidence is relevant implies that the party requesting production must also bear the burden of proof for the invoked fact.[91] Under Swedish law, the position is the opposite.[92] The question is not settled under Norwegian law.[93]

Furthermore, both in Sweden and Norway, it is not only required that the requested document(s) should broadly be able to shed light on a disputed issue. It is also required that it may have some evidentiary value. Under Swedish and Norwegian arbitration law, this results from the tribunal's competence to reject the evidence of its own initiative if the evidence '*is* manifestly irrelevant to the dispute' (Sw. '*uppenbart saknar betydelse i tvisten*').[94] The DAA does not contain a similar provision. Thus, at least in a Norwegian and Swedish context, the relevance consideration in practice also includes an element of 'materiality'.[95] In this regard, we note that in Denmark (and internationally), it is accepted that if other evidence is available and can prove the disputed claim, the requested documents are not material to the outcome of the case and need not be produced.[96] In Swedish jurisprudence, it is established that a request for documents for the purpose of supporting a claim which cannot be granted on the merits shall be rejected.[97]

90. Sweden: Lindskog, *supra* n. 18, pp. 720-721; Heuman (1989-1990), *supra* n. 38, p. 247.
Norway: HR-2019-997-A, para. 61.
Denmark: Pihlblad et al., *supra* n. 38, p. 147; Gomard & Kistrup, *supra* n. 15, p. 611.
91. Sø- og Handelsrettens dom af 3. november 2023, p. 21.
92. *See* NJA 2015 p. 651 para. 10.
93. Hjort, *supra* n. 36, p. 107, seems to indicate that Norwegian law is similar to Swedish law at this point.
94. Sweden: SAA § 25 second paragraph; Lindskog, *supra* n. 18, pp. 723-726; Heuman (1999), *supra* n. 38, pp. 439-440. NJA 1988 p. 652; Ekelöf, Edelstam & Heuman, *supra* n. 36, p. 265. Norway: NAA § 28 second paragraph, first sentence; Berg, *supra* n. 26, pp. 241-243; Woxholth, *supra* n. 38, pp. 639-642.
95. HR-2019-997-A para. 56.
96. Denmark: Gomard & Kistrup, *supra* n. 15, p. 612; Petersen & Werlauff, *supra* n. 38, p. 310.
Internationally: Philipp Habegger, 'Document Production – An Overview of Swiss Court and Arbitration Practice', in ICC Publication Document Production in International Arbitration, 2006 Special Supplement to ICC International Court of Arbitration Bulletin (ICC, 2006), p. 33.
97. NJA 2014 p. 651 para. 9.

In the IBA Rules,[98] relevance and materiality are typically understood as cumulative requirements, a two-pronged test.[99] Thus, at first glance, the IBA Rules appear to set out an additional requirement compared to what is established in Scandinavian principles. However, as explained, the relevance requirement established in Scandinavian principles also includes a materiality requirement. In respect of whether the parties may request production of documents concerning factual issues for which they do not bear the burden of proof, the focus under the IBA Rules is on whether the requested document(s) are relevant and material to the outcome of the case, not who bears the burden of proof for the individual factual contention.[100] The parties should arguably also have the opportunity to respond to the opposing party's arguments and evidence presented.[101]

Distinguishing between relevance and materiality may be difficult. Guidance may be found in the IBA Rules' formulation 'relevant *to the case* and material *to its outcome*'. Relevant would then be any document which may inform the case, while a document that is material to its outcome would be necessary to facilitate a 'complete consideration of the invoked fact from which legal conclusions are drawn'.[102] It is, however, difficult to imagine a document which would be material to the outcome of the case but not relevant to it, at least from a Scandinavian perspective. The materiality requirement may therefore be referred to as a 'strict relevance requirement', as that is the tougher test.[103]

[2] The Tribunal's Assessment of Relevance (and Materiality)

In its assessment of whether the evidence is relevant, the tribunal must necessarily base its assessment on the requesting party's assertions as to the factual issues of the

98. *See also* the SCC Rules Art. 31(3), stating that he Arbitral Tribunal, at the request of a party, may order a party to produce any documents or other evidence that may be *relevant to the case and material to its outcome*; and the DIA Rules Art. 33 stating that at the request of a party, the Arbitral Tribunal may order another party to produce documents [...] that the Arbitral Tribunal considers may be relevant to the case. Relevance should be interpreted more similar to 'material' pursuant to Danish law, *see infra* n. 105.
99. Born, *supra* n. 1, pp. 2357-2359; Blackaby et al., *supra* n. 1, N 6.95.
100. *See* on this: Born, *supra* n. 1, p. 2539; Marghitola, *supra* n. 64, pp. 55-56; Kozlowska-Rautiainen, *supra* n. 59, p. 101; Khodykin, Mulkin & Fletcher., *supra* n. 38, N 6.134; Zuberbühler et al., *supra* n. 38, p. 70.
101. Some authors have taken the opposite position, *see* Zettermarck & Wikström, *supra* n. 35, p. 595; Ashford, *supra* n. 75, p. 71; Yves Derains, 'Towards Greater Efficiency in Document Production before Arbitral Tribunals – A Continental Viewpoint', in *ICC Publication Document Production in International Arbitration, 2006 Special Supplement to ICC International Court of Arbitration Bulletin* (ICC, 2006), p. 87; Hanotiau, *supra* n. 59, p. 117; B. Berger & F. Kellerhals, *International and Domestic Arbitration in Switzerland* (Stämpfli, 2021), pp. 488-489. *See also* Khodykin, Mulkin & Fletcher, *supra* n. 38, pp. 148 et seq., who gives several examples from practice.
102. Marghitola, *supra* n. 64, p. 52; Jeff Waincymer, *Procedure and Evidence in International Arbitration* (Kluwer Law International, 2012), p. 859.
103. Zuberbühler et al., *supra* n. 38, p. 68.

case.[104] The crux of the assessment is whether the requested documents are relevant to the requesting party's factual assertions. Whether something is ultimately of evidentiary value is for the tribunal to decide,[105] and the tribunal is not bound by the requesting party's assertions in this regard.[106]

Thus, the tribunal *can* accept a request if it finds it prima facie likely that the documents *can* be relevant (and material).

Ordering a party to produce documents that are only prima facie relevant is, in many ways, less risky for the tribunal than potentially refusing to order a party to produce documents that will contribute to the resolution of the dispute.[107] However, the threshold must not be set so high that it prevents the clarification of facts of importance to the case. The requesting party, whose request has been dismissed, can potentially challenge the validity of the tribunal's decision if it has not been given the opportunity to present its case in full.[108] It should be noted that the threshold for invalidating an arbitral award due to a refused request is high,[109] if at all possible.[110]

How the tribunal assesses relevance and materiality may depend on when the request is submitted. Although the threshold, in theory, is not more lenient later in the process, the tribunal will be better positioned to determine which documents may be relevant and material. The parties' claims and legal arguments will be sufficiently developed to enable the tribunal to decide whether the requests are adequately addressed and whether the documents are relevant and material. At an early stage, typically before the defence has been filed, the tribunal will usually not be able to assess the relevance and importance of the request in the same way.

It is incumbent on the requesting party to account for the relevance and materiality of the documents and to do this in as great a level of detail as possible to assist the tribunal in its prima facie assessment of the requested documents' relevance and materiality.[111] Relevance is not established solely by explaining why the requested document, in a general sense, is relevant to the dispute but also how it is relevant to a currently disputed issue, e.g., because it was authored by a specific person within a specific timeframe.[112]

The fact that the request must be tied to a current dispute issue also gives rise to another consideration, namely that the parties' factual and legal claims must be formulated in a sufficiently precise manner for a request to be considered at all. The claims must be contested, and a party may not request documents relevant to a factual

104. Sweden: Ekelöf, Edelstam & Heuman, *supra* n. 36, p. 264. Norway: HR-2019-997-A para. 57-58 and Hjort, *supra* n. 36, p. 361. Denmark: Gomard & Kistrup, *supra* n. 15, pp. 611-612.
105. NJA 2014 p. 651 para. 9.
106. *See* to this effect, e.g., HR-2019-997-A, para. 57.
107. Heuman (1989-1990), *supra* n. 38, pp. 245 et seq.; Habegger, *supra* n. 96, p. 32.
108. Marghitola, *supra* n. 64, pp. 196-202.
109. *Hochtief Airport GmbH v. ABB AG and Athens International Airport SA* Judgment of the High Court of Justice of England and Wales [2006] EWHC 388, paras 75 et seq.
110. Lindskog, *supra* n. 18, p. 719; Ramberg, *Sverige som skiljedomsland – några synspunkter med anledning av en nutkomen bok*, in JT 1990/91 p. 610; Heuman (1989-1990), *supra* n. 38, pp. 242 et seq.
111. Commentary on the IBA Rules 2020 p. 11.
112. Kozlowska-Rautiainen, *supra* n. 59, pp. 107-108.

assertion which has not been properly made or which shall be dismissed.[113] If a sufficiently detailed factual assertion has not been made, it is difficult to argue that the document is relevant to a properly invoked, disputed fact. For the same reason, a request made later in the proceedings may be easier for the tribunal to rule on, as the parties' factual and legal positions may be sufficiently developed at this point so that it is easier for the tribunal to determine whether the requested documents may be relevant and material to the dispute.

[D] Proportionality

In all Scandinavian countries, it is generally held that a request must be proportional.[114] The IBA Rules have adopted a slightly different approach when considerations of proportionality are set out as an objection rather than as a requirement to the request itself.[115] It is fair to say that the requirement of proportionality is significantly less pronounced under the IBA Rules than under the more traditional Scandinavian approach.[116]

In the Scandinavian legal systems, proportionality is typically understood to mean that ordering the production of documents should not impose burdens on the requested party which are not reasonable in light of the dispute, the possible evidentiary value of the documents, and the burdens imposed on the party. The tribunal must consider the likelihood that the requesting party is able to prove what it is seeking by the requested documents and whether the documents produced may be material to the outcome of the case against the interests of the requesting party in not disclosing the documents. As part of this assessment, the tribunal must consider the practical burdens and costs imposed on the requested party.

§10.04 CONCLUSIONS

In all three jurisdictions, it is generally accepted that the tribunal may conduct the arbitration as it deems appropriate, including regulating issues of document production. While there are significant similarities between the three Scandinavian countries in respect of the principles applied to document production in arbitral proceedings, there are also some differences which are important to keep in mind.

The largest difference concerns how there appears to be a weaker basis for invoking international sources in document production procedures in Sweden than in Norway and Denmark which are both Model Law Countries. However, it seems

---

113. Sweden: Ekelöf, Edelstam & Heuman, *supra* n. 36, pp. 264-265.
114. Sweden: NJA 1977 p. 254, NJA 1998 p. 829, NJA 2012 p. 289 and NJA 2014 p. 651; Fitger, *supra* n. 38, 38:8a; Westberg, *supra* n. 61, pp. 639 et seq.
Norway: HR-2019-997-A paras 79 et seq.; Hjort, *supra* n. 36, pp. 166 et seq.
Denmark: U.1950.761 H; U.1995.670 H; Gomard & Kistrup, *supra* n. 15, p. 613.
115. IBA Rules Art. 9(2)(g).
116. *See* more generally on considerations of proportionality internationally in Born, *supra* n. 1, p. 2538.

generally accepted that the tribunal may give due regard to international best practices, especially in international matters, in all three countries.

In respect of the requirements of specification, relevance, and proportionality, we note that the specification requirement as a starting point is stricter in Scandinavia than pursuant to the IBA Rules. However, in respect of relevance, the Scandinavian threshold appears lower than pursuant to the IBA Rules. However, that difference may, in the end, be minor since the tribunal in the document production phase of the proceedings shall consider the requirement on the basis of the requesting party's assertions. The weight the proportionality requirement has in Scandinavia appears to be an outlier in international arbitration and is a principle international parties should be aware of when participating in arbitral proceedings seated in Scandinavia.

CHAPTER 11

Content with Consent: SCC Emergency Arbitration in Investor-State Disputes

Anastasiia Dulska[*]

§11.01 INTRODUCTION

In the volatile landscape of international investments, both investors and host states occasionally face unforeseen risks that necessitate swift legal action. Emergency arbitration offers a mechanism for obtaining interim relief even before a dispute formally reaches an arbitral tribunal. This form of arbitration is particularly appealing to investors involved in disputes with states, as it protects their investments from being at the mercy of state actions. By providing an immediate forum for addressing urgent issues, emergency arbitration enhances the effectiveness of international arbitration as a means of dispute resolution. This, in turn, strengthens the principles of fairness and justice within the international legal framework.

The mutual consent of the host state and the investor forms the basis for the jurisdiction of any arbitral tribunal. Consent is also crucial for an emergency arbitrator to consider when assessing an investor's application for interim relief in emergency arbitration proceedings. Among the various arbitration rules that facilitate such emergency proceedings are those of the International Chamber of Commerce (ICC), the Singapore International Arbitration Centre (SIAC), and the SCC Arbitration Institute.

Notably, the SCC Rules offer a significant advantage for parties seeking urgent interim relief in investor-state disputes by presuming consent for emergency arbitration.[1] The presumed context reduces ambiguity regarding the availability of emergency

---

* The author has no affiliation with the SCC other than as counsel in proceedings under the SCC Rules, including emergency arbitration proceedings in investor-State disputes. The views expressed in this chapter are solely those of the author.

1. The new Arbitration Rules of the SCC Arbitration Institute (SCC Rules), effective from 1 Jan. 2023, retain the same preamble as the previous version, which was in force since 1 Jan. 2017 ('the

arbitration compared to other rules. This means that there is no need to prove explicit consent to emergency arbitration from the parties involved, provided they have agreed to the SCC Rules. However, some states challenge their consent to emergency arbitration provisions introduced to the SCC Rules, arguing that they did not anticipate the introduction of the emergency arbitration mechanism into the SCC Rules when they signed investment treaties. Despite such arguments made by states, emergency arbitrators consistently regard the reference to the SCC Rules as a 'dynamic reference', automatically applying the latest version of these rules and appendices from the outset of the proceedings. Against this background, this chapter will focus on the emergency arbitration proceedings under the SCC Rules.[2]

Emergency arbitration offers several benefits to investors who seek interim relief in investment disputes. First, it provides a speedy and efficient way to address urgent matters that may otherwise cause irreparable harm or frustrate the enforcement of a future award. Emergency arbitrators are usually appointed within a few days and render their decisions within a few weeks, depending on the applicable rules and the complexity of the case. This contrasts with the lengthier process of constituting a full arbitral tribunal, which may take several months or even years. Second, emergency arbitration enhances the legitimacy and acceptability of the interim measures, as the parties can tailor the scope and nature of the relief sought, depending on their specific needs and circumstances. Third, emergency arbitration may deter the host state from taking further adverse actions against the investor or prompt the state to negotiate a settlement. By invoking emergency arbitration, the investor signals its seriousness and determination to pursue its claim and protect its rights. The host state may then reconsider its position and refrain from aggravating the situation or engage in good faith discussions with the investor to resolve the dispute amicably.

Against this background, this chapter outlines the requirements for emergency relief under the SCC Rules (section §11.02) and discusses the prima facie review standard used by emergency arbitrators (section §11.03). It then examines the extent of states' implied consent (section §11.04) and the criteria for admitting emergency applications (section §11.05). The chapter concludes by detailing the powers of the emergency arbitrator to issue interim measures under the SCC Rules (section §11.06). Overall, it assesses the effectiveness of emergency arbitration as an interim relief mechanism in investor-State disputes (section §11.07).

---

parties shall be deemed to have agreed that the following rules, or such amended rules, in force on the date of the commencement of the arbitration, or the filing of an application for the appointment of an emergency arbitrator, shall be applied unless otherwise agreed by the parties'). The 2007 version of the SCC Rules did not contain the same language.

2. The SCC jurisprudence discussed in this chapter can be accessed either in the public domain or through specialized legal databases.

§11.02 REQUIREMENTS FOR EMERGENCY ARBITRATION PROCEDURE IN INVESTOR-STATE DISPUTES

Emergency arbitration in investor-State disputes serves as an important mechanism in dispute resolution, analogous to interim relief under national procedural laws and standard arbitral proceedings. Emergency arbitration is a mechanism that 'allows a disputing party to apply for urgent interim relief before an arbitration tribunal has been formally constituted.'[3]

A distinctive requirement of emergency arbitration is the need to clearly demonstrate the necessity for immediate relief that cannot be delayed until an arbitral tribunal is constituted. In other words, applicants seeking interim relief from an emergency arbitrator must convincingly demonstrate that it is not feasible to delay relief until an interim award is made – or even until the arbitration tribunal is constituted. Consequently, emergency arbitration provides an essential short-term remedy for parties who cannot afford to wait for the formal constitution of an arbitral tribunal.

Although many international arbitral institutions have revised their rules to include emergency arbitration provisions,[4] only a select few offer investors the option to pursue interim relief through an investment arbitration context. Notably, the key frameworks governing investment arbitration – the ICSID Arbitration Rules[5] and the UNCITRAL Arbitration Rules – lack specific provisions for appointing an emergency arbitrator. In contrast, the SCC Rules, along with the 2017 SIAC Investment Arbitration Rules (SIAC Investment Rules)[6] and the ICC Rules,[7] do incorporate measures for appointing an emergency arbitrator applicable to disputes involving investors and states. However, the SIAC Investment Rules only apply if the parties explicitly agree to use the emergency arbitrator provisions.[8] Meanwhile, the emergency arbitrator provisions in the ICC Rules do not apply to investment arbitration proceedings at all.[9]

---

3. Lars Markert and Raeesa Rawal, Emergency Arbitration in Investment and Construction Disputes: An Uneasy Fit?, Journal of International Arbitration, Vol. 37, Issue 1, 2020, p. 132, available at: https://doi.org/10.54648/joia2020005; Cameron Sim, Chapter 7, Emergency Arbitration Meets the Courts, in Stockholm Arbitration Yearbook 2023, pp. 96-98.
4. *See, e.g.*, Swiss Rules of International Arbitration (Swiss Rules), 2021, Art. 43 – Emergency relief; ICC Rules of Arbitration, 2021, Art. 29 – Emergency Arbitrator and Appendix V; the LCIA Arbitration Rules, 2020, adopted by the London Court of International Arbitration, Art. 9B – Emergency Arbitrator; the HKIAC Administered Arbitration Rules, 2018, adopted by Hong Kong International Arbitration Centre, Art. 23 – Interim Measures of Protection and Emergency Relief; the International Dispute Resolution Procedures (Including Mediation and Arbitration Rules), 2021, adopted by the American Arbitration Association and its International Centre for Dispute Resolution, Art. 7 – Emergency Measures of Protection.
5. Note: Under the ICSID Rules, a party may seek provisional measures at any time after proceedings have been instituted. If the request is made before the tribunal has been constituted, the Secretary-General fixes a briefing schedule so that the tribunal may consider the request as soon as possible after constitution.
6. SIAC Investment Rules, Rule 27 – Interim and Emergency Interim Relief and Schedule 1 – Emergency Arbitrator.
7. ICC Rules of Arbitration, 2021, Art. 29 – Emergency Arbitrator and Appendix V.
8. SIAC Investment Rules, Schedule 1, para. 1.
9. ICC Rules, Art. 29(6)(c) ('The Emergency Arbitrator Provisions shall not apply if: [...] c) the arbitration agreement upon which the application is based arises from a treaty').

Consequently, absent states' explicit consent, the SCC Rules are the only procedural framework available to investors seeking emergency relief.[10]

Under the SCC Rules, a party may apply for the appointment of an emergency arbitrator until the case is referred to an arbitral tribunal.[11] The emergency arbitrator possesses essentially the same powers to grant interim measures as a constituted arbitral tribunal, specifically 'any interim measures it deems appropriate'.[12]

Article 37 of the SCC Rules does not set out the specific requirements that must be satisfied in order to issue interim measures. Swedish law, which frequently serves as the *lex arbitri* set by the SCC Board's decision in emergency arbitration proceedings, also grants the authority to order interim measures.[13] However, neither the SCC Rules nor the Swedish Arbitration Act specify the conditions that must be met for such measures to be granted. Nevertheless, as pointed out by the emergency arbitrator hearing the application brought by Evrobalt LLC against Moldova under the SCC Rules: '[t]hese requirements are [...] substantially uncontroversial, whether one applies Swedish law (as the law of the seat of the present Appendix II proceedings) or international law (as the law which governs the Treaty claims asserted by the Claimant). Articles 17-17A of the 2006 UNCITRAL Model Law on International Commercial Arbitration and Article 26 of the UNCITRAL Arbitration Rules 2010 helpfully codify these requirements'.[14]

Among the traditional requirements for granting interim relief, in addition to the criteria of necessity, urgency, and proportionality as outlined in Article 26 of the UNCITRAL Arbitration Rules 2010 cited in *Evrobalt v. Moldova*, the applicant seeking emergency relief must also demonstrate prima facie jurisdiction and a prima facie case on the merits. Emergency arbitrators generally apply these five requirements, which closely mirror those used in interim measure proceedings before domestic courts.[15]

10. SCC Rules, preamble.
11. SCC Rules, Appendix II, Art. 1(1).
12. SCC Rules, Appendix II, Art. 1(2), referring to Art. 37(1)-(3).
13. Swedish Arbitration Act, (The Swedish Code of Statutes (SFS) 1999:116, updated as per SFS 2018:1954, section 25(4).
14. *Evrobalt LLC v. The Republic of Moldova*, SCC Case No. EA 2016/082, Award on Emergency Measures, 30 May 2016, para. 33, available at: https://jusmundi.com/fr/document/decision/en-evrobalt-llc-and-kompozit-llc-v-moldova-award-on-emergency-measures-monday-30th-may-2016 (cited further as '*Evrobalt LLC. v. Moldova*'). The claimant filed its application under the 2010 SCC Rules, whereby Art. 32 grants the arbitral tribunal the authority to issue interim measures.
15. *See, e.g., Mohammed Munshi v. The State of Mongolia*, SCC Case No. 2018/007, Award on Emergency Measures, 5 Feb. 2018, para. 40, available at: https://jusmundi.com/fr/document/decision/en-mohammed-munshi-v-mongolia-award-on-emergency-measures-monday-5th-february-2018 (cited further as '*Munshi v. Mongolia*'); *Komaksavia Airport Invest Ltd. v. Republic of Moldova*, SCC Case No. 2020/130, Emergency Award on Interim Measures, 2 Aug. 2020 para. 77, available at: https://jusmundi.com/en/document/decision/en-avia-invest-v-republic-of-moldova-thursday-23rd-april-2020 (cited further as '*Komaksavia v. Moldova*'); *Kompozit LLC v. Republic of Moldova*, SCC Case No. 2016/95, Emergency Award on Interim Measures, 14 Jun. 2016, paras 50, 72, 67-77 et seq., available at: https://jusmundi.com/fr/document/decision/en-kompozit-llc-v-republic-of-moldova-emergency-award-on-interim-measures-tuesday-14th-june-2016 (cited further as '*Kompozit v. Moldova*'); *Evrobalt v. Moldova*, para. 17, 33; *TSIKinvest LLC v. Republic of Moldova*, SCC Case No. EA 2014/053, Emergency Decision on Interim Measures, 29 Apr. 2014, paras 61-65 et seq., available at: https://jusmundi.com/fr/document/

First, emergency arbitrators shall be satisfied that they have prima facie jurisdiction.[16] This requirement means that the jurisdictional basis invoked by a party initiating emergency arbitration proceedings shall appear to be reasonably sound. This implies that an investor must meet the underlying treaty's criteria for the arbitral tribunal's jurisdiction over its case, including personal jurisdiction (*ratione personae*), subject-matter jurisdiction (*ratione materiae*), and temporal jurisdiction (*ratione temporis*).

Second, emergency arbitrators shall be satisfied that on a prima facie basis investors have a case, i.e., that on first sight, there is a reasonable possibility that they will succeed on the merits.[17]

Third, investors seeking emergency relief should demonstrate that the requested measures are necessary to prevent serious prejudice to their rights, which otherwise would be at risk of harm. If there is a risk of irreparable or imminent harm to investors or their investments if the sought measures are not granted, the necessity requirement is considered to be met. It is important to note in this context 'irreparable harm' (understood as implying non-compensation by an award of money) has a flexible meaning in international law and investment arbitration in particular.[18] The potential

decision/en-tsikinvest-llc-v-republic-of-moldova-emergency-decision-tuesday-29th-april-2014 (cited further as '*TSIKinvest v. Moldova*'). Emergency arbitrators operating under other procedural rules applied similar conditions. *See, e.g.*, *Kosmos Energy Sao Tome and Principe v. ERHC Energy (BVI) Limited*, ICC Case No. 23177/TO, Order of Emergency Arbitrator, 13 Nov. 2017, para. 10.3, available at: https://jusmundi.com/en/document/decision/en-kosmos-energy-sao-tome-and-principe-v-erhc-energy-bvi-limited-order-of-emergency-arbitrator-monday-13th-november-2017; *Sergei Paushok, CJSC Golden East Company and CJSC Vostokneftegaz Company v. The Government of Mongolia*, UNCITRAL, Order on Interim Measures, 2 Sep. 2008, para. 45, available at: https://jusmundi.com/fr/document/decision/en-sergei-paushok-cjsc-golden-east-company-and-cjscvostokneftegaz-company-v-the-government-of-mongolia-order-on-interim-measures-tuesday-2nd-september-2008#decision_5525 (cited further as '*Paushok v. Mongolia*'); *Sergei Viktorovich Pugachev v. The Russian Federation*, UNCITRAL, Interim Award, 7 Jul. 2017, para. 212, available at: https://jusmundi.com/en/document/decision/en-sergei-viktorovich-pugachev-v-the-russian-federation-interim-award-friday-7th-july-2017 (cited further as '*Pugachev v. Russia*').

16. *Komaksavia v. Moldova*, para. 64; *Munshi v. Mongolia*, para. 33; *Kompozit v. Moldova*, para. 50; *Evrobalt v. Moldova*, para. 17; *TSIKinvest v. Moldova*, para. 61.a.
17. *OAO Gazprom v. The Republic of Lithuania (I)*, SCC Case No. V125/2011, para. 79, available at: https://jusmundi.com/fr/document/decision/en-oao-gazprom-v-the-republic-of-lithuania-award-tuesday-31st-july-2012 (cited further as '*Gazprom v. Lithuania*'). *See also*, *Komaksavia v. Moldova*, para. 77; *Kompozit v. Moldova*, para. 72; *Evrobalt v. Moldova*, para. 33; *TSIKinvest v. Moldova*, para. 62.
18. Marc J. Goldstein, A Glance into History for the Emergency Arbitrator, Fordham International Law Journal, Vol. 40, Issue 3, 2017, pp. 780-798, p. 788: 'An early (in relative terms) exponent of caution in adopting the common law notion of irreparable harm into an international customary principle governing arbitral provisional relief, Professor Caron in his 1986 survey (1) noted a mixed record of embrace and reluctance in the jurisprudence of the Iran-US Claims tribunal; (2) took note of the risk of oversimplification of the common law concept of irreparable harm (non-compensability by an award of money) in its adoption into international jurisprudence, which might overlook more nuanced aspects of the common law (such as the exception for money damages not easily or precisely measured) that cause injury to be seen as irreparable despite the possibility of a monetary award; (3) cautioned that assumptions about effective enforcement and execution of monetary judgments in common law courts may be inapplicable to international arbitral awards; and (4) maintained that an inflexible insistence that provisional relief may only be issued if the injury is not compensable by money might often

for monetary compensation from a future award on damages does not automatically negate the need for interim measures. In theory, although all losses might be compensable by an award on damages,[19] the possibility of future monetary compensation does not automatically imply that such compensation would adequately remedy the harm. Therefore, it does not eliminate the necessity for interim protection.[20]

Fourth, the measures sought in an emergency arbitration must be urgent, reflecting the inherent urgency of such proceedings as outlined in Appendix II of the SCC Rules.[21] This requirement implies that it would be impractical for an investor to wait for the constitution of an arbitral tribunal. Therefore, intervention by an emergency arbitrator is justified. Indeed, in twelve known SCC emergency arbitration proceedings reviewed by the author, the timeframe for these proceedings is notably short, varying from one to a maximum of two weeks.[22]

---

be at odds with the fundamental purpose of arbitral provisional relief to preserve the rights of the parties up to the time of a final award'.

19. The requirement of 'harm not adequately reparable by an award of damages' is included in the UNCITRAL Model Law, Art. 17A 'Conditions for granting interim measures' ('the party requesting an interim measure [...] shall satisfy the arbitral tribunal that: a) harm not adequately reparable by an award of damages is likely to result if the measure is not ordered [...]'). The emergency arbitrator referred to this provision in the context of emergency arbitration proceedings under the SCC Rules in *Evrobalt v. Moldova.*
20. Gary Born, 'International Commercial Arbitration, Chapter 17: Provisional Relief in International Arbitration', 3rd ed., pp. 2601-2758, p. 2653: 'Most authorities have reasoned that the injury required for provisional measures is not "irreparable" harm in what is perceived to be the Anglo-American sense, but instead only a showing of grave, substantial, or serious injury. Thus, one award required a showing of "substantial" (but not necessarily "irreparable" as known in common law doctrine) prejudice for the requesting party.' Indeed, as another authority reasoned, '[t]he US definition of "irreparable harm" is a harm that cannot readily be compensated by an award of damages. If this standard were strictly applied, most commercial disputes arbitrated under the UNCITRAL Rules would not qualify for interim protection under Article 26, since the award of money damages can, at least in theory, rectify nearly all commercial losses'.
21. For instance, the SCC Board shall seek to appoint an emergency arbitrator within merely within twenty-four hours of receipt of the application, and the emergency arbitrator shall make any emergency decision no later than within five days once the Secretariat has referred the application to the emergency arbitrator. SCC Rules, Appendix II, Arts 4, 6 and 8.
22. In a chronological order: (1) *Gazprom v. Lithuania*, Application – 13 Jun. 2011, Order – 24 Jun. 2011; (2) *TSIKInvest v. Moldova*, Application – 23 Apr. 2014, arbitrator appointed on 24 Apr. 2014, Award – 29 Apr. 2014; (3) *GPF GP S.à.r.l v. Poland*, SCC Case No. 2014/168, available at: https://jusmundi.com/fr/document/decision/en-gpf-gp-s-a-r-l-v-poland-final-award-wednesd ay-29th-april-2020 (cited further as '*Griffin Group v. Poland*'), Application – 30 Dec. 2014, Award 6 Jan. 2015; (4) *JKX Oil & Gas plc, Poltava Gas B.V. and Poltava Petroleum Company v. Ukraine (I)*, SCC Case No. EA 2015/002, available at: https://jusmundi.com/en/document/decision/en-jkx-oil-gas-plc-poltava-gas-b-v-and-poltava-petroleum-company-v-ukraine-resolut ion-of-the-kyiv-city-court-of-appeal-tuesday-17th-may-2016 (cited further as '*JKX Oil & Gas v. Ukraine*'), Application – 7 Jan. 2015, Award – 14 Jan. 2015; (5) *Evrobalt v. Moldova*, Application – 24 May 2016, arbitrator appointed on 25 May 2016, Award – 30 May 2016; (6) *Kompozit v. Moldova*, Application – 9 Jun. 2016, arbitrator appointed 10 Jun. 2016, Award – 14 Jun. 2016; (7) *Puma Energy Holdings SARL v. the Republic of Benin*, SCC Case No. EA 2017/092, Emergency Award, 8 Jun. 2017, available at: https://jusmundi.com/en/document/decision/en-puma-energy-holdings-sarl-v-the-republic-of-benin-monday-1st-january-2018 (cited further as '*Puma Energy v. Benin*') where the emergency arbitrator rendered an emergency award on 8 Jun. 2017, while the proceedings on the merits started on 1 Jan. 2018; (8) *Munshi v. Mongolia*, Application on 19 Jan. 2018, arbitrator 31 Jan. 2018, Award – 5 Feb. 2018; (9) *Zaza Okuashvili v. Georgia*, SCC Case No. V 2019/058, Partial Final Award on Jurisdiction and Admissibility, 31 Aug. 2022,

Finally, the measures sought should be proportional.[23] In this respect, the ICSID tribunal in *City Oriente v. Ecuado*r explained that the key factor for provisional measures is not solely preventing irreparable harm but ensuring that the harm prevented by such measures is substantially greater than any damage inflicted on the affected party as a result of interim measures.[24]

The above requirements pose a very high bar to be met by a party who seeks interim relief from an emergency arbitrator. Therefore, it is not surprising that emergency arbitrators operating under the SCC Rules only granted the requested emergency relief (in full or in part) in 60% of the decisions rendered to date in treaty-based investor-State-related emergency arbitrations.[25] The outcome of twelve known SCC emergency arbitration proceedings reviewed by the author[26] confirms these statistics, with only several emergency awards being rendered in favour of the investor.[27]

---

available at: https://jusmundi.com/en/document/decision/en-zaza-okuashvili-v-georgia-ruling-of-the-emergency-arbitrator-tuesday-2nd-april-2019 (cited further as '*Okuashvili v. Georgia*'), Application – 22 Mar. 2019, Award – 2 Apr. 2019; (10) *State Development Corporation 'VEB.RF' v. Ukraine*, SCC Case No. 2019/113 and V2019/088, available at: https://jusmundi.com/en/document/decision/en-vnesheconombank-veb-v-ukraine-original-proceedings-wednesday-21st-august-2019 (cited further as '*VEB v. Ukraine*'), Application – 21 Aug. 2019, arbitrator appointment – 22 Aug. 2019, Award – 28 Aug. 2019; (11) *Komaksavia v. Moldova*, Application – 24 Jul. 2020, arbitrator appointed 27 Jul. 2020, Award – 2 Aug. 2020; (12) *Carlos Manuel de São Vicente v. Republic of Angola*, SCC, Decision in Interim Relief dated 16 Jun. 2021, available at https://jusmundi.com/fr/document/decision/en-carlos-manuel-de-sao-vicente-v-republic-of-angola-decision-on-interim-relief-wednesday-16th-june-2021#decision_16858 (cited further as '*Vicente v. Angola*'), proceedings lasted thirteen days resulting in the decision dated 16 Jun. 2021.

23. The same requirements are mirrored in the arbitral tribunals' decisions on interim measures. *See, e.g., Lao Holdings N.V. v. The Government of the Lao People's Democratic Republic*, ICSID Case No. ARB(AF)/12/6, Decision on Claimant's Second Application for Provisional Measures, 18 Mar. 2015, para. 16, available at https://jusmundi.com/en/document/decision/en-lao-holdings-n-v-v-lao-peoples-democratic-republic-i-decision-on-claimants-second-application-for-provisional-measures-wednesday-18th-march-2015#decision_1542 ('The elements the Claimant must establish to obtain Provisional Measures are the following: (i) prima facie jurisdiction, (ii) prima facie establishment of the right to the relief sought, (iii) urgency or (imminent danger of serious prejudice), (iv) necessity, and (v) proportionality.') (with further references).
24. *City Oriente Limited v. The Republic of Ecuador and Empresa Estatal Petróleos del Ecuador (Petroecuador)*, ICSID Case No. ARB/06/21, Decision on Revocation of Provisional Measures and Other Procedural Matters, 13 May 2008, para. 72, available at: https://jusmundi.com/fr/document/decision/en-city-oriente-limited-v-republic-of-ecuador-and-empresa-estatal-petroleos-del-ecuador-petroecuador-i-decision-on-revocation-of-provisional-measures-and-other-procedural-matters-tuesday-13th-may-2008 (cited further as '*City Oriente v. Ecuador*').
25. Alexey Pirozhkin, 'Emergency Arbitrator's Decisions in Investment Treaty Disputes at the SCC' (2014-2019), SCC Practice Note, May 2020, p. 6, available at: https://sccarbitrationinstitute.se/sites/default/files/2022-11/emergency-arbitrators-decisions-in-investment-treaty-disputes-at-the-scc-2014-201.pdf; Anja Havedal Ipp, 'SCC Practice Note: Emergency Arbitrator Decisions Rendered' (2015-2016), pp. 11-14; Lotta Knapp, 'SCC Practice: Emergency Arbitrator Decisions Rendered' (2014).
26. *See supra* n. 23.
27. The requested measures were granted in full or partially in: *TSIKInvest v. Moldova*, Emergency Decision, Order, paras 1 and 2; *JKX Oil & Gas v. Ukraine* (Emergency Award, 14 Jun. 2015, available at: https://jusmundi.com/en/document/decision/uk-jkx-oil-gas-plc-poltava-gas-b-v-and-poltava-petroleum-company-v-ukraine-decision-of-pechersk-district-court-tuesday-9th-june-2015#decision_1504); *Kompozit v. Moldova*, paras 92-93; *Puma Energy v. Benin* (Emergency

§11.03 THE STANDARD OF A PRIMA FACIE REVIEW IN EMERGENCY ARBITRATION

Emergency arbitrators dealing with investor-State disputes follow the standard of a prima facie review as adopted in international law. The international law standard of a prima facie review originally stems from the jurisprudence of the International Court of Justice (ICJ). It was further reaffirmed by arbitral tribunals and emergency arbitrators. It is clear from the ICJ rulings and decisions of emergency arbitrators and arbitral tribunals that the standard of a prima facie review for the purpose of interim measures is considerably low, both as regards the requirement of prima facie jurisdiction and of a prima facie case on the merits.

The prima facie review standard was initially set out by the ICJ in the case of *Military and Paramilitary Activities in and against Nicaragua*. In this case, ICJ found that 'whereas on a request for provisional measures the Court need not, before deciding whether or not to indicate [provisional measures], finally satisfy itself that it has jurisdiction on the merits of the case, or, as the case may be, that an objection taken to jurisdiction is well-founded, yet it ought not to indicate such measures unless the provisions invoked by the Applicant appear, prima facie, to afford a basis on which the jurisdiction of the Court might be founded'.[28]

As also explained by Judge Singh in the *Nuclear Tests* case, the reason for the limited threshold for the condition of prima facie jurisdiction is that, if the ICJ were to thoroughly investigate the possible basis for its jurisdiction beyond prima facie 'the Court is inevitably left no option but to proceed to the substance of the jurisdiction of the case to complete its process of adjudication which, in turn, is time-consuming and therefore comes into conflict with the urgency of the matter coupled with the prospect of irreparable damage to the rights of the parties. It is this situation which furnishes the "raison d'être" of interim relief'.[29]

The ad hoc UNCITRAL tribunal in *Paushok v. Mongolia* emphasised that, essentially, it only needs to decide that the claims made are not, on their face, frivolous or clearly beyond the tribunal's competence. Going further would necessitate a

---

Award dated 8 Jun. 2017 is not public, reviewed by the Global Arbitration Review, 'Benin challenges emergency arbitrator decision', 10 Jul. 2017, available at: https://globalarbitrationreview.com/article/benin-challenges-emergency-arbitrator-decision); *Okuashvili v. Georgia*, (award is not public, reviewed by the Global Arbitration Review, *see* Sebastian Perry, 'Georgian businessman gets emergency relief in Stockholm', 12 Apr. 2019, available at: https://globalarbitrationreview.com/article/georgian-businessman-gets-emergency-relief-in-stockholm); *VEB v. Ukraine*, para. 15; and *Komaksavia v. Moldova*, para. 130.

28. *Military and Paramilitary Activities in and against Nicaragua (Nicaragua v. United States of America)*, Provisional Measures, Order of 10 May 1984, I.C.J. Reports 1984, p. 169, para. 24. *See also LaGrand (Germany v. United States of America)*, Provisional Measures, Order of 3 Mar. 1999, I.C.J. Reports 1999, p. 9, para. 13; *Fisheries Jurisdiction (United Kingdom of Great Britain and Northern Ireland v. Iceland)*, Interim Protection, Order of 17 Aug. 1972, I.C.J. Reports 1972, p. 12, para. 20, in which the Court held that a decision on prima facie jurisdiction does not constitute a prejudgment of the question of whether this tribunal has jurisdiction to deal with the merits of the case.
29. *Nuclear Tests (New Zealand v. France)*, Interim Protection, Order of 22 Jun. 1973, I.C.J. Reports 1973, p. 135, p. 146.

determination of the facts and, practically, a hearing on the merits of the case. Such a lengthy and complicated process would undermine the very purpose of interim measures.[30]

The emergency arbitrator in *Evrobalt v. Moldova* and *Kompozit v. Moldova* concluded with regard to the prima facie jurisdiction review that they simply need to consider whether a reasonable case demonstrating that the emergency arbitrator has jurisdiction over the subject matter of the dispute has been made.[31] For that matter, the emergency arbitrator only needs to 'be satisfied that the jurisdictional basis invoked by [an investor] appears to be reasonably sound' on a prima facie basis, in 'circumstances where [an arbitral tribunal] is yet to pronounce it'.[32] This has also been confirmed by the emergency arbitrator in *Komaksavia v. Moldova*, where he stated that he is not required to delve into the merits of the dispute. Instead, an emergency arbitrator must review the submitted documentation to determine whether the investor's case is prima facie covered by the BIT.[33] Establishing prima facie jurisdiction requires more than just the state's prima facie consent to emergency arbitration procedures. There must also be prima facie jurisdiction under the relevant treaty, which includes meeting the conditions of *ratione personae*, *ratione materiae*, and *ratione temporis* jurisdictions.[34] Essentially, in the context of emergency arbitration, the emergency arbitrator only needs to decide that the claims made are not, on their face, obviously outside its jurisdiction. Given the urgent nature of emergency arbitration, emergency arbitrators are not expected to delve into jurisdictional issues as deeply as an arbitral tribunal would before rendering a final award. Their scrutiny should be limited to 'a manifest lack of jurisdiction', similar to the interim relief proceedings before the national courts.[35]

30. *Paushok v. Mongolia*, para. 55.
31. *Evrobalt v. Moldova*, paras 17-18; *Kompozit v. Moldova*, paras 48-50. *See also, Victor Pey Casado, Président Allende Fondation v. République du Chili*, ICSID Case No. ARB/98/2, Decision on Provisional Measures, 25 Sep. 2001, para. 8, available at: https://jusmundi.com/en/document/other/en-victor-pey-casado-and-president-allende-foundation-v-republic-of-chile-introductory-note-tuesday-25th-september-2001#other_document_6620.
32. *Evrobalt LLC v. The Republic of Moldova*, SCC Case No. EA 2016/082, Award on Emergency Measures, 30 May 2016, para. 17. *See also Komaksavia Airport Invest Ltd. v. Republic of Moldova*, SCC Case No. 2020/130, Emergency Award on Interim Measures, 2 Aug. 2020, paras 64-65.
33. *Komaksavia Airport Invest Ltd. v. Republic of Moldova*, SCC Case No. 2020/130, Emergency Award on Interim Measures, 2 Aug. 2020, para. 65.
34. Although the standard of review is low, it did not prevent emergency arbitrators to deal with complex jurisdictional issues. For example, in *Munshi v. Mongolia*, the investor's dual nationality (UK and Australian passports) did not trigger major issues and the application under the Mongolia-UK BIT was partially granted. Similarly, in *Okuashvili v. Georgia*, the SCC emergency arbitrator was satisfied that there was *prima facie* jurisdiction notwithstanding the fact that the claimant was a dual national of the UK and Georgia and granted interim relief against Georgia under the UK-Georgia BIT. *See* Global Arbitration Review, Sebastian Perry 'Georgian businessman gets emergency relief in Stockholm', 12 Apr. 2019, available at: https://globalarbitrationreview.com/article/georgian-businessman-gets-emergency-relief-in-stockholm.
35. Rania Alnaber, 'Emergency Arbitration: Mere Innovation or Vast Improvement', in William W. Park (ed.), Arbitration International, Oxford University Press 2019, Volume 35 Issue 4, pp. 441-472, at p. 450.

Such an approach is well illustrated by two emergency arbitration proceedings previously initiated by dual nationals under the SCC Rules. In *Munshi v. Mongolia*, the SCC emergency arbitrator was satisfied that the claimant, Mr Mohammed Munshi, established prima facie jurisdiction under the Mongolia-UK BIT by merely submitting his passport as a UK citizen (together with his Australian passport).[36] In *Okuashvili v. Georgia*, the SCC emergency arbitrator was satisfied there was prima facie jurisdiction under the UK-Georgia BIT and granted the interim relief requested against Georgia by a UK-Georgian dual national, Mr Zaza Okuashvili.[37] In these cases, emergency arbitrators dealing with applications for interim relief from dual nationals did not broaden the limited scope of the jurisdictional inquiry typically conducted during emergency proceedings. They maintained a focused and restricted examination of the personal jurisdiction, consistent with the nature and purpose of emergency arbitration.

However, in *Vicente v. Angola*,[38] the emergency arbitrator refused to hear the emergency application brought under the Angola-Portugal BIT and the SCC Rules based on the lack of prima facie jurisdiction. The emergency arbitrator concluded that issues regarding the interpretation of the said treaty and whether it could be interpreted as a broad consent of the host state to resolve disputes with investors that the investor submitted 'to any other [not ICSID or UNCITRAL] arbitration institution or in compliance with any other arbitration rules'[39] should be comprehensively analysed, emphasising that the prima facie standard is relevant only to the factual aspects of the application for emergency relief, not to the interpretation of the treaty itself.

It is important to note that even if the emergency arbitrator accepts jurisdiction on a prima facie basis, this determination has little impact on the arbitral tribunal's own assessment of jurisdiction. In *Komaksavia v. Moldova*, the emergency arbitrator was satisfied that the claimant made 'an investment in the Republic of Moldova for purposes of the BIT, by acquiring a shareholding in the locally incorporated entity.[40] Nevertheless, the tribunal later unanimously dismissed Komaksavia's claims on the basis of lack of jurisdiction *ratione materiae* under the BIT.[41]

As for the establishment of a prima facie case on the merits, it appears that the emergency arbitrator likewise does not need to go into details of the merits if they are 'satisfied that the Claimant has provided evidence sufficient to determine that it has established at least a prima facie case on the merits'.[42] In the very first known emergency arbitration proceedings of *Gazprom v. Lithuania*, the emergency arbitrator

36. *Munshi v. Mongolia*, paras 29 and 33.
37. Global Arbitration Review, Sebastian Perry 'Georgian businessman gets emergency relief in Stockholm', 12 Apr. 2019, available at: https://globalarbitrationreview.com/article/georgian-businessman-gets-emergency-relief-in-stockholm.
38. The author has been part of the team representing Mr. Vicente. All opinions are the ones of the author.
39. Angola-Portugal BIT 2008, Art. 11(1)(e), available at: https://investmentpolicy.unctad.org/international-investment-agreements/treaties/bit/101/angola---portugal-bit-2008-.
40. *Komasksavia v. Moldova*, para. 19, paras 24-25.
41. *Komasksavia v. Moldova*, Final Award, 3 Aug. 2022, available at: https://jusmundi.com/en/document/decision/en-komaksavia-airport-invest-ltd-v-republic-of-moldova-final-award-wednesday-3rd-august-2022#decision_26589, para. 200.
42. *Komaksavia. v. Moldova*, para. 100.

denied the investor's request for relief due to a perceived lack of urgency. However, he noted that the evidence presented by the claimant suggested a reasonable possibility of success on the merits, seemingly without engaging in the analysis of the said evidence.[43]

Legal commentators further note that in light of the early stage of the case and the limited time frames for both deciding the case and for the duration of the measure if granted, most emergency arbitrators seem to apply a relatively low threshold for determining the reasonable likelihood of success on the merits of the case.[44] The level of merits review in the emergency arbitrator procedure should not be so high as to conflict with its purpose and nature. By definition, 'prima facie' means 'at first sight' or 'on first appearance but subject to further evidence or information'. The prima facie test should maintain a low threshold, serving merely to prevent frivolous or vexatious claims that are 'manifestly without merit'.[45]

In *TSIKinvest v. Moldova*, the emergency arbitrator determined that the claimant need not show a likelihood of success on the merits but merely a reasonable possibility of succeeding.[46] Therefore, in order to satisfy the requirements of the emergency arbitrator's prima facie case on the merits, the claimant must 'demonstrate that, prima facie, there is a reasonable possibility to succeed on the merits'[47] or, in other terms, that 'it has a reasonable chance to succeed on the merits, or that there is at least a serious issue to be tried'.[48]

Furthermore, the SCC Rules require that an emergency arbitrator shall render his or her decision on interim measures no later than five days from the date the application was referred to the emergency arbitrator.[49] It would virtually be impossible for an emergency arbitrator to delve into in-depth jurisdiction and merits analysis within the time allocated by the rules. Emergency awards rendered by SCC emergency arbitrators have devoted one paragraph[50] or, at most, a couple of paragraphs to the issues of prima facie jurisdiction and a prima facie case on the merits.[51] Case law based on the SCC Rules thus seem to suggest that the emergency arbitrator is neither expected nor required to conduct an in-depth analysis of jurisdiction and the merits of the case.

43. *Gazprom v. Lithuania*, para. 79.
44. Patricia Louise Shaughnessy, 'Chapter 32: The Emergency Arbitrator', in Patricia Louise Shaughnessy and Sherlin Tung (eds), The Powers and Duties of an Arbitrator: Liber Amicorum Pierre A. Karrer, Kluwer Law International, 2017, p. 346.
45. Kyongwha Chung, Prima Facie Case on the Merits in Emergency Arbitrator Procedure, Kluwer Arbitration Blog, 8 Sep. 2017, available at: https://arbitrationblog.kluwerarbitration.com/2017/09/08/prima-facie-case-merits-emergency-arbitrator-procedure/.
46. *TSIKinvest v. Moldova*, para. 54.
47. *Kompozit v. Moldova*, para. 74.
48. *Smart King Ltd. v. Season Smart Limited, Yueting Jia*, HKIAC Case No. A18176, Award of Emergency Arbitrator, 25 Oct. 2018, para. 86, available at: https://jusmundi.com/en/document/decision/en-smart-king-ltd-v-season-smart-limited-yueting-jia-award-of-emergency-arbitrator-thursday-25th-october-2018.
49. SCC Rules, Appendix II, Art. 8(2).
50. TSIKinvest v. Moldova, para. 61.
51. Komaksavia. v. Moldova, paras 64-66; Evrobalt v. Moldova, paras 17-19; Munshi v. Mongolia, paras 32-33.

Such analysis shall instead be undertaken by the arbitral tribunal appointed in the course of the arbitration proceedings.

§11.04 CONSENT TO THE EMERGENCY ARBITRATION PROCEDURE UNDER THE SCC RULES

When states conclude investment treaties that include dispute resolution mechanisms, they create a framework that allows disputes between a contracting party and an investor from another contracting party to be resolved through investor-state arbitration. This arrangement effectively serves as a standing offer by the host state to engage in arbitration and empowers investors to initiate arbitration in the event of a dispute. This chapter explores whether such an offer includes emergency arbitration and examines the nature and extent of such consent.

[A] Implied Consent to Emergency Arbitration When the Parties Chose to Arbitrate under the SCC Rules

The SCC Rules offer a distinct advantage to the parties in investor-State disputes by implying consent to the emergency arbitration mechanism. Unlike the SIAC Investment Rules and the ICC Rules, which require explicit consent from all parties to be applicable, the SCC Rules assume consent once parties opt for arbitration under these rules. Consequently, if parties select the SCC Rules, they are automatically considered to have consented to the version of the rules effective at the time when they file an application for an emergency arbitrator. The current 2023 version of the SCC Rules includes specific provisions for appointing an emergency arbitrator and applies to investment treaty disputes without necessitating separate state consent for emergency proceedings.

According to the preamble of the SCC Rules, the parties shall be deemed to have agreed that the applicable rules are those in force on the date of the commencement of the arbitration, or the filing of the application for the appointment of an emergency arbitrator unless otherwise agreed by the parties. In accordance with this provision, emergency arbitrators have systematically confirmed that the reference to the SCC Rules implies the application of the version of the SCC Rules, including the appendices, in force as of the date on which the proceedings commenced.[52]

52. *TSIKinvest LLC v. Republic of Moldova*, SCC Case No. EA 2014/053, Emergency Decision on Interim Measures, 29 Apr. 2014, para. 3; *Komaksavia Airport Invest Ltd. v. Republic of Moldova*, SCC Case No. 2020/130, Emergency Award on Interim Measures, 2 Aug. 2020, para. 63; *Evrobalt LLC v. The Republic of Moldova*, SCC Case No. EA 2016/082, Award on Emergency Measures, 30 May 2016, para. 29; *Kompozit LLC v. Republic of Moldova*, SCC Case No. 2016/95, Emergency Award on Interim Measures, 14 Jun. 2016, paras 46-47. In *Munshi v. Mongolia*, the emergency arbitrator did not even address the issue of the version of the applicable rules or the applicability of appendices, but took for granted the application of the 2017 SCC Rules, *see Mohammed Munshi v. The State of Mongolia*, SCC Case No. 2018/007, Award on Emergency Measures, 5 Feb. 2018.

In particular, in *Evrobalt v. Moldova*, the emergency arbitrator held that the state's standing offer to arbitrate shall be construed as implying a '*dynamic reference*' to the arbitral rules in force on the date of the commencement of the proceedings.[53] He further pointed out that '[a]t the time they signed the Treaty in 1998, and when they came to ratify it thereafter, the Contracting Parties would have known that the SCC Rules had been reissued several times in the past. If they so wished, it would have been straightforward to freeze the applicable version of the SCC Rules by inserting a few words in Article 10(2)(b). This they did not do'.[54]

In *Munshi v. Mongolia*, the emergency arbitrator did not even address the issue of the version of the applicable rules or the applicability of appendices but took for granted the application of the 2017 SCC Rules.[55] Other decisions of the emergency arbitrators operating under the SCC Rules further confirm that the consent of the host state to emergency proceedings is implied.[56]

[B] Consent to Emergency Arbitration under the SCC Rules When the Applicable Treaty Does Not Contain an Explicit Reference to These Rules

Investors seeking emergency relief under the SCC Rules might face difficulties when the applicable investment treaty does not specifically and unambiguously provide for SCC arbitration. Based on the limited case law that is publicly available so far, it seems that emergency arbitrators are hesitant to conflate the state's readiness to arbitrate as expressed in the underlying treaty with their readiness for emergency proceedings. This assumption particularly holds true when the underlying treaty is subject to interpretation and cannot be construed as an unequivocal offer to arbitrate under the specific set of procedural rules.

For instance, in one of the most recent (known) SCC emergency arbitration proceedings in investor-state disputes, the emergency arbitrator refused to hear an application submitted by Carlos Manuel de São Vicente against Angola under the Portugal-Angola BIT and the SCC Rules.[57] In his application, the investor requested to be released from what he claimed to be unjust pre-trial detention in Angola or relaxation of his detention regime, allowing him to receive medical treatment and

53. *Evrobalt LLC v. The Republic of Moldova*, SCC Case No. EA 2016/082, Award on Emergency Measures, 30 May 2016, para. 30.
54. *Evrobalt LLC v. The Republic of Moldova*, SCC Case No. EA 2016/082, Award on Emergency Measures, 30 May 2016, para. 30.
55. *Mohammed Munshi v. The State of Mongolia*, SCC Case No. 2018/007, Award on Emergency Measures, 5 Feb. 2018.
56. *TSIKinvest v. Moldova*, para. 3; *Komaksavia v. Moldova*, para. 63; *Evrobalt v. Moldova*, para. 29; *Kompozit v. Moldova*, paras 46-47.
57. The emergency arbitrator's Decision on Interim Relief was rendered on 16 Jun. 2021. It is not yet been made public. For an overview of the case, *see* Global Arbitration Review, Cosmo Sanderson, 'Jailed businessman fails in emergency claim against Angola', 21 Jun. 2021, available at: https://globalarbitrationreview.com/jailed-businessman-fails-in-emergency-claim-against-angola.

access to his legal counsel without surveillance or interference from the authorities.[58] He also asked for the removal of a freeze on his investments in Angola's hospitality sector, citing mismanagement as the reason that could have led to the destruction of their value.[59]

In contrast with the decisions cited above, where the underlying treaties explicitly provided for the applicability of the SCC Rules to the disputes between investors and States, the dispute resolution clause in the Portugal-Angola BIT does not include an explicit reference to the SCC Rules. Instead, it contains an open-ended offer to arbitrate 'in compliance with any other arbitration rules'.[60] More specifically, Article 11(2) of the Angola-Portugal BIT allows investors to submit disputes with the host state to local courts, UNCITRAL or ICSID arbitration, or 'in compliance with any other arbitration rules'.[61]

This provision could be construed as a standing offer of the host state to arbitrate which allows the investor to submit the dispute against the host state to any arbitration institution. Since Article 11(2)(e) of the Angola-Portugal BIT does not contain any limitation regarding the investor's choice of the arbitration institution or the arbitration rules, it allows the investor to submit his dispute to the SCC under the SCC Rules. Nevertheless, the emergency arbitrator hearing the investor's emergency application in the *Vicente v. Angola* case concluded that she lacked jurisdiction because neither the BIT in question nor Angola's investment law provided for jurisdiction for SCC emergency arbitration.[62]

It appears that on a prima facie basis, the emergency arbitrator was not convinced that the broadly worded dispute resolution clause of the Angola-Portugal BIT embodied Angola's consent to emergency arbitration and, in particular, emergency arbitration under the SCC Rules.[63] Thus, in *Vicente v. Angola*, the emergency arbitrator applied a rather strict test for assessing jurisdiction.

A prevailing view in investment arbitration, as first expressed by the *Amco v. Indonesia* ICSID arbitral tribunal in 1983, is that the state's offer to arbitrate is not to be 'construed restrictively, nor, as a matter of fact, broadly or liberally'.[64] This conclusion

58. Global Arbitration Review, Cosmo Sanderson, 'Jailed businessman fails in emergency claim against Angola', 21 Jun. 2021.
59. Global Arbitration Review, Cosmo Sanderson, 'Jailed businessman fails in emergency claim against Angola', 21 Jun. 2021.
60. Angola-Portugal BIT 2008, Art. 11(2)(e), available at: https://investmentpolicy.unctad.org/international-investment-agreements/treaty-files/5675/download.
61. Angola-Portugal BIT 2008, Art. 11(2)(e), ('[i]f the dispute cannot be resolved in accordance with the provisions of paragraph 1 of this article, [...], the investor may, at his request, submit the dispute: [...] e) To any other arbitration institution or in compliance with any other arbitration rules'), available at: https://investmentpolicy.unctad.org/international-investment-agreements/treaty-files/5675/download.
62. Global Arbitration Review, Cosmo Sanderson, 'Jailed businessman fails in emergency claim against Angola', 21 Jun. 2021.
63. Global Arbitration Review, Cosmo Sanderson, 'Jailed businessman fails in emergency claim against Angola', 21 Jun. 2021.
64. *Amco Asia Corporation and others v. Republic of Indonesia*, ICSID Case No. ARB/81/1, Decision on Jurisdiction, 25 Sep. 1983, para. 14, available at: https://jusmundi.com/fr/document/decision/en-amco-asia-corporation-and-others-v-republic-of-indonesia-decision-on-jurisdiction-sunday-25th-september-1983 (cited further as '*Amco v. Indonesia*').

is often quoted with approval by subsequent investment tribunals.[65] The ad hoc UNCITRAL tribunal in *Ethyl v. Canada* further considered that the sole basis for jurisdiction is the parties' consent to arbitration, which an investor expresses by the very act of commencing it.[66] The consent of the host state usually takes the form of a standing offer in an investment treaty which is accepted by the investor by filing a claim against the host state.[67] The *Garanti Koza v. Turkmenistan* tribunal further explained that there is no basis in the Vienna Convention on the Law of Treaties (VCLT) for imposing a requirement that the state's consent to arbitration must be 'clear and unambiguous'.[68]

In *Vicente v. Angola*, although the investor demonstrated consent to arbitration by filing an emergency application and the host state's consent to arbitration was clear under the Angola-Portugal BIT, the emergency arbitrator appears to question specific type of arbitration agreed upon by the parties and whether it included emergency arbitration proceedings.[69]

In principle, the powers of an emergency arbitrator to grant interim relief under the SCC Rules are equivalent to those of the arbitral tribunal. However, there is room for debate on whether consent to the emergency arbitration, as implied under the SCC Rules, can be inferred from a treaty that does not explicitly incorporate the SCC Rules, such as through the operation of an MFN clause. In contrast with emergency arbitration, in usual arbitral proceedings, it may be permissible to imply such consent based on an MFN clause. Lack of clarity on the applicability of broad treaty interpretations in emergency proceedings thus potentially suggests that more complex treaty interpretations might be more appropriate outside of the context of the expedited review in emergency arbitration.

For instance, in *Okuashvili v. Georgia*, although the underlying UK-Georgia BIT provided only for arbitration at ICSID,[70] the consent to SCC arbitration was invoked through the most-favoured-nation (MFN) clause in the Georgia-UK BIT[71] by reliance on the Georgia-Belgium-Luxembourg Economic Union BIT.[72] The emergency arbitrator

65. *See, e.g., ST-AD GmbH v. The Republic of Bulgaria*, PCA Case No. 2011-06, Award on Jurisdiction, 18 Jul. 2013, para. 383, available at: https://jusmundi.com/en/document/decision/en-st-ad-gmbh-v-the-republic-of-bulgaria-award-on-jurisdiction-thursday-18th-july-2013.
66. *Ethyl v. Canada*, ad hoc arbitration, Award on Jurisdiction, 24 Jun. 1998, para. 59, available at https://jusmundi.com/en/document/decision/en-ethyl-corporation-v-the-government-of-canada-award-on-jurisdiction-wednesday-24th-june-1998 (cited further as '*Ethyl v. Canada*').
67. *See, e.g., American Manufacturing & Trading INC v. Republic of Zaire*, ICSID, Award, 21 Feb. 1997, para. 5.23, available at https://jusmundi.com/en/document/decision/en-american-manufacturing-trading-inc-v-republic-of-zaire-award-friday-21st-february-1997.
68. *Garanti Koza LLP v. Turkmenistan*, ICSID Case No. ARB/11/20, Decision on the Objection to Jurisdiction for Lack of Consent, 3 Jul. 2013, para. 22, available at: https://jusmundi.com/fr/document/decision/en-garanti-koza-llp-v-turkmenistan-decision-on-the-objection-to-jurisdiction-for-lack-of-consent-wednesday-3rd-july-2013 (cited further as '*Garanti Koza v. Turkmenistan*').
69. Global Arbitration Review, Cosmo Sanderson, 'Jailed businessman fails in emergency claim against Angola', 21 Jun. 2021.
70. Global Arbitration Review, 'Georgian businessman gets emergency relief in Stockholm', 12 Apr. 2019.
71. Exhibit CLA-119, UK-Georgia BIT 1995, Art. 3.
72. BLEU (Belgium-Luxembourg Economic Union) – Georgia BIT 1993, Art. 10(3).

was satisfied, under these circumstances, that there was prima facie jurisdiction under the SCC Rules to order the interim measures requested by the investor.[73] In other words, an investor successfully[74] replaced a particular arbitration forum with another based on a different treaty.[75] In *Okuashvili v. Georgia*, along with three other non-SCC cases,[76] the arbitral tribunal recognised that an MFN clause could be invoked to initiate proceedings before a forum not explicitly specified in the underlying treaty. As explained above, the emergency arbitrator in *Vicente v. Angola* took a different approach, requiring unequivocal consent to the SCC Rules.

In any event, as discussed above, the applicable test is that of a prima facie assessment. While some emergency arbitrators might not delve into treaty interpretation on an issue of consent in emergency proceedings, seemingly satisfied that the mere acceptance of the application by the arbitral institution is enough, others might be more stringent in establishing their jurisdiction to decide on the emergency application.

§11.05 ADMISSIBILITY OF THE EMERGENCY ARBITRATION UNDER THE SCC RULES

Typically, investment treaties stipulate specific conditions that must be satisfied before initiating investment proceedings. These conditions often require the disputing parties to engage in negotiations for a specified period to amicably resolve their differences, during which they must refrain from starting formal arbitration proceedings. This period is known as a 'cooling off period'.[77] If these conditions are not met, a claim may be deemed inadmissible. Consequently, an important question arises: Are these same preconditions applicable to emergency applications under the SCC Rules? Such applications are often filed by investors on an urgent basis, sometimes immediately after a formal 'trigger letter' has been issued to the host state.

73. *Okuashvili v. Georgia*.
74. However, the affirmative answer was accompanied by a dissenting opinion of Professor Rolf Knieper finding that the MFN clause did not contain an explicit agreement that consent to an arbitral system as well as to arbitral rules could be displaced by the MFN provision. For discussion on same, *see* Mark Mangan, 'Substantive Protections: MFN, in The Guide to Investment Treaty Protection and Enforcement', Mark Mangan and Noah Rubins (eds), 2nd ed., 2023, Global Arbitration Review – Law Business Research, pp. 198-199.
75. *Okuashvili v. Georgia*.
76. *Garanti Koza LLP v. Turkmenistan*, ICSID Case No. ARB/11/20, Decision on the Objection to Jurisdiction for Lack of Consent, 3 Jul. 2013, available at https://jusmundi.com/fr/document/decision/en-garanti-koza-llp-v-turkmenistan-decision-on-the-objection-to-jurisdiction-for-lack-of-consent-wednesday-3rd-july-2013, *Venezuela US, S.R.L. v. Bolivarian Republic of Venezuela*, PCA Case No. 2013-34, Partial Award (Jurisdiction and Liability), 5 Feb. 2021, available at https://jusmundi.com/en/document/decision/en-venezuela-us-s-r-l-v-bolivarian-republic-of-venezuela-partial-award-jurisdiction-and-liability-friday-5th-february-2021; and *Krederi Ltd. v. Ukraine*, ICSID Case No. ARB/14/17, Award, 2 Jul. 2018, available at https://jusmundi.com/en/document/decision/en-krederi-ltd-v-ukraine-none-currently-available-monday-21st-july-2014.
77. The duration of the cooling-off period may vary, the most common being six months.

Article 7 of Appendix II of the SCC Rules acknowledges the urgent nature of emergency proceedings.[78] On this point, arbitrators in emergency proceedings under the SCC Rules seem to agree that the pendency of the cooling-off period does not bar an emergency arbitrator from deciding on interim measures by such an arbitrator.[79] This position seems practically justified and sound, as any alternative approach would contradict the very purpose of the emergency proceedings.

For instance, in *TSIKinvest v. Moldova*, the emergency arbitrator held that 'it would be procedurally unfair to Claimant and contrary to the purpose of the Emergency Arbitrator procedure to apply the Cooling-Off Period to the appointment of an Emergency Arbitrator or to an emergency decision on interim measures to be made by the Emergency Arbitrator, not least since Claimant seems to be facing a serious risk of suffering irreparable harm before the expiry of the Cooling-Off Period if interim measures are not granted.'[80]

Moreover, when the application of the cooling-off period provided in the treaty would, in any event, be 'manifestly futile', emergency arbitrators have also considered that the cooling-off period was not applicable, in accordance with established case law and the view of legal commentators.[81] For instance, the emergency arbitrator in *Kompozit v. Moldova* considered that, due to the respondent state's refusal to engage in settlement discussions, the cooling-off period was not applicable, and the claimant could refer the dispute to arbitration without having to wait until the expiration of the period.[82] In this respect, the emergency arbitrator laid specific emphasis on the language used by the treaty that the parties in dispute will try to resolve their disputes amicably '"as far as possible", which implies that when the parties are not able to resolve the dispute amicably, then the investor is entitled to submit the dispute to arbitration'.[83]

78. SCC Rules, Appendix II, Art. 7 ('Article 23 of the Arbitration Rules shall apply to the emergency proceedings, taking into account the urgency inherent in such proceedings.').
79. Alexey Pirozhkin, 'Emergency Arbitrator's Decisions in Investment Treaty Disputes at the SCC (2014-2019)', SCC Practice Note, May 2020; *TSIKinvest v. Moldova*, para. 66; *Evrobalt v. Moldova*, para. 22. *See also* in *Puma Energy Holdings SARL v. the Republic of Benin*, SCC Case No. EA 2017/092, Emergency Award, 8 Jun. 2017 (not public), where the emergency arbitrator rendered an emergency award on 8 Jun. 2017, while the proceedings on the merits started on 1 Jan. 2018. The emergency arbitrator's decision was reported by the Global Arbitration Review. For an analysis of the award, *see* Global Arbitration Review, Alison Ross, 'Swedish emergency arbitrator halts enforcement of Benin court judgment', 13 Jun. 2017, available at: https://globalarbitrationreview.com/article/swedish-emergency-arbitrator-halts-enforcement-of-benin-court-judgment. *See also*, IA Reported, Jarrod Hepburn, 'Analysis: Stockholm arbitrator finds emergency measures justified against Benin where entire investment faces extinguishment due to alleged denial of justice', 14 Jun. 2017, available at: https://www.iareporter.com/articles/analysis-stockholm-arbitrator-finds-emergency-measures-justified-against-benin-where-entire-investment-faces-extinguishment-due-to-alleged-denial-of-justice/.
80. *TSIKinvest v. Moldova*, para. 66.
81. *Evrobalt v. Moldova*, para. 22; *Kompozit v. Moldova*, paras 55-56.
82. *Kompozit LLC v. Republic of Moldova*, SCC Case No. 2016/95, Emergency Award on Interim Measures, 14 Jun. 2016, paras 55-56.
83. *Kompozit LLC v. Republic of Moldova*, SCC Case No. 2016/95, Emergency Award on Interim Measures, 14 Jun. 2016, para. 55.

Nevertheless, particularly in some of the earlier SCC emergency arbitration proceedings involving investor-state disputes, respondent states have tried to limit the enforcement of emergency arbitrators' awards. They argued that investors had not adhered to the cooling-off periods mandated by the underlying investment treaties when submitting their applications. For instance, Ukraine made such an argument in the enforcement proceedings initiated by UK- and Dutch-based investors JKX Oil & Gas, Poltava Gas B.V., and Poltava Petroleum Company following a favourable decision from the emergency arbitrator in January 2015.[84] The state, however, did not participate in the emergency proceedings.[85]

In conclusion, while investment treaties typically impose a mandatory negotiation phase before formal arbitration can commence, it is evident from the analysis of SCC case law that such requirements do not apply uniformly to emergency proceedings. This exemption is clearly justified by the urgent and potentially irreversible harm that the emergency measures aim to prevent. Reviewed jurisprudence under the SCC Rules further endorses a pragmatic approach where emergency arbitrators may waive the cooling-off period to promptly address significant risks to investors and their investments, ensuring that emergency arbitration procedure under the SCC Rules is efficient and responsive.

§11.06 THE EMERGENCY ARBITRATOR'S POWER TO ORDER INTERIM MEASURES UNDER THE SCC RULES

Article 1(2) of Annex II of the SCC Rules provides that '[t]he powers of the Emergency Arbitrator shall be those set out in Article 37(1)-(3) of the Arbitration Rules'. In other words, under the SCC Rules, an emergency arbitrator has the same powers to grant interim relief before the case is referred to an arbitral tribunal as the arbitral tribunal itself would have.

Article 37 of the SCC Rules provides that the Arbitral Tribunal may, at the request of a party, 'grant any interim measures it deems appropriate' and order that the party requesting the interim measure is provided appropriate security.[86] As the emergency arbitrator noted in *Munshi v. Mongolia*, Article 37 of the SCC Rules calls for a broad interpretation. If the intention had been to restrict the interim measures to specific types, the SCC Rules would have set out a list of specific interim measures that a tribunal or emergency arbitrator could grant. Instead, the use of the word 'any' in the rules suggests that the intention is to afford both arbitral tribunals and emergency

84. *JKX Oil & Gas plc, Poltava Gas B.V.* and *Poltava Petroleum Company v. Ukraine* (I), SCC Case No. EA 2015/002, available at: https://jusmundi.com/en/document/decision/en-jkx-oil-gas-plc-poltava-gas-b-v-and-poltava-petroleum-company-v-ukraine-emergency-award-wednesday-14th-january-2015 (the emergency award is not public, but discussed in the available resolutions of the Ukrainian courts, in Ukrainian).
85. Global Arbitration Review, Sebastian Perry, 'SCC emergency award enforced against Ukraine', 13 Jun. 2016, available at: https://globalarbitrationreview.com/article/scc-emergency-award-enforced-against-ukraine.
86. SCC Rules, Art. 37 (1).

arbitrators' wide discretion to grant interim measures as the case demands.[87] The arbitral tribunal and the emergency arbitrator have therefore broad discretion as to the type of interim measures they can order.

The emergency arbitrator also has broad discretion as to the form in which the interim measures shall be ordered. As it stems from Article 37(3) of the SCC Rules, the 'interim measure shall take the form of an order or an award'. In practice, since the introduction of the emergency arbitration proceedings in the 2010 SCC Rules,[88] the SCC emergency arbitrators have systematically rendered their decisions in the form of '*award*' or '*emergency award*'.[89] However, perhaps the first known emergency arbitrator's decision in the investment arbitration context took the form of an 'Order on Interim Measures'. It was issued on 24 June 2011 in the emergency arbitrator proceedings in *Gazprom v. Lithuania* conducted immediately prior to the main proceedings.[90] In a few other instances, emergency arbitrators have issued 'decisions' rather than 'awards'.[91] It is disputable whether a particular form of an emergency arbitrator's decision has a practical effect on its enforcement. For instance, two known enforcement proceedings initiated by investors after they received interim measures granted in their favour by the SCC emergency arbitrators dealt with both 'Emergency Arbitrator Decision on Interim Measures' granted in *VEB v. Ukraine* and with 'Emergency Award' rendered in *JKX Oil & Gas v. Ukraine*. Both were eventually dismissed in Ukraine following a thorough consideration by several local courts, including the Supreme Court of Ukraine, which refused to enforce them.[92]

The scope of the emergency arbitrator's powers under the SCC Rules is sufficiently wide to enable the emergency arbitrator to grant any measures that might be sought by investors, provided that the requirements for such measures are met. Emergency arbitrators have consistently ruled that emergency relief is justified when the health or life of individuals, the safety of their properties, or the viability of a business is at risk - particularly in situations where there is a threat of assets being subjected to state-enforced sale or cancellation. Such circumstances are considered to potentially cause irreparable damage, warranting the urgent and necessary measures being sought. This justifies the issuance of emergency relief, as will be discussed in more detail below.

87. *Munshi v. Mongolia*, para. 39.
88. The prior to the 2010 version of the SCC Rules, in force as of January 2007, did not contain emergency arbitration provisions. In January 2010, the SCC introduced into its Rules Appendix II, which provided for emergency arbitration.
89. For the publicly available awards, *see, e.g.*: *Komaksavia v. Moldova*; *Munshi v. Mongolia*; *Kompozit v. Moldova*; *Evrobalt v. Moldova*; *TSIKInvest v. Moldova*.
90. *Gazprom v. Lithuania*, para. 278.
91. For instance, emergency arbitrators issued 'decisions' in *VEB v. Ukraine*, *Vicente v. Angola*, *TSIKInvest v. Moldova*.
92. *JKX Oil & Gas v. Ukraine*, Decision of the Supreme Court of Ukraine dated 19 Sep. 2018, available at: https://jusmundi.com/en/document/decision/uk-jkx-oil-gas-plc-poltava-gas-b-v-and-poltava-petroleum-company-v-ukraine-postanova-verkhovnogo-sudu-ukrayini-wednesday-19th-september-2018#decision_2410; *VEB v. Ukraine*, Judgment of the Supreme Court of Ukraine – 14 Jan. 2021, available at: https://jusmundi.com/en/document/decision/en-vnesheconombank-veb-v-ukraine-original-proceedings-wednesday-21st-august-2019.

[A] Measures Adopted by Emergency Arbitrators to Protect Investments

Investment arbitration often deals with measures to protect assets and investments from adverse administrative or judicial actions by host states, such as stays of enforcement of local administrative or court decisions, prohibitions on the forced sale of property by auction, and other provisional measures to safeguard investments pending resolution of disputes. The following case law demonstrates the outcomes of a few emergency proceedings that are of practical significance.

In *VEB v. Ukraine*, Vneshekonombank (VEB), a Russian state-owned development bank, faced significant challenges in its investment in Prominvestbank, a Ukrainian commercial bank. The dispute arose from Ukraine's alleged expropriation and interference with VEB's investment, leading to arbitration under the 1998 Russian Federation-Ukraine BIT.[93] An emergency arbitrator awarded interim conservatory measures requested by the claimant to protect its investment in Ukraine. These measures were intended to prevent Ukraine from enforcing specific administrative decisions that could undermine VEB's investment during the arbitration process.[94] However, the enforcement of this emergency award in Ukraine proved contentious. The Kyiv Court of Appeal initially refused enforcement, citing public policy concerns and procedural issues, but the Supreme Court later overruled this, emphasising the dynamic application of SCC Rules and Ukraine's opportunity to present its case despite procedural constraints.[95]

In *JKX Oil & Gas and Poltava v. Ukraine*, investors faced similar challenges at the enforcement stage. The Dutch and English investors initiated arbitration proceedings against Ukraine on 7 January 2015, citing violations of the Energy Charter Treaty and Ukraine's bilateral investment treaties with the UK and the Netherlands due to a law enacted by Ukraine that increased gas royalties from 28% to 55%. An emergency arbitrator was appointed under the 2010 SCC Rules on 8 January 2015, and on 14 January 2015, he ordered Ukraine not to collect royalties exceeding the previous rate of 28%. In the main arbitration proceedings, JKX claimed compensation for losses amounting to USD 270 million.[96] Although it appears that the increase of gas royalties could have been compensated by an award on damages, the emergency arbitrator nevertheless was satisfied that the investors' application for emergency relief was

93. Russian Federation-Ukraine BIT, 1998, available at: https://investmentpolicy.unctad.org/international-investment-agreements/treaties/bit/2859/russian-federation---ukraine-bit-1998-.
94. *VEB v. Ukraine*, Partial Award on Preliminary Objections (Case No. V2019/088) dated 31 Jan. 2021 discusses in para. 16 of the Emergency Arbitrator Decision on Interim Measures dated 28 Aug. 2019.
95. *VEB v. Ukraine*, Decision of the Kyiv Court of Appeal dated 15 Sep. 2020 and Judgment of the Supreme Court of Ukraine dated 14 Jan. 2021, available at: https://jusmundi.com/en/document/decision/en-vnesheconombank-veb-v-ukraine-original-proceedings-wednesday-21st-august-2019.
96. Kluwer Arbitration Blog, Yaroslav Petrov, 'JKX vs. Ukraine: An Update on the Enforcement of Emergency Arbitrator's Award', 12 Aug. 2016, available at: https://arbitrationblog.kluwerarbitration.com/2016/08/12/jkx-vs-ukraine-an-update-on-the-enforcement-of-emergency-arbitrators-award/; Global Arbitration Review, Sebastian Perry, 'SCC emergency award enforced against Ukraine', 13 Jun. 2016, available at: https://globalarbitrationreview.com/article/scc-emergency-award-enforced-against-ukraine.

sufficiently substantiated and complied with the requirements of urgency, proportionality, and necessity.

In *Komaksavia v. Moldova*, investment arbitration was initiated by Komaksavia Airport Invest Ltd., a Cyprus-incorporated company, against the Republic of Moldova under the 2007 Cyprus-Moldova BIT. The dispute arose in relation to Komaksavia's alleged investment into the Moldovan entity Avia Invest SRL, an operator of the forty-nine-year concession contract concluded in 2013 with Moldova's Public Property Agency to modernise and operate the Chisinau International Airport.[97] In 2016, Komaksavia acquired a controlling shareholding (95%) in Avia Invest, 'thereby making an investment in the Republic of Moldova for purposes of the BIT'.[98] The core of the conflict arose when in July 2020 Moldova's Public Property Agency terminated the concession contract due to alleged breaches by Avia Invest.[99] In response to Moldova's actions, Komaksavia sought emergency interim measures to prevent the termination of the concession and to safeguard its investment during the arbitration proceedings. The SCC emergency arbitrator granted these interim measures in August 2020, ordering Moldova to refrain from any actions that would affect Komaksavia's rights under the concession agreement. This included prohibiting the enforcement of administrative decisions that could jeopardise the investor's interests.

In *Puma Energy Holding v. Benin*, an SCC emergency arbitrator stayed the enforcement of a Benin court judgement which represented a clear danger of effectively extinguishing the commercial operations of Puma Benin. The emergency arbitrator relied on the *Perenco v. Ecuador* tribunal's view that an award of provisional measures is justified where a business faces the risk of being complete cessation. Consequently, the emergency arbitrator ordered Benin to refrain from any action that could threaten the *status quo* pending the determination of Puma's investment claims against Benin.

In *Kompozit v. Moldova*,[100] the arbitrator emphasised that monetary compensation alone does not suffice to prevent irreparable harm, echoing the flexible interpretation of 'irreparable harm' adopted by the Paushok tribunal. The tribunal recognised that monetary compensation might not adequately capture the real value of the shares at the time of their cancellation.[101] Accordingly, the emergency arbitrator ordered Moldova to refrain from implementing the National Bank's decision to cancel the shares, acknowledging that such interim measures were necessary to preserve the claimants' rights pending arbitration.

Similarly, in *TSKIinvest v. Moldova*, interim relief was granted under comparable circumstances. However, in *Evrobalt v. Moldova*, despite a similar factual background,

97. *Komasksavia v. Moldova*, paras 20-23.
98. *Komasksavia v. Moldova*, para. 19, paras 24-25.
99. *Komasksavia v. Moldova*, paras 38-39 et seq.
100. Note: That case involved the Moldovan National Bank's decision that Kompozit, together with nineteen other shareholders of Agroindbank, the country's largest commercial bank, had acted in concert and acquired a substantial shareholding without its prior permission. As a result, the National Bank suspended the shareholders' rights and required them to dispose of the shares within a three-month period, failing which the shares would be cancelled after this period.
101. *Kompozit LLC v. Republic of Moldova*, SCC Case No. 2016/95, Emergency Award on Interim Measures, 14 Jun. 2016, para. 88.

the application for interim measures was dismissed, highlighting the case-by-case nature of emergency decisions.

In *Paushok v. Mongolia*, the tribunal ordered Mongolia to refrain from seizing or obtaining a lien on the claimants' assets, allowing the claimants to continue their ordinary business operations. This decision further underscores the necessity of interim measures to maintain the status quo and prevent irreparable harm, even when future monetary compensation is possible.

From the decisions in the above-mentioned emergency arbitrations, it follows that the potential for monetary compensation does not negate the necessity of interim measures in international investment arbitration. Preserving the actual value and operational status of investments is paramount to ensure that claimants do not suffer irreparable harm that cannot be remedied by financial compensation in future awards. Emergency arbitrators are advised to take this into account when rendering their decisions.

[B] Measures Adopted by Emergency Arbitrators to Safeguard Investors' Rights

Another group of interim measures in international investment arbitration aims at ensuring that the *status quo* is maintained and that disputes are not aggravated while substantive claims are being adjudicated.[102] These measures serve a critical function in preserving the balance between the parties and protecting the integrity of the arbitral process. In the context of emergency arbitration, interim measures play a crucial role by preventing parties from taking actions that could disrupt the status quo or exacerbate the dispute. This helps protect investments from immediate threats.

In *Gazprom v. Lithuania*, Gazprom initiated the emergency arbitration proceedings in June 2011 in an attempt to preserve its right to resort to arbitration pursuant to the SCC Rules, aiming to have its dispute settled by an arbitral tribunal that would be constituted later.[103] The emergency arbitrator, however, declined to grant the relief sought by Gazprom due to a lack of urgency.[104]

Maintaining the *status quo* is often a challenging endeavour, particularly when ongoing investigations or administrative actions predate the initiation of arbitration proceedings. In such instances, these actions are considered part of the status quo and may not be halted by interim measures. The case of *Pugachev v. Russia* exemplifies this complexity. In *Pugachev*, the arbitrator declined to issue interim measures to stop an ongoing investigation into the investor because the investigation predated the arbitration and was thus deemed part of the *status quo*.[105] This decision underscores the

102. Similar requests were made in emergency arbitration proceedings related to investment treaty disputes in 2014-2019, which outcomes are confidential. Alexey Pirozhkin, 'Emergency Arbitrator's Decisions in Investment Treaty Disputes at the SCC (2014-2019)', SCC Practice Note, May 2020, p. 9.
103. *Gazprom v. Lithuania*, para. 78.
104. *Gazprom v. Lithuania*, para. 79.
105. *Pugachev v. Russia*, para. 283.

nuanced nature of interim measures and the need for emergency arbitrators to carefully consider the historical context of the actions in question.

In addition to preserving the status quo, tribunals have also issued interim measures to ensure the safety of investors and their access to legal counsel. Ensuring access to legal representation is fundamental to maintaining the procedural fairness of arbitration proceedings. Without adequate legal counsel, an investor might be unable to effectively present their case, potentially skewing the arbitration process in favour of the host state.

The investor's ability to pursue their claim is jeopardized even more in situations where the physical safety and freedom of key individuals involved in the arbitration are at risk. For instance, in *Igor Boyko v. Ukraine*, the tribunal responded to the application of the incarcerated investor by ordering Ukraine to '*take immediate measures to protect, and to refrain from taking [...] any measures that could endanger the health, life, physical safety, and psychological integrity of the Claimant*'.[106] *Boyko v. Ukraine* is a good example of how arbitration tribunals can intervene to ensure that the physical and psychological well-being of investors is not compromised during the arbitration process.[107] The tribunal recognised that the claimant's ability to participate in the arbitration and manage his investments was severely hampered by his detention. By ordering immediate protective measures, the tribunal aimed to mitigate these risks and maintain the integrity of the arbitration proceedings.

In *Hydro v. Albania*, the tribunal ordered the respondent to release the claimant's key individuals and suspended investigation into them, confirming that the arrest of the central persons involved in the arbitration from the claimants' side would prevent them from effectively managing the claimants' businesses and fully participating in the arbitration. In *Border Timbers v. Zimbabwe*,[108] the arbitral tribunal granted the claimant interim measures and ordered to immediately take all necessary measures to protect the life and safety of the claimants. It is noteworthy that the latter case demonstrates that tribunals are, in general, though not as a rule, willing to intervene decisively when the lives and safety of investors are at risk, thereby ensuring that the arbitration can proceed without endangering the participants.

Such an approach can also be seen in *Perenco v. Ecuador*, where the tribunal directed Ecuador to refrain from instituting or pursuing any action against the claimant or its officers and employees in connection with the subject of the arbitration. This order was essential to ensure that the claimant and its associates were not subjected to

106. *Igor Boyko v. Ukraine*, PCA Case No. 2017-23, Procedural Order No. 3 on Claimant's Application for Emergency Relief, 3 Dec. 2017, available at https://jusmundi.com/en/document/decision/en-igor-boyko-v-ukraine-saturday-1st-december-2018 (cited further as '*Boyko v. Ukraine*').

107. *Boyko v. Ukraine*, PCA Case No. 2017-23, Procedural Order No. 3 on Claimant's Application for Emergency Relief, 3 Dec. 2017.

108. *Border Timbers Limited, Timber Products International (Private) Limited, and Hangani Development Co. (Private) Limited v. Republic of Zimbabwe*, ICSID Case No. ARB/10/25, Procedural Order No. 5 (Provisional Measures), 3 Apr. 2013, available at https://jusmundi.com/fr/document/decision/en-border-timbers-limited-timber-products-international-private-limited-and-hangani-development-co-private-limited-v-republic-of-zimbabwe-procedural-order-no-5-provisional-measures-wednesday-3rd-april-2013, para. 65.

retaliatory actions that could hinder their participation in the arbitration. By ordering Ecuador to refrain from any actions against the claimant and its personnel, the tribunal aimed to prevent any form of harassment or intimidation that could disrupt the arbitration.

However, there are opposite decisions with regard to investors and their rights, such as *Munshi v. Mongolia* and *Vicente v. Angola*, rendered by the emergency arbitrators in two recent emergency proceedings under the SCC Rules.

In *Munshi v. Mongolia*, the claimant sought interim measures for his release from detention, which had been ordered by Mongolian authorities on fraud charges related to his investment in the mining sector. The emergency arbitrator, however, did not grant the request for release, determining that the detention did not constitute irreparable harm that could not be compensated by monetary damages, disagreeing with the claimant, who argued that his detention severely hampered his ability to manage his investment and participate in the arbitration. The emergency arbitrator was of the view that the potential harm could be addressed through monetary compensation.[109] It seems that in this case, the emergency arbitrator had to strike a balance between ensuring the procedural integrity of the arbitration and respecting the host state's judicial processes.

A comparable outcome was seen in *Vicente v. Angola*, where the emergency arbitrator dealt with a request for interim measures related to the detention of the claimant, who faced serious charges in Angola. The emergency arbitrator issued a decision on 16 June 2021 rejecting the request by Angolan-Portuguese dual national Carlos Manuel de São Vicente on the basis that neither the BIT in question nor Angola's investment law provided jurisdiction for SCC emergency arbitration. Based on a prima facie assessment of the evidence, the emergency arbitrator expressed 'severe doubts' about the urgency of the request for interim relief, questioning whether it necessitated immediate action or could wait until a tribunal in the main proceeding was formed. The arbitrator emphasised that for an application to qualify as urgent in emergency arbitration, the remedy sought must be something that cannot be deferred until the arbitral tribunal is constituted.[110]

Whether these two decisions represent the correct approach remains debatable, particularly regarding the limits of emergency arbitrators' powers to address human rights issues.

Finally, interim reliefs aimed at safeguarding investors' rights might also take the form of an order to refrain from publicising details of criminal investigations, such as

---

109. The arbitral tribunal took a similar view in *Dawood Rawat v. Republic of Mauritius*, PCA Case No. 2016-20, Award on Jurisdiction, 6 Apr. 2018, available at https://jusmundi.com/en/document/decision/en-dawood-rawat-v-republic-of-mauritius-award-on-jurisdiction-friday-6th-april-2018. In this case, the tribunal denied the investor's application for interim measures, stating that Should Rawat ultimately prove that Mauritius has taken retaliatory actions against him or Iris's family in violation of the France-Mauritius BIT, any harm proven will be reparable via the monetary damages he claims.' *See Dawood Rawat v. Republic of Mauritius*, PCA Case No. 2016-20, Order Regarding Claimant's and Respondent's Request for Interim Measures, 11 Jan. 2017, para. 129.

110. Global Arbitration Review, Cosmo Sanderson, 'Jailed businessman fails in emergency claim against Angola', 21 Jun. 2021.

seen in *Teinver v. Argentina*. In this case, the tribunal found that a press conference by Argentinian authorities revealing the details of the arbitration, the criminal complaints and the allegations made therein amounted to an aggravation of the dispute and threatened the claimants' right to the preservation of the *status quo*.

As seen, there is a wide range of possible measures that could be justified by the particularities of specific facts underlying the emergency application for interim relief. What has not yet been seen, however, is an emergency application initiated by a host state to preserve its rights. Such a scenario cannot be completely ruled out, as host states may also face a situation where they would need to safeguard their rights, for instance, in case of an imminent ecological threat posed by the activity carried out by an investor.

§11.07 CONCLUSION

The effectiveness of emergency arbitration is evident in its ability to provide swift and decisive interim relief. By granting such measures, emergency arbitrators can prevent the investor from suffering irreparable harm and ensure that the *status quo* is preserved, thereby protecting the parties' interests during the arbitration process.

This is evidenced by successful applications in several known emergency arbitrator proceedings under the SCC Rules, as discussed in this chapter. Notable cases include *TSIKInvest v. Moldova*, *JKX Oil & Gas v. Ukraine*, *Kompozit v. Moldova*, *Puma Energy v. Benin*, *Okuashvili v. Georgia*, *VEB v. Ukraine*, and *Komaksavia v. Moldova*, where emergency arbitrators awarded the relief sought either partially or in full.

The powers conferred upon emergency arbitrators under the SCC Rules are broad, enabling them to grant any interim measures they deem appropriate. This broad discretion is similar to that of fully constituted arbitral tribunals, ensuring that emergency arbitrators can address the urgent needs of the parties effectively. The abundant case law discussed in this chapter confirms that emergency arbitrators typically do not doubt their authority to make decisions, as long as they are satisfied that the conditions for an emergency application have been met. Although not explicitly required by Appendix II of the SCC Rules governing emergency arbitration, the requirement of urgency has proven to be one of the most challenging aspects, often leading to the dismissal of an emergency application if it is not clearly demonstrated. For example, in cases like *Gazprom v. Lithuania*, *Evrobalt v. Moldova*, and *Vicente v. Angola*, the emergency arbitrators expressed concerns that the urgency claimed did not justify immediate action, as the measures sought could wait until the constitution of the arbitral tribunal.

From the case law reviewed above, when parties opt for arbitration under the SCC Rules, their consent to emergency arbitration is implicitly presumed. The author shares the prevailing opinion that the dynamic reference to any version of the SCC Rules means that the latest version of these rules applies unless the parties have explicitly agreed otherwise. Such a mechanism simplifies the process, allowing for a streamlined approach to obtaining interim relief under the SCC Rules, which is crucial in preventing irreparable harm and maintaining the *status quo* until an arbitral tribunal can be constituted.

Moreover, the standard for prima facie review of the emergency arbitrator's jurisdiction is intentionally low. A similar standard of review applies to assessing the prospects of success of a case on the merits. This is a welcome interpretation as it ensures that urgent matters can be addressed expeditiously without requiring a detailed examination of complex jurisdictional issues, such as dual nationality of investors or the merits. Emergency arbitrators need only be satisfied that there is a reasonable basis for jurisdiction and a prima facie case on the merits, facilitating the swift decision-making that is essential in circumstances of emergency.

Despite these established principles, several aspects of emergency arbitration in investor-State disputes remain unclear. Particularly, there is inconsistency in how emergency arbitrators interpret consent and jurisdiction, especially when the relevant treaties do not explicitly reference the SCC Rules or contain broad arbitration clauses. This variability challenges predictability and uniformity in emergency arbitration decisions, which could affect parties' confidence in the process.

Furthermore, the concept of irreparable harm in international law, a prerequisite for emergency relief, is notably broad and applied inconsistently by emergency arbitrators.

Demonstrating that an investor or investment would suffer irreparable harm if emergency relief was denied is challenging, especially given the short timeframe allowed for emergency proceedings under the SCC Rules because, arguably, any damage could ultimately be compensated through an award on damages. Therefore, the author recommends that emergency arbitrators should exercise particularly careful judgment when assessing the requirement of irreparable harm in emergency proceedings.

The emergency arbitrator's ability to address human rights concerns, such as the detention of investors, also remains a contentious issue. The different outcomes in cases like *Munshi v. Mongolia* and *Vicente v. Angola* add to the significance of the ongoing debate regarding the extent to which emergency arbitrators can and should intervene in matters involving allegations of human rights violations.

Finally, the possibility for states to utilise the provisions on emergency arbitration, potentially in cases involving ecological impacts or human rights violations, is untested. The scope and limitations of states using this mechanism have yet to be fully explored and understood, as there are no known instances to date of states lodging emergency applications against investors to date.

In conclusion, while emergency arbitration under the SCC Rules has demonstrated its value in providing swift and effective interim relief, its broader applicability and the authority of emergency arbitrators, particularly concerning human rights and state utilisation, is uncertain. In order to achieve certainty, it will be crucial to continue the ongoing development of international arbitration norms and adapt existing frameworks to better accommodate the needs of both states and investors.

CHAPTER 12

Dispute Resolution Boards: An Efficient Dispute Resolution Method in Sweden?

Mikael Linton-Wahlgren

§12.01 BACKGROUND

This chapter aims to explore the use of dispute resolution boards (DRBs) as a dispute resolution method in Sweden. It is my view that the use of a well-developed dispute resolution board process (DRB process) could work as an attractive dispute resolution method in, e.g., major construction, infrastructural and energy projects as well as long-term product or business development projects. The use of DRB processes has gained significant attention in the Nordic countries in recent years. This has led to some initial attempts to implement DRB processes in Swedish construction contracts, which I will return to later in this chapter.

The benefits of and arguments for the implementation of a DRB process as an alternative dispute resolution (ADR) method have also been fueled by the international organization DRBF,[1] which has addressed the concept of DRBs at several conferences, workshops, and articles in the Nordic countries. FIDIC[2] has also, through the introduction of its own DRB processes, i.e., the Dispute Adjudication Board (DAB) and the Dispute Avoidance and Adjudication Board (DAAB), which are set out in its standard

1. The Dispute Resolution Board Foundation, DRBF, is a nonprofit organization dedicated to promoting DRB processes for resolving disputes in construction and infrastructure projects. It provides resources, training, and guidance on the establishment and operation of DRBs.
2. FIDIC stands for the Fédération International des Ingénieurs-Conseils (International Federation of Consulting Engineers) and is an industry umbrella group based in Geneva, made up of approximately one hundred national associations of consulting engineers. The organization was founded in 1913 with the goal of promoting excellence in engineering management, including thorough study and publication of industry best-practice guides.

contract forms,[3] established a well-renowned and used structure for the use of DRBs worldwide. Furthermore, the World Bank's adoption of the FIDIC 1999 suite of contracts concept of the DAB and the FIDIC 2017 suite of contracts concept of the DAAB in the World Bank's General Conditions of Contract section of their Standard Bidding Documents and Standard Procurement Documents, for construction contracts, has further established the DRB process as a well-recognized and appreciated tool for dispute resolution in major construction projects.

In this chapter, I intend, based on DRBF's Guide to Best Practices and Procedures,[4] to shed light on if and why the DRB process could be a complement to the resolution of disputes by court litigation or arbitration and how the DRB process can streamline the resolution of disputes in major construction, infrastructural and energy projects as well as in long-term product or business development projects in Sweden.

§12.02 THE USE OF DRB PROCESSES INTERNATIONALLY

[A] The History of DRBs

The concept of DRBs has been developed by the construction industry, dispute resolution institutions (e.g., the ICC),[5] organizations involved in the development of standard contract forms (e.g., FIDIC), and other stakeholders. Traditionally, contractual disputes in the construction industry have been resolved using methods ranging from litigation to ADR processes, such as arbitration, mediation, and adjudication. The introduction of DRBs into construction contracts represents a significant advancement in resolving contractual disputes.[6]

In the 1950s, public construction contracts in the United States became more complex due to the number of contracting parties and additional nontechnical demands, such as environmental regulations and public interest pressures. Combined with the financial instability of contractors, there was a need for more pragmatic solutions to settle claims and disputes.[7] Initially, arbitration became popular as it was

3. The concept of a DAB was introduced in the FIDIC 1999 suite of contracts, which includes the Red Book (Construction), Yellow Book (Plant and Design-Build), and Silver Book (EPC/Turnkey Projects). In the FIDIC 2017 suite of contracts, the term DAB was replaced by Dispute Avoidance and Adjudication Board (DAAB). The 2017 suite includes updated versions of the Red, Yellow, and Silver Books, as well as the Green Book (Short Form of Contract) and the Gold Book (Design, Build and Operate Projects).
4. DRBF, *Dispute Board Manual—A Guide to Best Practices and Procedures* (SPARK Publications, 2019). This guide updates the DRBF's previous manual and explains practices and procedures that have evolved in the application of DRBs. This guide gives special attention to recommended best practices and cautions against modifications to the process which may be acceptable only in certain circumstances.
5. The International Chamber of Commerce provides dispute resolution services, including arbitration and mediation, and has developed rules and guidelines for the use of DRBs in international construction projects.
6. DRBF, *Dispute Board Manual—A Guide to Best Practices and Procedures* (SPARK Publications, 2019), 7.
7. DRBF, *Dispute Board Manual—A Guide to Best Practices and Procedures* (SPARK Publications, 2019), 6.

considered less expensive and faster than litigation. However, arbitration also eventually became costly and time-consuming, leading to the development of other ADR processes like mediation and, subsequently, the adoption of DRBs.[8]

The DRB concept continued to evolve in the United States between 1972 and the 1990s, driven by the construction industry, interest organizations, and national committees.[9] The success of the DRB process in the United States led to its increased use in international projects, supported by governments, professional engineering associations, and project-funding institutions like the World Bank.[10]

In the 1990s, several large international projects successfully utilized DRBs, such as the Channel Tunnel Project (UK/France), the new Hong Kong International Airport, and the Ertan Hydroelectric Project in China.[11] In January 1995, the World Bank included a mandatory three-person DRB for contracts exceeding USD 50 million in its standard bidding documents.[12] Later that year, FIDIC introduced the DAB concept in its "Orange Book,"[13] followed by the 1999 "Red Book," which provided for a standing DRB, and the Yellow and Silver Books, which offered the option of an ad hoc or standing DRB. In 2017, FIDIC's Rainbow suite of contracts[14] was revised to include the DAAB, focusing on both dispute avoidance and adjudication.[15]

Since the mid-1990s, there have been several significant milestones in the expansion of the DRB process, including its adoption by the Asian Development Bank and the European Bank for Reconstruction and Development in 1997 for their internationally funded projects.[16] In 2004, the ICC introduced its own DRB rules, which

8. DRBF, *Dispute Board Manual—A Guide to Best Practices and Procedures* (SPARK Publications, 2019), 6.
9. DRBF, *Dispute Board Manual—A Guide to Best Practices and Procedures* (SPARK Publications, 2019), 6.
10. DRBF, *Dispute Board Manual—A Guide to Best Practices and Procedures* (SPARK Publications, 2019), 6.
11. DRBF, *Dispute Board Manual—A Guide to Best Practices and Procedures* (SPARK Publications, 2019), 6.
12. DRBF, *Dispute Board Manual—A Guide to Best Practices and Procedures* (SPARK Publications, 2019), 7.
13. FIDIC, https://fidic.org/books/design-build-and-turnkey-1st-ed-1995-orange-book (1995).
14. The FIDIC Rainbow Suite of Contracts refers to a collection of standard forms of contracts published by FIDIC. Each colour of the "Rainbow Suite" represents a different type of contract tailored to specific types of work and project requirements. These include the FIDIC Red Book (1999)—designed for construction projects where the contractor is responsible for all of the engineering, procurement, and construction (EPC), the FIDIC Yellow Book (1999)—used for electrical and mechanical works, especially where the contractor designs and builds the plant or infrastructure, the FIDIC Silver Book (1999)—intended for projects delivered on a turnkey basis, the FIDIC Green Book (1999)—designed for smaller projects of relatively low value and short duration, the FIDIC Gold Book (2008)—covering projects delivered under a single contract where the contractor is responsible not only for the design and construction but also for the long-term operation and maintenance of the project, the FIDIC Pink Book (2010)—developed for use by multilateral development banks in financing projects, the FIDIC Blue Book (2017)—suited to large scale dredging and maritime engineering works and the FIDIC White Book (2017)—typically used for consultancy services where consultants provide professional services on a project.
15. FIDIC, https://fidic.org/node/13618 (2017).
16. DRBF, *Dispute Board Manual—A Guide to Best Practices and Procedures* (SPARK Publications, 2019), 7.

were updated in 2015 to include concepts of dispute avoidance and facilitation with appendices in force as of 2018.[17] In 2005, as part of the United Nations' Millennium Goals, procurement heads from various development banks collaborated with FIDIC to develop the "FIDIC MDB Harmonised Conditions of Contract" or "Pink Book"[18] (updated in 2010), widely used for major infrastructure projects in developing countries, with nine MDBs globally adopting this DRB process.[19] The UK-based Institution of Civil Engineers also published its "Dispute Resolution Board Procedures" in 2005.[20]

Since 2008, Japan's International Cooperation Agency (JICA) has promoted DRBs for projects financed by JICA Official Development Assistance loans, making them mandatory in JICA's procurement guidelines and standard bidding documents.[21] In 2014, the UK Chartered Institute of Arbitrators extended the DRB process beyond construction contracts to any medium- or long-term project with its "Dispute Board Rules."[22]

DRBs are increasingly used in private-public partnerships (PPP) projects and have seen hybrid rules for large projects with multiple contracts, such as the London 2012 Olympics & Paralympics, the Rio 2016 Olympics & Paralympics, and the European Union's "Fusion for Energy" (F4E) project.[23]

Today, DRBs are recognized as the leading contract-management process that proactively assists parties in a project to avoid or resolve disputes in a timely and cost-effective manner. They are an integral part of many major construction projects worldwide and are increasingly being employed in other industries, such as information technology, insurance, defence, and manufacturing for large and complex contracts.[24]

[B] The Most Common Rules Used for the Formation of DRBs

As illustrated in section §12.02[A] above, several key organizations have played a significant role in the development and promotion of DRB practices worldwide. DRBF, FIDIC and the ICC have each contributed to the development of the concept and practice of DRBs, and their guidelines are considered authoritative in the field.

These organizations and their suggested DRB process are described below.

17. ICC, Dispute Board Rules, in force as from Oct. 1, 2015, with Appendices in force as from Oct. 1, 2018 (2022).
18. FIDIC, Conditions of Contract for Construction (Multilateral Development Bank Harmonised Ed. Version 3 (2010).
19. DRBF, *Dispute Board Manual—A Guide to Best Practices and Procedures* (SPARK Publications, 2019), 7.
20. DRBF, *Dispute Board Manual—A Guide to Best Practices and Procedures* (SPARK Publications, 2019), 7.
21. DRBF, *Dispute Board Manual—A Guide to Best Practices and Procedures* (SPARK Publications, 2019), 7.
22. DRBF, *Dispute Board Manual—A Guide to Best Practices and Procedures* (SPARK Publications, 2019), 7.
23. DRBF, *Dispute Board Manual—A Guide to Best Practices and Procedures* (SPARK Publications, 2019), 7.
24. DRBF, *Dispute Board Manual—A Guide to Best Practices and Procedures* (SPARK Publications, 2019), 7-8).

[1] The DRBF

The DRBF is a nonprofit organization dedicated to promoting the DRB process for resolving disputes in construction and infrastructure projects. It provides resources, training, and guidance on the establishment and operation of DRBs. The DRBF's definitions and best practices are widely recognized in the industry.[25]

The DRBF's definition, in its Dispute Board Manual, of how a DRB should be structured is that a DRB consists of one or three independent, impartial, and respected individuals selected by the contracting parties. The DRB members are usually experienced professionals in the construction industry, such as engineers, architects, or construction lawyers. The DRB should be established at the commencement of the project and remain in place throughout its duration. The primary function of the DRB is to provide an informal and nonbinding process to resolve disputes that may arise during the course of the project. The DRB encourages the resolution of disputes at the earliest possible stage and aims to prevent disputes from escalating to arbitration or litigation. The DRBF emphasizes that the DRB process is preventative in nature, focusing on dispute avoidance and early resolution. The board typically reviews project progress, provides opinions on potential issues, and, when disputes do arise, offers recommendations or decisions to resolve them. While the DRB's decisions are not legally binding, they are generally respected and followed by the parties, helping to maintain the project's momentum and avoid costly and time-consuming legal proceedings.[26]

[2] FIDIC

FIDIC is an international standards organization that develops and publishes contract forms for the global construction industry. FIDIC's contract documents, including the Red Book, Yellow Book, and Silver Book, contain provisions for DABs or DAABs, which are similar to DRBs. FIDIC's definitions and developed procedures for these DRBs have been highly influential and ground-breaking for the acceptance and structuring of DRBs. FIDIC does not use the term "Dispute Resolution Board" in its standard contract forms. Instead, FIDIC uses the terms "Dispute Adjudication Board" (DAB) in its 1999 suite of contracts and "Dispute Avoidance and Adjudication Board" (DAAB) in its 2017 suite of contracts. In the 2017 suite of FIDIC contracts, the concept of a DAB evolved to include dispute avoidance as well, leading to the introduction of DAAB. These boards serve a similar function to DRBs, focusing on dispute avoidance and resolution.[27]

---

25. DRBF, *Dispute Board Manual—A Guide to Best Practices and Procedures* (SPARK Publications, 2019), 8.
26. DRBF, *Dispute Board Manual—A Guide to Best Practices and Procedures* (SPARK Publications, 2019), 14-16).
27. FIDIC, FIDIC Contracts Guide (2017 editions, as reprinted in 2022 with amendments) Guide 1st ed. (2022).

The abbreviations DAB and DAAB have specific meanings related to dispute resolution in FIDIC's standard form contracts. The two DRB processes, in summary, are characterized by the following:

(a) A DAB, as defined in the FIDIC 1999 suite of contracts, consists of a panel composed of one or three independent and impartial experts appointed by the parties to the contract. The DAB is established at the outset of the project and has the authority to make binding decisions on disputes that arise during the execution of the contract. These decisions are binding on the parties until superseded by an arbitral award or court judgment. The DAB process aims to provide a swift and efficient resolution to disputes, thereby avoiding lengthy and costly arbitration or litigation.[28]

(b) A DAAB consists of one or three independent and impartial experts appointed by the parties to the contract, with a dual role: to proactively work with parties to avoid disputes and to adjudicate disputes that do arise. The DAAB provides a proactive approach to dispute resolution, offering informal assistance and advice to the parties during the project and, when necessary, making decisions on disputed matters that are generally binding but can be superseded by an arbitral award or court judgment if either party is dissatisfied.[29]

FIDIC contracts are known for their comprehensive dispute resolution provisions, and the inclusion of either a DAB or DAAB is a key feature for ensuring the effective and timely resolution of conflicts in large construction projects. The DABs or DAABs play a crucial role in maintaining project continuity and reducing the need for more formal and lengthy dispute resolution processes.

As mentioned in section §12.02[A] above, the World Bank's standard procurement documents for construction contracts also reference the use of DRBs, which can be either DABs or DAABs, depending on the version of the used FIDIC contract form. These provisions are typically included in the General Conditions of Contract (GCC) section of the World Bank's Standard Bidding Documents (SBDs) or Standard Procurement Documents (SPDs) for construction contracts. The specific provisions regarding the establishment, composition, and procedures of the DRB will be detailed in the contract documents provided by the World Bank for each individual project. In addition, SBDs (2000 revision) provided that the recommendation of a DRB expert is binding and must be given effect unless or until an arbitral award or court judgment is rendered on the same issue.[30]

28. FIDIC, 1999 FIDIC suite of contracts, clause 20, titled "Claims, Disputes and Arbitration" (1999).
29. FIDIC, the 2017 FIDIC suite of contracts, clause 21, titled "Disputes and Arbitration (2017).
30. Jane Jenkins, *International Construction Arbitration Law*, 3rd ed. (Kluwer Law International, 2021) 125.

Both the DAB and DAAB concepts emphasize the importance of early and efficient dispute resolution in construction projects, with the aim of maintaining project progress and minimizing the impact of disputes on time and cost.[31]

[3] The ICC

The ICC provides dispute resolution services, including arbitration and mediation, and has developed rules and guidelines for the use of DRBs in international construction projects. The ICC refers to DRBs in its standard documents and guidelines.[32] In these documents, the ICC defines DRBs as a standing body, typically comprising one or three independent and impartial experts, appointed at the outset of a project either jointly by the parties or, if they fail to do so, by ICC's International Centre for ADR. The DRB's primary function is to assist the parties in avoiding disputes and, where disputes arise, to provide a forum for their resolution. The ICC's DRB processes operate under various names, including DRBs,[33] DABs,[34] or Combined Dispute Boards (CDBs),[35] depending on their specific mandate and the rules under which they operate. The ICC provides rules and guidelines for the establishment and operation of DRBs, which are used in international construction and infrastructure projects. The ICC Dispute Board Rules offer a framework for the prevention, management, and resolution of disputes, with the aim of reducing the time and cost associated with arbitration or litigation.

[4] The SCC

The Stockholm Chamber of Commerce (the SCC) provides rules and procedures for Swedish and international arbitration and other forms of dispute resolution. However, the SCC does not have a distinct set of rules for a DRB process similar to those provided by the ICC, FIDIC or DRBF. In general, the SCC focuses on administering and overseeing arbitration cases, including international commercial arbitration and investment treaty arbitration.[36] It is one of the leading institutions for international arbitration and is recognized for its expertise in handling complex cross-border disputes.

The closest the SCC comes to a DRB concept, while not being an actual DRB process, is the recently introduced SCC Express Rules.[37] The SCC states that "the aim of the SCC is to promote trade between companies. We do this by helping companies spend as little time as possible on dispute resolution, allowing them to spend more time

31. FIDIC, FIDIC Contracts Guide, clause 21, (2017 editions, as reprinted in 2022 with amendments) Guide 1st ed. (2022).
32. ICC, Dispute Board Rules, in force as from Oct. 1, 2015, with Appendices in force as from Oct. 1, 2018 (2022).
33. ICC, Dispute Board Rules, Art. 4 (2022).
34. ICC, Dispute Board Rules, Art. 5 (2022).
35. ICC, Dispute Board Rules, Art. 6 (2022).
36. SCC, https://sccarbitrationinstitute.se/om-scc (2024).
37. SCC, SCC Express, https://sccarbitrationinstitute.se/en/our-services/scc-express (accessed Mar. 28, 2024).

on their core business."[38] Furthermore, the SCC presents SCC Express as being a "service primarily aimed at parties with an ongoing contract. The priority is on the business relationship and the parties have a legal dispute they want to resolve quickly and at a fixed price. The service can also be used by parties who want to test their legal position before a settlement discussion or a decision to initiate legal proceedings through arbitration or in court."[39]

Moreover, SCC Express is described as "a consent-based and confidential dispute resolution process. The contracting parties may jointly decide to choose SCC Express as the dispute resolution method, either when the contract is written or when the dispute arises. The SCC appoints a neutral legal expert to give their opinion on the merits of the case within three weeks."[40] Like in a DRB process, it is said that "this assessment is neither enforceable nor binding on the parties, unless they have specifically agreed to this. The main purpose of the service is to help the parties move forward in their contractual relationship."[41] The process for dispute resolution services is set out in the SCC Express Rules.[42]

[C] The Basics of DRBs

While the DRB process is a relatively recent method for resolving disputes in major projects, its effectiveness is well-established. The unique attribute of the DRB process has become evident over many years of application. When adequately implemented, the DRB process offers an economical and highly efficient way to help project parties not only resolve disputes swiftly but also, more crucially, prevent disputes and attain the best possible project results.[43]

A DRB is usually comprised of three members, though some DRBs may have only one member. The DRB member should be a reputable and trustworthy expert chosen for expertise, experience, and impartiality in the project's subject matter. In a construction project, a DRB typically consists of a diverse group, including engineers, contractors, architects, builders, consultants, and lawyers, all of whom are specialists in construction work. All members of the DRB must be approved by the contracting parties. It is essential that DRB members always maintain their independence and neutrality and do not represent a specific contracting party.[44]

---

38. SCC, SCC Express, https://sccarbitrationinstitute.se/en/our-services/scc-express (accessed Mar. 28, 2024).
39. SCC, SCC Express, https://sccarbitrationinstitute.se/en/our-services/scc-express (accessed Mar. 28, 2024).
40. SCC, SCC Express, https://sccarbitrationinstitute.se/en/our-services/scc-express (accessed Mar. 28, 2024).
41. SCC, SCC Express, https://sccarbitrationinstitute.se/en/our-services/scc-express (accessed Mar. 28, 2024).
42. SCC, SCC Rules for Express Dispute Assessment (2023).
43. DRBF, *Dispute Board Manual—A Guide to Best Practices and Procedures* (SPARK Publications, 2019), 14.
44. DRBF, *Dispute Board Manual—A Guide to Best Practices and Procedures* (SPARK Publications, 2019), 14.

During the project, the DRB regularly convenes with the parties to assist in preventing and, if required, resolving issues and disputes. The DRB achieves this by offering an unbiased platform for the real-time resolution of disputes at minimal expense. The mere presence of a readily accessible dispute avoidance and resolution mechanism—utilizing mutually chosen, technically proficient, and experienced "neutrals" who are well-acquainted with the project—promotes consensus on matters that might otherwise lead to protracted and expensive arbitration or litigation.[45]

The DRB is typically established when the parties sign a contract for the project's delivery. At this point, the parties also sign a formal agreement with each DRB member (DRB Agreement). However, a DRB can be established at any stage if there is mutual agreement between the parties. The DRB Agreement outlines the responsibilities of the parties as well as the roles and duties of the DRB. The costs associated with the DRB are generally split equally between the owner and the contractor.[46]

Regular meetings between the contracting parties and the DRB usually take place at the project site and often include a site inspection. These meetings, attended by both off-site executives and senior on-site personnel, provide the DRB with updates on the overall progress of the project. The DRB is informed about potential issues that may lead to increased costs or delays, as well as any unresolved matters that could escalate into disputes. The DRB engages in discussions and consultations with the parties to explore ways to resolve these issues.[47]

In between the scheduled DRB meetings, the DRB is kept informed about the project's progress through monthly reports, meeting minutes, and any other documentation deemed necessary by the parties or the DRB to ensure that the DRB always remains fully informed.[48]

Should any issue under the contract remain unresolved after negotiations between the parties and discussions with the DRB, either party has the right to formally refer the dispute to the DRB for a recommendation or decision.[49]

The methods for selecting DRB members differ, and several widely used approaches exist. Both the owner and the contractor must select their preferred DRB candidates, considering factors such as qualifications, availability, experience, and background. Candidates may need to submit a formal statement affirming their impartiality and independence from any parties or individuals connected to the project. After the DRB nominees receive approval from the parties, the DRB is officially formed when the parties and the DRB members jointly sign a DRB Agreement.[50]

45. DRBF, *Dispute Board Manual—A Guide to Best Practices and Procedures* (SPARK Publications, 2019), 14.
46. DRBF, *Dispute Board Manual—A Guide to Best Practices and Procedures* (SPARK Publications, 2019), 14-15.
47. DRBF, *Dispute Board Manual—A Guide to Best Practices and Procedures* (SPARK Publications, 2019), 15.
48. DRBF, *Dispute Board Manual—A Guide to Best Practices and Procedures* (SPARK Publications, 2019), 15.
49. DRBF, *Dispute Board Manual—A Guide to Best Practices and Procedures* (SPARK Publications, 2019), 15.
50. DRBF, *Dispute Board Manual—A Guide to Best Practices and Procedures* (SPARK Publications, 2019), 15.

In most construction contracts without a DRB, a specific dispute resolution procedure is outlined that must be adhered to in the event of a dispute. By contrast, the DRB's role in dispute avoidance is not restricted to any set process, allowing the DRB to implement the most appropriate dispute avoidance strategies for the issue at hand.[51]

Establishing the DRB as early as possible after the contract is signed enables the DRB to become acquainted with the project from the beginning, i.e., at a time when issues and disputes are likely to emerge. The early formation of a DRB also commits the parties to a framework designed to resolve issues and prevent disputes by fostering positive relationships and open communication at all levels.

As the DRB stays informed about the progress of the work and any ongoing issues, it is prepared to assist the parties in addressing issues in real time as they arise. Resolving issues early, before they escalate into disputes, helps maintain relationships and significantly reduces both costs and the loss of productive project time.[52]

In addition, the participation of senior off-site personnel in DRB meetings not only keeps the DRB better informed about the project's progress but also provides it with the opportunity to use its authority to prevent potential disputes.

However, if the parties are unable to resolve an issue and it turns into a dispute, the DRB can settle it quickly once a formal referral has been made by one of the parties. When a dispute is referred to the DRB for resolution, the DRB process is cost-effective compared to other dispute resolution methods.[53]

The DRB employs a variety of dispute avoidance techniques tailored to the specific issue at hand. Typically, the DRB adopts a proactive approach, promoting dispute avoidance by focusing on project management and the resolution of various issues during regular DRB meetings. The DRB inquires routinely into potential issues, claims, or disputes and reviews and monitors their status together with the parties. The DRB also encourages the parties to seek early resolution of issues and to utilize the DRB for facilitating informal sessions or special meetings with the parties or interested third parties.[54]

The possibility of referring a dispute to the DRB for its resolution motivates the parties to resolve issues that could escalate into disputes. Feedback from the DRB prompts the parties to critically evaluate their positions on the issue at hand.

Moreover, before formally referring a dispute to the DRB, the parties may request an informal, nonbinding advisory opinion from the DRB.[55] The advantage of such an advisory opinion is that it can often be provided by the DRB on short notice and

51. DRBF, *Dispute Board Manual—A Guide to Best Practices and Procedures* (SPARK Publications, 2019), 15.
52. DRBF, *Dispute Board Manual—A Guide to Best Practices and Procedures* (SPARK Publications, 2019), 15.
53. DRBF, *Dispute Board Manual—A Guide to Best Practices and Procedures* (SPARK Publications, 2019), 15.
54. DRBF, *Dispute Board Manual—A Guide to Best Practices and Procedures* (SPARK Publications, 2019), 15.
55. DRBF, *Dispute Board Manual—A Guide to Best Practices and Procedures* (SPARK Publications, 2019), 15.

frequently leads to the resolution of an issue that might otherwise have been formally referred to the DRB for a recommendation or decision.

When the parties are unable to resolve disputes promptly on their own or with the help of the DRB, either party may formally refer the dispute to the DRB. The process leading to a recommendation or decision by the DRB is typically outlined in the DRB Agreement and/or the project contract. This process usually involves each party submitting position papers, documents, and evidence related to the dispute, followed by an opportunity for each party to respond to the other party's submissions.[56]

A hearing or conference is convened either by mutual agreement of the parties or at the request of the DRB.[57] This provides an opportunity for the parties to further articulate their positions and respond to the opposing side's arguments. Whether legal counsel to the parties are allowed during such hearings depends on the terms of the DRB Agreement.

When all relevant information has been presented and submitted, the DRB issues a written recommendation or decision, which includes the DRB's analysis and reasoning, within the timeframe stipulated in the DRB Agreement.[58]

Depending on the contract's terms and conditions, the DRB's issuance may be a nonbinding recommendation or a binding decision (subject only to subsequent arbitration). In either scenario, experience has demonstrated that a well-reasoned analysis of the dispute by a panel of neutral, highly experienced professionals almost always leads to the settlement of the dispute without further legal action.[59]

Finally, it should be noted that the interim binding nature of a DRB's decision emanates from the parties having contractually agreed that they will implement and abide by the DRB's decision until the dispute is finally resolved. The decisions are, accordingly, not enforceable in the same way as arbitral awards or judgments.

[D] The Benefits of Using the DRB Process

Over time, owners and contractors engaged in significant projects have utilized various methods to resolve their contractual disputes, ranging from court litigation to various forms of ADR, such as arbitration, mediation, and adjudication. The incorporation of DRBs into the contract and dispute-management framework has also proven to be a successful innovation in the field of ADR.[60]

The use of DRBs has proven to be a crucial element of best-practice project management. Especially in the construction industry, major projects often entail

56. DRBF, *Dispute Board Manual—A Guide to Best Practices and Procedures* (SPARK Publications, 2019), 16.
57. DRBF, *Dispute Board Manual—A Guide to Best Practices and Procedures* (SPARK Publications, 2019), 16.
58. DRBF, *Dispute Board Manual—A Guide to Best Practices and Procedures* (SPARK Publications, 2019), 16.
59. DRBF, *Dispute Board Manual—A Guide to Best Practices and Procedures* (SPARK Publications, 2019), 16.
60. DRBF, *Dispute Board Manual—A Guide to Best Practices and Procedures* (SPARK Publications, 2019), 8.

considerable risks for the participants, which can vary based on the project's type, complexity, duration, and allocated budget. Some of the major benefits of using DRBs as a means of avoiding or resolving disputes are listed below:[61]

(a) DRBs can help the parties to facilitate agreement on contract-related matters, e.g., time and cost-related issues, and, as a result, can prevent future disputes. Accordingly, a DRB process plays an important role as a dispute avoidance process. The DRB can aid the parties in addressing contentious issues and contractual disagreements before they escalate into a formal dispute. As regards dispute resolution, the DRB offers the parties an impartial recommendation or decision on formal disputes, thereby allowing the parties to settle such matters at the project level and avoiding disruption in the progress of the project.

(b) Unresolved and prolonged disputes can lead to delays and disruptions in the project, increasing costs and causing a breakdown in relationships and communication between the parties. In the case of public or government projects, such disputes can also lead to community and political issues (along with additional costs and delays) that may have repercussions far beyond the project's scope. By using a DRB process, a DRB decision can make the parties adopt a "comply-now, argue-later" approach. The DRB process acts as a motivation for the parties to resolve their disagreements and help the parties maintain their business relationship. Research shows that when a DRB is used in a project, up to 98 % of disputes are resolved at the project level, with the remaining 2 % being referred to arbitration or litigation.[62]

(c) The parties sometimes view the use of a DRB as an added expense rather than a cost-effective management tool.[63] However, comparing DRBs to project insurance can highlight their value.

   The parties invest heavily in various insurance policies, including general liability, professional liability, workers' compensation, builder's risk, loss of profit/production and other policies to mitigate project risks. For larger projects, party-controlled insurance programs are implemented, incurring costs beyond the actual policies for management and administration. These programs aim to prevent or reduce losses and cover any losses that occur by transferring the risk to insurers. DRBs serve a similar function but have a broader and more positive impact on project outcomes.

   Insurance programs are successful if they prevent and cover losses during a project. Investing millions in insurance premiums and administrative costs is considered prudent as it mitigates and absorbs project risks. However,

61. DRBF, *Dispute Board Manual—A Guide to Best Practices and Procedures* (SPARK Publications, 2019), 10.
62. DRBF, Workshop on Dispute Boards in Multilateral Development Bank Financed Projects (2021).
63. DRBF, *Dispute Board Manual—A Guide to Best Practices and Procedures* (SPARK Publications, 2019), 9.

statistics from the DRBF show that the cost of insurance on major projects almost always exceeds the cost of using a DRB by a significant margin, even before considering the additional benefits of a DRB,[64] e.g., preserving relationship and cooperation between the parties, limiting cash flow problems and avoiding delays in the project.

(d) DRBs deliver decisions in a timely and cost-effective manner, serving as an efficient means to resolve disputes quickly and affordably. Conducting a cost-benefit analysis for the use of DRBs on a project involves comparing the relatively fixed costs of a DRB with the benefits of minimizing the cost and time impact of disputed issues. When conducting such a cost-benefit analysis, there are several key factors to consider, e.g., including:

   (i) The carrying costs of a DRB relative to the project's budget are small, typically ranging from 0.05% to 0.15% of project costs.[65]

   (ii) A DRB is integrated into the project's management structure to reduce project costs. For instance, the DRB often participates in senior management meetings in conjunction with DRB meetings and can arrange on-site meetings convenient for the parties aimed at optimizing project outcomes.

   (iii) The additional marginal cost of a DRB is lower than any other formal dispute resolution process. The DRB is relatively informal, usually does not involve external consultants or lawyers, lacks a document-discovery procedure, and utilizes real-time information readily available to both the parties and the DRB.

   (iv) Comparative studies between projects with and without DRBs almost always show positive results. Projects with DRBs, compared to those without, typically experience significantly fewer and smaller cost overruns and schedule delays.[66]

   In summary, the cost of a DRB yields a positive return on investment due to faster project delivery times, minimizes cost overruns, prevention of most disputes, and a much lower cost of resolution for unavoidable disputes.[67]

(e) DRBs offer additional "soft" benefits to a project. Regular meetings between DRBs and project teams foster open communication and collaborative behaviour, which help maintain contractual relationships. DRBs prompt parties to address potential problems early on when they are most easily resolved. Additionally, DRBs can facilitate solutions that are best for the project, minimizing cost and time overruns.

64. DRBF, *Dispute Board Manual—A Guide to Best Practices and Procedures* (SPARK Publications, 2019), 9.
65. DRBF, *Dispute Board Manual—A Guide to Best Practices and Procedures* (SPARK Publications, 2019), 10.
66. DRBF, *Dispute Board Manual—A Guide to Best Practices and Procedures* (SPARK Publications, 2019), 10.
67. DRBF, *Dispute Board Manual—A Guide to Best Practices and Procedures* (SPARK Publications, 2019), 10.

Even when disputes arise, the DRB hearing process allows for the orderly and neutral management of conflict. The DRB process is unique among alternative dispute resolution methods as it occurs in real time. Disputes can be resolved quickly while the project continues, enabling management to concentrate on achieving better project outcomes. Furthermore, the outcomes of the DRB process uphold the contract provisions and risk allocation, as the DRB is required to apply the terms agreed upon in the contract documents.

(f) Lastly, DRBs offer a dispute resolution process characterized by integrity and procedural fairness. The DRB process is grounded in factual records, project documentation, and applicable law. The DRB provides well-reasoned and detailed findings by experienced and independent experts who understand the project, the participants, and the facts of the dispute. This merit-based process should instil confidence in both owners and contractors.

§12.03 THE USE OF THE DRB PROCESS AS A COMPLEMENT TO ARBITRATION IN MAJOR INFRASTRUCTURE AND CONSTRUCTION PROJECTS IN SWEDEN

[A] The Development of Dispute Resolution in Swedish Construction Project

Based on my background as a former in-house counsel and nowadays acting as arbitrator, mediator, and adjudicator, this section sets out my views of how disputes, specifically in the construction industry, have been resolved and can be resolved in the future. When I worked for Skanska, ABB, Rolls-Royce and NCC on their international projects, I frequently had to work under the then-applicable FIDIC standard conditions. I also had the privilege to represent ABB in the contractor group (consisting of some of the other multinational electro-mechanical companies), who addressed the contractors' view on the World Bank and other MDBs intended implementation of the FIDIC's then-newly released 1999 suite of contracts.

In Swedish construction projects, as well as in construction projects around the world, conflicts frequently emerge early on due to alterations in the original scope of the contract. While technical adjustments to address the unforeseen can usually be settled through agreement between the contractor and the owner, the financial and time-delaying implications of these changes can be problematic. Stalemates on these matters can adversely impact the liquidity and cash flows of the involved parties. The Swedish standard contracts for commercial construction projects, i.e., the AB 04[68] and ABT 06,[69] which are the most frequently used standard terms in Swedish construction projects, often necessitate interpretation and legal analysis. However, legal expertise is

68. Byggandets Kontraktskommitté (BKK), *Allmänna Bestämmelser "FÖR BYGGNADS-, ANLÄGGN INGS- OCH INSTALLATIONSENTREPRENADER" AB 04* (2004).

69. Byggandets Kontraktskommitté (BKK), *Allmänna Bestämmelser "FÖR TOTALENTREPRENA DER AVSEENDE BYGGNADS-, ANLÄGGNINGS- OCH INSTALLATIONSARBETEN"AB 06* (2006).

seldom present in the projects, leading engineers to interpret relatively complex contracts, which can result in varying outcomes. In such situations, swift interim dispute resolution by a DRB can offer an appealing solution. Ideally, a "pay-first, build-later, resolve-last" approach allows a party with a valid payment claim but weak financial standing to survive and ultimately pursue its rights in a comprehensive hearing.

In AB 04 and ABT 06, a condition has been introduced offering a simplified dispute resolution, allowing the parties, in the event of a contractual dispute, to jointly refer the matter to an appropriate impartial arbitrator. This simplified dispute resolution provision regulates, e.g., the appointment of the impartial arbitrator, the procedural rules, and the timelines for the parties' actions and when and in what format the impartial arbitrator shall deliver the decision. The arbitrator's decision shall be binding on the parties until they agree on another solution or the matter is finally settled by either a court of law or an arbitral tribunal, following a notice of dissatisfaction by either of the parties.[70]

Should the parties decide not to use the abovementioned simplified dispute resolution option in AB 04 or ABT 06 or wish to finally settle the dispute through litigation or arbitration based on a notice of dissatisfaction, this will trigger the other dispute resolution conditions set out in AB 04 and ABT 06.[71] These dispute resolution provisions stipulate, e.g., that disputes are to be settled in court if the value in dispute does not exceed a certain amount[72] and that if the value in dispute exceeds that amount, it can be settled by arbitration.[73]

Public authorities now tend to bring nearly all their disputes to court, resulting in an increased workload for the judiciary with construction disputes of varying sizes. There are numerous instances demonstrating that the resolution of such disputes can be notably slow, with a single district court process potentially spanning several years. Given this trend, the prospect of obtaining swift interim judgments pending a full trial becomes appealing.

Accordingly, disputes in the Swedish construction industry are still predominantly settled through litigation or arbitration. The reasons for this are probably tradition, comfort, and the lack of knowledge among the involved parties of DRBs and other ADR processes.

Sweden is, in my opinion, underdeveloped when it comes to the use of ADR methods to resolve commercial disputes. However, even if it is still early days, there are some ADR solutions that are being tried out in Sweden. Apart from a few DRBs, as mentioned below, the main ADR methods that have been tested or developed in Sweden are mediation, adjudication, and the SCC Express procedure.

---

70. BKK, AB 04 and ABT 06 Chapter 10 ("SIMPLIFIED DISPUTE RESOLUTION") § 1 (2004 respectively 2006).
71. BKK, AB 04 and ABT 06 Chapter 9 ("DISPUTE RESOLUTION) §§ 1-3 (2004 respectively 2006).
72. The threshold being 150 price base amounts (*Sw: "prisbasbelopp"*).
73. In accordance with the Swedish Arbitration Act (SFS 1999:116).

As mentioned earlier in this chapter, the use of DRBs should be looked upon as both an alternative method to handle disputes as early as possible and, more importantly, as a tool to prevent disputes and conflicts with the use of one or more independent adjudicators. The three dominants of dispute prevention could be summarized as follows: the contract and its conditions should (i) offer a clear management support and guidance, (ii) have a legally and operationally easy-to-use function and setup, and (iii) be usable as a manual for all parties involved in the contract management.[74]

In creating a sustainable long-term contractual relationship, one should keep in mind that it is not only a matter of winning the contract but also of making sure that the contract works efficiently during the performance of the project[75] and delivering an outcome that both contracting parties are satisfied with. In this sense, it could, based on my own experience, be well-invested time for both parties to put extra focus on making a thorough pre-risk analysis, trying to map out all the unknowns and potential risks and disputes in a project. Furthermore, the parties should put effort into drafting and negotiating an efficient and conflict-preventive contract that will, preferably, work as a project contract manual as well.[76] The lawyer's role is accordingly to be not only the drafter and advocate but also a designer of the contract and problem-solver.[77]

Essential for dispute prevention is, accordingly, for the parties to put sufficient efforts into identifying and handling likely risks, misunderstandings, and potential disputes in the contract. In the attempt to create a well-functioning contract, the inclusion of a DRB process, like the DAB and DAAB, is, in my opinion, recommended, as it permits binding decisions on unresolved contractual matters. A DRB can either be a standing or an ad hoc DRB, but I would recommend the standing DRB because it will provide a well-updated and experienced DRB panel that can give efficient support to the parties throughout the project.

As mentioned before, the use of DRBs is highly recognized internationally in the construction industry, especially if the DRB process is based on FIDIC's DAB and DAAB rules included in its standard forms. It is important, however, to use the right version of FIDIC's standard forms and not try to squeeze in conditions and issues that could be handled better by another FIDIC standard form.[78]

---

74. Anette Kavaleff, Licentiate in Law, owner of Oy Kavaleff Consulting AB, an energy lawyer with professional past as company lawyer, director for investments and project finance and vice president for the legal department in Imatran Voima Oy and its successor Fortum Oyj, *DRBF Webinar—"DBs in the Nordics"* (video recording from Jan. 13, 2022).
75. Helena Haapio, Contract Strategist, Lexpert Ltd, Associate Professor of Business Law, University of Vaasa, Senior Researcher, Tampere University JARGONFREE Research Group, Professor of Practice and Docent, University of Lapland, *DRBF Webinar—"DBs in the Nordics"* (video recording from Jan. 13, 2022).
76. Torbjörn Ström, Legal Counsel at Skanska Sverige AB.
77. Aisha Nadar, Attorney at law, Vice Chair at ICC Commission on Arbitration and ADR, DRBF Country Representative for Sweden, Board Member at FIDIC, *DRBF Webinar—"DBs in the Nordics—The Swedish Roundtable,"* (video recording from Mar. 18, 2022).
78. Kai Möller, Head of Export at Sweco AB, Committee member of FIDIC's Contract Committee, FIDIC Ambassador in Sweden, *DRBF Webinar—"DBs in the Nordics—The Swedish Roundtable,"* (video recording from Mar. 18, 2022).

As regards the legal effect of a DRB recommendation or decision, it is not enforceable under Swedish law like an arbitral award or judgment. However, my view is that especially a DRB decision ought to be considered as an agreed interpretation of the concerned contract condition or as an amendment to the contract.[79] That means that noncompliance with the agreed DRB procedure and/or the DRB's recommendations or decisions ought to be considered a breach of contract, warranting available remedies under Swedish law.

One common argument against using DRBs is that it adds unnecessary costs and diversion from the work and completion of a project. However, the use of a DRB process in a contract can, as mentioned in section §12.02[D] above, be viewed as an insurance program. Considering the previously mentioned insurance cover involved in a major construction project, the use of a DRB process should be considered an insurance that can cater for an efficient resolution of upcoming unknown and unforeseen claims or disputes.

[B] The Use of DRBs in Sweden

Despite a number of major infrastructure and construction projects in Sweden during the past twenty-five years—e.g., the Öresund Bridge (completed in 2000), the City railway (*Sw: "Citybanan"*) in Stockholm (opened in 2017), the Northern Link (*Sw: "Norra Länken"*) in Stockholm (completed in 2014), the Southern Link (*Sw: "Södra Länken"*) in Stockholm (completed in 2004), the Malmö City Tunnel (*Sw: "Citytunneln"*) (opened in 2010) and the Bothnia Line (*Sw: "Botniabanan"*) (completed in 2010)—only one of them has used the DRB process.

A DRB was used in the Öresund Link projects. However, the use of this DRB was limited during the execution of that project.[80]

One of the main owners of Swedish infrastructure projects in Sweden is the Swedish Transport Administration (*Sw: "Trafikverket"*). Even if I know, from my own contacts with that body, that it has considered the introduction of a DRB process in some of its projects, it is currently using the dispute resolution processes based on AB 04 and ABT 06.[81]

However, the New Metro Administration at Region Stockholm has introduced a DRB process in its contract for the execution of the Green Line metro extension project, which is planned to be in service by 2028.[82] This is done by amending AB 04's Chapter. 9, section 1. Under the amended condition, a DRB consisting of three members is appointed as a standing body for dispute settlement. The DRB's recommendations or decisions in respect of disputes, not exceeding a fixed maximum value, shall be final and binding on the parties if they do not notify, within the prescribed time, that they do

79. *See* Christina Ramberg, Professor in civil law at Stockholm University, *DRBF Webinar—"DBs in the Nordics—The Swedish Roundtable,"* (video recording from Mar. 18, 2022).
80. Torbjörn Ström, Legal Counsel at Skanska Sverige AB.
81. Jennie Magnusson, Acting General Counsel and Acting Head of Legal and Planning Assessment at the Swedish Transport Administration.
82. Julia Tavaststjerna, Chief Legal Officer at the New Metro, Region Stockholm.

not agree with such a recommendation or decision.[83] In that case, the dispute shall be referred to court. Accordingly, this DRB condition seems to be similar to FIDIC's DAAB conditions.

§12.04 CONCLUDING REMARKS

In conclusion, I have tried, in this chapter, to present the benefits and, in my view, the rationale behind using a DRB process in contracts for major construction projects. However, based on my industry experience, I am convinced that the DRB process could also be introduced in other forms of long-term contracts, e.g., cooperation, manufacturing, and product development contracts.

Despite its international success, the DRB process is not widely used in major construction contracts in Sweden. This is notable given its popularity in the US, UK and internationally, and considering its inclusion in standard contract forms by the World Bank and other MDBs.

The ICC ADR rules could also be considered. According to the Chairman of the ICC Task Force, charged with drafting the ICC ADR rules, the main factor differentiating the ICC's approach from others is that the ICC's system is intended to be adaptable to medium- and long-term contracts in any industry anywhere in the world.[84]

The DRB process offers several advantages:[85]

(a) It provides a swift and less costly alternative to court or arbitration proceedings.
(b) It allows projects to continue while disputes are resolved.
(c) It enables parties to select DRB members with appropriate expertise, ensuring technically sound decisions while allowing for judicial review if necessary.

The growing recognition of the effectiveness of DRBs has led experts to suggest their broader adoption in Sweden. As stated by two Swedish commentators:

> [i]t seems that roughly the same reasons that motivated the introduction of adjudication in the UK are also valid in the Swedish construction industry. However, given the reluctance of the legislator to interfere with commercial contracts and the legislator's very traditional attitude towards newer forms of alternative dispute resolution, the natural first step would be for the BKK[86] to introduce something similar to [DRBs] in the next version of AB and ABT.[87]

83. The New Metro Administration at Region Stockholm, *Administrative regulations to the AB 04 governing the Green Line metro extension project,* AB 04's Chapter 9 § 1.
84. Jane Jenkins, *International Construction Arbitration Law,* 3rd ed. (Kluwer Law International, 2021) 128.
85. Jane Jenkins, *International Construction Arbitration Law,* 3rd ed. (Kluwer Law International, 2021) 76.
86. Byggandets Kontraktskommitté.
87. Anders Ingvarsson and Daniel Holmblad, *Tvistlösning inom affärsrätten—en antologi,* (Nordstedts Juridik, 2020) 112 (translated from Swedish to English by the author).

One interesting and encouraging step towards establishing DRBs as a common ADR process in Sweden is that the New Metro Administration at Region Stockholm has adopted the DRB process by introducing a DRB into its contract for the execution of the Green Line metro extension project.[88]

While discussing the potential of DRBs in Sweden, it is important to note the existing efforts and their shortcomings. As highlighted in recent observations:

> The BKK has already considered similar models in the form of the simplified DRB procedure currently provided for in Chapter 9 of AB 04 and ABT 06. However, this procedure has not had any impact. The reasons for this appear to be, not least, that the procedure is based on voluntariness in terms of both implementation and compliance with decisions. The rules have also been considered less well thought out.[89]

A particular challenge against DRBs in Sweden is the limited pool of suitable and competent individuals for DRB assignments.[90] Nevertheless, considering the limited number of available contractors, sub-contractors and owners in Sweden, the use of DRBs ought to be an appealing alternative, and parties should be incentivized to use a DRB process, as it is (in most cases) an effective way to preserve the parties' business relationship and facilitate the possibility of them working together in the future.

However, despite the fact that the use of DRBs has been proven internationally to be a fast and cost-effective procedure, some of the resistance in the Swedish construction industry to use DRBs is probably due to, e.g., that it is considered to compromise the transparency of the case or that the disputing parties believe that they would benefit from a more detailed presentation of evidence or hearings.

DRBs are effective in many disputes but are considered less suitable for complex issues like professional liability and final project costs. Nevertheless, they reduce insolvency risks and project delays due to payment disputes.[91]

In summary, the use of DRBs is, in my opinion, a process that conveniently helps the parties in a long-term contract to avoid disputes. Having a DRB process in place in a contract will assist the parties in focusing on their performance and commitments under the contract and will prevent delays in the execution of the contract due to disputes that could be resolved if addressed at an early stage, which will save costs in the long run despite upfront costs. The DRB process also promotes that all concerned parties in a project can be involved in the attempt to resolve a claim or dispute when the parties are still up to date with all the facts in the matter. Thus, by this chapter, I wish to encourage the adoption of DRB procedures in Swedish construction and long-term contracts.

88. Julia Tavaststjerna, Chief Legal Officer at the New Metro, Region Stockholm.
89. Anders Ingvarsson and Daniel Holmblad, *Tvistlösning inom affärsrätten—en antologi*, (Nordstedts Juridik, 2020) 112 (translated from Swedish to English by the author).
90. Anders Ingvarsson and Daniel Holmblad, *Tvistlösning inom affärsrätten—en antologi*, (Nordstedts Juridik, 2020) 112 (translated from Swedish to English by the author).
91. McCafferty, L., *Adjudication: Pros and Cons of Adjudication* (Thomson Reuters, uk.practicallaw.thomsonreuters.com 2019). (translated from Swedish to English by the author).

CHAPTER 13

The Authority to Interpret Awards Without Support in Statutory Provisions or Arbitration Rules: Where Does the Tribunal's Jurisdiction End, and the Court's Begin?

Christopher Stridh

§13.01 INTRODUCTION

The finality of the award is often described as one of the advantages of arbitration. However, unfortunately, awards occasionally contain shortcomings or imperfections. For example, it is sometimes the case that the operative part of the award, also called the award's dispositif, by itself or in combination with the award's reasoning, is phrased in an unclear manner, thereby creating doubt as to the proper interpretation of the award.

As a means to address this issue, the Swedish Arbitration Act of 1999[1] (hereinafter referred to as the 'Arbitration Act' or simply the 'Act'), like many national arbitration laws, allows the arbitrators to interpret the award at the request of either party within thirty days of the date when the award was rendered. This follows from section 32(1), which states that (emphasis added):

> If the arbitrators find that an award contains any obvious inaccuracy as a consequence of a typographical, computational, or other similar mistake by the arbitrators or any another person, or if the arbitrators by oversight have failed to

1. Lagen (1999:116) om skiljeförfarande. The original wording of the act has been translated by the Swedish Ministry of Justice (Ds 1999:22). Translations into English of Swedish authorities referred to in this submission have been made by the author.

> decide an issue which should have been dealt with in the award, they may, within thirty days of the date of the announcement of the award, decide to correct or supplement the award. *They may also correct or supplement an award, or interpret the decision in an award, where any of the parties so requests within thirty days of receipt of the award by that party.*[2]

By way of comparison, under Article 33(1)(b) of the UNCITRAL Model Law, a party may 'request the arbitral tribunal to give an interpretation of a specific point or part of the award', but only 'if so agreed by the parties' that is, typically, where the applicable arbitration rules allow it.

Most commonly used sets of rules for administered and non-administered (ad hoc) arbitrations – domestic and international – also allow for interpretation of awards within a certain period of time.[3] For example, Article 47 of the 2023 Stockholm Chamber of Commerce Arbitration Rules (SCC Rules) allows for an application 'for the interpretation of an award' to be made 'within 30 days from receipt of the award'.[4]

However, disagreements regarding the interpretation may also arise at a later stage of the parties' dispute. The issue is particularly prominent at the enforcement stage, where, for example, the losing party may seek to limit the scope of the binding effect of the award. Issues of interpretation may also arise where the award in question contains one or more declaratory relief(s). For example, a claimant may rely on a declaratory relief on liability issues in a subsequent arbitration relating to quantum. In such cases, the issue of whether the tribunal possesses the mandate to interpret an arbitral award in the absence of explicit support from statutory provisions or arbitration rules holds significant practical implications. This contribution delves into the existing literature and case law relevant to this topic from a Swedish law perspective. It also endeavours to provide practitioners and arbitrators with a more comprehensive understanding of issues relating to the interpretation of arbitral awards.

---

2. The meaning of the wording 'interpret the decision in an award' used in the provision relates only to the operative part of the award, *see* SOU (Eng. *Official Swedish Government Report*) 1994:81 p. 168 and prop. (Eng. *Government Bill*) 1998/99:35 p. 135. The provision further refers to the 'arbitrators', while the interpretation of the award is carried out by the arbitral tribunal as a judicial body. Hence, the award may be interpreted by a tribunal with a new composition. In the following, the term 'tribunal' refers to the judicial body, without distinction as to which individual arbitrators are members of the tribunal.
3. *See* 2021 UNCITRAL Rules, Art. 37(1); 2021 Swiss Rules, Art. 37(1)(a); 2018 HKIAC Rules, Art. 39(1); 2016 SIAC Rules, Art. 33(4); 2022 ICSID Rules, Rules 69 and 70; 2018 DIS Rules, Art. 40(2)(3); and 2021 VIAC Rules, Art. 39(1)(2).
4. Unlike the Arbitration Act, the SCC Rules do not limit the scope of interpretation to the operative part of the award but refer to a 'specific point or part of the award'. In order for a request to be entertained, however, it should in most cases need to concern the operative part of the award, *see* Annette Magnusson et al. (eds), *International Arbitration in Sweden: A Practitioner's Guide*, p. 322 (2nd ed., Kluwer Law International 2021) and Jakob Ragnwaldh et al., *A Guide to the SCC Arbitration Rules*, p. 143 (Kluwer Law International 2020).

§13.02 SOURCES AND LIMITATIONS OF THE TRIBUNAL'S INTERPRETATION MANDATE UNDER SWEDISH LAW

Under Swedish law, the scope of the arbitrators' mandate is determined by the arbitration agreement.[5] The scope of the arbitration agreement is, in turn, determined by, first, the interpretation of that particular agreement and, second, the legal limitations imposed by mandatory law, including the requirement in section 1(1) of the Arbitration Act that disputes referred to arbitration must concern an identified legal relationship (the *identification requirement*).[6] In other words, the determination of the tribunal's mandate to interpret an arbitral award involves both contractual and statutory interpretation. Each of these matters will be considered below, subject to a general preliminary comment.

The question of the tribunal's interpretation mandate is linked to the doctrine of res judicata. While there is no express provision on the res judicata effects of an arbitral award in the Act, the Supreme Court has stated that the binding effect of an arbitral award in principle has the same objective scope as a court judgment.[7] In very simple terms, according to the doctrine of res judicata, as applicable in arbitration, a final award typically prohibits subsequent proceedings involving the same parties concerning the same cause of action as covered by the award. This means that a request for relief that has been put forth and ruled upon in previous proceedings cannot be re-examined in subsequent proceedings. It also means that all facts which were or could have been invoked in favour or against the relief sought in previous proceedings can generally not be invoked in subsequent proceedings.[8]

According to former Supreme Court Justice Stefan Lindskog, the leading academic commentator on Swedish arbitration law, an arbitration agreement does not *in dubio* give a broader mandate to interpret awards than what follows from section 32(1) of the Act. If a dispute arises regarding the meaning of the award and the thirty-day period under section 32(1) has expired, it is thus for a court of general jurisdiction to

5. *See, e.g.*, Stefan Lindskog, *Skiljeförfarande En kommentar* (Eng. *Arbitration A commentary*), Chapter I.0-1, p. 91 and section 34:4.3.1, p. 936 (here disregarding the instances of statutory based arbitration) (3rd ed., Norstedts Gula Bibliotek 2020) (cit. 'Lindskog'); Magnusson et al., *supra* n. 4, p. 138; Fredrik Andersson et al, *Arbitration in Sweden*, p. 57 (Jure Förlag 2011); Finn Madsen, *Commercial Arbitration in Sweden*, p. 40 (5th ed., Jure Förlag 2020); and Lars Heuman, *Skiljemannarätt* (Eng. *Arbitration law*), p. 46 (6th ed., Norstedts Juridik 1999).
6. *See, e.g.*, Lindskog, Chapter I:0-6.1.1, p. 194 (n. 799) and Magnusson et al., *supra* n. 4, p. 110.
7. *See Esselte AB v. Allmänna Pensionsfonden et al.* (NJA 1998 p. 189). Notably, the rules on res judicata are among the most complex and debated under Swedish procedural law, and caution may be called for in the application of the principle in international arbitration, *see, e.g.*, Lindskog, Chapter III:0:3.2.3-3.2.4, p. 595; Magnusson et al., *supra* n. 4, p. 324; and Kaj Hobér, *International commercial arbitration in Sweden*, p. 259 at para. 7.105, (2nd ed., Oxford University Press 2021).
8. *See, e.g.*, Robert Nordh, *Processens ram i tvistemål* (Eng. *Procedural framework in civil cases*), p. 40 (4th ed., Iustus Förlag 2019) and Per Olof Ekelöf et al., *Rättegång III* (Eng. *Trial III*), p. 165 (8th ed., Norstedts Juridik 2018). Notably, for the res judicata effect to apply, the first award must be invoked in the subsequent proceedings, *see*, e.g., Lindskog, Chapter III:0:3.2.3, p. 595 and Andersson et al, *supra* n. 5, p. 146.

decide on its interpretation unless the arbitration agreement expressly states otherwise.[9] In other words, the parties are free to enter into an arbitration agreement that gives the arbitral tribunal the mandate to interpret an award that goes beyond the mandate given under section 32(1) of the Act.[10]

Lindskog further adds to this point that, according to section 32(1) of the Act, an award may only be interpreted by the tribunal that rendered the award in question.[11] Thus, if a question of interpretation of a previously rendered award arises in a new arbitration, any interpretation issue rests with the first tribunal – that is, in the unlikely event that the time limit for taking recourse to the specific provision in section 32(1) of the Act or the applicable arbitration rules has not expired.

As mentioned, these considerations are relevant when a request for specific performance is based on an award of declaratory nature, such as an award on liability. If a declaratory award has been issued, then, as a rule, the examination of a request for performance as such is covered by the arbitration agreement.[12] However, according to Lindskog, in the described scenario, if the respondent raises defences such as alleged insufficient causation or contributory negligence by the claimant, any interpretation issue regarding the final determination of such defences through the first award would fall under the jurisdiction of a court of general jurisdiction to resolve.[13] Another highly regarded commentator, Professor Lars Heuman, however, seems to take the opposite position, holding that the arbitration agreement should be considered applicable to any new disputes based on a previously rendered award.[14]

It is well established that a request for interpretation under section 32(1) of the Arbitration Act can only seek to clarify the award. In other words, the request cannot seek to modify or annul the award.[15] If an interpretation goes beyond what is allowed

9. *See* Lindskog, Chapter I.0-4.3.2, p. 146 (n. 585 *in fine*), Chapter I:0-6.1.4, p. 200, Chapter IV.0-4.4.4, p. 775, Chapter IV.0-5.2.7, p. 788, Chapter IV, section 29-4.3.3, p. 844 and Chapter IV, section 33:4.3.1, p. 880.
10. *See* Lindskog, Chapter I.0-6.1.4, p. 201 (n. 797) and Chapter IV, section 32:3.5, p. 877. It may be noted that one commentator holds that caution should be exercised in upholding an agreement to restrict the right to interpretation under section 32(1) of the Arbitration Act, *see* Cars, *Lagen om skiljeförfarande En kommentar* (Eng. *The Arbitration Act A commentary*), p. 153 (2nd ed., Tierp 2000).
11. *See* Lindskog, Chapter I:0-6.1.4, p. 200 and Chapter IV, section 33:4.3.1, p. 880.
12. *See* Lindskog, Chapter I.0-4.3.2, p. 146 (n. 585 *in fine*) and Chapter I:0-6.1.4, p. 201 (n. 799).
13. For a fuller discussion on the separation between liability and quantum under Swedish law, *see* Henrik Johansson, *Mellandom – nu och i framtiden* (Eng. *Partial award – now and in the future*), SvJT 2001 pp. 505 et seq. and the *dictum* by Lindskog in *Handelsbolaget Tylöbaden v. Halmstads kommun* (NJA 2008 p. 339, '*Handelsbolaget Tylöbaden*').
14. *See* Heuman, *supra* n. 5, p. 560. It is worth noting that Heuman's analysis lacks a distinction between scenarios where the arbitral tribunal derives a subsequent award from its own earlier decision and cases where an award is based on a previous tribunal's ruling, *see further* section [B] (The relevance of section 32(1) of the Arbitration Act).
15. *See* Lindskog, Chapter IV, section 32:4.3.1, p. 880. It may be mentioned that such agreements may be concluded in advance, i.e., before the question of interpretation arises, without prejudice to the identification requirement, *see* Lindskog, Chapter I.0-6.1.4, p. 200 (nn. 797 and 801).

under section 32(1) of the Act, the award may be challenged. If not set aside, the interpretation becomes a part of the award.[16]

§13.03 DETERMINATION OF THE PARTIES' INTENTIONS REGARDING THE TRIBUNAL'S INTERPRETATION MANDATE

[A] Introduction

As noted, the first step in determining the tribunal's mandate to interpret an award is to assess the parties' arbitration agreement. As confirmed by the Swedish Supreme Court in, among other cases, *Belgorkhimprom v. Koca* (NJA 2019 p. 171, '*Belgor*'), the scope of an arbitration agreement is determined in accordance with general principles of contract interpretation.[17] This means that the scope of an arbitration agreement regarding the tribunal's mandate to interpret awards is determined based on the parties' mutual intention, provided that such a mutual intention is ascertainable. If discerning a specific mutual intention among the parties proves unattainable, other objective factors must be considered.[18]

The primary manifestation of the parties' mutual intent typically resides within the confines of the written contract. However, arbitration agreements often adhere to standardised templates, rendering the language insufficient for deducing any distinct

16. *See* Lindskog, Chapter IV, section 32:6.2.1, p. 887. The error most likely constitutes an excess of mandate according to section 34(1) p. 3, as the (wrongful) interpretation becomes part of the award unless challenged.
17. *See Belgor*, para. 13. *See also Components Plastunion AB v. Husqvarna* (NJA 2023 p. 437, '*Husqvarnas skiljeavtal*'), where reference is made to *Belgor* (para. 14) (although in another context than questions of interpretation). The Supreme Court's ruling in *Belgor* has received considerable attention in the legal debate, *see, e.g.*, Christer Danielsson, *Swedish Arbitration-Related Case Law*, in *Stockholm Arbitration Yearbook 2019*, pp. 9 et seq. (The Netherlands: Kluwer Law International 2019); Reldén & Frank, *The Belgor Case: Towards an Extensive Interpretation and Application of Arbitration Agreements*, in *Stockholm Arbitration Yearbook 2020*, pp. 65 et seq. (The Netherlands: Kluwer Law International 2021); Heuman, *Har det skett en omsvängning eller omläggning av praxis från restriktiv till extensiv tillämpning av skiljeavtal?* (Eng. *Has there been a shift or change in practice from restrictive to extensive application of arbitration agreements?*), SvJT 2019 pp. 534 et seq.; and Patrik Schöldström, *Har Belgor förändrat prövningen av en skiljenämnds behörighet och handläggningsfel)* (Eng. *Has Belgor changed the review of an arbitral tribunal's jurisdiction and procedural errors?*), JT 2019 pp. 243 et seq.
18. *See Belgor*, para. 13. Here, reference was made to *Grant Thornton Sweden AB v. Hans Nilsson* (NJA 2015 s. 741, '*Partneravtalet*'). Similar statements from the Swedish Supreme Court, confirming this order of interpretation objectives are found in numerous cases, *see, e.g., Det Andra Bolaget House Sweden AB v. John Svensson Byggnadsfirma AB*, paras 21-25 (NJA 2014 p. 960, '*Det andra bolaget*'); *Bilstudion Sverige AB v. Anders Fredling*, para. 11 (NJA 2021 p. 597, '*Mätarställningen*'); and *Idermark och Lagerwall Reklam AB v. Nordens Välfärdscenter*, para. 11 (NJA 2021 p. 643, '*Ramavtalet*'). It may be noted that Swedish contract law also protects unilateral intentions that remain uncontested by the other party who is aware of that (real) intention, *see, e.g.*, Ramberg & Ramberg, *Allmän avtalsrätt* (Eng. *General contract law*), p. 182 (12th ed., Norstedts Juridik AB 2022) and Adlercreutz & Gorton, *Avtalsrätt II* (Eng. *Contract law II*), p. 130 (6th ed., Juristförlaget i Lund 2010). Given the rarity of scenarios prompting the utilisation of this rule of interpretation within the realm of arbitration agreements, it will not be expounded upon any further in this contribution.

common intent.[19] Consequently, when determining the scope of the tribunal's mandate to interpret an award, reliance on other factors is often, if not always, necessary.

In this context, the Supreme Court held in *Belgor* that where the language permits varied interpretations and other relevant factors fail to provide direction, it is natural to assume that the arbitration agreement should serve a rational purpose (Sw. '*förnuftig funktion*') and take the parties' interests into account in a reasonable manner. It further went on to state that '[i]n such situations, the parties must be assumed to have wanted that the disputes shall be solved without delay and in one proceeding before an arbitral tribunal chosen by them'.[20]

[B] The Relevance of Section 32(1) of the Arbitration Act

Consistent with the precedent set by the Supreme Court in *Belgor*, in cases where an arbitration agreement is silent on the tribunal's mandate for interpretation, reliance should be placed upon 'other relevant interpretation data'. Such relevant interpretation data could potentially be the content of non-mandatory legal provisions.[21] As explained earlier, section 32(1) of the Arbitration Act clearly defines the limits of an arbitral tribunal's mandate to interpret its own award. Therefore, a primary question is whether, in the absence of an express agreement to the contrary, section 32(1) of the Arbitration Act is to be regarded as an interpretative factor supporting the conclusion that a tribunal may not interpret an arbitral award beyond the scope of the statutory provision.

As stipulated in section 27(4) of the Act, section 32 is one of two explicit exemptions from the general principle that arbitrators lose jurisdiction over the dispute upon issuing a final award.[22] This is commonly known as the tribunal becoming *functus officio* (the other exception being the remittance of the award back to the arbitrator for reconsideration in response to a setting-aside application, as per section 35 of the Act).[23] Section 32(1) of the Arbitration Act is based on Article 33(1)(b) of the Model Law,[24] which departs from the principle of the finality of the award. During the drafting phase of the Model Law, a strong view of the United Nations Commission on International Trade Law (UNCITRAL) favoured the removal of this provision, fearing its potential to undermine the finality of the award and provoke unwarranted attempts to reopen settled matters. Others argued for the necessity of an interpretative mechanism, particularly in international commercial arbitrations where awards are often not drafted in the arbitrators' native language. After discussion, it was unanimously agreed to accept the retention of the provision, subject to its reformulation to contain a

19. *See Belgor*, para. 13.
20. *Ibid.*
21. *See, e.g., Bilstudion Sverige AB v. Anders Fredling*, para. 12 (NJA 2021 p. 597, '*Mätarställningen*'); Ramberg & Ramberg, *supra* n. 18, p. 195; and Bert Lehrberg, *Avtalstolkning* (Eng. *Contract interpretation*), p. 234 (10th ed., Iusté 2023).
22. *See also* prop. 1998/99:35 p. 99.
23. The provision does not specify exhaustively when an arbitrator's mandate ends, *see* prop. 1998/99:35 p. 100.
24. *See* SOU 1994:81, p. 167 and prop. 1998/99:35, p. 136.

requirement that a request for interpretation might be made only if agreed between the parties.[25]

Against this background, the underlying reasons for the inclusion of section 32(1) in the Arbitration Act can be seen to point in different directions, depending on the situation in which the question of interpretation arises.

The expression 'final award' is often used to mean different things. The expression 'final award' in section 27(4) of the Act, which terminates the tribunal's mandate and renders the tribunal *functus officio*, refers to an award which concludes the case (such that no other issues are left to be decided).[26] The parties may also decide that the arbitrators shall rule on a particular aspect of a dispute in a *separate award* (Sw. *särskild skiljedom*) according to section 29(1) of the Act. A separate award could – for instance – be rendered when there are a large number of claims that could be ruled upon separately. Separate awards are subject to the same formal requirements as other types of awards and have the same legal status as 'regular' final awards.[27] Accordingly, a separate award on specific performance is enforceable immediately upon being rendered.[28] Such awards are therefore sometimes referred to as 'final' awards, even though they are not final within the meaning of section 27(4) of the Arbitration Act.

If an award on specific performance is final according to section 27(4) of the Act, it is clear based on the wording of the Act alone that the mandate to interpret the award – unless the parties have expressly agreed otherwise – ceases at the end of the 30-day period stipulated in section 32(1) of the Act.[29] The fundamental principle of finality of the award justifies this restrictive approach.[30] This view is confirmed by the *travaux préparatoires* to the Arbitration Act, where the legislator held that (emphasis added):[31]

> The starting point should be that the mandate ceases when a final arbitral award has been rendered. [...] *This means that the arbitrators are not authorised to deal with the dispute after a final arbitral award has been rendered, unless specifically provided for by law or the parties' agreement.* Explicit exceptions to this general rule should apply to the possibilities for correction, interpretation, supplementation and remission [of a dispute to the arbitrators] provided for by the act.

---

25. *See* Commission Report, UN Doc A/40/17, paras 265-269.
26. *See also* Art. 43 of the SCC Rules.
27. *See, e.g.*, Lindskog, Chapter IV, section 29:3.1. p. 840 and Magnusson et al., *supra* n. 4, p. 304.
28. *Ibid.*
29. An exception may be if the award is so vague or incomplete that the tribunal's assessment on the merits cannot be ascertained from it. In such instances, however, it may be called into question whether this constitutes an interpretation in the truest sense. Instead, it appears to be more about the tribunal fulfilling its duty of issuing a legally enforceable award, *see* Lindskog, Chapter IV, section 33:4.3.1, p. 880 (n. 3481 *in fine*).
30. In this context, a party intending to use the final award as basis for an enforcement application arguably has little reason to hesitate in requesting interpretation under section 32(1) of the Arbitration Act (or applicable arbitration rules) if the award appears unclear. Conversely, the respondent may raise arguments – whether genuine or not – alleging ambiguity in the final award during the enforcement phase. The fact that such an objection is deliberately raised after the expiry of the time limit for taking recourse to the specific provision in section 32(1) of the Arbitration Act (or the applicable arbitration rules) does not seem to have been intended to affect the question of the mandate of the arbitral tribunal to interpret the award, *see infra* nn. 31-32.
31. Prop. 1998/99:35 p. 99.

In line with this, the *travaux préparatoires* also state that disputes concerning the interpretation of awards at the enforcement stage should primarily be resolved by general courts.[32]

In relation to declaratory awards, the conclusion becomes less evident. Notably, such awards may be both final and non-final within the meaning of section 27(4) of the Act. In the example where issues of liability and quantum are separated, it may be the case that both the determination of liability and any subsequent request for specific performance are adjudicated by *the same tribunal*, with the first award having the form of a separate award according to section 29(1) of the Act. The tribunal then retains its mandate to render a final award based on the separate award without being rendered *functus officio*, while section 32(1) of the Act, as explained above, is an *exception* to the principle that the arbitral tribunal may not interfere with an award that is final according to section 27(4) of the Act.[33] As such, it appears misplaced to view section 32(1) of the Act as a manifestation of the parties' contractual intentions. It is worth noting the following remark from the legislator, which pertains to how the arbitral tribunal's mandate to interpret awards under section 32(1) of the Act should be modelled (emphasis added):[34]

> The next question then becomes whether a mutual agreement between the parties should be required for interpretation to take place [according to Section 32(1) of the Act]. However, it can be immediately stated that it appears incomprehensible why there should be a requirement for a mutual agreement regarding interpretation but not have a corresponding requirement concerning the correction and completion of an arbitral award. *Parties surely do not contemplate the need for interpretation until they receive an unclear arbitral award. In that situation, one party generally does not have an interest in clarification.*

The Swedish legislator thus seems to reject the notion of a general requirement for an *explicit agreement* from the parties for interpretation to fall under the scope of their arbitration agreement. As further discussed below, it may also appear artificial to assume that the parties to an arbitration agreement would prefer to have the general courts decide on issues of interpretation simply because of the separation of different issues in dispute and that thirty-day time limit (or whatever time limit that is applicable under the arbitration rules) have lapsed.

It is possible that these considerations apply even in scenarios where there is separation between different issues in dispute between *different arbitral tribunals*, and the tribunal must rely on a final award of declaratory nature by a *previous tribunal* in rendering its own subsequent award. In such instances, however, the new arbitral

32. *See* SOU 1994:81 p. 214 and prop. 1998/99:35 p. 178.
33. It is worth noting that although the origin of the *functus officio* principle shows that it was intended to protect the integrity and finality of awards, it may have the opposite effect if the mandate to interpret an award requires an express agreement, since the arbitral proceedings may extend to judicial proceedings, i.e., by forcing parties to seek an authoritative decision on the correct interpretation of the award before a court.
34. Prop. 1998/99:35 p. 137.

tribunal, unlike the first tribunal, would admittedly lack the advantage of being considered best placed to carry out the interpretation.[35]

To summarise, it appears uncontroversial that the tribunal, save for what is provided for under section 32(1) of the Act or applicable arbitration rules, may not interpret a final award on specific performance unless specifically provided for in the parties' arbitration agreement. Whether the scope of the arbitration agreement covers interpretation of awards of a declaratory nature is less clear. At heart is the question of how the principle of *functus office* operates in situations that are outside of its primary intended scope. This issue is further complicated by the fact that declaratory awards may be interpreted by the tribunal that issued the award as well as by subsequent tribunals.

[C] The Significance of the General Courts' Ultimate Jurisdiction in Interpreting Arbitral Awards

In support of the position that an arbitration agreement does not *in dubio* give a broader mandate to interpret awards than what follows from section 32(1) of the Act, Lindskog relies primarily on the statement made in the *travaux préparatoires* that, at the enforcement stage, it is for the general court to resolve any disputes of interpretation.[36] In doing so, Lindskog abstains from exploring the presumed intentions of the parties in consideration of both section 32(1) of the Arbitration Act and the underlying purposes of the provision, as previously discussed. Lindskog also argues that this conclusion does not depend on whether the award is for performance or declaratory relief or on the stage of the arbitral proceedings at which the dispute over the interpretation of the award arises.[37]

Instead, Lindskog asserts that the mandate for interpreting the award by the general court aligns best with its ultimate jurisdiction to adjudicate the legal effects of arbitration awards.[38] In support of his position, Lindskog also cites the following (relatively old) rulings:[39]

> NJA 1918 p. 478. A clause in an insurance contract provided for a dispute concerning a certain causal relationship to be settled by an arbitration tribunal. During the proceedings of the policyholder's claim in the general court, an arbitration tribunal was established. Two of the arbitrators found, with different reasons, that a relationship 'in all probability' existed, while the third arbitrator came to the opposite conclusion. Whether a causal link had thus been established by the tribunal was examined by the general court.
>
> NJA 1932 p. 73. In the case, an arbitration award initially addressed various matters, including the timeframe for the delivery of goods. Subsequently, a later

35. Cf. *supra* n. 2.
36. *See* Lindskog, Chapter I:0-6.1.4, p. 200 (n. 796) and Chapter IV:0-4.4.4, p. 775 (n. 3059). Here, Lindskog also relies on statements from Professor Mæland's work *Voldgift*, p. 86 and 177 (Universitetsforlaget, 1988).
37. *See* Lindskog, *supra* n. 9. *See also* Lindskog, Chapter IV, section 29:4.3.3, p. 844.
38. *See* Lindskog, Chapter IV:0-4.4.4, p. 775.
39. *See* Lindskog, Chapter I.0-6.1.4, p. 201.

award established a revised delivery date due to intervening circumstances. An application to enforce the latter award was rejected, citing that it relied on an interpretation of the former award.

NJA 1936 p. 663. An arbitral tribunal held that an insurance company was entitled to withhold compensation until an issue of criminal liability had been resolved by a general court. In a subsequent arbitration, a new tribunal awarded the claimant insurance compensation. The Supreme Court held that the award of the first arbitral tribunal was binding and that the second arbitral tribunal was prevented from considering the claim for insurance compensation since the issue of criminal liability had not yet been decided by the general court.

It is unclear how Lindskog views the issue of the parties' presumed intention regarding the tribunal's right to interpret an award.[40] Possibly, Lindskog, in his determination of the scope of the typical standardised arbitration agreement, attaches decisive importance to what could be characterised as systematic considerations and, more specifically, the ultimate distribution of jurisdiction between tribunals and courts of general jurisdiction. In addition to the fact that the age of these judgments raises doubts about their relevance in contemporary contexts, Lindskog acknowledges that only one of the cited judgments (NJA 1936 p. 663) concerns the tribunal's mandate to interpret a previous award of declaratory nature. Additionally, that case is arguably not immediately relevant to the issue at hand, as it concerned whether the condition imposed by the first arbitral tribunal, that the right to insurance compensation was dependent on the outcome of criminal proceedings, was in fact a binding declaratory award and, if so, whether this condition was fulfilled at the time of the second arbitral award.[41]

[D] The Significance of a Swift Resolution Before a Tribunal Appointed by the Parties

As already mentioned, the Supreme Court in *Belgor* held that where the wording and other factors relevant to the interpretation of the arbitration agreement give no clear guidance as to the parties' genuine contractual intentions, the arbitration agreement should be construed as serving a rational purpose, which implies that the parties must be assumed to have intended that disputes are to be solved without delay and in one proceeding before an arbitral tribunal chosen by them.[42]

If one were to concede that the tribunal's mandate to interpret an award under uncertain circumstances lies beyond the scope of the arbitration agreement for any of the reasons given by Lindskog, it might be contended that this statement by the Supreme Court holds no relevance in determining the scope of the parties' arbitration agreement concerning a potential interpretation mandate. In the view of the author, there are at least two fundamental objections to be raised against this approach.

40. It may be mentioned that the Supreme Court's judgment in *Belgor* has been subject to severe criticism by Lindskog, *see* Lindskog, Chapter I, section 1:5.1.2, p. 262 (n. 1049).
41. *See* Lindskog, Chapter I:0-6.1.4, p. 201 (n. 799).
42. *See Belgor*, para. 13.

First, general principles of contract interpretation say that due consideration should be given to *all relevant circumstances*.[43] It would thus not be correct to completely overlook the parties' presumed desire for a swift dispute resolution within a single forum.

Second, the legal sources relied on by Lindskog cannot, at least not in the author's view, be said to speak unequivocally either in favour or against the conclusion that an interpretation mandate is inherent within the parties' arbitration agreement. Hence, the presumption established in *Belgor* should serve as the basis for determining the scope of the arbitration agreement regarding the tribunal's interpretation mandate.

Indeed, Lindskog's position would incentivise resorting to judicial review when the tribunal is faced with interpreting an award of declaratory nature – regardless of whether the award was rendered by the tribunal itself or by a previous arbitral tribunal. There may, for instance, be little point in presenting the costly and complex damages case before a tribunal based on a previous award on liability if the scope of liability as correctly recognised in the first award cannot be established by interpretation by a subsequent arbitral tribunal. At this point, the uncertainty over the tribunal's interpretation mandate may bring the proceedings to a halt pending judicial review. To allow the arbitration agreement to fulfil a sensible function, it seems most reasonable that a question of interpretation is first resolved in the context of arbitration. In line with the statements of the Swedish legislator,[44] it is also hard to see that the parties to the arbitration agreement intended for the general court to intervene and decide on a question of interpretation. The author therefore submits that an arbitration agreement should, as a starting point, include the mandate to interpret awards of declaratory nature, whether final or not, in the meaning of section 27(4) of the Act.

§13.04 DEALING WITH DISAGREEMENTS ON INTERPRETATION

As will be recalled, the absence of a mandate to interpret the award does not prevent the tribunal from considering a request for specific performance based on a previously rendered award.[45] Nor does necessarily the fact that an arbitral tribunal encounters a question of interpretation that such request should be dismissed for lack of jurisdiction.

This is because the tribunal retains the discretion to address the interpretation of the initial award as a preliminary matter (Sw. *prejudiciell fråga*), even though such a decision is not legally binding on the parties involved.[46] To this end, Lindskog submits that a tribunal should only render an award based on a preliminary (non-binding) decision on the interpretation of a previous award if it is 'obvious' what the result of the interpretation will be. Otherwise, the tribunal should refer the party whose claim

43. *See supra* n. 18.
44. *See supra* n. 34.
45. *See supra* n. 12.
46. *See* Lindskog, Chapter I.0-6.1.4, p. 200 (n. 800).

depends on the question of interpretation to initiate proceedings in a court of general jurisdiction.[47]

Lindskog's statement initially raises the question of what is meant by the result of an interpretation being 'obvious'. Contrary to its supposed purpose, this proposed discretion for the tribunal to decide whether it should decide on the interpretation issue as a preliminary matter rather contributes to increasing the degree of difficulty for tribunals and parties faced with questions of interpretation.

It is further not entirely obvious for what underlying reasons the general court should decide on the issue of interpretation. Particularly, a wrongful decision by the tribunal on the interpretation issue as a preliminary matter may be challenged.[48] Hence, having the tribunal decide on the interpretation issue as a preliminary matter does not alter the ultimate distribution of jurisdiction between tribunals and courts of general jurisdiction, which is a factor on which Lindskog bases his fundamental position. On this point, however, Lindskog seems to be of the opinion that *if* the tribunal is given a mandate to interpret a previously rendered award of declaratory nature, its decision on the interpretation issue will not be of preliminary nature but binding on the parties.[49] As such, a wrongful decision by the tribunal may no longer constitute grounds for challenging the award. Since the parties have control over the res judicata effects of the award, it is certainly possible for the parties to give such mandate to the tribunal, at least once an interpretation issue has arisen.[50] At the same time, Lindskog holds that if the parties argue for different interpretations of the award and neither of them claims that the arbitral tribunal lacks the mandate to decide the interpretation issue, then normally, this matter is deemed to have been referred to the tribunal's discretion through an implicit arbitration agreement.[51] A party wishing to preserve the possibility of having the effects of a special award examined by a general court is therefore well advised to make this clear.

As for the tribunal's considerations, once an issue of interpretation arises, they likely depend on how confident it feels in its conclusion. If the tribunal is confident that a preliminary decision will be upheld if challenged before a general court, there is much to gain by continuing the arbitration based on the decision, possibly even pending the

47. *See* Lindskog Chapter IV, section 32:4.3.1, p. 881 (n. 3482). Notably, the forum provisions in section 43 of the Arbitration Act are not applicable and the district court is the court of first instance.
48. *See* Lindskog, Chapter I:0-6.1.4, p. 201 (n. 800). However, it may be noted that the fact that an issue is first assessed by a tribunal may affect any subsequent assessment by general courts. Particularly, the Supreme Court in *Belgor* established yet another presumption, namely that it is the tribunal that is best positioned to determine the issue of its own jurisdiction. *See further* Schöldström, *supra* n. 17.
49. *See* Lindskog, Chapter V, section 34:5.2.5, p. 971. Cf., however, Lindskog, Chapter I:0-8.1.1, p. 206 (n. 854), where Lindskog (although with some doubt) expresses that an arbitration agreement *in dubio* may be understood as including the mandate of the arbitral tribunal to decide on issues of interpretation as a preliminary matter.
50. *See supra* n. 15.
51. *See* Lindskog, Chapter V, section 34:5.2.5, p. 971 (n. 3864).

court's final determination.[52] Conversely, if the outcome of a general court's assessment seems more questionable, there are arguably advantages of 'getting it done right' over 'getting it done fast'.

§13.05 SUMMARY

The question of whether the arbitral tribunal has the mandate to interpret an arbitral award in the absence of explicit backing from statutory provisions or arbitration rules ultimately hinges on the interpretation of the arbitration agreement. Legal literature and case law suggest that, as a rule, an arbitration agreement should not be construed to allow for the interpretation of the award beyond what is stipulated in section 32(1) of the Arbitration Act or applicable arbitration rules. However, neither these provisions nor previous statements in the legal literature and case law appear to primarily address cases where a prior declaratory award serves as the basis for an award for specific performance. Furthermore, modern principles of contract interpretation emphasise the importance of swift dispute resolution in a single proceeding before an arbitral tribunal chosen by the parties. Therefore, the author submits that the tribunal's mandate to interpret an award, whether in the form of a separate award or a final award rendered by a previous arbitral tribunal, is inherent in its mandate until it becomes *functus officio* under section 27(4) of the Act.

Even if it is accepted that arbitration agreements typically do not cover interpretation of awards, the limited references to such situations do not suggest that a request for performance should be dismissed for lack of jurisdiction because of a question about interpretation. Instead, they suggest that the tribunal, in later proceedings, might assess the content of the declaratory award as a preliminary matter. Although making a mistake on this matter could be seen as a challengeable error, the advantages of taking such a decision are likely to be many, not least if the question of interpretation is clear.

52. According to section 2(2) of the Arbitration Act, the tribunal may continue the arbitration pending the court's determination on the tribunal's jurisdiction.

STOCKHOLM ARBITRATION YEARBOOK

1. Axel Calissendorff & Patrik Schöldström (eds), *Stockholm Arbitration Yearbook 2019*, 2019 (ISBN 978-94-035-0692-0).
2. Axel Calissendorff & Patrik Schöldström (eds), *Stockholm Arbitration Yearbook 2020*, 2020 (ISBN 978-94-035-2410-8).
3. Axel Calissendorff & Patrik Schöldström (eds), *Stockholm Arbitration Yearbook 2021*, 2021 (ISBN 978-94-035-3524-1).
4. Axel Calissendorff & Patrik Schöldström (eds), *Stockholm Arbitration Yearbook 2022*, 2022 (ISBN 978-94-035-1876-3).
5. Christer Danielsson & Patrik Schöldström (eds), *Stockholm Arbitration Yearbook 2023*, 2023 (ISBN 978-94-035-0358-5).
6. Christer Danielsson & Patrik Schöldström (eds), *Stockholm Arbitration Yearbook 2024*, 2024 (ISBN 978-94-035-4428-1).

www.ingramcontent.com/pod-product-compliance
Lightning Source LLC
LaVergne TN
LVHW020642300926
849161LV00004B/776
* 9 7 8 9 4 0 3 5 4 4 2 8 1 *